JESUS IN THE GOSPELS

Leander E. Keck

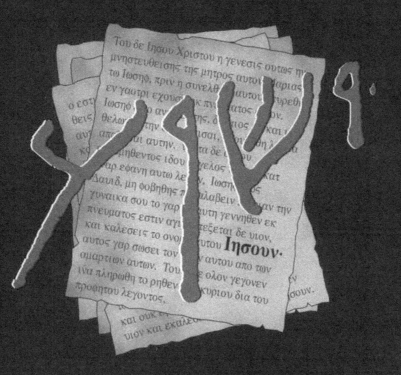

Study Manual

DISCIPLE
Second Generation Studies

Leander E. Keck, writer of the JESUS IN THE GOSPELS study manual, served as New Testament consultant on the four-phase DISCIPLE Bible study and convener of the consultation on the development of CHRISTIAN BELIEVER. Dr. Keck, Winkley Professor of Biblical Theology Emeritus and former Dean of Yale University Divinity School, was the convener of the Editorial Board of *The New Interpreter's Bible*.

JESUS IN THE GOSPELS
DISCIPLE Second Generation Studies
Study Manual

Copyright © 2003 by Abingdon Press
All rights reserved

Nellie M. Moser, Senior Editor; Mark Price, Development Editor; Amy Cain, Production Editor; Linda O. Spicer, Unit Assistant; Ed Wynne, Production & Design Manager.

For more information about JESUS IN THE GOSPELS seminars or DISCIPLE training seminars, call toll free 800-251-8591 or 800-672-1789
fax 615-749-6049
www.cokesbury.com/services/secondgeneration.asp

03 04 05 06 07 08 09 10 11 12 — 10 9 8 7 6 5 4 3 2 1

Contents

	Reading's Promise	4
	A Word to the Reader	6
1.	Jesus *in* the Gospels	8
2.	When Words Became Events	16
3.	Celebrating Beginnings	24
4.	The Wilderness Voice	32
5.	Gifted by the Spirit and Tested by the Choices	40
6.	When God's Reign Becomes Real	48
7.	Called and Commissioned	56
8.	Mission With Healing Power	64
9.	Conflicts Over Obedience	72
10.	The Inaugural Word	80
11.	Counting on God	90
12.	The Choice	98
13.	Faith as Wonder	106
14.	Destiny Disclosed	114
15.	Merciful Discipline	124
16.	The Journey Is the Way	132
17.	Destiny Symbolized	142
18.	Sharp Words in the Temple	152
19.	Signs of Danger and Dangerous Signs	164
20.	Destiny Seized	176
21.	Destiny Achieved	188
22.	This Jesus God Raised Up	200
23.	In the Beginning Was the Word	212
24.	We Have Seen His Glory	222
25.	In Him Was Life	232
26.	Yet the World Did Not Know Him	242
27.	That They May Believe	250
28.	Jesus' Legacy	262
29.	Mission Completed	274
30.	Looking Back at Jesus' Future	284
	Glossary	296

Reading's Promise

When we think about it, there's nothing quite like reading. Unfortunately, we seldom do think about it. However, since reading is such a vital part of disciplined Bible study, it is worth a few moments to think about what can happen when we read Scripture. But first consider a few simple aspects of reading itself.

Thinking About Reading

All of us learned to read; few of us recall how we did it. Yet we should not take for granted the ability to read, to understand someone else's marks on paper or screen, and to say the marks into words that we may not have heard or seen before. The more we do think about reading, the more awesome this ability becomes—especially when we recall how many things can happen as we read or as a result of reading: We acquire information; we meet ideas that had not occurred to us; we remember what we had forgotten or overlooked; we simply enjoy an author's way with words; at times we disagree with what we are reading. And sometimes we do not understand but keep on reading, hoping the next page will be more comprehensible.

From the time we began to read, the kind of writing before us affected how we expected to respond. The child does not expect the same experience from the rhyme of a Dr. Seuss book as from the plot of a fairy tale, nor does a parent expect the same reaction to a letter from a daughter halfway around the world as to an owner's manual. Knowing what to expect from the writing is a condition for reading profitably.

Knowing what to expect from the writing is a condition for reading profitably.

Expectations are not the only thing we bring to our reading, whatever the text. We bring habits of thought, convictions about what is right and wrong, curiosity, physical conditions such as poor vision, or a sense of urgency ("I've got to get this read before ..."). In other words, we bring ourselves—the selves that have been built up across the years, the selves we are because of where we live, our gender, and our skin color. Reading can help us see better who we really are, as well as who we aren't and perhaps want to be. Self-discovery is an important aspect of reading, especially when we read literature with substance.

The fact that we most often read sitting down, whether in a comfortable chair or at a desk, does not mean we are passive. Reading can be taxing as well as exciting. Not just because unfamiliar words or complex sentences demand sustained attention, but also because in reading we are engaging the person who wrote what we read—and perhaps letting the author engage us as well. Underlining and writing comments in the margins are ways of conversing with what the writer has written. When talking with a person directly, we can say, "I'm not sure I understand; what do you mean?" The person spoken to can respond, but the author cannot; so we put a comment or question in the margin to record our part of the conversation. Sometimes we still don't get it until later. Then the book or essay opens up, perhaps unexpectedly, and we too open up to what it says. Significant reading is like that.

Reading Scripture

All the preceding observations about reading apply also to reading Scripture. The distinctive character of the Bible, however, suggests that a few additional observations are appropriate.

To begin with, unless we read to someone, we normally read silently, to ourselves, by ourselves. But Scripture was written to be read aloud, even when it was read alone. We cannot skim when reading aloud. The slower pace allows us to attend to all the details. Reading aloud also invites us to use the voice to emphasize certain words, to distinguish questions from statements, as well as the words of one speaker in the story from those of another person. By reading the text aloud, especially the Gospel stories that report exchanges between Jesus and his hearers, we become interpreters. Indeed, since the stories in the Gospels had been told and retold for years before they were written down, the person who today reads these stories aloud is a successor of the early Christians who first *told* these stories.

Furthermore, Scripture was meant to be read publicly, in the faith community assembled for worship and for instruction. So if we read it as intended, we will read it in the company of others whether they are present or not. Because the Christian Bible is the church's book, in reading it we join a community of readers and hearers who repeatedly have pondered it, struggled with it, and have been grasped by its power to change and renew faith and life. This community spans centuries and cultures and now circles the globe as well. Participating in this community provides the occasion to open ourselves to our fellow readers who well may understand our shared Scripture in ways that would not occur to us.

> **Scripture was meant to be read publicly, in the faith community assembled for worship and for instruction. So if we read it as intended, we will read it in the company of others whether they are present or not.**

Some of us read all sorts of things—newspapers and magazines, novels, "how to" books, poetry, jokes, to name a few—in keeping with our interests, tastes, or desire to know. Usually we easily understand their subject matter. When we read Scripture, however, we often have difficulty knowing what it says and what it means. That experience should neither surprise nor dishearten us. Like all good literature, the Bible often discloses its meanings to those who stay with it long enough to get something out of it. Curiously, what we get out of it may or may not be what the author put into it, for what the author put into it is not always obvious. Still, the author's efforts can help us grasp the subject matter more clearly, at least clearly enough to know that our understanding is moving in the right direction.

In the long run, what matters most is not whether we have grasped something of the subject matter but whether the subject matter has somehow grasped us. When the Bible's subject matter grasps us, we find ourselves confronted by something that challenges and changes us. We cannot require our reading of Scripture to produce such an experience, but we can be open to it. And then, if we *are* grasped, we will be surprised by the gift.

Reading the Gospels

The subject matter of the Gospels is Jesus, not just the man himself but also the meaning of a whole event whose center is Jesus. And that event includes Jesus' relation to the Jewish religion he inherited, to the circle of disciples around him, and to the early Christians who believed in him after his death and resurrection—including those whose understanding of Jesus is built into the Gospels they wrote about him. The Jesus of the Gospels is not a detached figure but a person whose meaning cannot be separated from his impact on his contemporaries and on those who believed in him later.

Reading the Gospels attentively is essential if we are to grasp their subject matter. While any piece of writing requires attention, in the case of the Gospels attentive reading means bearing in mind that their purpose is to *form* their readers by the way they *inform* them about the subject matter. The Gospels achieve their purpose when we

> **While any piece of writing requires attention, in the case of the Gospels attentive reading means bearing in mind that their purpose is to *form* their readers by the way they *inform them* about the subject matter.**

grasp enough of what they tell us about Jesus that we can be grasped by him. That is the promise of reading the Gospels.

A Word to the Reader

Before You Begin

1. JESUS IN THE GOSPELS differs somewhat from the four phases of DISCIPLE Bible study, for it looks more closely at the Gospel texts. The title of this study suggests why this is so: We will be looking at Jesus *in* the Gospels. This focus requires attention to details.

2. Sometimes the first three Gospels (the Synoptics) report what Jesus said and did in almost the same way and in the same setting, but at other times they tell the same story differently or in a different setting; so too, nearly identical words of Jesus sometimes appear in different settings. We will use these differences to detect some aspect of what each Gospel writer wants to highlight about Jesus. When the Gospel of John tells the same story as the Synoptics, we will look at it briefly as well. But since John's Gospel has its distinct way of presenting Jesus, we will examine that Gospel at the end of our study.

3. The assigned daily Bible readings usually include passages from the Old Testament that are important to the Gospel readings, sometimes because the Gospels mention what the Old Testament says, and sometimes because the Old Testament passages reveal what the Gospels take for granted. From time to time, readings from the Apocrypha are assigned because they help us understand better the Jewish thought-world Jesus inherited.

Biblical references in the daily assignments generally follow the sequence of the lesson development and so are often not in biblical sequence. Expect to read some passages more than once and some passages several times because meaning can differ according to context.

4. While Scripture quoted here is from the New Revised Standard Version, from time to time other versions are cited as well because differences in translation often signal either different understandings of the Greek text or different words used in the manuscripts. As you read your Bible, watch for small, usually italic, letters of the alphabet that appear within or at the end of biblical verses indicating additional information in footnotes. The footnotes ordinarily appear at the end of the right-hand column in a two-column Bible or at the bottom of the page in a one-column Bible. Occasionally the study manual commentary refers to an alternative translation of a particular verse or mentions verses missing from or added to some manuscripts. You will find that information in the footnotes.

5. Sometimes the lessons quote from early Christian writings not in the New Testament. Such quotations remind us that second-and third-century Christians were producing a growing body of writings alongside and in response to the New Testament.

6. Topics that cannot be treated within the body of the lesson but that are pertinent to the subject matter of the lesson, such as historical information or explanation of a concept, appear as brief notes or in chart form within or near the lesson to which they relate. Not every lesson has such additional information. References to notes and charts by title and page number come within the lessons; for example, Lesson 1 includes the first reference to a note (See "The Gospels," page 15.)

7. Every field of study develops its own technical vocabulary to make talking about the subject matter more precise. This practice is true also of biblical study. For example, the Greek translation of the Old Testament, used by all New Testament writers, is called the Septuagint. To aid understanding, the study manual includes a glossary of such technical or unfamiliar terms. When such a word appears in a lesson, an asterisk indicates the word is included in the glossary (for example, Septuagint*). After the word has appeared in two lessons the asterisk is dropped.

As You Go

Things to look for. Accompanying each day's Scripture reading assignments are suggestions of things to look for that will take you deeper into Scripture. The words *note, notice,* and *observe* are used often in the suggestions to encourage close attention to detail.

If you *note* or *observe* carefully, you may discover things in the texts you might have missed otherwise. You also will make your own observations and find it useful to write them down. (In this study, "texts" refers to what is written in the Bible not to what is written in the study manual, as in "textbook".) Speaking of the "text" is a way of emphasizing first what is written, not the information it might contain.

Suggestions of things to look for sometimes amount to two or three sentences; other times, several sentences. As the study progresses, the suggestions increase in length and detail thereby developing and sharpening your ability to read carefully. As you become aware of detail in Scripture ask yourself repeatedly, What am I to make of this? The study manual provides space for recording insights, observations, and questions related to the Scripture. This approach to study of the Gospels requires and involves close reading of the text—not to be done on the run, in bits and pieces, or at the last minute. Scheduling enough time for reading and writing is crucial.

Study manual format. The lesson title and the printed Scripture that follows indicate the lesson's focus. The title of each lesson serves also as the heading for the commentary portion of the lesson in the study manual. Main elements in the study manual format are designated by scriptural phrases.

"They Have No Wine" is Mary's word to Jesus at the wedding in Cana (John 2:3). The words appear in each lesson as the heading for a brief statement about some aspect of the human condition that is addressed, sometimes indirectly, in the week's study. This statement may not apply to everyone, and it is never a complete description. It intends to be suggestive, to alert the reader to some part of daily life that needs attention.

"Beginning With Moses and All the Prophets" is from Luke 24:27, where the writer of the Gospel reports what Jesus said to the two persons he met on the road to Emmaus. "Moses and all the prophets" is a way of referring to Scripture as a whole, which Jesus interpreted in relation to himself. Here the phrase signals that to understand Jesus in the Gospels we must attend also to the Old Testament.

"Do You Want to Become His Disciples, Too?" comes from John 9:27 (NIV), where the man whose blindness Jesus had healed asks this question of those who questioned him. Even though that setting differs from ours, the question itself goes to the heart of what this study is about. These paragraphs do not tell you what to do; rather, they are designed to stimulate thoughtful reflection so that you can come to your own conclusions about what your following Jesus calls for.

This section always includes a question or a suggestion requiring written response as a starting point for describing the Jesus you see in the week's Scripture.

All the prayers come from the Psalms and are quoted from The Contemporary English Version (CEV) published by American Bible Society in 1995. The freshness of this readable (especially aloud) and understandable translation makes it especially useful for prayer. From time to time you may wish to use other translations, as well as use the quoted psalm as a starting point for composing your own prayer.

Gospel Comparisons. Daily individual study and weekly group study involve use of three components—the Bible, the study manual, and Gospel Comparisons.

Gospel Comparisons contains selected Gospel portions from the New Revised Standard Version printed in multicolumn format to facilitate the comparing of similarities and differences in Gospel accounts of an event, teaching, or story. The printed selections follow the sequence of Scripture treated in the study manual.

GC 1-1 is an example of the symbol that appears in the study manual at the point in any lesson where the Gospel Comparisons is to be used during daily study. (GC means Gospel Comparisons. The first number indicates the lesson and the second number, the Gospel portion to be used at that point in the lesson.) The symbol may appear one or more times in a lesson. A few lessons do not call for use of Gospel Comparisons during daily study. Brief instructions accompany each Gospel portion.

Some Gospel portions are included for use during weekly group study and therefore are not referred to in the study manual. References to their use appear in the leader guide.

Completing daily assignments. Follow these steps in completing daily assignments:

First: Look at the biblical references to get a sense of what portions of the Bible you are going to read.

Second: Glance at the suggestions of things to look for to get an idea of what to watch for while reading Scripture.

Third: Read all of the assigned biblical passages for the day and take notes on the passages.

Fourth: Go back and work through the suggestions of things to look for one at a time, writing notes as you *note* and *observe* so you can retrieve your ideas for group discussions.

Expect to spend at least forty-five to sixty minutes in daily study on Days 1–5. Allow at least one hour on Day 6 for reading the commentary in the study manual, which often requires looking up additional references, comparing Scripture passages in the Gospel Comparisons, and writing your response to the question or suggestion at the end of the lesson.

1 Jesus *in* the Gospels

I handed on to you as of first importance what
I in turn had received: that Christ died for our sins in
accordance with the scriptures.

(1 Corinthians 15:3)

They Have No Wine

Knowing what to do about the legacy of the past is hard. Sometimes we feel the past is a burden we carry because we can't get away from the effects of what happened long ago. Old beliefs seem to get in the way of the new. At the same time, we want something reliable to hold on to. Remembering an inheritance is part of discovering who we are. Tradition cuts both ways. What will we hand on to our children, and to their children?

Beginning With Moses and All the Prophets

None of this week's readings is from the Gospels. Nevertheless, they prepare us to read the Gospels fruitfully by showing us some of the ways the Bible tells us about events—ways that express the meaning of events for the life of faith.

Day 1 Exodus 14:21–15:21; Psalms 78; 136

All the assigned readings are about the same event—the Israelites' escape from Pharaoh's army. Note, however, the different ways this event is recorded, and the ways the event is used. Remember that in the Bible form follows function (that is, *how* something is told reflects *why* it is told).

Day 2 Deuteronomy 4:1-14; 6; 2 Timothy 2:8-15; 1 Peter 2:20-23

Note how the readings from Deuteronomy insist on remembering the past for the sake of the future. Observe the ways Jesus is remembered in the New Testament passages, and the purposes for this remembering.

Day 3 Acts 2:14-36; 10; 13:13-43; 17:16-34

While Jesus is essential in each of the sermons in today's readings, make note of how the setting for each affects what is emphasized about him.

Day 4 Romans 1:1-6; 1 Corinthians 11:17-34; 15:1-11; Philippians 2:1-13

In each of today's readings Paul apparently uses traditions about Jesus, though only in 1 Corinthians 11:23 and 15:3 does he point this out. (A "tradition" is something handed on repeatedly so that the wording becomes standardized. The Gospels contain the stories and teachings of Jesus that were handed on as traditions, mostly by word of mouth, before being written down. Philippians 2:5-11 may be a piece of tradition that Paul quotes.) Note that each of these traditions emphasizes some aspect of Jesus that was important enough to be handed on as a tradition.

Day 5 Hebrews 1:1-4; 2:1-9; 5:7-10; 11:1–12:2; 1 John 4:13–5:12

Today's readings are not from the Gospels, but note how they express the gospel.

Day 6 Read and respond to "Jesus *in* the Gospels" and "Do You Want to Become His Disciples, Too?"

Prayer Concerns

Jesus *in* the Gospels

Disciples study Jesus in the Gospels because they must. No one compels them to do so, of course. The obligation is implied in discipleship itself. As an apprentice learns from the master of a craft, so the disciple learns from the teacher, Jesus. We study Jesus because we are his followers already, whether we have long followed him closely, stumbled behind him, or have just begun to walk in his steps. And our apprenticeship does not end. Nor do we want it to.

The disciple does not study Jesus directly, however, but indirectly by studying the New Testament Gospels. (Throughout these lessons, *Gospels* always refers to these four writings—Matthew, Mark, Luke, and John; *gospels* refers to those not in the canon,* such as the *Gospel of Thomas.**) The Gospels were created, in fact, to assist people like us—believers at various stages in their discipleship—to understand who Jesus is and why following him changes a person's life at the core. Embarking on a study of Jesus in the Gospels can make us eager or apprehensive, but it will not leave us neutral. Jesus is that kind of person, and the Gospels are that kind of writing. Disciples have a stake in what they learn about Jesus in the Gospels. So we begin by remembering the sort of writing the Gospels are and what we can expect from them. (See "The Gospels," page 15.)

From Gospel to Gospels

Recall that the entire first generation of Christians believed the gospel before they read any of our Gospels, all written after Paul's letters (which were written in the 50's). None of the Gospels, not even Mark (probably the oldest), was written "from scratch"; all of them use traditions of Jesus' words and deeds that had been circulating in the early Christian groups (oral tradition). A saying or a story becomes a "tradition" when it is repeated frequently enough that its wording becomes stable, though not beyond change. Some of the Jesus traditions might have been written down before they were used by the Evangelists* to create the Gospels we have; other traditions continued to be handed on by word of mouth until they were included in the Gospels, and still others never were written down and so are lost to us. The point is that the gospel message is older than any Gospel text. If today people become believers by reading the Gospels, in the early decades of Christianity people believed the gospel message before there were

Gospels to read in worship or to study with other believers. (Few first-century Christians would have had their own copies.)

Our reasons for studying Jesus in the Gospels coincide with the reasons that produced them in the first place—to guide believers as they sought to be faithful disciples. The same was surely true of the Jesus traditions themselves. When we use the Gospels in Christian worship and preaching today, and study them together with other followers of Jesus, we are using these books in their native habitat, the Christian community. Because the Gospels were written in the service of the gospel message, they focus attention on what is important for the disciple to know in order to be a faithful follower. Consequently, the Gospels do not tell us some things we might want to know. What did Jesus look like? How much schooling did he have? Could he speak Greek or Latin as well as Hebrew and Aramaic? When did Joseph die? Did Jesus know, or know about, any of the writings we now call the Dead Sea Scrolls? Was he (or had he ever been) married? These are legitimate historical questions, but they are not "gospel questions"—questions that point to the good news of Jesus as God's gift by which humanity can be restored to God's intent.

The good news, the gospel message about the meaning of Jesus, accounts for one important feature of the Gospels—the strange proportion between the amount of attention given to what Jesus said and did during his mission and the last week of his life. In Mark, for instance, the last week gets five chapters but the whole public ministry before that gets only ten. This proportion reflects Mark's conviction that this last week, and particularly the Passion story,* is the narrative form of the gospel message: "Christ died for our sins in accordance

The Evangelists tell the story of Jesus from the beginning to the end, but they understand the beginning in light of the end.

with the scriptures" (1 Corinthians 15:3). In other words, the Gospels present the Jesus story from the standpoint of its outcome (his cross and resurrection), understood as the gospel. To restate it:

The Evangelists tell the story of Jesus from the beginning to the end, but they understand the beginning in light of the end. In studying the Gospels then, we should expect to meet the gospel message right from the start.

Although the New Testament contains four Gospels, the church has taught there is really *one* gospel expressed in four Gospels. That is why they have been given the title, "The Gospel According to . . . ." The names that follow are also traditional; the books never name their authors, nor do they say when and where they were written. This study will use the traditional names simply for the sake of convenience. The actual names of the Evangelists are not known and are not important here anyway. What is important is learning to hear each Gospel's gospel in its own right. Probably each Gospel was written for a particular cluster of house churches, perhaps in a major city such as Antioch. The Evangelists did not write their Gospels to be sold on the street or to contribute to a planned collection of Jesus books; but once the Gospels were assembled, we can do what their first readers could not—compare them. Comparing the Gospels in detail will be an important part of this study, for comparison repeatedly enriches our understanding of each Gospel and of the gospel itself. In the New Testament the gospel is not played by a solo violin but by a string quartet.

The very characteristic that enriches the disciple's understanding of the gospel—the diversity of the Gospels—frustrates the historian's quest for information about Jesus. The disciple desires understanding for the sake of fidelity to Jesus; the historian searches for information for the sake of an accurate picture of the past. The difference is not absolute, of course, because the disciple too wants to know what happened. Nevertheless, the difference is important enough to merit a few brief observations in order to clarify what we will undertake here.

Gospels and Historians

The core task of a historian is to reconstruct and illumine the past on the basis of evidence whose reliability has been tested, usually by appealing to a variety of considerations. The discipline of historical study is based on the premise that there is a difference between what happened and the report of what happened because even an accurate report may not be complete. Besides, the *way* something is reported is rarely free from the bias or point of view of the reporter. Because reports differ, often a person cannot learn what really was the case and so must

decide whether something reported is possible, plausible, probable, or reasonably certain. Often historians conclude that without further evidence, they simply do not know, and cannot know, the facts.

When historians take up "the quest of the historical Jesus" (to use Albert Schweitzer's phrase), they proceed as they would in studying Julius Caesar or Thomas Jefferson. They must reckon with the fact that the Gospels are biased toward the Christian understanding of Jesus; virtually all

In the New Testament the gospel is not played by a solo violin but by a string quartet.

evidence about him is Christian. We have no Roman records of Jesus' trial, and the few lines about Jesus in ancient Jewish writings were written long after the Christian Gospels. Furthermore, the Gospels themselves sometimes disagree when reporting the same event. A famous instance concerns the day Jesus died. According to John, Jesus died the day the lambs were being slaughtered to be eaten at the Passover meal that night; but according to the other three Gospels, he died the day after the Passover meal. Each date suggests something important about Jesus, but both cannot be right historically.

Historians also cast their nets widely in order to get all the evidence, from whatever source. They look at noncanonical gospels and gospel quotations in second-century and third-century Christian literature; they study ancient writers who describe Palestine and conditions there, especially Josephus* who wrote the history of the Jews. They study coins and other archaeological evidence and give special attention to other religious literature produced by Jews of the period, such as the Dead Sea Scrolls, and by the later rabbis whose understanding of Jewish life and faith had roots both before and in the time of Jesus. The information gathered and sifted this way does not tell us directly about Jesus or the Gospels, but it does allow historians to make the environment of Jesus—his times and circumstances—intelligible so that he and the earliest Christian traditions about him can be understood in their own setting. Our understanding of the historical context of Jesus and earliest Christianity has also been enriched through exploration of the ways institutions and communities functioned in first-century Palestine. We understand Jesus better when we realize that the Jerusalem Temple functioned also as a bank, that the synagogue was a school and meeting place, that much of the land was farmed by poor tenants while the owners lived abroad. Such information that illumines Jesus' environment is immense and varied; and because historians differ in what they emphasize, they produce different portraits of Jesus.

Today's disciples of Jesus also want to have reliable knowledge of the Gospels and of Jesus, for they want to know as much as possible about the person they are following. Information becomes important when it affects a person's discipleship. Simply knowing the facts about Jesus rarely makes anyone a disciple; were that the case, the devil would have been the chief disciple. Indeed, the Gospels themselves indicate that those who knew the facts— those who saw and heard what Jesus did and said—did not really understand what they saw and heard to be faithful until after the Resurrection. Even now without reliable knowledge of Jesus of Nazareth, we can easily create in our minds a Jesus who never was.

Our study, then, will be informed by "the quest of the historical Jesus" but will not be such a quest. We will study Jesus *in* the Gospels, not the historian's Jesus *behind* the Gospels, for that would have the effect of replacing the four Gospels with a fifth one. Nor will we create one gospel by blending the four. A theologian named Tatian tried such blending eighteen centuries ago when he wove the four Gospels into a single narrative that for a time became the gospel text for the churches in Syria. Elsewhere, this combined text, known as the Diatessaron (literally, "from four"), was rejected. Rather than accept Tatian's solution, the rest of the church decided, wisely, to live with the theological as well as historical problems generated by having four Gospels side by side. Do not four portraits of the same person enrich our understanding more than just one? Although the church included only four Gospels in the New Testament, some Christians also read other gospels that probably were produced in the second century. Today, some of them exist only in fragments or as quotations in later Christian writings.

An Early Summary of the Gospel Message

In 1 Corinthians 15 Paul interpreted the meaning of Jesus' resurrection by reminding the new Christians in Corinth of the gospel message he had preached there a few years before (in about A.D. 50–51). And to do so, he quotes one of the oldest pieces of tradition in the whole New Testament. We know it is a piece of tradition because the

language Paul uses—"had received," "handed on"—was used also by Jewish sages for the transmission of their traditions. (The Revised English Bible [REB] actually includes *tradition* in the translation.) Paul "received" it when he was baptized in Damascus (Acts 9:18), no later than A.D. 35. In receiving the tradition, he did not merely acquire the information it contains, for he surely had known believers were claiming Jesus had been buried and resurrected; otherwise he hardly would have harassed "the church of God" (1 Corinthians 15:9). In other words, within a few years after the Resurrection, this tradition had become so firmly fixed that Paul taught it as the core gospel message he took to the Corinthians in distant Greece. Now, when he reminds them of it, he adds the second line in 15:6, as well as the reference to his "Damascus road experience" in 15:8. Here is what he wrote:

15:3
"I handed on to you the tradition I had received:
that Christ died for our sins,
in accordance with the scriptures;
15:4
that he was buried;
that he was raised to life on the third day,
in accordance with the scriptures;
15:5
and that he appeared to Cephas [Peter],
and afterwards to the Twelve.
15:6
Then he appeared to over five hundred . . . at once,
most of whom are still alive, though some have died.
15:7
Then he appeared to James [Jesus' brother],
and afterwards to all the apostles.
15:8
Last of all he appeared to me too"
(1 Corinthians 15:3-8, REB).

This tradition provides a window through which we can glimpse the way the Jesus traditions circulated before the Gospels were written. On one hand, despite the early date of this tradition, the Gospels contain no story about an appearance of Jesus to James. On the other hand, none of the appearance stories in the Gospels mention this tradition (though Luke 24:34 mentions the appearance of the Risen One to Simon, Peter's original name). We may reasonably conclude that the same traditions simply were not known everywhere by all Christians. Remembering this likelihood helps us understand why some sayings and stories of Jesus are found in one Gospel but not in another, and why the Gospels differ from time to time. For instance, Matthew 16:13-18 and John 1:35-42 give quite different accounts of *when* Jesus said Simon would be called Peter (Cephas). In other words, we know *all* the Jesus traditions in our Gospels; the first-century Christians probably did not.

Paul's received tradition does agree with the other parts of the Gospels. First, the tradition asserts "Christ died for our sins"; this death is not seen here as a tragic event, something to be regretted. Rather, it was a death that dealt effectively with sin—though how it did so is not said, thereby inviting reflection that later was formulated as the doctrine of the Atonement. The death was for *our* sins; no one else is blamed for Jesus' death. The text does not say Jesus died because of Pilate's sins or the Pharisees' sins. Rather, the persons who created, used, transmitted, and received this tradition are united in a confession shared by all the beneficiaries of Christ's death. Presumably they were both awed by this event and deeply grateful for it. (We do, after all, still refer to that day as Good Friday!) In one way or another, each of the Gospels also teaches us this death is redemptive (see Matthew 26:28; Mark 10:45; Luke 24:45-47; John 6:51).

The tradition Paul quotes also asserts that Jesus' death and resurrection occurred "in accordance with the scriptures" (perhaps referring to Isaiah 53:4-9 and/or Hosea 6:2). In other words, the meaning of Christ's cross and resurrection is consistent with the will and way of God in Israel's Bible. The importance of this assertion is hard to overemphasize. Two observations are particularly significant here: (1) Each of the Gospels links Jesus to Scripture. Consequently, we simply cannot study Jesus in the Gospels while ignoring the Old Testament. Therefore each week's readings include appropriate passages from the Old Testament. (2) But the Old Testament is much more than the historical background for Jesus. For there we meet the God to whom Jesus prayed—the God he obeyed. Because of the conviction that God resurrected a man who was crucified as a criminal, Christians have developed their own way of reading the Scripture of Israel—namely, in light of Jesus' cross and resurrection as the decisive disclosure of God. Right from the start Christians have seen in Jesus' death and resurrection the new covenant Jeremiah had expected (Jeremiah 31:31-34); indeed, Jesus said as much when he instituted the Lord's Supper, for he said the wine was the new covenant in his blood (Luke 22:20). Christians adopted the Scripture of the synagogue and referred to it as the books of the old covenant (testament) and referred to selected Christian writings as the books of the new covenant. For Christians, these two collections belong together as one Bible, because if we have only the books of the new covenant, Christianity soon becomes a pagan religion with a god who is not the God of Israel, "the God and Father of our Lord Jesus Christ" (Romans 15:6). For us Gentile Christians, next to faith in Jesus as God's gift for our redemption, the most important thing that has happened for us is keeping Israel's Scripture as our Old Testament. Today, some people prefer to call it the first testament. What matters here is recognizing that the Gospels that tell us about Jesus are part of the Christian Bible that has both Testaments and that, for the Gospel writers, what we call the Old Testament was Scripture, the only Scripture they knew and used.

> For us Gentile Christians, next to faith in Jesus as God's gift for our redemption, the most important thing that has happened for us is keeping Israel's Scripture as our Old Testament.

The Way Ahead

We could study the Gospels one at a time, but that would be quite repetitive because Matthew and Luke are expansions of Mark. Instead, beginning with Lesson 4 we will study all three Synoptics* together, letting Mark provide the framework, and comparing Matthew and Luke with it. From time to time we will switch to Matthew and Luke because they include material Mark does not have. In each lesson, the reference to the lead passage will be printed in dark type. This should make it easier to follow the thread of the story. At certain points we will look also at John, though this Gospel will be studied last in order to hear its distinctive voice more clearly. Occasionally we will give attention to some stories and sayings of Jesus not in the New Testament Gospels, because looking at them will help us appreciate more what the New Testament does contain. Since the Jesus story did not occur "once upon a time" but in a particular place and time, we will also point to aspects of the historical setting in which Jesus lived and in which the earliest traditions were transmitted. We will, in short, be studying a rich and promising inheritance.

So Then

Some of us may be quite familiar with this inheritance, having received it in our youth and lived with it steadily ever since; others of us still may be discovering it. But even those already familiar with it can discover aspects not noticed before.

That discovery may include realizing we have new questions about the Gospels and about Jesus as well. We should expect this experience, for the Gospels, like the Jesus they portray, intend to do far more than provide answers to questions we already have. As does Jesus, the Gospels intend to question us—who we really are and how we relate to God and to our fellow human beings. If we read the Gospels "with the grain"—consistent with their intent—then we also should consider whether we are asking the right questions. And the right question for one person may not be the right question for another. But raising the right questions is an essential ingredient of faithful discipleship.

The right questions about the Gospels and the Jesus they portray often turn into questions about our own discipleship. Then we may discover few specific right answers, as the diversity of Christian faithfulness shows. Here we do well to bear in mind what Paul wrote: "For we know only in part, and we prophesy only in part. . . . For now we see in a mirror, dimly, but then we will see face to face. Now I know only in part; then I will know fully, even as I have been fully known" (1 Corinthians 13:9, 12).

Do You Want to Become His Disciples, Too?

Disciples do not write their own ticket; they follow the model, one they received from persons who live by it, and hand it on to others. Following the model, though, requires knowing it.

The disciple who has received the inheritance of the Gospels' witness to Jesus must also transmit it to contemporaries and to the next generation. So one question that should be asked again and again in the course of this study is this: What have we learned about Jesus that we want to hand on to others, especially to those who come after us?

Describe your perception, image, understanding of Jesus as you begin this study. Who is the Jesus you bring with you to this study?

Jesus is my Lord, my Savior, & my Redeemer. He is my strength & my example to follow day by day.

Prayer

Our LORD, you are eternal!

    Your word will last as long as the heavens.

You remain faithful in every generation,

    and the earth you created will keep standing firm.

All things are your servants,

    and the laws you made are still in effect today....

I won't ever forget your teachings,

    because you give me new life by following them.

(Psalm 119:89-91, 93, The Contemporary English Version [CEV])

The Gospels

This study assumes the following scholarly conclusions about the Gospels: (1) Mark is the oldest, written shortly before or shortly after the Jewish revolt against Rome in A.D. 66–70. Some think it was written in Rome, others in Galilee or in that vicinity. (2) Matthew and Luke used Mark for their overall framework, though both these Evangelists did not hesitate to put what they used into different settings, or to abbreviate or expand what they used. Both Gospels probably were written between A.D. 85–95. Where they were written is not known, though Matthew is often placed in Syria, perhaps Antioch. (3) Sometimes Matthew and Luke report Jesus' teachings in identical words *not* found in Mark. Many scholars have concluded, therefore, that in these instances both Gospels rely on another stream of tradition, which scholars have tagged "Q"* as a convenient way of distinguishing this material from what is found also in Mark. "Q" does not actually exist but must be reconstructed from Matthew and Luke. Whether it had been written down already (perhaps in Galilee) as some contend, remains unclear. In any case, "Q" consisted of a collection of Jesus sayings, and probably came into existence before Mark (around A.D. 50). (4) Matthew (M*) and Luke (L*) each has stories and sayings of Jesus found in no other Gospel, for example the Christmas wise men in Matthew and the Christmas shepherds in Luke. (5) John too probably was written around A.D. 90, traditionally in Ephesus though possibly in or near Syrian Antioch. It is unlikely the author of John used any of the other three Gospels, though he did know some of the stories and sayings in those Gospels. On the whole, John is an independent voice.

15

2 When Words Became Events

All this took place to fulfill what had been spoken by the
Lord through the prophet:
"Look, the virgin shall conceive and bear a son,
and they shall name him Emmanuel,"
which means, "God is with us."
(Matthew 1:22-23)

They Have No Wine

Empty words. Just talk. Unkept promises. Vain hopes. Who has not been let down, dismayed, crushed inwardly by trusted words that proved hollow? Is life only promise? Do the deepest yearnings for what is reliable ever come to pass?

Beginning With Moses and All the Prophets

The opening chapters of Matthew and Luke invite us to share these Gospels' distinctive angles of vision from which they will present Jesus in the chapters that follow. This week we focus on Matthew. All the Old Testament passages are mentioned or implied in Matthew 1–2. Sometimes the wording of a quoted Old Testament passage differs from the wording we find in our Old Testament. The reasons for this difference vary from passage to passage. Keep these three considerations in mind: (1) Our English versions of the Old Testament are translated from the Hebrew, but the Gospels quote the ancient Greek version (Septuagint*), which does not always agree with the Hebrew. The translators of the Gospels render what the Greek texts say, not the Hebrew behind them. (2) Sometimes the Evangelists* modified the wording so the quotation fits the point better. (3) The Evangelists may well have been quoting from memory.

Day 1 Matthew 1–2

Fulfill is a key word in Matthew, especially in Chapters 1–2, indicating how we are to read the story of Jesus. Try using other words to make the same point.

Day 2 Genesis 38; Ruth 1:1–2:13; 4:13-22; Joshua 2; 6:1-25; 2 Samuel 11:1–12:25

Notice the four women in Jesus' genealogy. The Old Testament readings for today provide clues to why they are included in the genealogy.

Day 3 Exodus 1–2

Note how elements of Matthew 1–2 suggest certain details of the passage from Exodus.

Day 4 Isaiah 7:1-17; Jeremiah 31:15; Hosea 11:1-9; Micah 5:1-4

Matthew claims that certain parts of these passages are "fulfilled" in what happened in connection with the beginning of Jesus' life.

Day 5 2 Samuel 7:1-16; Psalms 89:1-4, 19-37; 132:11-18; Jeremiah 23:5-6

Notice how the promise to David persists in these passages (as well as in Micah 5:1-4), written centuries apart.

Day 6 Read and respond to "When Words Became Events" and "Do You Want to Become His Disciples, Too?"

Prayer Concerns

When Words Became Events

Where does the story of Jesus really begin? In Luke it begins with Gabriel's promise to Mary (Luke 1:30-31); but in Matthew the life of Jesus began before the story begins, for Mary is already pregnant and Joseph is planning to "break the engagement," as we might put it. What a strange way to begin the story of the Messiah! In fact, almost everything in Matthew 1-2 is strange and unexpected. And that, of course, is the point. These chapters surprise us at every turn, beginning with the difference between what they contain and what we usually call them, "the birth stories." In fact, there is no birth *story* in Matthew; the birth itself is barely mentioned (2:1). Nevertheless, these chapters tell us who Jesus is and point to his meaning, several meanings in fact. To see them, we need to look at the chapters as a whole and to watch for various clues to the significance of Jesus built into them.

On Reading Matthew 1-2

The author created a continuing narrative by combining quite different kinds of material: genealogy, stories, and the narrator's* comments that tell the reader what is really going on, the meaning of it all. But the meaning is also built into the genealogy and the stories themselves. If we want to understand these chapters, we should put our own questions aside, at least to begin with, and look for what the author is telling us and for the kind of response he seems to expect of us. Having done that, we may discover—and that could prove to be the right word—that our own questions, while not wrong, are not as important as we had thought, and that Matthew is answering questions we might not have asked but should have. Matthew's overarching question, of course, is Who is Jesus? At the end of Matthew 2 we detect another question, also answered by Matthew: If the Messiah is to come from Bethlehem, why was Jesus' hometown a village in Galilee?

One feature that distinguishes these chapters from the rest of the Gospel is the emphasis on dreams (1:20; 2:12, 13, 19, 22). In Matthew, dreams have the same role as visions: They are manifestations of divine guidance made known to the one who dreamed.

Another feature of these chapters is they focus on Joseph. Mary is silent throughout; in Luke the focus is on Mary, and Joseph is ignored. In Matthew it is through Joseph that Jesus is legally

"the Messiah, the son of David" (Matthew 1:1, 20), because the blood line runs through him, even though he was not the father of Jesus. For that reason the genealogy, which uses the formula "the father of," suddenly changes at 1:16: "Joseph the husband of Mary, of whom Jesus was born." Given the virgin birth, there was no other way for Jesus to be a legal descendant of David.

A third feature of these chapters is the inclusion of the women: Tamar (1:3); Rahab and Ruth (1:5); Bathsheba, "wife of Uriah" (1:6); and Mary (1:16). Matthew assumes the reader knows who they are. The function of these women in the genealogy continues to be disputed, largely because no explanation seems to fit all of them. At times it is wise to admit we do not know the answer, and this appears to be such a time.

Since these two chapters begin Matthew's Jesus story, we should note also what they do not include — namely, the kind of information we usually expect in a biography, even if Matthew is not a biography in the modern sense. Matthew offers not a word of explanation about who Mary and Joseph are or how old either one of them was when Mary's pregnancy was discovered. We do not learn how many wise men came or where they came from ("from the East" doesn't tell us much), what their names were, or why from the appearance of the star they concluded the king of the Jews had been born. Matthew considers it neither necessary nor useful to explain why Joseph was afraid to return to Bethlehem, since the angel told him that "those who were seeking the child's life are dead" (2:20). We are left to infer that Joseph suspected Archelaus would prove to be as much a threat to the child as his father had been, but why Joseph thought so is not said. Nor does Matthew say how old the child Jesus was when he was brought back to "the land of Israel." Above all, we are not told what Mary thought of all these things, or even whether Joseph told her of his dream in which he learned how she had become pregnant. And Matthew is totally silent about the entire period, of unspecified length, between the family's arrival in Nazareth and the preaching of John the Baptist, which begins the next chapter. Matthew allows nothing to divert attention from what he wants us to see and understand. We will see the same is true of Luke, though he wants us to see different things and different people.

Jesus' Identity Stated

Identity is a word we use to say who a person really is, perhaps despite appearances. *Identity* is not found in isolation, however, but in relatedness. In Chapters 1–2, Matthew explicitly states Jesus' identity in terms of three relationships: relationship to Israel, to Scripture, and to God. He does not devote a paragraph to each, but weaves the relationships into the story.

In the first line Matthew announces Jesus' identity (1:1), not by mentioning his parents (as in "Simon son of Jonah," Matthew 16:17) or his hometown ("Jesus of Nazareth") but by using a title of an office—Messiah. (Had the New Revised Standard Version translated the Greek word used here, *Christos*, it would have used "Anointed"; instead it uses English letters [Messiah] to spell the Hebrew word [*mashiah*] behind the Greek; other versions use "Christ"—RSV, NIV, REB.) At the end of the genealogy, the same

> **Matthew explicitly states Jesus' identity in terms of relationship to Israel, to Scripture, and to God.**

identity is repeated twice more (1:16-17). For Matthew the Messiah is a royal figure; that is why the magi's question about the birthplace of the "king of the Jews" (2:2) and Herod's question about the birthplace of the Messiah (2:4) are the same question. As we will see in time, Jesus' identity as Messiah and King will reappear at the center of the story and at the end as well.

In Jesus' day it was not obvious to all Jews that the messiah would be a king, though many thought so. In fact, the writers of the Dead Sea Scrolls expected two messiahs, a priestly one alongside a royal one. Remember there was no single job description for the expected messiah, nor did all hopes for Israel's deliverance from oppression even mention a messiah; in such cases, God would bring the glorious future in unspecified ways. Indeed, not all Jews believed a messiah would come, but those who did assumed he would be a human being like everyone else. In Matthew, however, the understanding of the Messiah is somewhat different because of Jesus' virgin birth.

Matthew did not need to explain who Herod was, for though he wrote this book nearly a century after Herod's death, everyone knew who Herod was. Herod, sometimes called "the Great,"

was made king of Judea by the Romans in 40 B.C., and he remained Rome's friend until his death in 4 B.C. (Since Jesus was born before Herod's death, scholars generally date his birth around 6 B.C.) Herod's ruthless rule was marked also by great building projects, the best known being the harbor and city of Caesarea on the Mediterranean coast and the Temple in Jerusalem. At his death, Herod's domain was divided among his sons, one of whom, Archelaus, ruled the area around Jerusalem. Another Herod, Antipas but often called simply Herod, ruled Galilee and adjacent areas. This was the Herod who had John the Baptist arrested and executed.

Matthew needs only a few words to suggest one consequence of Jesus' identity as Messiah-King, and they appear in the magi's question when they arrived in Jerusalem, "Where is the child who has been *born* king of the Jews?" as well as in Herod's reaction, "he was frightened, and all Jerusalem with him" (Matthew 2:2-3). Why would a tyrant like Herod be afraid of a baby? Instead of rejoicing because the Messiah-King, the long-awaited (by some) bringer of God's righteous rule, is now born, there was fear because this infant who was *born* king would replace Rome's *appointed* king. To prevent this possibility, Herod ordered the slaughter of all children in and around Bethlehem who were two years old or less. Only Matthew reports this tragedy; the Jewish historian of Jewish history, Josephus,* does not mention it. The "slaughter of the innocents," as it has come to be known, appears from time to time in Christian art, though not often in recent times. Is it too gruesome for religious art? For Matthew even Herod's dastardly deed is not without meaning, though it is a dark meaning. Matthew finds its meaning in the lament that follows the fulfillment of Jeremiah's word (Jeremiah 31:15), spoken nearly six centuries before when the people were killed or deported to Babylon.

> "A voice was heard in Ramah,
>   wailing and loud lamentation,
> Rachel weeping for her children;
>   she refused to be consoled,
>   because they are no more"
>   (Matthew 2:18).

This quotation brings us to the second way Matthew stated the identity of Jesus—as the one in whom Scripture is "fulfilled." Matthew quotes the Old Testament more than does any other Gospel, often as a comment on an event that just happened: This occurred so that what was said through the prophet (sometimes named) might be fulfilled. In Matthew 1–2 this formula appears

19

at 1:22; 2:15, 17, 23—that is, it follows every incident except the story of the magi.

A few observations on the various uses of the Old Testament in the New are appropriate here:

(1) When Matthew was being written, there was no New Testament, so there was no "Old" Testament either. Paul's letters probably had been collected and copied, and of the Gospels at least Mark had been written; but these Christian writings were not yet collected into what was later called the New Testament. Until then, what we now call the Old Testament was simply Scripture, the sacred and authoritative writings used in the synagogues and early Christian communities. In Matthew's day, all Christians regarded Scripture as the authoritative Word of God. For that reason quoting it was important. Even today quotations often have a similar function: We quote recognized authority to support the argument.

> **Matthew quotes the Old Testament more than does any other Gospel.**

(2) The relation between the synagogue's Scripture and Christianity was seen in a variety of ways (and still is). One way emphasized agreement, as in 1 Corinthians 15:3-8 mentioned earlier: "Christ died for our sins in accordance with the scriptures." In other words, the meaning of Christ's death agrees with, and is consistent with, God's ways found in Scripture. The relation of Scripture to Christianity was seen also as promise made (by God) and promise kept, whether by God, Jesus, the Spirit, or the work of the apostles. Another way Scripture relates to Christianity is found in the opening chapters of Matthew (and elsewhere): A word in Scripture is "fulfilled" in Jesus' life, and later in the life of the church as well (Acts 13:32-33). A "fulfilled" word is one whose truth is confirmed by what actually happened; until then the word remained a promise or hope, true but not yet actual.

(3) Since the same Greek words can mean either purpose or result, Matthew's expression, "*so that* what had been spoken through the prophets might be fulfilled" (Matthew 2:23) probably means "this occurred, *with the result that* what had been a word has now become an event." This statement implies that what happened should not be understood simply as the result of human devising and circumstances, though these factors are real (as the story of the slaughter of the innocents shows), but primarily because God is guiding these events in accord with the purpose expressed long ago.

The third way Matthew stated Jesus' identity explicitly is the most complex because it relates Jesus to God, to his people, and to Scripture (1:20-25). In fact, in this passage the three aspects of Jesus' identity are so interwoven they cannot be separated. Although the angel does not actually say Mary's baby is the Son of God, he implies it, "for the child conceived in her is from the Holy Spirit." Moreover, the virgin birth fulfills, brings to pass, what the Lord had said through the prophet Isaiah (Isaiah 7:14). It is important to recall this verse's setting in Isaiah. There it is part of the promise that God would give King Ahaz a sign to confirm Isaiah's promise that the two kingdoms about to invade Judah would fall. "Look, the young woman is with child and shall bear a son, and shall name him Immanuel . . . . before the child knows how to refuse the evil and choose the good, the land before whose two kings you are in dread will be deserted" (7:14, 16). Matthew's Greek version uses *parthenos* (virgin) to translate the Hebrew *'almah* (young woman). Since Mary was still unmarried (and presumably still a virgin) when she became pregnant by the Holy Spirit, Matthew saw Isaiah's words actualized in what was occurring within Mary. Further, the name Isaiah mentioned, *Immanuel* (in Greek, *Emmanuel*), does mean "God is with us," which Matthew understands as confirming the child is in fact God's child. Matthew knows, of course, that Joseph actually named the child "Jesus," in Hebrew *Yehoshua*, meaning "God [Yahweh] will save." The actual name and the symbolic name complement each other, for only one in whom God is present (Immanuel) can save from sin (Jesus/ Yehoshua); to put it another way, when God is present, there is salvation from sin (as well as judgment on sin).

Jesus' Identity Implied

Clearly the question, Who is Jesus? can be answered, and in Matthew 1–2 is answered, in different ways. Matthew not only tells us who Jesus is but also implies a good deal more in his emphasis on the fulfillment of Scripture.

To begin with, fulfillment itself implies finality. This element of finality distinguishes fulfillment from allusion or comparison. An allusion reminds readers of something similar and so invites us to make associations by merely mentioning something in passing or by using a key word. For example, saying "that was Henry's Damascus road" invites us to recall Paul's dramatic turnaround and to interpret Henry's experience in its light. Fulfillment, on the other hand, is as final as a kept promise. Matthew does not explain this but implies it repeatedly. For Matthew, saying Scripture is fulfilled in Jesus means that Jesus is the decisive event, signaling the end toward which God's purposes have been directed. Matthew is not alone in this, for in one way or another, the whole New Testament assumes or asserts the same point. The fact of finality keeps the New Testament authors from saying that the same Scripture was fulfilled several times. History may repeat itself, they imply, but fulfillment does not.

Second, Matthew shows us fulfillment without actually saying so. Herod's murder of the children calls to mind Pharaoh's similar action against the Israelite male infants centuries before. Similarities between Moses and Jesus appear several times in Matthew. For instance, Jesus' teaching the Sermon on the Mount is often compared with Moses' giving the law on Mount Sinai. In fact, in Matthew, and only in Matthew, Jesus makes five speeches (Matthew 5–7; 10; 13; 18; 24–25), which are often regarded as a counterpart to the five books of Moses (the Pentateuch). This Moses-feature hardly seems accidental; it probably reflects Matthew's conviction that Jesus fulfills the promise that someday God would bring on the scene a prophet like Moses (Deuteronomy 18:15). In Acts 3 Peter claims this promise has been kept in Jesus (3:22). In other words, by showing Jesus doing Moses-like things, Matthew invites the reader to see in Jesus the one promised long ago. Also, in Jesus' day Moses often was regarded as almost a divine figure.

Finally, Matthew sees in the return of the Holy Family from Egypt (Matthew 2:20-21) the fulfillment of Hosea 11:1, "Out of Egypt I called my son." Hosea, of course, used *son* to refer to the people of Israel. When Matthew sees this word fulfilled in Jesus' return from Egypt, he implies that in some sense Jesus *is* Israel, that he personifies what Israel is meant to be in the purpose of God.

For Matthew, saying Scripture is fulfilled in Jesus means that Jesus is the decisive event, signaling the end toward which God's purposes have been directed.

Notice how well Matthew has prepared readers for the story of Jesus: Through the genealogy he placed Jesus in the history of God's people, beginning with Abraham; through Joseph's dream he identified Jesus as the Virgin's child; through Herod he accounted for the fact that though the messiah was to be a Bethlehemite, he, like Israel, came out of Egypt. Herod, moreover, reminds us of Pharaoh, who also slaughtered baby boys. Through the magi Matthew hinted that non-Jews would worship one who was "born king of the Jews." By explicitly quoting Scripture, he pointed out that in Jesus the prophets' words were becoming events. As a result, readers know what the characters in the rest of the book do not know but must learn—who Jesus is and why he is decisive.

So Then

Matthew's way of introducing Jesus is designed to elicit our joyous awe at the wonders that mark the arrival of God's Son on the human scene. Not even the time of his arrival is a coincidence, coming forty-two generations after Abraham (Matthew 1:17). The child's very existence results from the work of the Holy Spirit. God's guidance is conveyed by the angel of the Lord who appears in dreams. Somehow the magi know that the rising of this child's star means they must journey westward to pay homage and bring precious gifts. Again and again we are told that in these events the words of ancient Scripture come true, at last. And the real meaning of this child's arrival is "Immanuel"—God with us. Celebrating this birth is easy.

Too easy, in fact, when we neglect the dark underside of this introduction to Jesus, when we forget that Bethlehem's infants were slaughtered because Herod was threatened by this good news. This child's life was threatened by his own Pharaoh, and the Holy Family became refugees, fleeing to Egypt where their forebears had been enslaved. Even upon returning, they were afraid to go home, to Bethlehem, but settled in Galilee instead. In this introduction, the words of prophecy indeed became events, but they included "Rachel weeping for her children" the way mothers still weep when their offspring are the victims of tyrants. What kind of study about God's messiah can follow from such an introduction? What can we expect from such a beginning? This infant is called "Immanuel" while a child. How will God be with us when he grows up and goes to work? The rest of the story too is designed to elicit our joyous awe.

Do You Want to Become His Disciples, Too?

The disciple persists in trusting God to bring the divine promises to pass in God's good time. Often the promise is kept in ways we do not expect. Perhaps you can cite examples from your own experience.

What claim does the Jesus in Matthew's "birth story" make on you?

_____

_____

_____

_____

_____

Prayer

With all my heart I praise you, LORD.
    In the presence of angels I sing your praises.
I worship at your holy temple
    and praise you for your love and your faithfulness.
You were true to your word
    and made yourself more famous than ever before.
When I asked for your help,
    you answered my prayer and gave me courage.

(Psalm 138:1-3, CEV)

Name Him Jesus. The name *Jesus* appears on the cover in both Hebrew and Greek. The large letters are ancient Hebrew script and come from an inscription. They spell the name *Yeshu, Jesus*, and are to be read from right to left. *Yesu, Yeshu, Yeshua, Yehoshua* are English forms of the Hebrew/Aramaic name *Joshua*, which means "God is salvation." Matthew 1:18-22, printed in Greek over the representations of four manuscript pages, includes the words that translate into English as "you are to name him Jesus." *Iesous* is the English spelling of the Greek name *Jesus*. The Greek form of the name, as used in Matthew 1:21, appears in darker type. The four manuscript pages suggest the four Gospels. Of the four Gospels only Matthew and Luke include the instruction to "name him Jesus."

3 Celebrating Beginnings

Blessed be the Lord God of Israel,
for he has looked favorably on his people
and redeemed them.

(Luke 1:68)

They Have No Wine

Often we tire of hoping for a time when there will be peace because there is
also justice, when the good is not threatened by evil, and when joy has dispelled
anxiety. Yet we keep hoping because we must, for without hope we would be
powerless.

Beginning With Moses and All the Prophets

The first two chapters of Luke are the focus of this week's study. They firmly
situate both John the Baptist and Jesus in devout Jewish life. While these chapters, like the opening chapters of Matthew, also remind us of Old Testament stories, the stories Luke recalls are different. The tone of these chapters is festive
because they celebrate the wondrous beginnings of the time of salvation.

Day 1 Luke 1–2

Read Luke 1–2 carefully so you can keep it in mind as you read the Old Testament passages this
week. *Birth of John Bap. foretold - Zechariah's disbelieved - mutness. Birth of Jesus foretold, Mary visits Eliz. "Magnificat". John born Zechariah speaks & prophesies. Jesus born in City of David (Bethlehem) Shepherds visit. Jesus circumcised & named, presented in temple. Simeon & Anna recognize baby Jesus as saviour - Simeon to Mary: a sword will pierce your own soul.*

Day 2 1 Samuel 1:1–2:10; 1 Kings 16:29-33; 17:1-7; 18:17-40

In the stories of the births of John and Jesus are echoes of the story of Samuel. Note the
similarities among the song of Hannah (1 Samuel 2:1-10), the Magnificat (Luke 1:46-55), and the
Benedictus (Luke 1:68-79). The readings from First Kings help us understand the reference to
Elijah in Luke 1:16-17. *Hannah praying - has son Samuel - Gives him to the Lord Priest Eli whose sons were wicked.*

Day 3 Isaiah 40; 49

Simeon and Anna yearned for the time of salvation for Israel. How might today's readings have nurtured their hopes?

Chapter 40 "Comfort, O comfort my people" "In the wilderness prepare the way of the Lord" "The Glory of the Lord shall be revealed - all people shall see it"

Chapter 49 He will not forsake or forget his Children - He has inscribed us on the palm of His hand Those who wait for the Lord shall not be put to shame!

Day 4 Exodus 12:1-31; Leviticus 12; Deuteronomy 16:1-17

Today's readings portray the piety of Jesus' parents. If you could interview Luke, what questions would you ask about Jesus' childhood? Then ask yourself, "Why do I want to know such things?"

1-Passover 2- Festival of Weeks 3 Festival of Booths Who were his other relatives besides Ely & John the Baptist?

Day 5 1 Samuel 2:18-26; 3:1–4:1; Isaiah 52:7-12

The reading from First Samuel continues the story of Israel's important prophet. Notice how Luke 2:52 echoes 1 Samuel 2:26.

Samuel is called by the Lord + spoken to about the iniquity Eli's sons had brought on Eli's house - Samuel became a trustworthy prophet of the Lord Isaiah 52:7- How beautiful on the mountain are the feet of Him who brings good news -

Day 6 Read and respond to "Celebrating Beginnings" and "Do You Want to Become His Disciples, Too?"

Prayer Concerns

Celebrating Beginnings

Matthew's story of Jesus' infancy is somber because Jesus' life is in such danger only God's providential intervention (through dreams) assures his survival. But Luke's story is marked by celebration and joy. Only Simeon's saying reminds us Jesus' life will have tragic consequences as well (Luke 2:29-35). Each Gospel tells the story of Jesus' infancy in its own way, in keeping with each Evangelist's sense of what is important. No evidence indicates that either writer had the other's narrative in mind; neither story supplements the other. Rather, each narrative is complete in itself. Though Matthew and Luke differ, they agree on central points: Jesus was conceived through the Holy Spirit; he was born in Bethlehem but grew up in Nazareth; Mary and Joseph were devout Jews. But Herod plays no role in Luke's account, which obviously knows nothing of the flight into Egypt. And Matthew does not include a presentation visit to Jerusalem. We don't know why the stories differ; they probably circulated independently in different Christian circles. What is important is to hear what each says about Jesus.

The Annunciations

Luke shows Jesus and John must be understood together by telling the story of the two announcements in much the same way, often using the same words. **GC 3-1**

	John		Jesus
Luke	1:11-12	Luke	1:28-29
Luke	1:13	Luke	1:30-31
Luke	1:15	Luke	1:32
Luke	1:18	Luke	1:34
Luke	1:59-64	Luke	2:21
Luke	1:80	Luke	2:40

Luke regards the marvelous births to childless women as a sign of God's grace, uniquely so when the Holy Spirit "overshadows" Mary.

Compared with the story of the angel's annunciation to Joseph (Matthew 1:18-23), the story of Gabriel's annunciation to Mary (known as "the Annunciation") is more elaborate and sensitive to her responses (Luke 1:26-38), which move from deep perplexity (1:29) through implied disbelief (1:34) to acceptance (1:38). (Gabriel's "Do not be afraid" does not necessarily mean Mary trembled with fear; rather, this word of assurance is a standard feature of biblical stories about the appearance of the divine [an epiphany] or of an angel.) Gabriel's initial prediction is straightforward: Mary will become pregnant, give birth to a son, and call his name Jesus. The name is not interpreted, as in Matthew.

Gabriel then explains who this child will become—the permanent heir to the throne of David. As the Davidic king he will be called "the Son of the Most High." Thus Jesus fulfills the word of the prophet Nathan in 2 Samuel 7:8-17, where God says of David's offspring, "I will establish his kingdom. He shall build a house for my name, and I will establish the throne of his kingdom forever. I will be a father to him, and he shall be a son to me. [That is, he will be God's son, not a divine being but a human whose special relation to God is expressed in obedience.] When he commits iniquity, I will punish him . . . . But I will not take my steadfast love from him." The reference to a "house" points to Solomon, David's successor who built the Temple. But when Nathan continues, "Your house and your kingdom shall be made sure forever before me; your throne shall be established forever," the word *house* apparently means dynasty. Although Gabriel draws on 2 Samuel 7 to tell Mary who her son will be, Luke might not take these words to mean Jesus will rule over a political kingdom.

Mary has difficulty believing Gabriel because she does not have sexual relations with a man (literally, "I do not know a man," or a husband). Instead of our wondering why Mary did not think Gabriel was predicting what would happen after she became Joseph's wife, it is better to see how her puzzlement functions in the story: It sets the stage for Gabriel's word about the Holy Spirit coming upon her, with the result that the child himself will be "holy" and "will be called Son of God"

For Luke, both Jesus and the church are the work of the Holy Spirit.

(Luke 1:35). This time, "Son of God" means more than a specially obedient person like the king (as in 2 Samuel 7:14); it now means one who owes his very existence directly to God's Spirit. The two meanings are not mutually exclusive, of course; but the former does not require the latter. In fact, Matthew 5:9 shows that Godlike persons can be called "sons of God," though "children of God" (NRSV) obscures the point (as "children of the Most High" does also in Luke 6:35).

The Holy Spirit is one important thread that runs through these stories (1:35, 41, 67; 2:26-27), and it links them to what follows; for instance, Gabriel predicts John "will be filled with the Holy Spirit (1:15, perhaps actualized in 1:80); Jesus will receive the Spirit at baptism (3:22), as we will see later. Luke's companion volume, Acts, portrays the beginning of the church and its subsequent mission as the work of the Holy Spirit. For Luke, both Jesus and the church are the work of the Holy Spirit, which, as Peter explained on Pentecost, is nothing other than the fulfillment of Joel's prophecy that God's Spirit will be poured out on all people (Acts 2:17-21). What began with John the Baptist and Jesus became the hallmark of the early church.

Another feature of Luke's account is its emphasis on the Temple in Jerusalem, the center of the Jewish religion in Jesus' day but no longer standing when Luke wrote, since the Romans destroyed it in A.D. 70. Luke 1 begins in the Temple; the infant Jesus is taken to the Temple in Luke 2; and as a twelve-year-old Jesus engages the teachers there, foreshadowing his teaching ministry in the Temple during the last week of his life (19:47-48). Likewise, after Pentecost, the earliest believers attended the Temple daily (Acts 2:46), where they healed (3:1-10) and taught (5:21, 42) to the consternation of the authorities. And it was from the Temple Paul was dragged and arrested, bringing his public mission to an end (21:27-33). Thus Luke implies the gospel began at the center of Judaism and from there spread outward to "the ends of the earth." Luke is not encouraging his Gentile readers—whether in the first or twenty-first century— to think that in moving beyond Jerusalem, Christianity abandoned its roots; rather, he is implying they should remember those roots.

While Matthew orients the account toward Joseph, Luke's focuses on Mary (Joseph says nothing at all in either account). Luke does not actually say Jesus is conceived "from the Holy Spirit" (Matthew 1:20) but clearly implies it (Luke 1:31-35). When Gabriel tells Mary the elderly Elizabeth also is pregnant (for the first time), he implies his information is a sign that what is promised to Mary will really happen, "For nothing will be impossible with God" (1:36 37). Fortunately, Luke did not explain exactly what happened but pointed to the wonder-working power of God so his readers—then and now—can marvel, believe, and celebrate.

The announcement of John's coming birth, also marvelous but not to the same degree, emphasizes two things. First, his not drinking "wine or strong drink" will mark him as a Nazirite—a person living under a vow of consecration to God (see Numbers 6 for the rules for beginning and ending Nazirite lifestyle)—and he will be "filled with the Holy Spirit" and so be equipped to speak God's word. Second, he will be the one who fulfills the role of Elijah, whose return was promised in Malachi 4:5-6: "Lo, I will send you the prophet Elijah before the great and terrible day of the LORD comes. He will turn the hearts of parents to their children and the hearts

> Luke is not encouraging his Gentile readers— whether in the first or twenty-first century— to think that in moving beyond Jerusalem, Christianity abandoned its roots; rather, he is implying they should remember those roots.

of children to their parents, so that I will not come and strike the land with a curse." According to 2 Kings 2:9-12, Elijah did not die but was taken to heaven in a fiery chariot, so the expectation developed that he would return before God's great Judgment, as Malachi said later (as did also a book of the Apocrypha,* Sirach* 48:10, which climaxes a summary of Elijah's work as a prophet). Luke 1:17 says John "will go before him," namely "the Lord their God" mentioned in the preceding verse. In Jewish thought some expected Elijah to be the forerunner of the Messiah; the Gospels see John in this role.

Zechariah's inspired utterance, known as the Benedictus from its first word in Latin ("blessed"), actually celebrates the redemption of Israel through Jesus (1:68-75) before celebrating the future work of John (1:76-79). In this redemption God remembers the covenant with Abraham, and its goal is freedom for lifelong service to God "in holiness and righteousness" without fear of enemies. John's role is to be God's prophet who will prepare the way of the Lord, which Luke takes as John's preparation for Jesus. The whole passage uses words and phrases drawn from the

Greek Old Testament. The same is true of Mary's song, the Magnificat (from the opening Latin word "magnifies").

The Magnificat (1:46-55) begins with Mary's celebration of her role in God's work of redemption and then moves to characterize the effects of that redemption as reversal. The proud and mighty are humbled, and the lowly (poor) are exalted; the hungry are filled, and the (sated) rich are emptied. As in Zechariah's praise, in this mighty act of God's faithfulness the covenant with Abraham is now actualized. The reversal that Mary anticipates looks ahead to Luke's form of the beatitudes and woes (6:20-26).

> The focus throughout the Benedictus and the Magnificat is on the great and marvelous things God has done through specific persons, real people.

Both the Benedictus and the Magnificat look beyond the immediate circumstances of Zechariah and Mary as they celebrate God's redemptive achievement through Jesus. In terms of the story itself, that redemption had not yet happened when these two burst into poetry, nevertheless all the verbs are in the past tense as if it had already happened. Because the poems use past tense, Christian readers, for whom redemption from sin has happened, are invited to join the celebration. Understandably both passages have come to be used in the liturgies of many churches. The focus throughout the Benedictus and the Magnificat is on the great and marvelous things God has done through specific persons, real people.

Good News at Night

The story of Jesus' birth (Luke 2:1-20)—and the circumstances that accompanied it—is probably the best known part of the Gospel of Luke. Here Jesus no longer shares the stage with John; here attention is focused on Jesus himself. Compared with Matthew's account, nothing here threatens the Christ Child, and Caesar's decree is merely the reason Jesus was not born in his hometown. When the news of the Savior's birth comes to the shepherds (disdained by "polite society"), already one line of Mary's Magnificat begins to come true: God has lifted up the lowly. The story concludes with the shepherds' praise on earth echoing the angels' praise in the heavens. By dawn the shepherds (presumably) were back with their sheep as before; yet in due course, nothing would be the same again.

Luke subtly reminds us Jesus was born during the reign of Augustus Caesar (27 B.C. to A.D. 14), revered in his lifetime for bringing peace to a strife-torn empire and who in its eastern domains was called "god" and "savior." A well-known inscription celebrated the date of his birth: "[the birthday] of the god has marked the beginning of the good news [*euangelion!*] through him for the world." In Luke the angels too announce "good news" for all the people: "To you is born this day in the city of David a Savior, who is the Messiah [Christ], the Lord," as well as "peace on earth" (CEV)—adding up to a different good news about a different peace from a different savior.

Right as Luke was in what he portrayed theologically, he apparently did not get the date exactly right historically. Nowhere else do we read of an empirewide census that required all people to be registered in their ancestral home. Besides, Quirinius was governor of Syria in A.D. 6–7. Here Matthew's dating is to be preferred: Jesus was born in the last years of Herod's reign, which ended in 4 B.C. In any case, Luke's mistaken date should not keep us from seeing the point: Jesus the Savior *was* born in the heyday of Augustus the savior. The contrast is deliberate, and it calls for faith's perception of its significance.

No less important is the faith required of the shepherds with respect to the sign that the good news is true: Instead of the trappings of a royal birth, this baby is wrapped in "swaddling cloths" (RSV) or simple "bands of cloth" (NRSV) and lying in a manger. Nothing visibly royal there! So, instead of believing their eyes and doubting their ears, the shepherds believed both and "returned, glorifying and praising God for all they had heard and seen."

A week later, Jesus' parents too remembered God's covenant with Abraham, for the child was circumcised; nor did they forget Gabriel had already said his name would be Jesus.

Obedience and Prophecy in Jerusalem

Luke next frames the scene in the Jerusalem Temple by emphasizing that Jesus' parents conscientiously observed the law of Moses (Luke 2:22-24, 39). Here two laws are obeyed. The first pertains to ritual impurity brought about by the flow of blood in the birth process. According to

Leviticus 12, the new mother is ritually impure for forty days (the week before the circumcision plus 33 days) if she gives birth to a son, twice that if the baby is a girl. At the end of this time, she is to present an offering of a young lamb and a turtledove or pigeon; if she cannot afford a lamb, the number of birds is doubled. Mary and Joseph, being poor, offer only the birds. After purification Mary may enter the Temple. The second law pertains to the fact that the firstborn is a boy. According to Exodus 13:2 the firstborn, animal as well as human, belongs to God. Exodus 13:11-16 makes clear the rules for "redeeming" the firstborn—that is, giving it back to God by giving God a substitute. Luke omits the redemption of the baby Jesus, probably because he regards presenting him "to the Lord" in the Temple as acknowledging that he belongs to God. "Every firstborn male shall be designated as holy to the Lord"

> When the news of the Savior's birth comes to the shepherds (disdained by "polite society"), already one line of Mary's Magnificat begins to come true: God has lifted up the lowly.

(Luke 2:23) is Luke's paraphrase of Exodus 13:2. Luke's retention of the Old Testament idiom "opens the womb" (RSV; "firstborn," NRSV) shows he assumes Jesus' birth process was normal, not miraculous as in later legend. In the noncanonical *Protevangelium of James,** a midwife determines that even after Jesus' birth the womb remained closed, intact. (Whether this story became the basis of the doctrine of the "perpetual virginity of Mary" or an expression of that belief is not evident.)

Simeon speaks as an inspired prophet (Luke 2:27-35). His oracle known as the Nunc Dimittis, from the initial words in Latin ("now dismiss"), both confirms what has been said already about Jesus' identity and significance, and goes beyond it as well. In the child he sees nothing less than the salvation that is to be

> "a light for revelation to the Gentiles and for
>   glory to your people Israel."

He sees that through Jesus Israel's vocation to be a "light to the nations" (Isaiah 49:6, 9; the word for "nations" also means "Gentiles") will be fulfilled.

This prophecy is especially important for Luke, whose second volume (Acts) shows how this mission to the Gentiles actually happened.

But Simeon also foresees that

> "this child is set [by God] for the fall and rising
>   of many in Israel, and for a sign that is spo-
>   ken against" (Luke 2:34, RSV).

That is, Jesus will be opposed in Israel, as will become plain precisely in Nazareth (4:16-30, especially 4:28-29). As a result, "the inner thoughts of many will be revealed"; it will become evident who will and who will not accept the salvation prepared (2:30-31). In the Greek, the word to Mary in 2:35, "and a sword will pierce your own soul too," interrupts the saying; but some English versions (NRSV, NIV) take the liberty of placing it at the end. That even Mary will have trouble accepting the ministry of her son will be noted in 8:19-21. The aged widow Anna, a prophet like Simeon, confirms to the public what Simeon had said privately.

The summary comment in 2:40 ("the child . . . became strong, filled with wisdom; and the favor of God was upon him") prepares us for the story that follows—the twelve-year-old Jesus in the Temple (2:41-51). Luke does not explain why the lad stayed in Jerusalem or where his parents looked for him for three days before finding him in the Temple. What matters is what he was doing there—"sitting among the teachers, listening to them and asking them questions"—a precocious boy endowed with wisdom, engaged in give-and-take with the teachers, the sages who knew the Scriptures. Mary's rebuke (understandable to every parent who has finally found a child who was absent without permission) sets the stage for Jesus' reply, the point of the story: "Why were you searching for me? Did you not know that I must be in my Father's house?" (literally, "be about my Father's interests" or "affairs"). In fact, his parents did not know. And even now, they "did not understand what he said to them." To infer that they must have forgotten Simeon's words, or Gabriel's announcement, is to spoil the story, whose double purpose is to show that Jesus sensed his vocation even as a lad, and to give the readers a preview of Jesus the wise man who will be a teacher of Israel in the Temple (19:47; 21:37; in fact, all of Jesus' teaching in Luke 20–21 appears to be given in the Temple). Appropriately, Luke ends Chapter 2 by saying, "Jesus increased in wisdom . . . and in divine and human favor."

The story of the young Jesus in the Temple (not found in the other New Testament Gospels) is quite different from stories about the child Jesus in the

*Infancy Gospel of Thomas.** Here, for example, already at the age of five Jesus is a miracle worker. One day, while playing at a brook, he made pools of water "by his word alone," and made twelve clay sparrows; when Joseph reprimanded him for violating the sabbath, Jesus "clapped his hands and cried to the sparrows: 'Off with you!' And the sparrows took flight and went away chirping." When a boy took a willow branch and destroyed the pools of water Jesus had made, Jesus was furious and said, "You insolent, godless dunderhead, what harm did the pools and the water do to you?" So Jesus caused the boy to wither up completely. This boy Jesus was also impertinent, for on his first day at school, he rebuked the teacher for not knowing the mysterious meanings of the alphabet. The *Infancy Gospel of Thomas* ends with Luke's story of Jesus in the Temple, to which such details were added as the comment that Jesus "put to silence the elders and teachers of the people" and the words of the scribes and Pharisees to Mary: "Blessed are you among women, because the Lord has blessed the fruit of your womb [notice the use of Luke 1:42]. For such glory and such excellence and wisdom we have never seen or heard."

These stories are not based on Christian traditions about Jesus; they are the products of pious (and not so pious) imagination. Such stories have been put into circulation again and again, down to our own time. Perhaps those who repeat them think they are honoring Jesus.

So Then

Although Matthew 1–2 and Luke 1–2 are commonly called "the birth stories," they are both more than and less than that—and for the same reason: They do not narrate Jesus' birth at all. In Matthew the birth is mentioned in passing, "until she had borne a son" (Matthew 1:25); and in Luke 2:7 the birth itself gets only part of the sentence, "And she gave birth to her firstborn son and wrapped him in bands of cloth, and laid him in a manger, because there was no place for them in the inn." Both Gospels show more interest in Mary's conceiving than in the delivery, because the latter is not unusual, while the former is miraculous. But the miracle itself is not described. In Matthew, when the story begins, Mary is already pregnant; and the angel tells Joseph that "the child conceived in her is from the Holy Spirit" in order to stop his plan "to dismiss her quietly" and so avoid public shame (Matthew 1:18-20). In Luke, the conception through the Holy Spirit is simply promised by the angel (Luke 1:35) but not reported; what is reported is that Elizabeth's unborn child "leaped for joy" when Mary, now pregnant with Jesus, arrived (1:39-45). In other words, both Gospels direct our attention to the circumstances attending the central event. And though Matthew explains and Luke celebrates, neither argues a doctrine of Jesus' divine origin. As regrettable as it is understandable, these four chapters have sometimes generated more argument over "what really happened" than praise of God for the coming of John and Jesus.

At no point do these Gospels (or Acts) later use what is told in these opening chapters to *elicit* faith in Jesus. The "birth stories" *express* Christian faith; they play no role in persuading anyone in the Jesus story as a whole that Jesus deserves to be heeded because he was "conceived by the Holy Spirit, born of the Virgin Mary," as the Apostles' Creed will put it later. These stories provided early Christians a means of saying, in effect, that God was at work in Jesus from the start of his life, that the very existence of Jesus was an act of God on our behalf, that the whole Jesus event is a gift from God. Early Christians surely would not have thought this way had Jesus not been the sort of person he was, and had his death not been followed by his resurrection. That's why Christmas and Easter belong together.

Do You Want to Become His Disciples, Too?

The festal joy at Christmas can continue after the decorations are packed up. Without celebration and gratitude the disciple's life easily becomes a grim and joyless determination to get on with life. It need not be that way. Each day, give God thanks for one good thing that has come your way. Above all, give God thanks for the whole event of Jesus, not just for his birth.

What aspects of Luke's birth story combine to express your faith in Jesus?

Annunciation - visitation - birth in "City of David - Fulfillment of Old testament prophesies.

Prayer

I offer you my heart, LORD God, and I trust you....
Show me your paths and teach me to follow....
You lead humble people to do what is right
    and to stay on your path.
In everything you do, you are kind and faithful
    to everyone who keeps our agreement with you.

(Psalm 25:1, 4, 9-10, CEV)

4 The Wilderness Voice

The voice of one crying out in the wilderness:
"Prepare the way of the Lord,
make his paths straight."

(Mark 1:3)

They Have No Wine

The local newscast is often more depressing than the network news. It's not just the fires and train wrecks. It's the violence in the streets and in the schools, the corruption, the physical abuse of women and children and of prisoners. How long can it go on like this? Can anyone straighten it out?

Beginning With Moses and All the Prophets

This week's study explores how the Gospels portray the mission of John the Baptist and its significance for understanding the mission of Jesus. Because Matthew and Luke used Mark, we find both repetition and difference. Seeing both with regard to John the Baptist will prepare us to find repetition and difference also in what the Gospels tell us about Jesus.

Day 1 Isaiah 40:1-11; Malachi 3:1-5; 4; **Mark 1:1-8**; 6:7-29; 9:9-13; 11:27-33

Today's Gospel readings come from Mark. Its first readers did not know the stories in Luke 1–2, which had not yet been written. Note the way Mark 1:4-8 "fulfills" the quotation in 1:2-3. Remember that the Herod in Mark 6 is Herod Antipas, the son of the Herod in Matthew 2.

*John Bapt. → preaching repentance & baptizing in the Jordan —
King Herod has J the B. beheaded in prison.
⓶ Disciples speak of Elijah?*

Day 2 Matthew 3:1-12; 14:1-12; 21:23-32; Luke 3:1-20; 9:7-9

(1) This day's readings allow us to compare how Matthew and Luke introduce John.
(2) **GC 4-1** Observe that Matthew and Luke report the content of John's preaching of repentance (Matthew 3:7-10; Luke 3:7-14), whereas Mark does not. Observe carefully that except for the opening phrases, Matthew 3:7-10 and Luke 3:7-9 are nearly identical. Note also that only Luke contains John's words spelling out what repentance entails (Luke 3:10-14).

(3) Note that whereas in Mark 1:7-8 John promises that the "more powerful" one will baptize "with the Holy Spirit," in Matthew 3:11 and Luke 3:16 John says he will baptize "with the Holy Spirit and fire," and that "with fire" adds threat to the promise. Observe that in both Matthew and Luke John goes on to spell out this threat (Matthew 3:12; Luke 3:17). Note that in 3:18 Luke considers John's exhortations as "the good news." Observe that Luke gets John off the stage at 3:19-20, and so does not tell the story of John's murder.

"His winnowing fork is in his hand, to clear his threshing floor and gather wheat into his granary; but the chaff he will burn with unquenchable fire."

Luke leaves John B. in prison - Matthew has him killed in prison.

Day 3 1 Kings 17:1–19:18; 2 Kings 1; Sirach 48:1-14

The readings from First and Second Kings suggest why John is an "Elijah figure." The passage from Sirach* shows how Elijah was remembered in this book in the Apocrypha.* Whether or not the Evangelists read this book, it helps us understand the thought world of Judaism in Jesus' day.

Elijah lived in the wilderness ; was hairy & wore a leather belt - (similar to John B.)

Elijah was taken to heaven in a whirlwind of fire in a chariot with horses of fire (Sirach 48:9)

Day 4 John 1:5-8, (19-28) 10:40-42; Acts 19:1-7

(1) Notice that the Fourth Gospel emphasizes John's role as a witness to Jesus. (Remember that "witness" and "testimony" translate the same Greek word.)

(2) **GC 4-1** Observe that whereas the Evangelists Mark, Matthew, and Luke interpret John as the one who fulfills the words of Isaiah (Matthew 3:2-3; Mark 1:2-3; Luke 3:4), in the Fourth Gospel John himself claims this (John 1:23).

Jews sent priests & Levites to ask John B.: "Who are you?" He answers: "I am the voice of one crying out in the wilderness, 'Make straight the way of the Lord,' as Isaiah said. "I baptize c̄ water. There is one coming after me — — —

Day 5 Isaiah 29:18-19; 35:5-6; 61:1; Matthew 11:2-19; Luke 7:18-35

 (1) **GC 4-2** Observe that Matthew 11:2-19 is quite similar to Luke 7:18-35, yet at certain points the two Gospels diverge (for example, compare Matthew 11:12 and Luke 16:16, and note that Luke 7:29-30 has no parallel in Matthew 11, and conversely, that Matthew 11:14 has no parallel in Luke 7). Recall that most scholars account for the similarities and differences by proposing that here Matthew and Luke used Q,* which each Evangelist edited. None of these teachings is found in Mark.

 (2) Note how Jesus uses the language of the Isaiah passages to characterize his ministry (Matthew 11:4-5; Luke 7:22-23).

 (3) Observe that while Jesus speaks highly of John (Matthew 11:11; Luke 7:28), he also contrasts his mission with John's (Matthew 11:16-19; Luke 7:31-35).

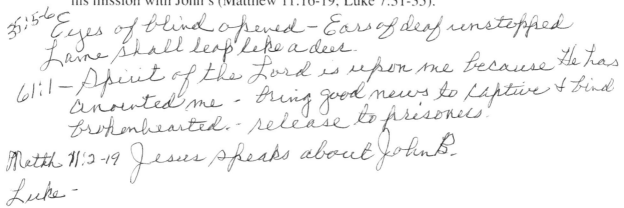

35:5-6 Eyes of blind opened - Ears of deaf unstopped
Lame shall leap like a deer.
61:1 - Spirit of the Lord is upon me because He has anointed me - bring good news to capture & bind brokenhearted. - release to prisoners.
Matth 11:2-19 Jesus speaks about John B.
Luke -

Day 6 Read and respond to "The Wilderness Voice" and "Do You Want to Become His Disciples, Too?"

Prayer Concerns

The Wilderness Voice

What an austere figure he was—living in the wilderness through which the Jordan ran to the Dead Sea, surviving on locusts and wild honey, dressed in camel's hair, threatening God's wrath for all except those who believed him and were baptized. Even so, he was looking for a deliverer. So different was he from Jesus that it is difficult to see why this man should be regarded as Jesus' forerunner. How could such a stern figure with such a severe message set the stage for Jesus?

We know little about John, for apart from the Gospels and Acts the rest of the New Testament does not mention him; and each Gospel has its own view of him. The only Jewish writer of the time to mention him is Josephus, who portrays him somewhat differently from the way the Gospels do. What concerns us here, however, is the way the Gospels understand his place in the story of Jesus. For them it is the significance of Jesus that makes John important enough to include.

Mark's Interpretation

Mark tells us why John is important: His mission in the wilderness fulfills the Scripture that announces a voice "in the wilderness" (Mark 1:3). (Although Mark claims to quote Isaiah, the quotation itself actually combines Malachi 3:1 with the line from Isaiah 40:3.) John's mission is to "prepare the way of the Lord" (which Mark assumes is the Lord Jesus). John himself spoke of a "more powerful" one who would come (Mark 1:7), but he did not say who this would be. Mark, of course,is convinced that it is Jesus, and that John's baptizing mission prepared the way for the mission of Jesus.

According to Mark 1:4, John proclaimed "a baptism of repentance for the forgiveness of sins." That God forgives those who repent was, and remains, a basic teaching of the Bible and the Jewish faith. What was remarkable about John's mission, however, was that he insisted that those who sought God's forgiveness must also be baptized. In Jewish life, this connection between baptism and forgiveness was new, and it was different. As a result, John was remembered even by Josephus, who wrote half a century later, as "the Baptist." Since we have nothing from John himself, we do not know why he insisted on baptism. Probably he expected water baptism to save his hearers from the coming fiery judgment (mentioned in Matthew 3:12 and Luke 3:17 but not in Mark).

Nor does Mark explain why John ate and dressed as he did (Mark 1:6). Perhaps Mark regards John's attire as evidence he was Elijah (promised to return before the Judgment; see Malachi 4:5), for according to 2 Kings 1:8 Elijah could be identified by what he wore: "a garment of haircloth, with a girdle of leather about his loins" (RSV).

Given the brief introduction to John at the beginning of Mark, it is somewhat surprising this Gospel tells the story of John's murder in great detail (Mark 6:17-29). Mark uses this gruesome story as a flashback to explain why some people, including Herod Antipas, were regarding Jesus as as another John the Baptist—literally, "John the baptizer has been raised from the dead" (6:14-16; also 8:27-28). In Mark the story of John's death provides the only clue to the political aspect of John's moral preaching: He did not hesitate to tell the puppet king that in marrying his sister-in-law he violated the prohibition in Leviticus 18:16; 20:21 ("uncover the nakedness" is a term for sexual relations). In this story, however, the villain is not Herod but Herodias, just as Jezebel was the villain in the reign of Ahab during the time of Elijah (1 Kings 19:2).

> In Mark, John does not interpret Jesus but Jesus interprets John.

John's death underlies Jesus' reply to the disciples' question in Mark 9:9-13, "Why do the scribes say that Elijah must come first?" (before the Messiah comes). Jesus affirms this expectation of Elijah's coming and adds, "But I tell you that Elijah has come, and they did to him whatever they pleased, as it is written about him [that is, about John]" (9:13). In other words, the view that John, as the expected Elijah, is the Messiah's forerunner goes back to Jesus himself. Matthew, perhaps recognizing that Mark's reference to what is "written about him" is not clear, replaces this phrase with "So also the Son of Man is about to suffer at their hands" (leaving "their hands" unclear). Whereas Mark does not say whether the disciples understood what Jesus had said, Matthew adds, "Then the disciples understood that he was speaking to them about John the Baptist" (Matthew 17:10-13). In Mark, John does not speak explicitly of Jesus as the Coming One; instead, it is Jesus who says the expected forerunner has come. In other words, in Mark, John does not interpret Jesus but Jesus interprets John. That Jesus thought highly of John is clear also in the last reference to the Baptizer in Mark (Mark 11:27-33).

To sum up, Mark does not allow our interest in John to deflect our attention from the central point: John is the forerunner whose mission prepared the way for Jesus. Mark shows no interest at all in John's impact on Jewish life; nor does Mark treat John's mission as the historical setting for Jesus' mission. John's mission is not the context for that of Jesus, but its preparation.

> **John insisted that the repentance he called for meant changing the way one lived.**

Matthew's Portrait of John

Matthew often follows Mark, so a somewhat different view of John emerges where Matthew's account diverges from Mark's. This divergence appears in the first sentence of Matthew 3, where Matthew, and only Matthew, gives the theme of John's preaching: "Repent, for the kingdom of heaven has come near." At 4:17 Matthew uses exactly the same words to state the theme of Jesus' preaching. In doing so, he aligns John and Jesus much more closely than does Mark; indeed, the understanding of John as the forerunner is now explicit, for John's preaching actually anticipates that of Jesus. Like Mark, Matthew too claims John fulfills the words of Isaiah, but he omits Mark's "See, I am sending my messenger . . . , / who will prepare your way" because, as a careful student of Scripture, Matthew knows this line is not from Isaiah 40:3 but from Malachi 3:1.

Matthew 3:7-10 reports John's preaching. Remarkably, John attacked those who came to him for baptism. In Luke he attacked "the crowds"; but in Matthew, the "many Pharisees and Sadducees," who in this Gospel will be Jesus' opponents. John denounces them for thinking that by confessing sin and being baptized they will be saved from the coming Judgment ("the wrath to come"). What really is required is "fruit worthy of repentance"—the results in a changed life. Although _repentance_ translates the Greek _metanoia_, which literally means "changed mind," the Greek surely translated the Hebrew or Aramaic _teshubah_, from the verb _shub_ ("turn," or "turn around"). Here as elsewhere in the Gospels, repentance is not sorrow for having sinned or regret for getting caught at it but turning one's life around, making a U-turn. In other words, John insisted that the repentance he called for meant changing the way one lived.

The next saying in this paragraph (3:9) denies that in the Judgment the hearers can rely on being members of the covenant people of God. On that day, a birth certificate will not suffice, nor can Abraham's descendants assume God needs them in order to keep his part of the covenant, because God can make descendants of Abraham from stones. On that day, only repentance and baptism will see them through the wrath of God.

The paragraph ends with a warning that time for repentance is running out: The ax is already cutting the root of the trees, and every tree that does not bear good fruit (a changed life as the result of repentance) will be cut down and burned. In the Sermon on the Mount Jesus will use the same image (Matthew 7:15-20), for Matthew another sign that the message of John anticipated the message of Jesus.

In Matthew, the report of John's preaching turns without interruption to his words about the Coming One (3:11-12), which are like his words in Mark 1:7-8—except for one important difference. In Mark John says, "I have baptized you with water; but he will baptize you with the Holy Spirit" (Mark 1:8). In Matthew, John says, "He will baptize you with the Holy Spirit and fire" (Matthew 3:11). Even though the next verse changes the image of the Judgment from the endangered orchard (3:10) to the grain harvest, the threat of fire remains. Not only will the Coming One separate wheat from chaff, but also he will burn the chaff "with unquenchable fire" (3:12).

Matthew's story of John's murder is less detailed than Mark's and makes Herodias less villainous while making Herod more responsible. In Mark, Herodias wanted John killed, "but she could not, for Herod feared John, knowing that he was a righteous and holy man, and he protected him . . . and . . . liked to listen to him" (Mark 6:19-20). In Matthew, Herod wanted to kill John yet did not do so because "he feared the crowd, because they regarded him as a prophet" (Matthew 14:5). Matthew ends the story with a new detail: John's disciples, having buried him, "went and told Jesus." This accounts for Jesus' knowledge of what had happened to John when later he says, "Elijah has already come, and they did not recognize him [another new detail], but they did to him whatever they pleased" (Matthew 17:12).

Mark 11:27-33 reports that Jesus rebuffed the question about his authority by asking whether John's baptism was from God or not. Matthew 21:23-27 repeats the story almost word for word. But in Matthew Jesus adds to his reply the parable of the two sons (21:28-32), which Jesus uses to rebuke the religious leadership who had asked him about his authority: "John came to you in the way of righteousness and you did not believe him, but the tax collectors and the prostitutes believed him; and even after you saw it, you did not change your minds and believe him." In this paragraph, found only in Matthew, Jesus affirms John's mission, using a key word in Matthew—*righteousness*. We will meet this word again when we study the Sermon on the Mount.

Even more important are Jesus' words about John that appear in both Matthew 11:2-19 and Luke 7:18-35 but not in Mark. This material brings together several of Jesus' sayings about John; but it is introduced by the question that John, while in prison, put to Jesus through John's disciples, "Are you the one who is to come, or are we to wait for another?" Because John had emphasized that the Coming One would bring fiery Judgment, he evidently was puzzled to hear Jesus' mission had a different character.

Instead of answering yes or no, Jesus answers in such a way that John now must answer his own question: "Go and tell John what you hear and see: the blind receive their sight, the lame walk, the lepers are cleansed, the deaf hear, the dead are raised, and the poor have good news brought to them. And blessed is anyone who takes no offense at me" (Matthew 11:4-6). Two things must not be missed here. First, up to this point in the Gospel, Matthew has told a story for every activity Jesus mentions; second, these activities show Jesus is indeed doing what Scripture expected in the time of salvation as portrayed in Isaiah 29:18-19; 35:5-6. In other words, Jesus challenges John to see in Jesus' mission the fulfillment of Scripture, and thus implies he is indeed "the one who is to come." Jesus' response also implies that as the expected one, he did not bring what John expected. That is why he pronounces "blessed" those who are not offended by what he does and says.

Jesus did not rebuke John for asking the question. To the contrary, after John's disciples left, Jesus told the crowds that John is "more than a prophet." In fact, he is the one who fulfills the promise in Malachi 3:1, omitted from Matthew 3:3 but which Jesus himself now quotes (11:10). Jesus goes on to say that no person ever born is greater than John. "Yet the least in the kingdom of heaven is greater than he."

Jesus' next significant saying about John (Matthew 11:12-13) is difficult to understand. No one knows for sure how 11:12 should be translated because the key word about the kingdom can mean either "suffered violence" or "has been coming violently"; so what Jesus has in mind is not clear. Matthew 11:13 also is unclear, for it is not obvious whether "until John came" means he is included with the prophets and the law or whether he is the beginning of the time of salvation. (Here too, Jesus declares John is the expected Elijah.)

The passage concludes with Jesus' words comparing his mission with that of John (11:16-19). He first compares responses to both their missions with children who complain among themselves that their playmates would not play wedding (alluding to Jesus' mission) and others would not play funeral (symbolizing John's mission). Likewise, some people complain about John because he was so ascetic: "He has a demon"; while others complain about the way Jesus lives: "a glutton and a drunkard, a friend of tax collectors and sinners." By these comparisons Jesus implied the forerunner's rejection anticipated his own. Neither was what people wanted.

Luke's View of John

Zechariah had foreseen that his son would be called "the prophet of the Most High" (Luke 1:76); accordingly, Luke begins the account of John's mission by saying, "The word of God came to John"—an expression used often for the biblical prophets (for example, Jeremiah 1:2; Ezekiel 1:3; Hosea 1:1; Jonah 1:1). What is surprising is Luke uses this event (Luke 3:1-2) to date the ministry of John (around A.D. 28–29). Luke sees John's mission as the fulfillment not only of Isaiah 40:3, as do Matthew and Mark, but also of Isaiah 40:3-5, which ends with the promise that "all people shall see it together." (Luke's wording of this promise diverges from the Hebrew because he is using the Septuagint:* " 'All flesh shall see the salvation of God,' " Luke 3:6.) By citing this extended passage, Luke points to the mission to the Gentiles, a major theme in his second volume, Acts. In other words, with John begins the time of salvation. The same perspective appears in Peter's sermon in Acts 10:34-37.

Matthew assumes his readers, most of whom may have been Christian Jews, will understand what John meant by calling for "fruit worthy of repentance" (Matthew 3:8). But Luke assumes (perhaps because he is writing for Christian Gentiles) he must insert a paragraph—found only here—that gives concrete instances of repentance

(Luke 3:10-14): Those who have must share with those who have nothing, tax collectors are to collect only what is owed, and soldiers are to refrain from extortion and to be satisfied with their wages. These instances show readers how John does what the angel had told Zechariah: "He [John] will turn many of the people of Israel to the Lord their God . . . and the disobedient to the wisdom of the righteous, to make ready a people prepared for the Lord" (1:16-17). Each exhortation provides a fascinating glimpse into the society in which John and Jesus taught.

John's requirement, "Whoever has two coats must share with anyone who has none; and whoever has food must do likewise," (3:11) calls for compassionate sharing by all who truly repent—not because having two coats or food is sinful but because keeping both when the neighbor has neither *is* sinful. The saying itself does not refer to the coming Judgment, but by placing it after the dire warnings of the preceding paragraph, Luke suggests the demand is more urgent than the need to retain what one has with an eye to "a rainy day." But what if the imminent Judgment *is* the rainy day? Then sharing with the needy is the right way to prepare for it.

John's word to the tax collectors (local customs officers who collected tolls) is remarkable for what it does not say—to resign their jobs because collecting tolls was itself sinful. Instead, they were to be honest civil servants, not using their positions to enrich themselves at other people's expense. The same is required of soldiers (local Jews in Antipas's service; Roman troops were not quartered in the area in John's time). What John forbids is a practice still found in parts of the world where the military extorts by intimidation.

John in the Fourth Gospel

Here we will focus on those features that distinguish this Gospel's treatment of John from that of the Synoptics.* Everything this Gospel says about John makes one point: John is significant only because he points to Jesus. He is not so much the forerunner as the witness. In this Gospel he is not called "the Baptist" or "the baptizer."

In the Prologue (John 1:1-18) John appears twice (1:6-8, 15). Though "sent from God" like a prophet, he is not to be confused with the light (Jesus) because his role is to witness to the light, to say who Jesus is and why he is decisively significant. In 1:15 we have John's first testimony: "This was he of whom I said, 'He who comes after me ranks ahead of me because he was before me.'" This sentence sounds like a restatement of what the baptizer had

said in Mark 1:7: "The one who is more powerful than I is coming after me." In the Fourth Gospel's version, higher rank has replaced greater power, for here John is alluding to the Incarnation,* stated in John 1:14: "The Word became flesh." John's first witness in 1:15 is for the benefit of everyone, including us, the readers of the narrative.

John's second testimony, on the other hand, was for the benefit of specific persons in the narrative (1:19-28). According to this passage, John's witness came in response to two questions: "Who are you?" (1:19, repeated in 1:22), and "Why . . . are you baptizing?" (1:25). In reply to the first question, John disavowed three roles: He is not the Messiah nor Elijah nor "the prophet" (the expected prophet like Moses; see Deuteronomy 18:15). But then he also claimed who he was—the voice in the wilderness of whom Isaiah spoke. John does not answer the second question, but responds to it by first stating what his questioners already know: "I baptize with water" (John 1:26). But now he does not contrast his water baptism with the Coming One's Spirit baptism as in Mark 1:8 (or with Spirit and fire as in Matthew and Luke) but instead continues, "Among you stands one whom you do not know, the one who is coming after me; I am not worthy to untie the thong of his sandal" (John 1:26-27). Although the unrecognized one is Jesus, his being "among you" does not mean he is actually present during the conversation but that he is a Jew among Jews and is not recognized for who he really is. As the Prologue put it, "He came to what was his own, and his own people did not accept him" (1:11). Thus John's witness to the Incarnation also points to its nature: The incarnate one is not recognized because outwardly he looks like everyone else. There is no halo over Jesus' head.

As the public ministry of Jesus in the Fourth Gospel nears its end, the writer says that after Jesus eluded arrest, he returned to where John had baptized. Here many people sought him out because "they were saying, 'John performed no sign [wondrous deed], but everything that John said about this man was true.' And many believed in him there" (10:40-42). In other words, John's witness was not in vain.

> **John is significant only because he points to Jesus. He is not so much the forerunner as the witness.**

So Then

John the Baptist is one of the most fascinating figures in the whole New Testament. The story of his imprisonment and beheading has inspired many paintings, as well as an opera, Richard Strauss's *Salome*. Yet little is known of him. (The strange story in Acts 19:1-7 tells just enough to stimulate our curiosity; the same is true of the brief description of John in the writing of Josephus.) For the Gospels John is significant for two reasons: His work, while differing in character and tone from that of Jesus, did prepare the way for Jesus' mission; and he baptized Jesus. We can only speculate about his influence on Jesus, which might have been greater than the Gospels indicate.

John the Baptist appears to have disciples today as well—namely those earnest Christians who seem to be more concerned with the coming Judgment than with the good news of the kingdom of God. Nevertheless, Christians are to be disciples of Jesus, not of John.

Do You Want to Become His Disciples, Too?

Many people respect Jesus yet wonder whether he is adequate for what we need (or think we need) right now. At times John's question to Jesus is also our question: "Are you the Coming One or shall we look for someone else?" The disciple answers yes to the first part and no to the second. Neither answer should be taken for granted.

Who is this Jesus John the Baptist points to? What is it about Jesus that makes John important?

Jesus is Son of God → Identified as such by John at his baptism

Prayer

Listen, LORD, as I pray! Pay attention when I groan.
You are my King and my God. Answer my cry for help
     because I pray to you.
Each morning you listen to my prayer,
as I bring my requests to you
     and wait for your reply. . . .

Let all who run to you for protection
     always sing joyful songs.
Provide shelter for those who truly love you
     and let them rejoice.

(Psalm 5:1-3, 11, CEV)

5 Gifted by the Spirit and Tested by the Choices

Because he himself was tested by what he suffered,
he is able to help those who are being tested.

(Hebrews 2:18)

They Have No Wine

We are so vulnerable, so open to the lure of choices we suspect are wrong and to the attraction of what we know is not right. We can even give good reasons for doing what is not good. To a large extent, the choices we make, and the patterns and habits of our choosing, determine the sort of person we become because choices test us. Making the right choice is rarely easy.

Beginning With Moses and All the Prophets

This week we study the stories of Jesus' baptism and temptation. We also consider why it is important to remember Jesus too was tempted, as well as what he had to say about temptation itself.

Day 1 **Mark 1:9-13;** Matthew 3:13–4:11; Luke 3:21–4:30; John 1:29-34

> **GC 5-1** Note how closely the first three Gospels link Jesus' baptism and temptation. Observe also that John has no temptation story, and think about the difference this omission makes in the way you picture Jesus.

Day 2 Deuteronomy 6:4-19; 8:1-16; Psalms 2; 91; Isaiah 42:1-4; 1 Kings 17:1; 18:1-2; 2 Kings 5:1-14

> Observe how today's readings from Deuteronomy, Psalms, and Isaiah are used in the stories of Jesus' baptism and temptation. Note also that in Luke 4:16-30 Jesus refers to the stories in First and Second Kings.

Day 3 Genesis 25:27-34; Hebrews 2:14-18; 4:14-16; 12:3-17

As you read the passages from Hebrews, remember the same Greek word means "tempt" as well as "test." What temptations do we resist if we heed the exhortations in Hebrews 12:12-17?

Day 4 Exodus 32:1-6; Numbers 21:4-9; 25:1-9; 1 Corinthians 10:1-13; James 1

Note how alert Paul and James are to the reality of temptation. In 1 Corinthians 10 see how Paul uses Israel's disobedience as a series of negative examples in order to warn the Corinthians against *their* temptation to idolatry.

Day 5 Mark 4:1-10, 13-20; 14:32-42; Luke 8:4-9, 11-15; 22:31-34

(1) **GC 5-2** In comparing the parable of the sower and its interpretation in Mark and Luke, attend to the difference between Mark 4:16-17 and Luke 8:13.

(2) To what temptation does Peter succumb in Luke 22:31-34?

(3) Note the different renderings of the same Greek word in Mark 14:38: "temptation" (RSV, NIV); "time of trial" (NRSV); "test" (REB).

Day 6 Read and respond to "Gifted by the Spirit and Tested by the Choices" and "Do You Want to Become His Disciples, Too?"

Prayer Concerns

Gifted by the Spirit
and Tested by the Choices

Given the sort of person John was and the sort of message he had, his baptism of Jesus is a remarkable fact. After all, John sought to save people from the wrath of God by calling them to repentance and baptism. Why would Jesus respond positively to such a mission? Even more remarkable is what the four Gospels say also happened: The Spirit came to Jesus at his baptism. In addition, the first three Gospels say the heavenly voice declared him to be God's Son. Each Gospel—as well as several gospels not in the New Testament—tells the story in its own way in order to express what the writer wanted to emphasize. The differences in these accounts make it difficult to know exactly what happened (what a video camera might have recorded). Also remarkable is the fact that in all three Synoptic Gospels the newly baptized Jesus must encounter Satan before he begins his mission.

Accounts of Jesus' Baptism and Temptation

Mark 1:9-13. Mark's account is so brief our attention is riveted on what the Evangelist wants us to know. The focus of the story is not on the baptism itself but on what happened as Jesus emerged from the water. (Immersion is assumed; Christian art portrays the baptism by affusion [water poured on the head] because artists could hardly paint the immersed Jesus.) Jesus saw the heavens "torn apart" (literally, "split"). A split sky signals that a revelation is about to occur (as in Revelation 4:1). And here the disclosure is both visual and auditory—seen and heard. Jesus, like John, is silent because the story is interested in what happened, not in what they think. He receives the gift of the Spirit and accepts what the voice says. The Spirit is power, for it "immediately drove him out into the wilderness" where he met Satan and "the wild beasts." The abrupt change from a high moment to a low one could hardly be expressed more vividly.

The climax of the scene is the voice from heaven (that is, God's voice) announcing Jesus' relation to God in two statements, both derived from Scripture. The first ("You are my beloved Son," Mark 1:11, REB) quotes a line from Psalm 2:7 that originally was God's word to the king on the occasion of his enthronement as indicated in the next line, "This day I become your father." That is, from now on, the king enjoys a special relation to God and also is expected to obey God as a son is supposed to obey his father. The second statement, "in you I take delight," comes from Isaiah 42:1, where God says, "Here is my servant, whom I uphold, my chosen one, in whom I take delight" (REB). Mark's use of this line is appropriate here because Isaiah continues, "I have put my spirit on him." (Mark does not quote this line, however; he probably assumes the readers know what Isaiah says.) Thus Mark shows the reader that Jesus now knows himself to be the Spirit-endowed Son designated by God to carry out God's will; furthermore, he is the "more powerful" one John had proclaimed (Mark 1:7), for Jesus is the bearer of Spirit-power.

That the Spirit is power is shown by the word Mark uses to say what happened next: The Spirit "drove" Jesus into the wilderness, the same word Mark uses to say Jesus "expelled" demons (1:34; "cast out," NRSV). According to Mark, Satan "tempted" Jesus throughout the forty days in the wilderness, though Mark probably understands the Greek word to mean "tested." Only Mark mentions the "wild beasts"—perhaps to suggest Jesus was the counterpart to Adam: In Eden Adam failed the test; in the wilderness Jesus passed it. The beasts might also suggest a place of danger and vulnerability. In any case, Mark implies (but does not describe) a conflict between Spirit-power and Satan-

> **In Eden Adam failed the test; in the wilderness Jesus passed it.**

power. Having won this conflict in the wilderness, Jesus continues his victory in the first act of his ministry: He expels an unclean spirit, one of Satan's agents (1:21-28). In contrast with Mark, the Gospel of John reports no exorcisms and reports no wilderness test either; compared with Mark, both Matthew and Luke understand the wilderness test as triple temptations.

Matthew 3:13–4:11. What we notice first in Matthew's account is that Matthew, assuming the greater baptizes the lesser, reports that John resisted Jesus' request for baptism and wanted Jesus to baptize him instead. John consented, however, when Jesus said, "It is proper for us in this way to fulfill all righteousness" (Matthew 3:15). Every word in this reply is significant. Jesus did not say he was required, for whatever reason, to be baptized; nor did he imply he knew he did not need John's baptism "with water for repentance" (3:11) because he was sinless. Instead, he said it was "proper for us"—that is, in keeping with God's purpose for both of them, because in this action each did what was right for him. Jesus did not keep aloof from those who were baptized "confessing their sins" (3:6) but identified with them, even though he had no sins to confess. Recall that repentance is wholehearted turning to God and God's will. Since the Godward turn was to be at the core of Jesus' appeal, Matthew's story implies Jesus did not ask anyone to do what he had not done. He too turned his life Godward. So it was "proper" for Jesus to be baptized along with others turning to God, and it was "proper" for John to baptize him.

Interestingly, in Matthew John does *not* connect his baptism with forgiveness of sins, for Matthew omits Mark 1:4. In Matthew forgiveness is linked to Jesus' death. Only in Matthew's account of the Last Supper does Jesus say, "This is my blood of the covenant, which is poured out . . . for the forgiveness of sins" (Matthew 26:28).

Matthew uses Mark's account of the baptism but makes subtle changes. The heavens are "opened" (not "torn apart," "split"), and Jesus sees "the Spirit of God" (not simply "the Spirit") descending. And the voice does not address Jesus as in Mark but makes a public announcement—"This is my Son"—implying John too hears it.

The noncanonical *Gospel According to the Hebrews** describes the baptism somewhat differently. "When the Lord ascended from the water, the whole fount of the Holy Spirit descended and rested upon him and said to him, 'My son, in all the prophets I was waiting for you, that you might come, and that I might rest in you. For you are my rest; and you are my firstborn son, who reigns forever.' " What the Synoptic accounts of the voice imply—the gift of the Spirit to Jesus fulfills the prophetic words—here is made explicit. Some paintings of Jesus' baptism include a small fountain overflowing with water—an attempt to show what this noncanonical gospel says.

Matthew uses Mark's brief report of Jesus in the wilderness (Mark 1:12-13) to frame the report of the temptations (notice how part of Mark appears at the beginning [Matthew 4:1] and the rest at the end [4:11]); but in doing so Matthew also makes some changes. The Spirit does not "drive" Jesus but "led" him into the wilderness "to be tempted." In Matthew, the temptations apparently began after Jesus had fasted and "was famished," suggesting this hunger made Jesus vulnerable to the first temptation. In Matthew the angels "waited on" Jesus after the devil had left him. In other words, he faced the diabolical one hungry and alone. In Luke, the angels are not mentioned; Jesus does not benefit from their service at all.

Luke 3:21–4:13. Luke gets John off the stage (3:19-20) before reporting Jesus' baptism. Nothing is to distract the reader from Jesus and the Spirit. In fact, the baptism doesn't even get its own sentence, as in Mark. Instead, it is simply mentioned as one detail of the setting for what is important in this Gospel—the coming of the Spirit and the word of the voice: "Now when all the people were baptized [implying that as far as Luke is concerned, John's preparatory ministry has now been completed], and when Jesus also had been baptized and was praying [a new detail], the heaven [singular] was opened" (3:21). Luke makes it clear he is not reporting a vision (as in Matthew and Mark) but an event. To underscore the reality of this event, Luke says, "The Holy Spirit descended upon him in bodily form like a dove." At this point Luke inserts the genealogy. But instead of beginning with Abraham and coming forward (as in Matthew), it begins with Joseph and runs backward all the way to Adam, who also was "son of God." In doing so Luke suggests Jesus is significant for the whole of humanity.

Luke too connects the temptation story with Jesus' baptismal experience: "Jesus, full of the Holy Spirit, returned from the Jordan and was led by the Spirit in the wilderness," where he was tempted throughout the forty days. He fasted the whole time and so "was famished" (Luke 4:1-2). We probably should understand Luke to mean the temptations reported next actually took place during the forty-day period. Accordingly, the story ends this way: "When the devil had finished every test, he departed from him until an opportune time" (4:13)—leaving us wondering just when that will be. By adding this detail, Luke implies the devil did not accept his defeat. (Does he ever?)

In the meantime, "Jesus, filled with the power of the Spirit, returned to Galilee" (4:14). Mark and Matthew simply assumed Jesus' Spirit-power, but Luke emphasizes it because the Spirit is the link that ties all these individual stories together.

Remember, for Luke the story of Jesus, like that of the church in Acts, is the story of what the Holy Spirit did.

As mentioned earlier, in Mark Jesus' victorious conflict with Satan in the wilderness is resumed in the first act of Jesus' Spirit-empowered mission. Luke too connects Jesus' first public act with the Spirit but in a completely different way—Jesus' preaching in his hometown synagogue (Luke 4:16-30), a story Mark and Matthew put much later (Mark 6:1-6; Matthew 13:54-58). Luke's version of the story is much longer because it is important for the overarching view of both Luke and Acts: (1) It brings to a head the entire narrative to this point, especially beginning at Luke 3:21. (2) It explains the significance of the Spirit's coming to Jesus, for he reads from Isaiah

"The Spirit of the Lord is upon me,
    because he has anointed me to bring good
        news to the poor"

and says these words are now being fulfilled. (Luke 4:18-19 combines Isaiah 61:1-2 with a line from Isaiah 58:6, neither following the Septuagint exactly.) (3) It begins Jesus' rejection as well, thereby reminding us of Simeon's prediction in Luke 2:34. (4) By pointing out that in the past Elijah went only to a widow in Sidon (a Phoenician city outside Israel) and that in Elisha's time the only leper healed was a Syrian, Jesus implies that the Gentiles will benefit from his mission more than his own people. With this story, Luke points ahead to the book of Acts.

The Triple Temptations

Matthew and Luke report the same three temptations; but in each Gospel the temptation story as a whole has a different climax because the sequence of the second and third temptation differs, giving each temptation story a different climax. GC 5-3 Two temptations begin the same way, "If you are the Son of God" (meaning, "If you are really the Son of God"). Jesus responds to each temptation by quoting Scripture.

Temptations is the right word for these allurements because they present attractive possibilities. After all, we can be tempted only by what seems attractive, by what holds desirable opportunities, by what promises self-fulfillment or self-enhancement, and by what suggests a shortcut to a goal. We are not tempted by something (or someone) in which we have no interest. In temptation the bad conceals itself in the guise of a possible good. If its badness were obvious, it would be far less attractive; it might even be repellent. In temptation, the

choices we face do not come labeled "good" or "bad," nor do they come graded ("this is better than that"). Because temptation appeals to something already in us, the response to it discloses who we really are as well as what we will be as a result of the choice. We are not surprised, then, that the tempter began by saying, "If you *are* the Son of God." By saying "if" instead of "because," the devil first tempts Jesus to doubt who he is, who God's voice said he is. We miss the story's impact if we simply watch Jesus repel the devil; the story can

> **Because temptation appeals to something already in us, the response to it discloses who we really are as well as what we will be as a result of the choice.**

alert us to the words that often begin our own temptations, "If you are a disciple." The story can also point us to Jesus' way of handling temptation.

We impoverish our reading of Scripture by assuming it has but one meaning; then we easily lapse into arguing over what that meaning is. Frequently, however, the biblical text invites us to discover meaning not only in what is said but also in what is suggested and implied. Matthew's and Luke's accounts of Jesus' temptations clearly offer meaning beyond the obvious, especially when we pay attention to details. Every word counts; there are no "throwaway lines."

Matthew alerts his readers to multiple meanings in Matthew 2:15, where he quotes Hosea 11:1: "Out of Egypt I have called my son." In Hosea this line refers to Israel's coming out of Egypt in Moses' day. Matthew claims this verse is actualized when the infant Jesus, after staying in Egypt, is taken to Nazareth, implying the Israel story will give us clues to the Jesus story. But Matthew also tells the Jesus story in ways that remind us of Moses. This dual meaning—Jesus as Israel and Jesus as Moses—is evident when we look closely at Matthew's temptation story.

Only Matthew says that Jesus fasted "forty days *and forty nights*" (Matthew 4:2). In the Old Testament, only Moses and Elijah fasted "forty days and forty nights" (Exodus 34:28; 1 Kings 19:8); and the report of Elijah's fast on the way *to* Horeb (Sinai) recalls Moses' fasting *at* Sinai. Further, Jesus overcomes the first temptation by quoting from Deuteronomy 8:3, where God reminds Moses of Israel's experience: God "humbled you by letting you hunger, then by feeding you with manna ... in order to make you understand that one does not live by bread alone, but by every word that comes from the mouth of the LORD."* The angels who "waited on" Jesus afterward remind the reader that Israel also was fed wondrously with manna and that an angel had provided food for Elijah during his travel to Horeb.

Likewise, Jesus' response to the second temptation in Matthew quotes from God's command to Israel, "Do not put the LORD your God to the test, as you tested him at Massah" (Deuteronomy 6:16). According to Exodus 17:1-7, the Israelites, having camped at a waterless place, demanded that Moses give them water, and Moses in desperation cried out to God, "What shall I do with this people? They are almost ready to stone me." God told him to strike the rock, and water flowed out. Moses "called the place Massah [meaning test] and Meribah [meaning quarrel], because the Israelites quarreled and tested the LORD, saying, 'Is the LORD among us or not?'" Even though Matthew's temptation story does not quote this question, Matthew probably assumes it, for it expresses precisely the issue in the temptation, "If you are the Son of God, throw yourself down" from the pinnacle of the Temple. Indeed, the devil tempts Jesus to do so by quoting Scripture (Psalm 91:11-12), implying, "Let's see if this really is true." What is more tempting than to find a detail in Scripture that might justify a choice that actually dares God to do something so stupendous it shows everyone we really trust God and God is really trustworthy?

The way to world power climaxes the temptations in Matthew. Only in Matthew does this test occur on "a very high mountain" where "all the kingdoms of the world and their splendor" are visible. The Evangelist doesn't need to be told that no mountain in the wilderness is high enough for such a view, not even if the earth were flat. The point probably reflects the assumption that this temptation depends on *seeing* the world's glory, not simply imagining it, because it is attractive first to the eye, then to the will. Here may also be an echo of Moses on Mount Nebo, where God showed him "the whole land" (Deuteronomy 34:1). But while God promised, "I will give it to your descendants" as was promised to Abraham, the devil promises to give it on the assumption (true? false?) it is his to give, which Jesus is to acknowledge by worshiping the devil ("All these I will give you, if you will fall down [prostrate yourself] and worship me," Matthew 4:9). What Matthew assumes, Luke

makes explicit (Luke 4:6-7). Jesus is not seduced, but responds with "Worship the Lord your God, / and serve only him," a paraphrase of Deuteronomy 6:13, which is part of what God said to Israel in Deuteronomy 6: "When the LORD your God has brought you into the land that he swore . . . to give you—a land with fine, large cities that you did not build, houses . . . , hewn cisterns . . . , vineyards and olive groves . . . , take care that you do not forget the LORD." As the obedient Son of God, here too Jesus shows himself fulfilling the command given to Israel.

In Matthew the angel's word to Joseph implies Jesus will be God's Son (Matthew 1:20-23), and in Luke Gabriel says so explicitly (Luke 1:35). But that sonship was made effective only by Jesus' obedience, his resolute commitment to make choices in accord with the deepest, and so most difficult, dimensions of God's will for Israel, also God's "son." Nor was it enough for Matthew and Luke to report that at the baptism God said Jesus was Son of God; they also show us that for Jesus being Son of God means obedience in a moral task with moral choices. If that was the case even for Jesus, it is no less true for his followers.

Matthew and Luke did not include the story of Jesus' temptations simply to inform us about what went on privately between Jesus and the tempter, for elsewhere they show little interest, if any, in Jesus' inner life until his agony in Gethsemane. This silence about Jesus' inner life and struggle makes the temptation story all the more significant, even if the Evangelists did not explain that significance. But we can surmise, for precisely in Gethsemane Jesus urges the sleepy disciples to pray they may be spared "the time of trial" (as he instructed them to pray in the Lord's Prayer). In Mark and Matthew Jesus gives the reason this prayer is needed: "The [human] spirit indeed is willing, but the flesh is weak" (Matthew 26:41; Mark 14:38). Whatever be "the time of trial," we dare not assume *our* flesh is strong enough to withstand the tempter's lure.

Looking Beyond the Gospels

The Gospels remind us that although Jesus was "born of the Virgin Mary," as the creeds put it, and gifted by God's Spirit and the words of the voice, he was also truly human, so human that he was vulnerable to demonic distortion of his vocation. Occasionally some people have argued whether in reality Jesus could have been tempted, and so could have sinned or not. The issue was formulated crisply in Latin: *posse non peccare* (possible not to sin) or *non posse peccare* (not possible to sin). Matthew and Luke clearly assume Jesus' temptations were real. They also imply that had that not been the case, Jesus' call to follow him would have been hollow, for who can follow one who is invulnerable to temptation, who cannot lose, and who has not learned the cost of obedience? The author of the letter to the Hebrews understood this need well: "Because he himself was tested by what he suffered, he is able to help those who are being tested" (Hebrews 2:18). Fortunately, the text does not say how he helps, for that is something each follower can discover.

Hebrews, which interprets the risen Christ as the high priest who represents us before God, goes on to say, "Since, then, we have a great high priest who has passed through the heavens, Jesus, the Son of God, let us hold fast to our confession. For we do not have a high priest who is unable to sympathize with our weaknesses, but we have one who in every respect has been tested [or tempted] as we are, yet without sin. Let us therefore approach the throne of grace with boldness, so that we may receive mercy and find grace to help in time of need" (4:14-16). The author surely did not think that in the Judean wilderness Jesus had faced every kind of temptation faced by Christians in the cities of the empire. In fact, it is not obvious this author was thinking only of Jesus' wilderness experience; he might have had in mind also Jesus' test in Gethsemane—or even his whole life as a test of obedience. Nor does Hebrews ask us to imitate Jesus whenever our temptation coincides exactly with his. Instead it asks us, precisely the vulnerable ones, to be bold in asking Jesus for help because as our representative before God he too was once vulnerable.

So Then

Whether we focus on Jesus' wilderness experience as a test (as in Mark) or as triple temptations (as in Matthew and Luke), we face our own temptations, beginning with the temptation to explain how the Gospel writers knew what had gone on in the wilderness. They never report that Jesus mentioned his experience to his disciples or that he regarded his responses as examples for them to follow. Nor do they satisfy our curiosity about what went through Jesus' mind at his baptism and what followed. Pursuing such questions is a way of seeking Jesus behind the Gospels rather than in them.

The real challenge of the stories of Jesus' baptism and wilderness experience is not to figure out what really happened but rather to discover what they tell us that is significant for the ways we understand Jesus, the Jesus whose disciples we want to be.

We can begin by pondering the fact that in Matthew and Luke Jesus begins his ministry with the temptations behind him. Their Jesus story has no reference to any ongoing struggle in Jesus' mind, no wrestling with alternatives, because the issues were settled before he began his lifework. A look at the issues in these temptations suggests how remarkable this portrayal is—using his status as Son of God to preserve his life (stones to bread), forcing God to preserve him from death (jumping from the pinnacle of the Temple), gaining sovereignty over the world (by worshiping the devil himself). Although neither Evangelist actually says so, both tell the story of Jesus' mission in such a way that the consequences of Jesus' wilderness experience are evident throughout. None of his wondrous deeds are for his own benefit. He does not force God's hand or test God's faithfulness but entrusts himself and his

> **The story of Jesus' temptations serves as the lens through which we are to read these Gospels.**

mission to God's hands, even unto death. He never acknowledges the devil's sovereignty over the world but challenges it by his wholehearted devotion to God and by his acts of power. In short, the story of Jesus' temptations serves as the lens through which we are to read these Gospels.

The same is true of the baptism story. Not only does it tell us that Jesus is the Spirit-empowered Son of God; it also implies that he who joined those who acknowledged their sins (by accepting John's baptism) would be prepared to eat with the despised tax collectors, consort with the downtrodden, and heal the sick even on the sabbath, for his wholehearted resolute obedience to God had been acknowledged by the voice at the Jordan and confirmed by the gift of the Spirit.

What then are we to make of the statement in Hebrews that Jesus was tempted in every respect as we are? To point out that as far as we know, he was not tempted by what our beautified language calls "substance abuse," lust for sexual gratification, suicide, faithlessness in marriage, or cheating on his income tax report is to evade the issue.

Precisely here we are tempted to rely on such observations, correct as they are, in order to conclude that our temptations have nothing to do with his; and besides, he was the Son of God. On closer examination, however, the issues Jesus faced appear also in what we face, though they appear in current garb. If we say Jesus really doesn't touch our situation because he was God's Son and we are very human, we should go on to ask, Just how human did he have to be in order to understand us? Are we more human than he? So where did Jesus find the right way to respond to temptation? In Scripture that pointed him to God. And he didn't have to look it up first; he knew his Scripture because he knew his God. Is there a better way to deal with temptation?

Do You Want to Become His Disciples, Too?

Choices test our loyalty and form our character. Temptation is experiencing the lure of wrong choices. The disciple is no more exempt from choices than the Master was. Actually, becoming a disciple is choosing a life of choosings in order to be a disciple.

In what ways does the tempted/tested Jesus challenge and comfort you?

_____

_____

_____

_____

_____

Prayer

Please listen, LORD, and answer my prayer!
    I am poor and helpless.
Protect me and save me because you are my God.
    I am your faithful servant, and I trust you.
Be kind to me! I pray to you all day.
Make my heart glad!
    I serve you, and my prayer is sincere.
You willingly forgive, and your love is always there
    for those who pray to you.
Please listen, LORD! Answer my prayer for help.
When I am in trouble, I pray, knowing you will listen.

(Psalm 86:1-7, CEV)

6 When God's Reign Becomes Real

The time is fulfilled, and the kingdom of God has come
near; repent, and believe in the good news.

(Mark 1:15)

They Have No Wine

Are not the confusions, chaos, and contradictions evident in the world around
us repeated within us? No one seems to be in charge in either place. And it
doesn't help to say we must get our priorities right, because we first need to
know the standard by which we can judge whether they are right. To order our
priorities, we need to know what we are most deeply loyal to.

Beginning With Moses and All the Prophets

Jesus spoke of "the kingdom of God"; Matthew often uses "kingdom of
heaven" to express the same thing since in Jewish custom "heaven" was a way
of referring to God without the risk of misusing the Lord's name (as in our "for
heaven's sake"). This week's lesson is one of the most important in the entire
study. You will soon see why.

Day 1 Psalm 93; Zechariah 14:9-11; **Mark 1:14-15;** Matthew 4:12-17; Luke 4:14-15;
Matthew 6:9-15; Luke 11:2-4; 17:20-21

Notice the different ways God's kingdom is imaged in these texts. Observe that for Matthew
Jesus' return to Galilee fulfills Scripture.

Day 2 Judges 8:22-23; 1 Samuel 8; Psalms 95; 97; Isaiah 44:6-8; Tobit 13

These readings document the persistence of the image of God as king, first of Israel, then of the
world. Tobit,* a book in the Apocrypha, was probably written about 200 B.C. It shows how the
theme of God's kingdom was emphasized also by Jews in the Diaspora.*

Day 3 John 3:1-15; 1 Corinthians 15:35-57; Galatians 5:16-26; Revelation 11:15-20

Observe the different ways the kingdom of God is understood in non-Gospel parts of the New Testament. Look carefully at what is and is not said about the Kingdom.

Day 4 Isaiah 6:1-10; Daniel 4; Mark 4:1-34; Matthew 13:1-35; 20:1-16; Luke 8:4-18; 13:18-21

The Gospel passages focus on the parables that concern the kingdom of God explicitly. Notice that Mark quotes Isaiah to explain Jesus' use of parables. Daniel 4 may provide part of the background for the parable of the mustard seed.

Day 5 Exodus 20:1-17; Leviticus 19:11-18, 29-37; Mark 10:13-31; Matthew 19:13-30; Luke 18:15-30

Observe how the Gospel passages accent the demands of the Kingdom.

Day 6 Read and respond to "When God's Reign Becomes Real" and "Do You Want to Become His Disciples, Too?"

Prayer Concerns

When God's Reign Becomes Real

The center of Jesus' message and mission was the kingdom of God. It was the hub to which the spokes were attached. Most of Jesus' teachings do not actually mention the Kingdom, and only one saying connects his exorcism with the Kingdom: "If it is by the finger of God that I cast out the demons, then the kingdom of God has come to you" (Luke 11:20). Nor does the kingdom of God figure in the accusations brought against Jesus during his trials in Jerusalem. Nevertheless, if Jesus' words and deeds had any animating center, it was his perception of the kingdom of God. There was no other center.

Yet, the more we recognize the centrality of the Kingdom in Jesus' mission, the more we are puzzled by the fact he never defines it, though the Synoptics show him speaking of it in a variety of ways. This variety is most evident in the verbs used with the phrase. Luke 11:20 is not the only time Jesus speaks of the kingdom of God as something that *moves toward people*, for the Lord's Prayer asks that it "come." On another occasion Jesus commends a person for being near to the Kingdom, implying the man has *moved toward the Kingdom* (Mark 12:34). Jesus also speaks of the Kingdom as a space one *enters*, as in Matthew 5:20 (see also Mark 9:47; 10:25; Matthew 21:31), as something that can be *received* (Mark 10:15), or can also be *taken away* (Matthew 21:43). Jesus can also identify those to whom the kingdom *belongs* (the poor, Luke 6:20; the poor in spirit, Matthew 5:3; the persecuted, Matthew 5:10). Evidently, what Jesus had in mind when he referred to the kingdom of God could not be conveyed with only one image.

Equally fascinating is the way Jesus used parables to talk about the kingdom of God. The connection between the Kingdom and the parables is particularly important because we expect the language to fit the subject matter. What about the kingdom of God prompts Jesus to speak of it with parables? Or what about parables makes them appropriate for talking about the kingdom of God?

The Parables in the Gospels

Before we explore particular parables, let's note what the Gospels show about Jesus' use of parables in general. (1) The parables of Jesus are found only in the first three Gospels. In John Jesus does use metaphors; for example, he speaks of himself as bread. But parables such as those in the Synoptics are absent from John.

(2) Each of the first three Gospels treats the parables in its own way. Mark 4:1-2 says one day Jesus taught the crowd "many things in parables"; but Mark then gives only three parables (the soils, the secretly growing seed, and the mustard seed); 4:33-34 repeats the generalization about many parables, adding he spoke only in parables. In Mark Jesus interprets the first parable and also explains why he speaks in parables. Not until Jesus gets to Jerusalem does he tell another parable (12:1-12). Matthew 13 is a collection of seven parables, two from Mark 4; each of the five new parables concerns the kingdom of heaven. Matthew also has parables elsewhere; indeed, the last of Jesus' five discourses in Matthew has its climax in parables (Matthew 25). Jesus' parables are found throughout Luke's Gospel, and some of his best known parables (for example, the good Samaritan and the prodigal son) are in a section devoted to Jesus' journey to Jerusalem (Luke 9:51–18:14).

(3) Sometimes parables are simply recorded, with no application stated (Mark 4:26-29; Matthew 13:33); readers—like the original hearers—are left to ponder the meaning. At other times, an application is added (read Matthew 18:10-13 plus 14; 18:23-34 plus 35; Luke 12:13-20 plus 21; 14:7-10 plus 11). Sometimes we find both an application and additional sayings (read Luke 16:1-8 plus 9 plus 10-12 plus 13). Both the application and the additions show how the early church understood and used the parables in its own teaching. Jesus probably ended the parable with the punch line.

(4) The parables reveal Jesus' significant skill as a storyteller. He was an astute observer who could use ordinary, simple acts of everyday life to convey his insights about a reality beyond the ordinary—a woman putting yeast into dough, seed scattered on various kinds of soil, the fisherman's net with both marketable and unmarketable fish, the day laborers waiting to be hired, the unexpected arrival of the absentee landlord, the farmer who builds more granaries because he assumes he will prosper indefinitely, the estate manager's request to give the fruitless fig tree one more chance by loosening the soil and adding manure, a man locking the door on his eating and drinking buddies from the night before claiming he doesn't know them. Moreover, the imagination that used the ordinary also created the extraordinary: Someone sows weeds in a neighbor's grain; a manager

cooks the books to save his skin; a pearl merchant sells everything to buy one magnificent pearl. The parables, like Jesus' striking metaphors (white-washed tombs, blind guides, the log in the critic's eye, tasteless salt) show Jesus to have been a folk poet who knew well the ways of his neighbors. Acknowledging the imaginative artistry of Jesus' parables and metaphors does not diminish Jesus' stature but enhances it. Indeed, our recognizing his skill enables us to understand his Kingdom parables better.

The Kingdom of God in the Gospels

We are talking here about the Synoptic Gospels, for in John Jesus mentions the kingdom of God only when talking with Nicodemus (John 3:3-5). Both Matthew and Mark begin their accounts of Jesus' mission with statements that summarize the theme of his preaching: The kingdom of God "has come near" and "repent" (turn life toward the God whose reign "has come near"). In Luke, Jesus' first mention of the Kingdom is at Luke 4:43, well into the story of his mission. Both Matthew and Luke later remind their readers that the theme of Jesus' message is the Kingdom (Matthew 9:35; Luke 8:1; 9:11).

The Gospels imply that Jesus intended his mission to enable people to grasp the Kingdom's meaning in a new way—and to be grasped in a new way by the Kingdom. When that occurred, he changed people's ideas of the Kingdom and the way they reasoned with the ideas, for a changed life and a changed way of thinking belong together. The task of the parables, especially those that speak of the kingdom of God, is to let their hearers experience this unity of changed thought and changed life.

Mark writes that Jesus proclaimed "the good news of God" and said, "The time is fulfilled, and the kingdom of God has come near; repent, and believe in the good news" (Mark 1:14-15). In Jesus' time and place, the idea that God is king (sovereign) was not news; for while the actual phrase *the kingdom of God* does not appear in the Old Testament, the idea that God is sovereign over creation—and especially over the people of Israel—was deeply rooted in the Jewish faith Jesus inherited and shared with his hearers. God is king and always has been despite the fact that Rome ruled most of the world people knew about and despite the fact that the people of God were deeply divided over how to respond to this rule created and sustained by the sword.

What was news, good news, is the announcement that the time of waiting for God's kingship to assert itself decisively is now complete; God's kingdom (the word *basileia* means both king*dom* and king*ship*) "has come near," so near that whoever believes this message must, and can, respond by turning life Godward before the Kingdom actually arrives for all to see. Jesus' message can be illustrated by the simple experiment often done in beginning science classes: Iron filings on a sheet of paper begin to stand up as the magnet under the paper comes closer and closer. Just as the filings respond before the magnet actually touches the paper, so those who believe Jesus' message respond by reordering their lives, by repenting, before the Kingdom fully arrives as a public event. Instead of living as they had always lived, out of the past, believers now live out of the future, by what is not yet actual but has come so near they begin living as if it had arrived. Because the Kingdom is not yet here (when everything and everyone will be right), those who live by the Kingdom are out of step with the present; they march by the drum they hear but cannot yet see but are confident it will soon be here. Believers live *already* by the *not yet* visible. Moreover, just as the filings respond to the magnet, so repentance is a response—a turning—to the God whose kingship has moved near. Turning life Godward can be as dramatic as a U-turn. And if Jesus is right, the person who turns Godward finds the neighbor.

> **Those who live by the Kingdom are out of step with the present; they march by the drum they hear but cannot yet see but are confident it will soon be here. Believers live *already* by the *not yet* visible.**

This turn Godward does change our thinking about God, not because our ideas *about* God (such as, God is the Creator) are changed but because the point of having these ideas has become real in a new way. That reality we call "God" is no longer primarily an idea we think is true but a transforming presence and power. When transformation occurs, ideas about God may change too. Did not Jesus point out, "The kingdom of heaven is like yeast that a woman took and mixed in with three measures of flour until *all* of it was leavened"

(Matthew 13:33)? The Kingdom eventually affects everything, ideas included.

God's Kingship and Jesus' Parables

In Mark 4:26-32 we find two parables that compare the Kingdom with typical situations. In the first the sower sows the seed and then does nothing until the harvest because he can do nothing more anyway. The sprouted seed grows without his help. The parable does not teach that the Kingdom, "seeded" by Jesus, grows in history the way an idea, such as human rights, steadily grows until it is accepted everywhere. Nor should we allegorize the parable by asking who is the sower, what is the seed, what are the three stages of growth, or when is harvest time. Rather, the situation of the seed and the situation of the Kingdom are similar. But how? It depends on the setting in which the parable is told. It might rebuke those who think they must help the Kingdom along. It might issue a challenge to believe that when the grain is ripe the harvest will come suddenly—that is, that the full arrival of the Kingdom will occur when, according to the plan of God, "the time is fulfilled." The kingdom of God is not a project but a promise. To live by that promise is to allow one's life to be released from ceaseless striving—even for something good. To live by that promise is to learn that everything does not depend on us (that would be news to God).

> The kingdom of God is not a project but a promise. To live by that promise is to allow one's life to be released from ceaseless striving—even for something good.

The second parable contrasts the tiny mustard seed with the giant shrub (in Matthew and Luke, a tree) with branches large enough to provide shade where birds may nest. What is Kingdom-like about that? In Ezekiel 31:2-14 Assyria is symbolized by the tallest tree in which "all the birds . . . made their nests" but which God destroyed; in Daniel 4 Nebuchadnezzar is a tree "in whose branches the birds . . . had nests" but he too will fall; he will eat grass like an ox until he has learned "that the Most High has sovereignty over the kingdom of mortals, and gives it to whom he will" (4:25). If Jesus has these trees in mind, the parable might mock the idea that God's kingdom will be a glorious earthly powerhouse—Jesus would be using irony, meaning the opposite of what he is saying. Or the parable might simply contrast the tiny beginning with the great result in order to challenge the hearer/reader to believe that Jesus and his few followers are the beginning of the Kingdom's arrival.

An even greater challenge is implied in the twin parables found only in Matthew 13:44-46. In the first parable, a man finds a treasure in someone else's field; but instead of telling the owner, he hides it, sells everything he has, and buys the field in order to have the treasure. To worry about the morality of the buyer is to miss the point. In the second parable, the merchant sells everything to buy one exceedingly valuable pearl. To ask what he will do with it now that he is broke is also to miss the point. Nor should we be misled by the fact that both men *find* what is valuable, as if the Kingdom were something waiting to be discovered. Actually the plot of the parables requires that persons *find* what is valuable (they do not earn it) as an unexpected event. Their unexpected opportunity to acquire a precious item is like the news of the Kingdom; it challenges Jesus' hearers to invest everything in order to receive it. These parables are especially suggestive: They show that when God's kingship becomes real, the response is to be total. When the Kingdom comes we do not haggle over the terms; it is all or nothing. How we respond to the parable—whether we get the point or regard the men as fools—shows our own relation to the Kingdom. In other words, the reader is put in the same situation as Jesus' hearers and as the men in the parables. When the coming of the Kingdom happens to a person, the stakes are high indeed. Few people are comfortable with these parables. One more thing: What gives Jesus the right to say such things? Is it not that he had invested everything in the one pearl?

But determined response is not the whole story. What comes next? The parable at the beginning of Mark 4 addresses just this question. Again the parable describes a typical situation: A sower scatters seed that falls in various places—on the path, on rocky ground, among thorns, and in good soil. We are not told how much fell in each place, but the odds do not look favorable for a crop. Some was eaten by birds, some was scorched by the hot sun because its roots were shallow, some was choked by its environment, but some did yield a crop of varying quantities. Strictly speaking, the parable is not about the Kingdom itself but about what happens when the Kingdom's coming is announced. When Jesus told the parable, he probably meant to reassure his hearers that among some people his message would bear fruit.

The parable's many details invited the allegorical interpretation* in each Gospel (Matthew 13:18-23; Mark 4:13-20; Luke 8:11-15). **GC 6-1** Now the relation of the seed to soil explains the fate of the preached gospel: The seeds on the path are people in whom the word has no chance because Satan (the birds) takes it away immediately; the seeds on the rocky ground are those who wither away in persecution because they have no deep roots; the seeds among thorns are those in whom the word is choked, not by persecution but by its opposite—the lure of the world. Only the seed in good soil, the faithful believer, bears fruit. The explanation assures, but it also warns: Don't let your response to the gospel be like the seeds in the wrong places.

Why Parables?

Few passages in Mark are as perplexing as Mark 4:10-12, the first of several places where Jesus explains privately what he had said publicly (see 4:34; 7:17-23; 9:28-29; 10:10-12; 13:3-4). Here the disciples ask "about the parables" as a whole, and Jesus answers comprehensively. First, Jesus' reason for speaking in parables is based on the difference between insiders and outsiders. At the end of Mark 3 Jesus implies that even his family, "standing outside," are outsiders. The insiders are those gathered around Jesus: "Here are my mother and my brothers! Whoever does the will of God is my brother and sister and mother." Now in Mark 4, Jesus first says to the insiders (the disciples), "To you has been given [the passive form of the verb implies God is the giver] the secret [literally, the mystery] of the kingdom of God"—its hidden, inner meaning that by nature is not observable. In Luke 17:20-21 Jesus makes the same point to the Pharisees: "The kingdom of God is not coming with things that can be observed; nor will they say, 'Look, here it is!' or 'There it is!' For, in fact, the kingdom of God is among you"—in Jesus its unrecognized bearer.

What Jesus goes on to say in Mark 4 is more troublesome: "But for those outside, everything comes in parables; *in order that*

>	'they may indeed look, but not perceive,
>		and may indeed listen, but not understand;
>	*so that* they may not turn again
>		[repent] and be forgiven.'"

But aren't parables supposed to communicate instead of prevent communication? Jesus' answer

might reflect the fact that *mashal*, the Hebrew word behind *parable*, can refer to all sorts of figurative speech and not only to what we call parables. If so, Jesus might mean that for outsiders everything comes in *riddles* because, as outsiders, they have not been given the secret of the Kingdom. Jesus' answer then implies that those who hear his words as riddles show they are still outsiders.

Especially troublesome is the twofold purpose of parables—to prevent outsiders from understanding and repenting and to prevent their being forgiven. Notice that the words in quotation marks (4:12) abbreviate and paraphrase Isaiah 6:9-10, where Isaiah is told to say such things to Israel. In Mark Isaiah's words are introduced by the Greek *hina* ("in order that"). As we saw earlier in connection with Matthew's formula, "so that the word spoken by the prophet might be fulfilled," purpose and result are not clearly distinguished in Greek, sometimes not even in English. So Mark probably means that for outsiders everything comes in riddles, and *as a result* they do not understand. This interpretation avoids having Jesus say that he speaks in parables in order to keep people from understanding and repenting. Mark also implies that what was true in Isaiah's time is repeated in Jesus' mission.

According to Matthew 13:13, lack of understanding is not the *outcome* of Jesus' use of parables, as in Mark, but the *reason* he uses parables in the first place. "The reason I speak to them in parables is that 'seeing they do not perceive, and hearing they do not listen, nor do they understand.'" And then Matthew quotes the whole passage from Isaiah 6:9-10 according to the Septuagint. To emphasize the contrast between the disciples and unperceiving Israel, Matthew adds a beatitude, "Blessed are your eyes,

> **Most of our language about God relies on metaphors or images because no human words can describe literally the reality that no one in this life has seen or can see.**

for they see, and your ears, for they hear," and explains that the prophets and the righteous longed to see and hear what the disciples now are privileged to see and hear (Matthew 13:16-17; Luke 10:23-24). In fact Matthew's chapter of parables contains the following exchange between Jesus and the disciples: When Jesus asked, "Have you understood all this?" they replied without hesitation, "Yes" (Matthew 13:51). But even in Matthew, they spoke too soon. They were not the last disciples to do so.

The Parable and the Kingdom

We come now to the relation between form and content, to the relation between the parable (form) and the news of God's kingship coming near (content). How does the form fit the content?

To talk of God as king and of God's kingdom or kingship, God's reign or rule, is to use a metaphor, an image or word picture, to express an important conviction about what is true—that we are subject to the character and will of that invisible reality we call God, whether we recognize this sovereignty or rebel against it. Most of our language about God relies on metaphors or images because no human words can describe literally the reality that no one in this life has seen or can see. Each metaphor allows us to express a distinct understanding of God—as father, mother, rock, fortress, or shepherd.

> **Since life is a story, the believer lives with parable stories because Jesus himself is the parable of God's reign.**

We are also aware of a gap between the way things are and the way they ought to be. When we use king-kingdom-kingship language about God to think about this gap, we find ourselves saying that if God really is king-sovereign, then this gap cannot be permanent. If it were permanent, God would never actually function as king but would only claim to be king (or, the image of God as king would be wrong). For this reason the Bible says both that God *is* king (as in Psalms 95 and 97) and that God *will be* king, that the truth of God's kingly rule which we now believe will become actual, that there will be no gap between what is and what ought to be.

The Lord's Prayer asks for exactly that:
"Your kingdom come.
Your will be done,
    on earth as it is in heaven."
At the same time, Jesus announced that God's kingdom-kingship was "at hand"—not actually here for all to see, but so near that already we can respond to God's kingly rule by anticipating the results of its arrival (that is, when what "ought to be" becomes what "is").

Jesus' parables fit this understanding because they are brief stories that show the impact of the nearness of God's kingdom on human life. Because the kingdom is "near" but not yet "here" (this distance language too is metaphorical), we can only believe the truth of Jesus' message, and we can believe it only if we believe the messenger. The parables too must be believed. They appropriately express the summons to anticipate the impact of the kingdom's arrival. And when we believe them, we also grasp them, and they grasp us as well.

One more thing: Since life is a story, the believer lives with parable stories because Jesus himself is the parable of God's reign.

So Then

Jesus' parables challenge the imagination because God's kingdom challenges the way we picture the world and our relation to God. The parables invite us to take a second look and a third because the image of God as king is itself a picture, one that requires us to recognize that God is sovereign, in charge, not a bystander. And Jesus' parables invite us to picture what our lives would be like—and will be like—when God's being in charge becomes real for us. Like the yeast in the dough, the presence of that reality will change everything.

Do You Want to Become His Disciples, Too?

Being loyal followers of Jesus requires our being loyal to what he was loyal to—God's reign. And that means believing persistently that God is indeed sovereign, and believing that means ordering our life so that it accords with God's will even before God's reign is acknowledged everywhere. Being a disciple takes imagination. It also gives hope.

What insights into Jesus do you get through the parables he told about God's reign?

_____

_____

_____

_____

_____

Prayer

Our LORD, you are King!
You rule from your throne above the winged creatures,
     as people tremble and the earth shakes.
You are praised in Zion, and you control all nations.
Only you are God! And your power alone,
     so great and fearsome, is worthy of praise.
You are our mighty King, a lover of fairness,
     who sees that justice is done everywhere in Israel.
Our LORD and our God, we praise you
     and kneel down to worship you, the God of holiness!

(Psalm 99:1-5, CEV)

7 Called and Commissioned

You did not choose me but I chose you. And I appointed you to go and bear fruit, fruit that will last, so that the Father will give you whatever you ask him in my name.

(John 15:16)

They Have No Wine

All too often, our heroes let us down. Maybe we expect too much of them. In any case, we want the heroes to pull us up to their level. When we learn they are on our level after all, we are deeply disappointed, cynical even. We need someone to show us the good in a real life, not just to tell us about it.

This Time: Beginning With Mark

We focus on the disciples, beginning with the stories of how Jesus acquired his first followers. The daily readings will bring into view each Gospel's portrayal of the disciples and their relation to Jesus. To allow time for careful reading and comparing of the Gospel passages, Old Testament readings are omitted.

Day 1 Mark 1:16-20; Matthew 4:18-22; Mark 2:13-17; Matthew 9:9-13; Luke 5:1-11; John 1:35-51

(1) Today's readings remind us of a fundamental principle in studying Bible stories. The first question to ask is not, What happened? but What do the stories want to tell us through what they report? GC 7-1 Using this principle, notice what each Gospel emphasizes about becoming a disciple of Jesus.

(2) Note how each story expresses John 15:16.

Day 2 Mark 3:13-19; 4:35-41; Matthew 8:23-27; Mark 6:7-13, 30-52; 8:1-21, 8:34–9:1; 9:30-37; 10:32-45; 14:17-54, 66-72; 16:1-8

Mark's portrayal of the disciples is the most negative of the four Gospels. Note the disciples' privileges that come from accompanying Jesus. What does the combination of privilege and failure suggest about Mark's understanding of discipleship itself?

Day 3 Matthew 8:18-22; Luke 9:57-60; Matthew 9:35–11:1; 13:16-17; Luke 10:23-24; Matthew 13:51-52; 15:29-39; 16:5-12; 17:14-21; 20:17-28; 25:14-46; 28:16-20

(1) **GC 7-2** To see how Matthew sometimes softens the harsh portrayal of the disciples in Mark, compare Mark 4:37-41 and Matthew 8:24-27; Mark 6:45-52 and Matthew 14:22-33; **GC 7-3** Mark 8:14-21 and Matthew 16:5-12; Mark 10:35-45 and Matthew 20:20-28 (but see also Mark 1:20).

(2) Notice also that Matthew adds 13:16-17 (Luke 10:23-24) to Jesus' teaching about the people's failure to understand the parables.

(3) The conclusion of Matthew (28:16-20) suggests that in Matthew, the teachers have understood the Teacher.

Day 4 Luke 8:1-3; 9:1-50; 9:51–10:24; 14:25-35; 17:1-10; 22:24-38; Acts 1:15-26; 10:34-43

    (1) Luke's portrayal of the disciples too is more positive than Mark's (Luke omits Mark 6:45-52 and 8:32-33). Only Luke 8:1-3 reports the presence and role of women in Jesus' group. Observe also that Luke 9:45 provides an explanation for Mark 9:32.

    (2) Notice the way Luke 14:25-35 emphasizes the cost of discipleship, and how Acts 2:44-45; 4:32-35 appear to be responses to Luke 14:33 (a saying found only here).

    (3) Note that the word of the risen Jesus in Luke 24:44-49 is carried out in Acts 1:15-26; 10:34-43.

Day 5 John 6:1-21, 41-71; 11:1-16; 12:1-8; 13

    (1) Note that according to John 6:60-63 the disciples have almost the same reaction to Jesus' words as "the Jews" in 6:41-42.

    (2) Note also that what Peter confesses in 6:68 corresponds to what the Evangelist says in 20:30-31.

    (3) Note the way Judas is characterized in 12:1-8.

Day 6 Read and respond to "Called and Commissioned" and "Do You Want to Become His Disciples, Too?"

Prayer Concerns

Called and Commissioned

Becoming, and remaining, Jesus' disciple is not easy. The Gospels show clearly it never was easy. Even those who accompanied Jesus found it hard to understand him and harder yet to live by what they did understand. Despite the first disciples' unique privilege, they are not portrayed as heroic figures. Even so, Jesus entrusted his word and way to them; indeed, after his resurrection he came precisely to those who had abandoned him. His appearances enabled them to remain his disciples in circumstances they did not foresee and made it possible for others to become disciples through their witness. The Gospels are one result of that ongoing witness. So our aim in learning about the disciples is not to look up to them (they were not heroes during Jesus' lifetime) nor to look down on them (we are not better than they) but to join them in following the lead of Jesus.

Of course, we are curious about how they came to be Jesus' disciples in the first place. Did they—at least some of them—really drop what they were doing and join a wandering teacher who suddenly interrupted their work? Or does his "Follow me" really summarize a conversation? Had they heard him before? What did they see in him, and what did he see in them? Clearly, the Gospels have little interest in providing answers to such questions. The Gospels imply these are not the right questions for our own discipleship.

The word *disciple* came to have two meanings in the New Testament. In the Gospels *disciple* refers to those who accompanied Jesus. Acts, however, uses it repeatedly to refer to people who had never seen Jesus but came to believe in him in response to the apostles' preaching (for example, Acts 6:1; 9:1; 14:22; 16:1; 21:16). Using the same word for those who had been with Jesus and for later believers suggests that what the Gospels report about the original disciples may apply also to us.

Disciples in Context

That Jesus had disciples is a historical fact, but its significance is not always obvious. For one thing, the crowds that followed Jesus from place to place, largely because he was a healer (Mark 6:53-56; Matthew 4:24-25; John 6:1-2), were not really disciples unless they followed Jesus as a way of life. Moreover, Jewish teachers, called "rabbi" (my master), also had disciples with whom they formed a group to study Torah and to share meals.

Customarily, a person sought a teacher because the teacher was known to be a wise and devout interpreter of Scripture. But Jesus had no such reputation, according to John 7:15: "The Jews were astonished . . . saying, 'How does this man have such learning, when he has never been taught?' " Nor had he been a disciple of a revered teacher, as was the case with the rabbis. An observer probably would have found it remarkable that Jesus had disciples and even more remarkable that he "called" them.

The Gospels show no modern biographical or psychological interest in explaining the mind, motivations, or strategies that prompted Jesus to acquire disciples. The Gospels give us reports of brief encounters and words of commendation and rebuke. Each report is worded in a way that discloses some aspect of Jesus' greatness as it touches the human condition of those who would follow him. The brief stories in which he summons certain individuals to follow him therefore simply say those persons did as he said (Mark 1:16-20; 2:13-14; John 1:35-39). To speculate why he called precisely them, or what thoughts went through their minds, detracts from the central point: Jesus calls; the called heed. To be sure, motives and interpersonal dynamics were at work then, as today when someone becomes a disciple, but the theological point remains paramount: Discipleship is a deliberate positive response to Jesus' call. According to Matthew 8:19-20, Jesus once discouraged a man who volunteered to become his disciple. On other occasions Jesus made clear that the invitation to become a disciple must not be taken lightly, for following him is costly (Luke 14:15-33). Also, since becoming a disciple is a personal response to Jesus, the Gospels never report that he called whole groups—tenant farmers, day laborers, Greek-speaking Jews. Jesus formed his group by calling individuals.

The Twelve

Within Jesus' followers was a special group, the Twelve (Matthew 10:1-4; Mark 3:13-19; Luke 6:12-16; John 6:70). And what a remarkable dozen they must have been! Despite the fact that the Gospels say nothing about half of them, we can conclude the group was remarkably diverse. Four were fishermen, and of these, two were in business with their father Zebedee (Mark 1:16-20). Zebedee's sons must have had forceful personalities, else Jesus would not have dubbed them "Sons of Thunder." They were the ones who wanted to "command fire to come down from heaven and consume" the Samaritans who did not allow Jesus and the disciples to enter their village (Luke 9:52-54). Apparently Andrew and Philip came from families who were somewhat Hellenized, for their names were Greek. Matthew was a despised collector of tolls. In addition to Simon Peter, the circle included a second Simon, who in Matthew and Mark is called "the Cananaean" (the Greek form of the Aramaic word for "zeal" or "zealot") and in Luke is called "the Zealot"—a fervent nationalist, probably inclined toward insurrection. And then there was Judas Iscariot. Some connect *Iscariot* to Kerioth, a place in southern Judea; others have seen in *Iscariot* a thinly veiled allusion to *sicarius* (assassin). We have no indication any of the disciples came from a priestly family or had been associated with scribes, Pharisees, or the sect at Qumran.* Nevertheless, the disciples seem so diverse we wonder how Jesus got them to eat together.

The names of the twelve are listed in Matthew 10:2-4; Mark 3:16-19; Luke 6:14-16. (The lists are nearly identical, except Luke does not mention Thaddaeus, and Matthew and Mark do not mention "Judas son of James"; none of these lists includes Nathanael, mentioned only in John. Oddly, the name of the tax collector, Matthew, appears in all these lists; but in the story of his call to be a disciple, Mark and Luke give his name as Levi (Mark 2:14; Luke 5:27). Of these twelve, the Gospels report the call of only five—the two pairs of brothers (Simon [Peter] and Andrew, and Zebedee's sons James and John) and Matthew-Levi. How the other seven came to be part of the circle of twelve is not known, not even in the case of Judas, the betrayer (whose name is at the end of all the lists).

> **According to the Synoptics, Jesus did not call disciples in order to have someone to teach. Rather, his aim was to have a group who would extend his own mission.**

The tradition that Paul quotes in 1 Corinthians 15:5 says the risen Jesus appeared "to the twelve" (though according to Matthew 28:16-17 he appeared to "eleven disciples" since Judas had hanged himself, Matthew 27:3-10). In any case, twelve had long been a special number in antiquity, and Jews remembered there had been twelve tribes to which people still belonged (for example, Paul; see Philippians 3:4-5). The tribes no longer existed as organized groups, of course. But some Jews expected God would somehow restore the twelve tribes so Israel no longer would be scattered. By designating certain disciples to be the Twelve, Jesus probably was symbolizing his hope that God would use his mission to reconstitute Israel. In only one instance do the Gospels report what Jesus had in mind for the Twelve; in Matthew 19:28 Jesus says, "You who have followed me will also sit on twelve thrones, judging the twelve tribes of Israel." Luke 22:29-30 has different wording: "I confer on you, just as my Father has conferred on me, a kingdom, ... and you will sit on thrones judging the twelve tribes of Israel." The Synoptics report, however, that Jesus also had something else in mind for the disciples.

Discipleship and Mission

According to the Synoptics, Jesus did not call disciples in order to have someone to teach. Rather, his aim was to have a group who would extend his own mission. This intention is clear in the story of Jesus' summoning the fishermen (Mark 1:16-20), for "Follow me" is coupled with a promise, "I will make you fish for people." Here discipleship and mission are inseparable, and "Follow me" implies that Jesus' mission will define theirs. We will look at this connection between discipleship and mission in each of the four Gospels.

Mark. Mark reports that Jesus designates twelve as apostles "to proclaim the message, and to have authority to cast out demons" (3:14-15)—that is, to do what he has been doing. But they do not yet do so. Instead, they remain with Jesus, who in one way or another exposes the split between those who are with him and those who are not (as we saw in the discussion of the parables). This section (3:13–6:6) ends with Jesus' being rejected in his hometown synagogue (6:1-6). Mark shows that the Jesus who calls and sends is a Jesus who is misunderstood, opposed, rejected. Only after having made clear this reaction to Jesus does Mark report that Jesus sent the disciples on their mission (in six pairs), giving them remarkable instructions: As they go from place to place they are to have nothing to rely on but his authorization—"no bread, no bag, no money in their belts" and only one tunic. Like the master who sent them, they too can expect to be rebuffed (6:7-13). And when they returned, they told Jesus "all that they had done and taught" (6:30). Mark does not say whether they also had been rejected; what matters for the Evangelist is that the disciples did indeed "fish for people" as Jesus had promised.

Matthew. The fact that Matthew 4:18-22 repeats the story of the call of the four fishermen in Mark 1:16-20 almost word for word shows that Matthew also links discipleship and mission.

What is distinctive about Matthew's understanding of discipleship and mission appears in Matthew 10, which expands Mark 6:7-13. Here Matthew assembles numerous sayings (some taken from Mark) that pertain to the mission theme. In doing so he created the second of Jesus' major discourses in this Gospel; the Sermon on the Mount (Matthew 5–7) is the first. While Matthew too reports Jesus sent the Twelve, this Gospel does not report the disciples returned! This omission is hardly an oversight. Rather, it is Matthew's way of suggesting that what Jesus said then about mission is pertinent also to the mission of the church.

From this rich chapter (Matthew 10) three themes merit attention here. The first has to do with Israel. While all the Gospels assume Jesus' mission was to his own people, only in Matthew does he say, "I was sent only to the lost sheep of the house of Israel" (15:24); so too, only in 10:5-6 does he forbid the disciples to go to Gentiles or Samaritans. The risen Jesus, on the other hand, sends the disciples (the church) to all nations (Gentiles). Historians generally conclude Matthew got it right: There was no mission to Gentiles until after the Resurrection. But even today's largely Gentile church must not forget that Jesus saw himself sent to his own people, not to us Gentiles. The Resurrection created a new situation; the worldwide mission reflects Jesus' new status (28:16-20).

The second theme insists the disciples cannot expect to fare better than Jesus did; for "a disciple is not above the teacher, nor a slave above the master; it is enough for the disciple to be like the teacher, and the slave like the master" (10:24-25; see also John 13:16; 15:20). The wording of Matthew 10:17-18 reflects what actually happened to Christian missionaries later: "They will hand you over to councils and flog you in their synagogues; and you will be dragged before governors and kings because of me" (this happened to Paul; see 2 Corinthians 11:24). Nevertheless, when Christians are in court God's Spirit will tell them what to say (Matthew 10:19-20; Luke 12:11-12). The church's mission will divide families and communities (Matthew 10:34-39), as Jesus' mission had done (12:46-50; 13:54-58); indeed, they "will be hated by all because of my name" (10:22). Matthew 24:9 says they will be hated, tortured, and killed. Unfortunately, Jesus was right—even during our lifetime, in various parts of the world, Christians are being tortured and killed because of their faith.

According to the third theme, the disciples are assured that neither they nor those who respond positively to their witness will suffer hardship and hatred in vain, for "the one who endures to the end will be saved" (10:22). It is not those who can kill only the body that the disciples are to fear, but the one who can destroy both body and soul (10:28)—that is, God, at the Last Judgment. This is a hard saying. The second-century sermon known as *Second Clement** quotes a variation that elaborates the saying but does not make it easier: "The Lord said, 'You will be as lambs in the midst of wolves' [see Matthew 10:16]. And Peter answered, 'But what if the wolves tear the lambs to pieces?' Jesus answered Peter, 'Do not let the lambs fear the wolves after they die [note that here Peter is responsible for the lambs, an echo of John 21:16]; and do not fear those who kill you and are not able to do anything more to you. But fear the one who, after you die, has power over your soul and body, to cast them into the hell of fire'" (2 Clement 5:2-4).

God is not indifferent. On that day, Sodom and Gomorrah will be better off than the towns that rejected Jesus' emissaries (Matthew 10:14-15); on the other hand, whoever welcomes them welcomes Jesus, and "whoever gives even a cup of cold water . . . in the name of a disciple" will not lose their reward (10:40-42). In fact, "those who find their life will lose it, and those who lose their life for my sake will find it" (10:39).

The astringent realism in Matthew's portrayal of discipleship is an important reminder that becoming, and remaining, a disciple requires enduring commitment, that "signing on" with Jesus is not like signing a petition at the mall.

Luke. In Luke Jesus does not acquire disciples at the beginning of his mission but later. By this time he had preached his programmatic sermon in his hometown, where he was rejected (Luke 4:16-30), and had healed Peter's mother-in-law (4:38-39). Luke replaces Mark's account of the call of the four fishermen with the story of the marvelous catch of fish, climaxed by Jesus' commissioning Simon. Simon's brother Andrew is ignored, and Zebedee's sons are mentioned only in passing. The climax of the story remains Jesus' word: "Do not be afraid; from now on you will be catching people" (5:10).

Luke's account of the mission of the Twelve (9:1-6, 10) uses Mark's account, but only Luke reports a second mission, that of the seventy (some manuscripts have seventy-two), who were sent as an advance party (Luke 10:1). What the number of those sent symbolizes remains unclear. Luke reports what the seventy (or seventy-two) said on their return: "Lord, in your name even the demons submit to us!" (10:17). Jesus' response implies that their exorcisms signal Satan's defeat: "I watched Satan fall from heaven like a flash of lightning" (10:18). But Jesus also tells them that what should make them happy is not their power over evil spirits but knowing their names "are written in heaven." Their secure relation to God is more important than their success on earth, even over the demonic—a perspective we all too often forget.

John. John's Gospel tells the whole Jesus story quite differently. Consequently, John's portrayal of Jesus and the disciples also differs markedly from that of the Synoptics. For one thing, in John Jesus does not send his disciples on a mission during his lifetime, but does so on Easter evening: "As the Father has sent me, so I send you." Instead of telling them to wait for the coming of the Holy Spirit as in Luke 24:49, in John the risen Jesus himself gives them the Spirit, adding, "If you forgive the sins of any, they are forgiven them; if you retain the sins of any, they are retained" (John 20:21-23). This authority is similar to that given to Peter in response to his confession at Caesarea Philippi: "I will give you the keys of the kingdom of heaven, and whatever you bind on earth will be bound in heaven, and whatever you loose on earth will be loosed in heaven" (Matthew 16:19).

Even though the story of Peter's confession at Caesarea Philippi is not found in John, Peter (speaking for the Twelve) does make a confession at John 6:68-69: "Lord, . . . You have the words of eternal life. We have come to believe and know that you are the Holy One of God."

The truly distinctive feature of John's picture of Jesus' relation to his disciples, however, is found more in the structure of the book than in particular details. The Synoptic accounts of what Jesus said when he instituted the Lord's Supper are relatively brief, but in John Jesus uses the occasion to instruct his disciples at length (John 13–16).

On Following

Not to be missed is the similarity between the story of Matthew's call (Mark 2:14) and that of the four fishermen in Mark 1:16-20 (Matthew 4:18-22). In all these instances, Jesus said, "Follow me"; and they "left" what they were doing and "followed him." In these stories, *following* has its usual meaning: The men abandoned their former life-work and began to accompany Jesus. The Gospels imply the other seven had done the same, for they too were part of the group who went from place to place with Jesus.

This literal meaning of *follow* also came to have another meaning—to live according to Jesus' pattern, to learn from him. This, of course, is what the word *disciple* normally means. (*Disciple* comes from the Latin *discipulus*, a learner or pupil.) Somewhat like an apprentice, a disciple learns by observing, accompanying, and being instructed by one who has mastered the craft. As noted, Acts uses "disciples" for those persons who believed the gospel message about Jesus, though they lived in Asia Minor and had never seen Jesus. This use of "disciples" fits another detail in Acts—the use of "the Way" to designate the earliest believers (Acts 9:2; 19:23; 24:14, 22). Virtually from the start, believers in Jesus understood themselves to be following the way of Jesus even though they were not accompanying him.

Following the Jesus way has taken many forms. Some followers have imitated his original disciples and so have abandoned ordinary life to devote themselves as fully as possible either to worship and work in a monastery or to what some Christians used to call "full-time Christian service." Others, in keeping with Martin Luther and other reformers, have sought to follow Jesus by staying put—that is, by learning how to be his followers where they are—in the home or on the job. For these people, following Jesus does not so much require doing the extraordinary as reshaping ordinary life steadily until it somehow becomes extraordinary in its quality and direction.

> **Jesus has always had flawed followers. But all the Gospels show he never gave up on them.**

More important than the form one's following takes is remembering that the follower responds to Jesus. Disciples are to be not disciples of disciples but disciples of Jesus. Thanks to the Gospels, the sort of person Jesus was and the kind of things he did and said still call "Follow me."

So Then

We can be grateful the Gospels did not lionize the disciples or portray them as super-Christians. H*d that been the case, we could not identify with th*
u*
w*
w*

th*
n*

Jesus' mission by quoting Isaiah 42:1-4. Two sentences from that quotation are especially appropriate for Jesus' relation to his disciples—today's included:

*ed reed
*g wick
*ctory.
*ntiles will hope."
*isciples, in not break-
*, Jesus did not settle
*on teaching and
*today's disciples set-
*do that would be to

*nd
*d and

*illed and

(John 7:53—8:11 does not appear in all translation and editions of the Bible. The explanation is similar to that for John 5:4.) Chapter 8 opens with Jesus forgiving a woman caught in adultery, after calling upon any of her accusers who is without sin to "cast the first stone." It continues with Jesus' statement: "I am the Light of the World" and more explanations concerning who he is and His relationship with the Father who sent Him. He foretells His death. There is continued opposition from the Jews in general and the Pharisees in particular. He talks about the few Jews who believed in Him as being "true disciples" and invokes the common ancestry of Abraham as further explanation of Himself.

Chapter 9 involves the granting of sight to a man who had been born blind (the sixth sign) and the negative reaction of not only the Pharisees, but also of his neighbors. Note Jesus' explanation that the man's blindness is not the result of sin! Notde also the fear of the man's parents that they would excluded from the Temple because of their son's being able to see. Note also Jesus' comments about spiritual blindness.

Video Presentation:

Suggested Readings:

8 Mission With Healing Power

Go and tell John what you have seen and heard: the
blind receive their sight, the lame walk, the lepers
are cleansed, the deaf hear, the dead are raised,
the poor have good news brought to them.
And blessed is anyone who takes no offense at me.

(Luke 7:22-23)

They Have No Wine

Some of us pamper our bodies; others of us abuse them. Either way, our
physical self affects our inner and spiritual self, often in ways we cannot control,
for our bodies are vulnerable to accidents and illness. But our inner self also
affects the body. The inner self too needs care; it does not need pampering. Our
health *is* important, and rightly so; but do we know *why* it is important?

Beginning With Moses and All the Prophets

Jesus' healings and exorcisms are important aspects of his mission in the
Synoptics. John reports healings but no exorcisms. The week's Scripture readings
allow us to see how each Gospel presents Jesus' healing work in its own light.

Day 1 **Mark 1:21–2:12;** 3:1-6; 5:1–6:6; 7:31-37; 8:22-26; 9:14-29; 10:46-52

Remembering Mark's brief story of Jesus in the wilderness helps us understand why an exorcism
begins Jesus' mission. Notice that Jesus insists on keeping the healings secret, though nobody
heeds him. Why would he do that?

Day 2 Leviticus 6:1-7; 13–14; 1 Samuel 18:6-11; Isaiah 61; Tobit 6:1-9; 11:1-15

Today's readings from the Old Testament and the Apocrypha help us understand the Gospel stories. Leviticus 6:1-7 relates to Mark 10:46-52; Leviticus 13–14 shows how what then was called
leprosy was to be diagnosed and cured. The passage from First Samuel reports how Saul's jealousy could be understood at the time. Tobit* 6 shows how some Jews understood demons; Jesus'
way of healing blindness is similar to that used in Tobit 11.

Day 3 Matthew 4:23-25; 8:1-17, 28-34; 9:1-8, 18-35; 12:15-21, 43-45

Note how Matthew 4:23-25 sets the stage for the Sermon on the Mount. Observe also that Matthew shows Jesus as the Messiah in word and deed by putting the Sermon on the Mount (the word) before the deed stories in Chapters 8 and 9.

Day 4 Luke 4:14-44; 7:1-17; 17:11-19; Acts 2:14-24

Notice how Peter's sermon in Acts 2 refers to Jesus' activity. Review also Acts 10:34-43 from last week's readings.

Day 5 John 2:1-11; 4:46-53; 5:1-18

Observe that in John Jesus' inaugurating act is not a cure but a symbolic deed. What does it symbolize?

Day 6 Read and respond to "Mission With Healing Power" and "Do You Want to Become His Disciples, Too?"

Prayer Concerns

Mission With Healing Power

Keep three things in mind as we proceed. First, in antiquity Jesus was not the only figure about whom stories of wondrous healings were told. Some stories about these other healers, wonder-workers, and magicians report quite astounding things. Christians in the first and second centuries told stories also about the wondrous healings done by the apostles (for example, Acts 3:1-10; 5:12-16; 8:5-8; 16:16-18; 19:11-12). In fact, compared with some of the noncanonical stories, the wondrous deeds reported in the New Testament are rather tame. The *Acts of John*,* for example, reports that once when John and his followers found too many bedbugs in the beds at an inn, John simply commanded the bugs to go outside until morning—and they did. Some of the noncanonical gospels also reported amazing miracles done by Jesus, even as a boy. The *Infancy Gospel of Thomas* reports that the boy Jesus once stretched a board that had been cut too short. In antiquity (and not only then) people told such stories to express their belief that the hero was specially endowed with divine power. So it was only natural that such stories were told also about Jesus, particularly since the evidence indicates people were indeed healed through Jesus.

> **In the Bible, marvelous healings are usually understood to be the result of God's gracious power at work.**

Second, if we want to hear what the healing and exorcism stories intend to express, we should not call these events *miracles* because to some people that word often implies an act that violates the laws of nature. Biblical writers spoke of "signs and wonders" or of "deeds of power." *Luck* was not part of the Gospel writers' vocabulary (nor of Jesus'), for this word disconnects God from the good, wondrous event and leaves it without meaning for the life of faith. In the Bible, marvelous healings are usually understood to be the result of God's gracious power at work.

Third, each Evangelist used the stories of Jesus' mighty acts to accent something important about him.

Jesus—Healer and Exorcist: Three Interpretations

Mark. In Mark we find Jesus healing persons of various sicknesses, from a woman with a fever (1:30-31) to a child thought dead (5:39), plus performing four exorcisms—expelling an evil spirit or demon that has taken control of a person. Although healings differ from exorcisms, both actions show Jesus was concerned with the well-being of the whole person, not just with the person's mind, heart, or soul. Most of the stories are short, briefly stating the person's condition, Jesus' action, the fact of the cure, and the response of observers. While the healings usually generate wonder and amazement, the exorcisms produce controversy. The persons healed are not named (Bartimaeus is an exception, Mark 10:46), nor do the Gospels report the persons' responses to what has occurred to them. The stories focus on the power and authority of Jesus. The viewpoint of the stories is not that of the person healed but of the believers who use the stories as evidence of the significance of Jesus. This fact is unusually clear in Mark 9:14-29 (Matthew 17:14-21 and Luke 9:37-43), which reports Jesus was able to exorcise a demon after the disciples tried and failed. `GC 8-1`

Jesus healed in various ways ranging from a simple command (Mark 2:11; 3:5) to a combination of command, touching, and use of spittle (7:33-34). Healing also occurred without Jesus' doing or saying anything (5:25-34) or at a distance (7:24-30). Twice Mark, written in Greek, reports the Aramaic words Jesus used (5:41; 7:34) because people who told the stories thought the healer's words had special power. Historians have collected nonsense words and strange sounds used by healers and magicians in antiquity to gain power over the disease or demon. The Aramaic words used by Jesus, however, are intelligible and are translated for Greek-using readers, who are to conclude Jesus was not a magician.

The Gospels also contain statements summarizing Jesus' healing and exorcising activity without mentioning a specific incident (for example, Mark 1:39; 6:56). These summaries suggest that the individual stories are particular examples of what happened repeatedly. The summaries also allow the Evangelists to indicate their own emphases (Mark 1:32-34, 39; Matthew 4:23-25; Luke 6:17-19).

Mark does more than emphasize *that* Jesus healed and expelled evil spirits. He also places the stories at crucial points in the narrative where they convey a particular meaning without actually saying so. In three places an event takes on symbolic meaning because of its location in the story.

(1) Mark 1:21-34 reports the inaugural event of Jesus' mission, signaling what the reader is to look for in what follows. Jesus' first act is to expel an "unclean spirit"—in other words, he exorcises a demon. Because the story is so short, the details stand out all the more. A demon-possessed man shouts, "What have you to do with us, Jesus of Nazareth? Have you come to destroy us? [or, You have come to destroy us! The manuscripts have no punctuation.] I know who you are, the Holy One of God." The evil powers know their hold on the man is doomed, but they fight back by saying who Jesus of Nazareth really is. Since to name is to gain power over the named, the demonic takes the initiative in order to neutralize Jesus' power to destroy evil. But then Jesus asserts *his* power by commanding, "Be silent [Shut up!], and come out of him!" The quiet sabbath service has become the scene of a noisy power struggle between the demonic and the Holy One of God. But the unclean spirit does not slip away quietly. The man has convulsions and shrieks before the demonic power leaves, making Jesus' victory over Satan evident. This exorcism is Jesus' first public act and confirms what Mark implied in the short report of Jesus in the wilderness (1:12-13): Satan tested Jesus and lost—but Satan did not disappear from the scene. Through the unclean spirit in the synagogue, Satan fights back and loses again. In short, the Evangelist tells the readers they are to view Jesus' mission as a conflict with evil power. Matthew omits the story. For that Gospel, the inaugural event is the Sermon on the Mount.

(2) Mark 8:22-26 reports the two-step healing of a man's blindness. Only Mark has the story, but it is important because of what it signifies. To see that significance, we must pay attention to where the story is placed. The previous paragraph ends with Jesus' question to the disciples, "Do you not yet understand?" Then comes this healing story, which is followed by Peter's confession and Jesus' first prediction of his suffering and death—to which Peter objects (8:27-33). Again we get a struggle, not over power as in the synagogue but over understanding: Because Peter is blind to the nature of Jesus' messiahship (Peter got the title right but thought Jesus got the meaning wrong), he rebukes Jesus, and Jesus rebukes Peter. By placing the story of the healing of blindness just before Jesus' exchange with Peter, Mark suggests that Peter and the disciples will not understand Jesus'

messiahship and death unless their blindness is healed. And it proves to be so as the narrative continues; Jesus will speak of his suffering two more times, yet the disciples' responses show they are still unable to understand. But the full symbolic significance of this two-step healing story appears only when we see how it relates to the story of the healing of another blind man, recorded in Mark 10:46-52.

(3) Mark 10:46-52, the healing of Bartimaeus's blindness, follows the most glaring example of the disciples' failure to understand Jesus, reported in 10:35-45 and just before the entry into Jerusalem. The whole narrative from Peter's argument with Jesus at Caesarea Philippi to this healing at Jericho emphasizes Jesus' repeated effort to announce his death and the disciples' failure to understand. And the two stories that report blindness healed, like bookends, hold together the material between them.

Mark's story is about Jesus and his disciples; but Mark is also talking to readers, telling us that only in light of the cross and Resurrection do we really understand who Jesus is and what his life and death are all about. Before Jesus' death and resurrection, only the demons understand what is afoot because they know the Holy One of God will destroy their power. And just as the two blind men receive their sight by Jesus' act of power, so only a mighty act of God's power will overcome the disciples' resistance to the meaning of Jesus and his death.

The inaugural scene in the synagogue points to another feature of Mark's use of the healing and exorcism stories—Jesus' command to be silent. This command has two functions within the story itself: It shows Jesus' authority (1:26), and it prohibits the spirit from saying again who Jesus really is. Mark's summary statement that follows emphasizes this second function: "He would not permit the demons to speak, because they knew him" (1:32-34; in 3:10-12 Jesus prohibits unclean spirits from making his identity known; so also in Matthew 12:15-16 and Luke 4:41). These Gospels imply Jesus did not want his true identity publicized by demonic powers. However, in the long exorcism story of the Gerasene demoniac (Mark 5:1-20), Jesus tells the cured man, who wants to join him, to go home and tell his friends what the Lord has done for him. The demon-possessed man shrieking the identity of Jesus is one thing; the witness of the man restored to sanity is another.

But silencing demons is only part of the picture; at times Jesus insisted on silence when he healed people who were not demon-possessed, though obviously such an event could not remain unknown in a village (1:44; 5:43; 7:24, 36). Neither Jesus nor Mark explains why the wondrous healing events should be kept secret. Perhaps Mark 1:35-38 offers a clue. This story reports that after the inaugural day Jesus slipped away before daybreak to pray.

Jesus did not want to be diverted from his central task by being a full-time healer and exorcist, despite the need.

When the disciples found him, they said, "Everyone is searching for you"—understandable, given his many healings and exorcisms the night before. But instead of returning with the disciples and resuming his wonderworking, Jesus insisted on going to other towns so that he could proclaim his message there too, "for that is what I came out to do." Jesus did not want to be diverted from his central task by being a full-time healer and exorcist, despite the need. So, he may have insisted people not talk about their being healed, lest his healing activity overwhelm his teaching mission.

There is yet a third part to the picture: Jesus commands the disciples to say nothing about his being the Christ, the Messiah (8:29-30), the Son of God (9:2-10), or about his death (9:30-32). Mark reports that the healed ignored Jesus' command but implies that the disciples obeyed. After all, they did not understand Jesus anyway—not until after Easter.

Scholars have proposed various explanations of "the messianic secret," as it came to be called. Recently, those who have come to read Mark as a piece of literature have noticed that Mark regularly portrays Jesus as a mysterious figure, never fully understandable, repeatedly suggesting more than he says, often saying the opposite of what the reader expects. But these strange traits are just what draw us into the story because we too struggle to understand Jesus, and so are as challenged by him today as his disciples were then. Does anyone really need a completely intelligible, wholly transparent, fully explainable Jesus?

Matthew. When Matthew expanded Mark, he generally retained the healing and exorcism stories, but he used them somewhat differently. Three features of Matthew's portrayal of Jesus the healer and exorcist invite attention.

The first concerns the placement of the stories and summaries. In Matthew the inaugural event of

Jesus' mission is not an exorcism, as in Mark, but the Sermon on the Mount, for which Matthew prepares the way by reporting Jesus' preaching and healing ministry (4:23-25). After the Sermon (Matthew 5–7) presents Jesus as the Teacher par excellence, Matthew 8–9 presents him as the doer; so Matthew 5–9 portrays Jesus as the messianic Son of God in *word* and in *deed*. Matthew frames these chapters by summaries of Jesus' healing work (4:23-25; 9:35), showing readers that these chapters form a single section (9:36-38 prepares for Jesus' next discourse in Chapter 10).

In putting together Chapters 8 and 9 Matthew omitted Mark's inaugural story of the exorcism in the synagogue, rearranged the sequence of Mark's stories, and shortened what he retained from Mark. As a result, in Matthew 8:1-17 Jesus heals a leper (one whose disease puts him outside the community), the servant of a Roman soldier (one who never was in the community), and Peter's mother-in-law (one whose place in the community was restricted). Thereby Matthew showed Jesus redefining the boundaries of the people of God by healing the excluded and the marginalized.

The second feature appears at Matthew 8:17, which Matthew adds to Mark's summary statement describing the end of the first day: "This was to fulfill what had been spoken through the prophet Isaiah, 'He took our infirmities and bore our diseases'" (Isaiah 53:4). For Matthew, Jesus' healings and exorcisms show that in him God is bringing to pass the word of Scripture (so also Matthew 12:15-21). By quoting these lines from Isaiah's portrayal of God's servant, Matthew implies that in his healing ministry, Jesus is the servant of God.

The third feature, though shared with Mark, has more prominence in Matthew—Jesus' response to the charge that he can exorcise demons because he is in league with the devil (Matthew 9:32-34). In 12:25-29 Jesus makes four responses, the first found in all three Gospels. (1) Just as a kingdom or house (here *house* means dynasty) divided against itself is destroyed, so Satan's kingdom cannot survive if Satan fights Satan in the exorcisms. Therefore it is ridiculous, Jesus implies, to accuse him of expelling Beelzebul's subordinates with Beelzebul's power. The accusation self-destructs. (2) Jesus then points out that other exorcists are at work, implying that if he uses Beelzebul, so do they. The other exorcists will repudiate the accusation. (3) But then in a saying not found in Mark, Jesus gives the meaning of his exorcisms: They bring the kingdom of God—to the accusers! "But if it is by the Spirit of God [Luke has 'finger of God'] that I cast out demons, then the kingdom of God has come to you" (Matthew 12:28).

In other words, Jesus is God's "finger" by which the coming of God's reign rescues people from demonic power. The Kingdom comes to the possessed too, for its power liberates them from Beelzebul. But in saying that it comes "to you"— the accusers, Jesus confronts them with the need to decide for or against him. (4) One cannot plunder a strong man's house without first tying him up. Here Jesus implies that in expelling demons he is in fact tying up the strong man (Satan) in order to rescue the possessed from Satan's power.

Luke. In Luke the inaugural event is neither an exorcism nor the Sermon on the Mount but Jesus' appearance in his hometown synagogue where he claimed Isaiah 61:1-2 was being fulfilled through him, and where he infuriated his former neighbors by speaking of their rejecting him and by reminding them of times when God's favor came to Gentiles, not to Israel. The hometown folk did, in fact, reject him (Luke 4:16-30). What is important just now, however, is Luke's use of Isaiah.

The words of Isaiah 61 are apt, for "the Spirit of the Lord is upon me" calls to mind the descent of the Spirit at Jesus' baptism and its subsequent role (Luke 3:22; 4:1, 14). The words also point toward Jesus' mission—

"because he has anointed me
   to bring good news to the poor.
He has sent me to proclaim release to the
   captives
and recovery of sight to the blind,
   to let the oppressed go free,
to proclaim the year of the Lord's favor."

Readers of Matthew and Mark know Jesus' mission is empowered by the Spirit, but only in Luke does Jesus himself make this claim in public. Luke reports that Jesus healed the blind; perhaps releasing the captives refers to exorcisms, and the liberation of the oppressed to the story of the bent-over woman in Luke 13:10-17.

Only in Luke do we find the story of Jesus' bringing a dead boy back to life (7:11-17), the report that Mary Magdalene had once been possessed by seven demons (8:2), the healing of the woman who had not stood erect for eighteen years (13:10-17), and the story of the man afflicted with dropsy (14:1-6). Noteworthy is the story in 17:11-19 of ten lepers who were cured while going to show themselves to the priests (to verify their cure so they could return to society) as Jesus told them to do; to Jesus' amazement, only one came back to thank him—and he was a Samaritan. (The parable of the good Samaritan also is found only in Luke.)

Even though Luke adds four stories while omitting three of Mark's (Mark 7:24-30, 32-37; 8:22-24),

the healings and exorcisms are not as prominent in Luke's story of Jesus' mission as they are in Mark's. Because Luke also added a great many sayings not found in Mark, the proportion of word to deed changed. Not that the wondrous deeds were unimportant for Luke. To the contrary, in Luke's second volume, Jesus' wondrous deeds are a significant part of the apostles' preaching (Acts 2:22; 10:38); in fact, the apostles' acts of healing continue the healing work of Jesus (3:6; 4:9-10, 29-30).

Meanings of Jesus' Healings and Exorcisms

What meanings might Jesus' healings and exorcisms have for us who read about them centuries later? First, in the context of Jesus' mission the healings and exorcisms were a significant expression of his message about the kingdom of God, even if the Gospels report only one saying in which he connects his exorcism with the Kingdom (Matthew 12:28; Luke 11:20). Had Jesus been a theologian like Paul he might have explained how various elements of his mission fit together; but his calling was to be the bearer of the Kingdom's coming. Even so, we can see that his various activities are consistent with

> In the context of Jesus' mission the healings and exorcisms were a significant expression of his message about the kingdom of God.

the core of his message—the coming of the Kingdom, the actualized will of God on earth as in heaven. This message implies that the Kingdom's arrival will make everything, and everyone, right—including the condition of body and mind. The Kingdom's coming rectifies the whole person, including the relationships that give a person identity. In a male-dominated society, Jesus' healing and exorcising work, like his teaching, extended to women and children as well as to men—a feature unique to Jesus. Further, nowhere do the Gospels report that Jesus first required people to believe his message before he would heal them or that he said in effect, "If you repent properly, I will heal you." Rather, he healed them and freed them from demonic power so they *could* repent (turn life Godward as rectified persons responding to the nearness of the Kingdom).

Second, in Jesus' healings the role of faith is not always obvious, though some degree of faith in the healer is assumed. Mark's version of the story of Jesus' rejection at Nazareth (Mark 6:1-6) ends with the Evangelist's comment, "And he could do no deed of power there, except that he laid his hands on a few sick people and cured them. And he was amazed at their unbelief." Matthew 13:58 is more straightforward: "And he did not do many deeds of power there, because of their unbelief." In the story of Jesus' healing the paralyzed man, the faith to which Jesus responds is that of the friends who had dug a hole through the roof so they could lower the man to Jesus in a crowded house (Mark 2:4-5); not a word is said about the man's faith before, during, or after the healing. On the other hand, Jesus told the woman whose hemorrhaging stopped when she touched his clothes that her faith made her well (5:34). By no means should this word to her be used to justify saying to persons of faith who are not cured, "If you had real faith, you would be healed!" Neither Mark 6:5-6 nor Matthew 13:58 is Jesus' word *to* the folks

Nowhere do the Gospels report that Jesus first required people to believe his message before he would heal them.

in Nazareth, but the Evangelist's comment. Had Jesus said, "If you had faith, I would heal you," he would have broken the reed already bruised (Matthew 12:20)—that is, he would have made matters worse. But he was not that kind of healer.

Third, since the healings and exorcisms were essential expressions of the kind of person Jesus was and of the nature of his mission, his followers feel obliged to carry on healing ministries themselves. It has been so from the start. Christian missions have consistently brought medicines and sanitation to all parts of the globe, established infirmaries, and trained doctors and nurses to staff them, often under difficult conditions. Nor should we forget the many persons moved to do likewise though not deliberately committed to the Christian faith or to following Jesus' precedent. That development is one of Jesus' unacknowledged legacies. In such efforts to bring healing to a battered and bleeding world, Christians can see grace released—and give thanks.

So Then

Jesus' healings and exorcisms are not to be separated from his vocation of herald and harbinger of God's kingly rule in human life; they were an integral part of that vocation. What matters is not *how* he healed, but *that* he did. Why? Because as expressions of the Kingdom's coming the healings and exorcisms indicate what the King is like. That's why they are part of the gospel in the Gospels.

Do You Want to Become His Disciples, Too?

Jesus was never more spiritual than when he dealt with the body, whether his own or that of others. The same is true of his followers. Our body is not just matter inhabited by the self; it is also the necessary means by which the self comes to expression. Caring for the body is therefore a spiritual act, especially when we care for someone else's body.

What do Jesus' healing activities say about who Jesus is?

_____

_____

_____

_____

_____

Prayer

Our LORD, I will remember the things you have done,
    your miracles of long ago.
I will think about each one of your mighty deeds.
Everything you do is right,
    and no other god compares with you.
You alone work miracles,
    and you have let nations see your mighty power.
With your own arm you rescued your people,
    the descendants of Jacob and Joseph.

(Psalm 77:11-15, CEV)

9 Conflicts Over Obedience

New wine must be put into fresh wineskins.
(Luke 5:38)

They Have No Wine

Those who are determined to do what is right are often criticized most. Why? Does their zeal irritate others? Is their understanding of what is right too rigid? Are they too proud of being and doing right? Whatever the case, I need to know what is right and why it is right if I am not going to be deterred by criticism.

Beginning With Moses and All the Prophets

This week's study concentrates on Jesus' conflicts, especially conflicts with those who had other ideas about obeying God's will. Because some of these conflicts were linked with his healings and exorcisms, we will look again at some passages studied last week. Other conflicts resulted from his distinct understanding of God's will in Scripture. The readings from the Old Testament will help us understand what distinguished Jesus from his critics who used the same Bible.

Day 1 Mark 2:1–3:6; Matthew 9:10-17; 12:1-14; Luke 5:17–6:11; Luke 13:10-17; Exodus 20:1-17; Leviticus 24:1-9; Numbers 28:1-10; Deuteronomy 5:12-15; 1 Samuel 21:1-6; Hosea 5:13–6:6

Mark 2:1–3:6 looks like an earlier collection of conflict stories that Mark included. Notice how the call of Levi leads to the next scene and how the topic of eating leads to its opposite, fasting, in 2:18-22. Note also that one sabbath controversy leads to the next. Observe how early (3:6) Mark signals the outcome of the whole story of Jesus (the Pharisees and Herodians reappear at 12:13.)

Day 2 Mark 3:20-30; Matthew 12:22-37; Luke 11:14-23; James 3:6-12

While some of today's readings were studied last week, they are important for this week's work as well. "The unforgivable sin" is a much-discussed topic; notice what it refers to here.

Day 3 Leviticus 11–15

The long reading from Leviticus was the basis for many of the regulations of the Pharisees and of the community at Qumran.*

Day 4 Mark 7:1-23; Matthew 15:1-20; Romans 14; Isaiah 29:13-24

GC-9-1 Compare carefully the readings from Mark and Matthew. Note that Mark 7:3-4 (omitted from Matthew) implies Mark's first readers were not Jews. Note the use of the word *parable* in Mark 7:17; Matthew 15:15. Review what was said in Lesson 6 about the uses of this word. Note the Evangelist's interpretation (in parentheses) of Jesus' words at Mark 7:19, and observe how close the passage in Romans comes to this verse in Mark.

Day 5 Mark 12:38-40; Matthew 23; Luke 12:49-56; 13:31-35; 20:45-47; Numbers 15:37-41; 2 Chronicles 24:17-22

Observe how Matthew 23 (the first part of Jesus' last discourse in Matthew) expands Mark 12:38-40. Note the accusation against the scribes and Pharisees in Matthew 23:2-3, and how it is then detailed, beginning with 23:13.

Day 6 Read and respond to "Conflicts Over Obedience" and "Do You Want to Become His Disciples, Too?"

Prayer Concerns

Conflicts Over Obedience

This week's Scripture lets us see the obedient Jesus in conflict with those who understood obedience to God differently. Since both Jesus and his critics sought to obey God's will, the conflicts raise such questions as, Which deeds express obedience and which do not? and How can we determine the difference?

Although Jesus did have conflicts with the Pharisees, the stories were written down three to six decades later and so reflect what had happened in the intervening years. Here are the essential points.

(1) The Judaism the Evangelists knew differed markedly from the Judaism Jesus knew because the Jews' losing the war against Rome (A.D. 66–70) changed the whole religious landscape. When Luke and Matthew were written, the Temple had been in ruins for two decades and the priesthood scattered; the Sadducees and the people who produced and hid the Dead Sea Scrolls had disappeared. The Pharisees' way of being faithful, obedient Jews was continued and developed by their successors, the early rabbis. They sought to shape and consolidate a Judaism without Temple and priesthood. Because those parts of the Torah that pertained to the Temple and the priests could no longer be carried out as prescribed, obedience to other parts of the Torah became more important than ever to the continuing of Judaism and the Jewish communities.

(2) While the rabbis were redefining and consolidating Judaism, the increasingly Gentile churches too were developing their own thought, organization, and way of life, drawing in part on the words and deeds of Jesus to guide them. In other words, the churches in which and for which the Gospels were written were also defining themselves, partly by distinguishing their way of life from that of the synagogues.

The Gospels give us an incomplete and one-sided picture both of the Pharisees and of Jesus' relation to Judaism.

(3) During the years synagogues and churches were growing apart, the Christians found especially useful the stories and sayings of Jesus in which he criticized the Pharisees' understanding of obedience.

As a result, the Gospels contain more stories and sayings of Jesus that show him differing from the Pharisees than those that show what he shared with them. The Gospels give us an incomplete and one-sided picture both of the Pharisees and of Jesus' relation to Judaism. If in studying Jesus' conflicts today, we ignore the historical context *of* the Gospels and its influence *on* the Gospels, we do both the Pharisees and Jesus an injustice.

Mark 2:1–3:6

No clouds obstruct the bright sunlight in Mark 1, the beginning of Jesus' mission. Dark clouds appear abruptly, however, in Mark 2:1–3:6; indeed, the concluding comment at 3:6, "The Pharisees went out and immediately conspired with the Herodians against him, how to destroy him," is a clap of thunder announcing the coming storm, though its arrival is delayed until 12:13 where another clap signals the storm is at hand. The conflict stories here give little attention to time and place, and only once give the name of a person (Levi)—but the name is uncertain (he is called Matthew in Matthew 9:9, and some manuscripts of Mark say his name is James). One story follows another, but one event does not cause the next. The sequence of the stories is determined by the subject matter. Thus the setting of the third story (Mark 2:15-17) is a meal, but the setting of the fourth (2:18-22) is its opposite, fasting; the fifth and sixth stories occur on the sabbath, one in the grainfields, the other in a synagogue. The story of the healing in the synagogue (3:1-6) forms the climax of this series of stories because the response of the Pharisees is ominous.

The most serious charge against Jesus comes in the first story (2:1-12). Here four men, determined to bring their paralyzed friend to Jesus despite the crowd, dig a hole through the flat clay roof and lower the mat on which the man is lying. Mark writes that when Jesus saw the faith of the man's friends, he told the man that his sins "are forgiven." Though the words "are forgiven" imply God is the forgiver, the scribes recognize Jesus has spoken for God and object: "Why does this fellow speak in this way? It is blasphemy! Who can forgive sins but God alone?" In response, Jesus asks them a question: "Which is easier, to say . . . , 'Your sins are forgiven,' or to say, 'Stand up and take your mat and walk'?" A strange choice. In one sense, to say, "Your sins are forgiven," is easier because who would know whether they are or not?

But to tell the man to get up risks embarrassment: What if he could not or refused to do so? On the other hand, pronouncing forgiveness is not easier, for in doing this Jesus presumes to know what God would do. Jesus refuses to choose and commands the man to stand, take his mat, and go home—in order to show that "the Son of Man has authority on earth to forgive sins." Indeed Jesus does claim to speak for God.

The second conflict emerges during a dinner given by a tax collector who had responded to Jesus' call. These tax collectors collected tolls or tariffs on goods brought across the Sea of Galilee into Herod Antipas's territory on the western side. They were despised, partly because they got the job by bidding for it and then set the tax rate high enough to cover the cost of the job, pay the government, and make a handsome profit as well. If tongues began wagging when news got around that Jesus called Levi to be his disciple, they surely did so when he ate with Levi and his colleagues and other "sinners." Luke makes explicit what Mark and Matthew probably assume: "Levi gave a great banquet for him [Jesus] in his house" (Luke 5:29).

Eating together was a mark of mutual acceptance, so eating with "tax collectors and sinners" (Mark's story uses the phrase three times to drive the point home) was scandalous. If Jesus were really serious about the kingdom of God, he wouldn't associate with those people, would he? Levi had given up being a tax collector, but the other guests were what they always had been. But from Jesus' perspective, the scrupulous Pharisees missed the point of his mission: Just as the healthy do not need a doctor but the sick, so he came "to call not the righteous but sinners." Eating with these disreputable, despised people did not undermine his mission but expressed it. If these people would not come to him (even Levi had to be called), he would go to them. Nor did he require their repentance first; rather, in going to them he made their repentance possible.

In the next story (Mark 2:18-20), it is the disciples who are accused of not taking their religion seriously, for they do not fast. The Pharisees and John the Baptist's disciples show by their fasting they are earnest in their devotion. "Why don't yours, Jesus?" Jesus responds with a question of his own: "The wedding guests cannot fast while the bridegroom is with them, can they?" No one fasts during a wedding (the celebration was far more than a brief reception, or even a luncheon, after the ceremony). But where is the wedding? Jesus challenges the questioners to see that his mission is wedding time, a time of rejoicing

because God's kingship is now being realized. What John's disciples are earnestly preparing for by fasting, Jesus' disciples are already celebrating.

To Jesus' counter-question in Mark 2:19 have been added other sayings (2:20-22). The first takes account of the fact that early Christians did fast even if Jesus' disciples had not done so during his lifetime, and the saying legitimates later fasting by paying close attention to what Jesus said. True, there is no fasting during the wedding ("as long as they have the bridegroom with them"), but this

> Jesus challenges the questioners to see that his mission is wedding time, a time of rejoicing because God's kingship is now being realized.

explanation implies there will be time when he will not be with them (when he "is taken away from them"), that is, after Jesus' death. "Then they will fast" (2:20). But this fasting is not the same as that of the Pharisees and John's followers. That difference is the point of the next sayings about the unshrunk patch on an old coat and new wine in old wineskins; new wine goes into new skins. Don't mix the old with the new. Christian fasting is new, not a return to the old—even though the food they are not eating is the same. What makes Christian fasting new is what also distinguishes Jesus' understanding of repentance from John's: John's repentance is the discipline of getting ready for disaster; Jesus' repentance is in response to the Kingdom.

GC 9-2 Mark 2:23-28 has Jesus and his disciples going through the grainfields on a sabbath. The story does not even hint at why they were there, for an explanation might suggest that the truth of Jesus' crisp teaching was tied to that circumstance instead of being universally true. The emphasis falls on Jesus' response; what the disciples thought or said, like the Pharisees' reaction, is irrelevant. All the essentials are there, however—the disciples' action, the transgression (they work on the sabbath), and Jesus' word implying they are not breaking the rules after all. Luke shortens Jesus' word (Luke 6:1-5), but Matthew expands it by inserting another saying (Matthew 12:5-7). All three Gospels end with virtually the same saying, "The Son of Man is lord even of the sabbath," yet in no two Gospels is Jesus' response identical because in each of them Jesus actually gives more than one justification for the disciples' act.

In all three Gospels Jesus first responds by reminding the Pharisees that Scripture itself provides a lawful precedent, one that was a more serious violation of the rules than plucking heads of grain. David and his companions ate the sacred bread when they were hungry (Exodus 25:30; Leviticus 24:5-9; 1 Samuel 21:1-6). In other words, what David did shows rules can be broken in order to meet human need. Jesus then applies the story to the sabbath situation at hand: The sabbath was made for human benefit, not the reverse. A later rabbinic saying makes the same point: "The sabbath is delivered unto you, and you are not delivered to the sabbath."

Now comes another answer: "The Son of Man is lord even of the sabbath." Technically, the Hebrew/Aramaic phrase "son of man" simply means "human being" as in Psalm 8:4 ("What is man [*enosh*, human] that you are mindful of him, the son of man [*ben adam*] that you care for him?" [NIV]). Some interpreters therefore think Jesus too means "the human being is lord even of the sabbath"; but it is highly likely that Mark understands the words as a title for Jesus, the Son of Man. So, in effect, Jesus would be saying, "I am lord even of the sabbath." On this basis, the disciples' action is supported by the authority of Jesus, not as a teacher from Nazareth but as the Son of Man now on earth (as in Mark 2:10). A few manuscripts of Mark omit either all or part of 2:27; Luke omits all of it. Sabbath-keeping apparently was not a problem in Luke's church, for in Acts the sabbath is mentioned simply as a day when something happens.

Matthew's version of the story puts the accent elsewhere. (Matthew omits Mark's reference to Abiathar [Mark 2:26] because he knows that the priest's name was Ahimelech.) Like Luke, Matthew omits Mark 2:27, "The sabbath was made for humankind, and not humankind for the sabbath." But he also inserts two sayings of Jesus found only here. In the first (Matthew 12:5-6) Jesus points out that the Temple priests perform their duties on the sabbath yet are not guilty of transgressing the law against work (Numbers 28:9-10). Then he adds a loaded comment, "Something greater than the temple is here"—himself as the bearer of the Kingdom. Jesus next takes the initiative and becomes the accuser, saying that if the Pharisees had understood Hosea 6:6, "I desire mercy and not sacrifice," they would not have "condemned the guiltless" disciples in the first place (Matthew 12:7).

The last conflict story in Mark 2:1–3:6 is set in a synagogue, but the focus is not on the deed but on the day it occurs—sabbath. The story assumes Jesus had now gotten a reputation about his attitude toward the sabbath, for his opponents were looking to see whether he would heal a man with a withered hand. Jesus does not evade the situation but challenges the Pharisees by summoning the man (who had not asked for healing) to his side and confronts them with a question: "Is it lawful to do good or to do harm on the sabbath, to save life or to kill?" The opponents saw that the answer was self-evident, and was a trap: They could not say doing harm on the sabbath is lawful (any more than on any day); but if they said doing good is lawful, they would approve of Jesus' healing before he did anything. Besides, according to common Jewish teaching, any law could be broken in order to save a life. But this man's condition was not life-threatening; his healing could have been postponed until sundown. So the Pharisees were silent. Jesus was now angry (a detail not repeated by Matthew and Luke). So he deliberately healed the man, and in doing so provoked the plot to get rid of him.

In Matthew's story (12:9-14) the Pharisees raise the question to which Jesus responds with a saying, an analogy: If your only sheep falls into a pit on the sabbath, would you pull it out (and not wait until the next day)? Arguing now from the lesser to the greater, Jesus says the obvious: A person is more valuable than a sheep, so of course it is permissible to heal this man on the sabbath. Jesus argues the same way in the story about the woman who could not stand straight (Luke 13:10-17) and in the story of the man with dropsy (Luke 14:1-6).

Mark 7:1-23

Mark 7:1-23, like the stories in 2:1–3:6, reports Jesus' response to the Pharisees and scribes who ask him to justify his disciples' behavior. Having noticed that some of them "were eating with defiled hands, that is, without washing them," they asked, "Why do your disciples not live according to the tradition of the elders, but eat with defiled hands?" (7:2, 5). The Pharisees' question has nothing to do with cleanliness; the issue is ritual purification (by washing), an act that separates the group from the ordinary, profane world.

According to Numbers 18:8-13, priests must wash (purify themselves ritually) before eating the holy food people had given as a sacrifice (18:11; Exodus 30:17-21). The Old Testament has no rules that require such ritual washing by ordinary folk, or for washing things brought from the market. Nor do the rabbinic texts have such requirements for all faithful Jews. However, the Pharisees, who formed a close-knit group who ate and studied Torah together, applied the rules for the priests to themselves, even though they were not priests. Evidently they took literally Exodus 19:6, "You will be to me a kingdom of priests, my holy nation" (REB). The Pharisees and scribes who question Jesus in Mark 7:5 probably practiced such ritual washing as a mark of their obedience to God's command, and justified the practice by appealing to "the tradition of the elders"—that is, to the "elders" of their type of Pharisaism. (Mark's "all the Jews" in 7:3 exaggerates.) So the Pharisees' "Why . . . ?" does more than request information; it conveys an accusation: "Jesus, why aren't your disciples as serious about being a holy community as we are?"

Mark sees that the Pharisees' question goes to the heart of what it means to be a follower of Jesus and so reports Jesus' three-part response, each part addressed to a different audience: Mark 7:6-13 addresses the Pharisees' use of tradition; 7:14-15 tells the crowd what does and does not defile. (Most manuscripts add 7:16, "Let anyone with ears to hear listen," but this looks like a copyist's way of emphasizing 7:15.) Mark 7:17-23 addresses the disciples privately, just as in 4:10-20 Jesus explains privately the parable spoken in 4:1-9. Mark guides his readers' understanding by adding his own comments, which appear in parentheses (7:3-4, 11, 19). Matthew 15:1-20 generally retains Mark 7:1-23 but omits Mark's parenthetical comments. Matthew also adds a saying found only here, Matthew 15:13-14. Luke omits Mark 7:1-23 entirely, perhaps because he knew the issue was not a problem for his (presumably) Gentile readers.

In Mark Jesus' first response to the question of the Pharisees and scribes (7:6-13) concerns their misuse of tradition and has two parts. In the first (7:6-8) he applies Isaiah 29:13 to them and concludes, "You abandon the commandment of God and hold to human tradition."

Jesus does not attack tradition as such, nor does he explain the proper role of tradition; what he does is accuse the Pharisees and scribes of so misusing tradition that they hold to it and abandon the command. They assume that the tradition spells out the command; but Jesus drives a wedge between tradition and command, not as a matter of principle but as a way of challenging the Pharisees' assumptions about their tradition, for their question appealed to "the tradition of the elders."

The second part of Jesus' response concerning misuse of tradition (7:9-13) is a well-chosen example of "making void the word of God through your tradition that you have handed on." This example shows how a vow *to* God can be used as a loophole to evade the command *from* God. Jesus points out that a person can avoid supporting parents by saying to them, "The money is not available for you because it is Corban" (Hebrew for "offering to God"). That is, as "Corban" it has been vowed to God. Since vows to God cannot be broken, this form of obeying God can be used to avoid obeying even one of the Ten Commandments. This interpretation of Corban as a sacred vow is not found in Scripture but is the creation of tradition. However, what appears to have irritated Jesus was not its origin but the result of misusing it.

In 7:14-15 Jesus takes up the issue that gave rise to this whole passage—defilement. He tells the crowd that the idea that "defilement" results when the hands are not washed ritually before eating is off the mark. According to Jesus, "There is nothing outside a person that by going in can defile [make one impure before God], but the things that come out are what defile."

> If defilement comes "from within, from the human heart," then sinful deeds are really manifestations of the inner self; they are not simply foibles or mistakes.

This statement is so amazing we can assume the disciples were not the only ones who needed an explanation (7:17). After all, Jesus' Jewish hearers knew well that what comes out of the body does defile (urine, pus, menstrual blood), for many biblical laws dictated how such discharges must be dealt with (Leviticus 11–15). So this part of what Jesus says is unnecessary. Besides, the whole point of the food laws was to identify what defiles when it is eaten; so Jesus seems to annul the command of God about food that defiles (for example, pork, shrimp, horse meat). What Jesus says appears to be a riddle, referred to here as a "parable."

Jesus' response to the disciples (Mark 7:17-23)—to the church as well as to the Twelve—begins on a note more clever than profound, as might be expected of a riddle. Jesus says, "Of course nothing that enters a person can make one impure because what enters does not go into the heart [the core of the self] but into the stomach, and then goes on out; it never enters the *person* in the first place." What actually does defile is what comes out of the person, from the heart. Mark 7:21-22 provides a list of such "evil things" (Matthew 15:19 shortens it). The list in Mark is like other vice lists in the New Testament (Romans 1:29-31; Galatians 5:19-21) and in other Greek and Roman literature of the time. These vices defile the persons from whom they come and harm those around them as well. Vices are like that.

If defilement comes "from within, from the human heart," then the sinful deeds (the vices) are really manifestations of the inner self; they are not simply foibles or mistakes. "All these evil things come from within, and they defile a person" (Mark 7:23). The person is defiled before the deed is done, for the sinful deed expresses what is already in the heart. Jesus did not diminish the danger of defilement; in fact, he increased it by relocating it. He shifted defilement from something that happens *to* a person (who neglects ritual washing, for instance) to what a person *is* in the heart.

However, Mark, writing for Christian Gentiles (evident from the way he describes Jewish practices in Mark 7:3-4), sees something else in Jesus' words: "Thus he declared all foods clean" (7:19). Mark concludes that if nothing entering a person, such as pork, defiles, then the whole basis for Jewish dietary laws collapses. Such a conclusion was hardly what Jesus had in mind; had it been, he would have repudiated a fundamental feature of Judaism, and there is no evidence at all for such an attitude or action. Further, such an attitude would imply Jesus regarded this aspect of Judaism as a problem to be overcome. For Jesus the Law is not the problem; the human heart is the problem. But for Mark and his Gentile readers, the dietary laws were a hurdle; so it is no surprise Mark saw in the logic of Jesus' words a way to solve it.

> **Our problem is not Judaism, then or now, but any form of Christianity that thinks it can have Jesus without having his Scripture and loyal obedience to the God of whom it speaks.**

So Then

The Gospel's reports of Jesus' harsh words against the scribes and Pharisees offend many Christians—not only Jews. The latter are convinced that the Gospels have distorted Judaism; the former, that the Gospels have distorted Jesus. Yet, Jesus' criticisms are nowhere directed toward Judaism itself but at certain abuses. Jesus criticized the abuses because he cared passionately for the integrity of the faith of his forebears. He spoke as an offended insider, not as an outsider. Besides, his criticism was no more severe than that of the biblical prophets. At no point did Jesus say or imply he came to save his people or the world from Judaism, for Judaism was not the problem. Nowhere do the Gospels report Jesus said people should stop observing sabbath, start eating foods declared unclean, ignore the holy days of Pentecost or Day of Atonement, or despise the Temple in order to obey God more truly. In the name of the God of Israel and its Scripture he spoke fiercely against those who, in his view, abused their own heritage. He was doing in his time what the prophets did in theirs. That he had a different view of his inherited religion from that of his critics does not imply he was pressing for an alternative religion.

Looking carefully at what Jesus said and did not say about the Pharisees is essential; also essential is trying to understand their viewpoint. Both efforts are needed if we are to avoid distorting the picture. But something else must be said as well: We would make a serious error in assuming the abuses Jesus addressed were so peculiarly Jewish that we Christians can simply watch Jesus criticize *them*—as if the same abuses were not found also among us.

Some of us—and probably our parents and grandparents—observed the Christian "sabbath" as rigidly as any Pharisee observed the Jewish sabbath. Today's society is much more complex. We all depend on those who must work on Sunday (nurses and doctors, police officers and firefighters), and many of us garden and shop on Sunday afternoon and engage in all sorts of recreation. Our work pattern has other days "off" or is more likely oriented toward the weekend. And for some faithful church folk, Sunday seems especially busy. Today's hectic pace makes the issues raised by Jesus' attitude toward the sabbath all the more pressing, not less. Is there no "day of rest," no release from ceaseless activity, no time to ponder and to pray in quiet? Disciples do not evade such questions but find an appropriate way to keep the

Christian sabbath, not because we must but because we may.

Our problem is not Judaism, then or now, but any form of Christianity that thinks it can have Jesus without having his Scripture and loyal obedience to the God of whom it speaks. Such a Jesus soon becomes just another pagan god.

Do You Want to Become His Disciples, Too?

Jesus found himself in conflict situations because he saw clearly what was of greatest importance and dared to live by it and endure the hostile reaction he provoked. The disciples are not above the master; they too can expect to be in conflict, to be criticized and misunderstood because their loyalty to Jesus often generates unconventional obedience.

What side of Jesus comes through in the reports of his conflicts with religious leaders?

_____

_____

_____

_____

_____

Prayer

You bless all of those who trust you, LORD,
    and refuse to worship idols or follow false gods.
You, LORD God, have done many wonderful things,
and you have planned marvelous things for us.
    No one is like you!
I would never be able to tell all you have done.

Sacrifices and offerings are not what please you;
    gifts and payment for sin are not what you demand.
But you made me willing to listen and obey.
And so, I said, "I am here to do what is written
    about me in the book, where it says,
'I enjoy pleasing you. Your Law is in my heart.' "

(Psalm 40:4-8, CEV)

10 The Inaugural Word

I tell you, unless your righteousness exceeds that of
the scribes and Pharisees, you will never enter
the kingdom of heaven.

(Matthew 5:20)

They Have No Wine

Sometimes, what is called "the good life" turns out to be not so good; at other times, it seems out of reach. Is that because "the good life" is an ideal we strive for without expecting to achieve it because the striving itself is what matters? Or are we striving for the wrong things? What are the marks of "the good life"?

Beginning With Moses and All the Prophets

This lesson is the first of three on the Sermon on the Mount (and its shorter form in Luke). Mark does not have the sermon, but does have some of its sayings. Both Matthew's Sermon on the Mount and Luke's Sermon on the Plain bring together words of Jesus spoken on different occasions. Although each of the three lessons examines one chapter of Matthew 5–7, we will keep the whole in view.

	Matthew	Luke
Setting of the Sermon on the Mount and the Sermon on the Plain	4:23-25	6:17-19
Introduction to the sermon	5:1-2	6:20
Beatitudes	5:3-12	6:20-22
Woes		6:24-26
Salt of the earth	5:13	(*14:34-35*)*
Light of the world	5:14-16	(*11:33*)
On the Law	5:17-20	
No anger	5:21-22	
Be reconciled	5:23-24	
Settle out of court	5:25-26	(*12:57-59*)
No adultery	5:27-30	
No oaths	5:33-37	
No retaliation	5:38-42	6:29-30
Love enemies	5:43-48	6:27-28, 32-36

*Italic indicates different placement

Day 1 Matthew 4:23–7:29; Luke 6:12-49; 14:34-35; Mark 9:49-50

Note how both Matthew and Luke carefully set the stage for the sermons. See also that while Matthew has more beatitudes than does Luke, in Luke they are balanced by woes not found in Matthew. Observe that Matthew 5:17-20 prepares for 5:21-48.

Day 2 Psalms 24:1-6; 37; Micah 6:6-8; James 1; 5:1-6

To see how some of Jesus' teaching is rooted in the Psalms, compare Matthew 5:8 with Psalm 24:4; and Matthew 5:5 with Psalm 37:11. Note also how both Matthew 5:10-12 and James 1:12 understand the difficulty brought about by faithful discipleship.

Day 3 Psalm 119:25-40; Galatians 2:15-21; James 2

The passages in Galatians 2:15-21 and James 2 are sometimes understood as expressing opposite points of view. Do they?

Day 4 Leviticus 19:1-18; 24:10-23; Deuteronomy 5:1-21; 24:1-4; Isaiah 66:1-2

These passages help us see Jesus' teaching in relation to the Scripture he knew.

Day 5 Romans 12:14-21; 13:8-14; Galatians 5:16-26; James 3:13–4:17; 5:12; 1 Peter 3:8-17

Note how today's readings are consistent with the sermons in Matthew and Luke even though they do not quote Jesus. Note also that the passage from Galatians emphasizes the role of the Spirit in the Christian life—an emphasis absent from the sermons.

Day 6 Read and respond to "The Inaugural Word" and "Do You Want to Become His Disciples, Too?"

Prayer Concerns

The Inaugural Word

We will look at the two sermons as a whole before studying the parts in detail. This lesson's title applies only to Matthew, for only in Matthew do these teachings constitute Jesus' inaugural sermon. In Luke Jesus gives his inaugural sermon in his hometown synagogue (Luke 4:16-30). So each Evangelist puts up front what he regards as the best way to orient the reader to Jesus' teaching as a whole.

The Sermon on the Plain (Luke 6:17-49) comes *after* Jesus' inaugural sermon and is much shorter than the Sermon on the Mount. Each Evangelist placed the sayings of Jesus where he thought most appropriate. Evidently the Evangelists thought the impact of Jesus' teachings would be greater if those with a similar theme were grouped together. Though we do not know when or where Jesus spoke these words, what matters is the teaching itself.

The Sermon on the Mount as a whole can be interpreted in many ways. For example, some readers have regarded it as the new law given by the new Moses from a new mountain; others have viewed it as the requirements for entering the kingdom of God; still others see the sermon as a statement of moral absolutes that cannot be carried out literally and so exposes all the compromises we make—

The view taken here is that the sermon is a sketch of what life looks like when it turns Godward in response to the Kingdom's nearness.

thereby pointing to the need for grace and forgiveness. The view taken here is that the sermon is a sketch of what life looks like when it turns Godward in response to the Kingdom's nearness. That is, the sermon is an outline of what Jesus meant by repentance. The sermon is part of the good news; if we forget this, the sermon becomes bad news.

Matthew understands the sermon as good news, as "gospel." Consider the setting he gave it: At Matthew 4:17 we read, "From that time Jesus began to proclaim, 'Repent, for the kingdom of heaven has come near.'" Next comes the story of Jesus' calling the first disciples (4:18-22), followed by an overview of Jesus' mission (4:23-25; notice how 4:23 picks up 4:17) and the people's response to it. Jesus then withdraws to an unspecified mountain, where his disciples join him (5:1). And now begins the inaugural sermon. It addresses those who already have accepted "the gospel of the kingdom." When the sermon ends, the crowds have arrived, and are astounded by what they have heard (7:28). What the disciples hear turns out to be for everyone. Matthew's Gospel ends on exactly the same note (28:16-20).

The Beatitudes

When we compare the "blessed" sayings in Matthew 5:3-12 with Luke 6:20-23, we notice important differences. **GC-10-1** (1) While Matthew has nine beatitudes, Luke has only four. (2) Four woes follow Luke's beatitudes; the woes are absent from Matthew. (3) In Luke woes follow blessings just as curse follows blessing in Deuteronomy 11:26-28, but while Moses offers a choice (a life that leads to blessing or one that leads to cursing), Jesus promises a reversal of circumstances both for the currently poor, hungry, weeping, and hated and also for the currently rich, sated, laughing, and praised. In other words, Luke's version has both good news and bad news; but Matthew's has mostly good news. (4) In Luke Jesus speaks directly *to* these groups, whereas in Matthew he speaks *about* persons in the first eight beatitudes and addresses directly only the reviled and persecuted. In Luke Jesus confronts and speaks specifically; in Matthew he consoles and speaks generally. Some scholars think Luke's version comes closer to the way Jesus talked than does Matthew's. If they are right, then Jesus thought the Kingdom's coming could bring the great reversal in which what is now wrong will be made right. And that rightness will require the reversal of the present—not just improvement.

In Matthew the Kingdom's coming will bring both reversal and vindication or fulfillment. The first four beatitudes promise reversal: To the poor in spirit (a difficult phrase that probably means those whose vitality is depleted, who are depressed) belongs the Kingdom; the mourners will be comforted, the meek will inherit the earth, and those whose yearning for righteousness is now frustrated will be filled by God. The next four beatitudes promise vindication: The merciful will receive mercy themselves, the pure in heart will see God, the peacemakers will be called (by God) "children of God," and the Kingdom belongs to those who are persecuted because they already live by it. The ninth beatitude elaborates the eighth and promises reward "in heaven"—not simply after death (a matter of when) but also with God (where it counts). In emphasizing good news, Matthew has not eliminated bad news altogether, for the threat of judgment also runs through this whole Gospel. In fact, each of Jesus' five discourses (teachings grouped by theme) end with this threat of judgment.

Discourse	Theme	Threat
Matthew 5–7	Righteousness of the Kingdom	7:21-27
Matthew 10	Mission	10:39-42
Matthew 13	Parables	13:47-50
Matthew 18	Church discipline	18:23-35
Matthew 24–25	Judgment	25:31-46

We should not allow the differences between Matthew's and Luke's beatitudes to obscure what is important: Jesus declares what is or is to be. He does not say, "If you want in on the Kingdom, make yourselves poor or poor in spirit" or "If you want to be called a child of God, be sure you are a peacemaker." What is promised here is not reward for being good or for meeting requirements, but God's gracious response to the human condition as it actually is, especially that of the disciples. The reward in heaven promised in Matthew 5:12 and Luke 6:23 refers to God's faithful response to the faithful who must endure suffering. They will not have endured much for nothing because God remembers, though at present it might not seem so. In this century, as in many before it, uncounted Christians have suffered and died because of their faithfulness to Jesus. The last beatitude is as important today as in the Evangelist's time—perhaps more so.

> **What is promised here is not reward for being good or for meeting requirements, but God's gracious response to the human condition as it actually is.**

On Doing the Will of God

The greater part of the Sermon on the Mount is devoted to Jesus' interpretation of the Torah, the written will of God. Jesus first insists he did not come to abolish but to fulfill the Law and calls on his followers to do what it teaches (Matthew 5:17-19). Matthew 5:20, "Unless your righteousness exceeds that of the scribes and Pharisees, you will never enter the kingdom of heaven," introduces the sayings that follow, and 5:48 completes the section with its demand, "Be perfect, therefore, as your heavenly Father is perfect." The surpassing righteousness required is nothing less than Godlike perfection. Israel's obligation to reflect the character of God in its way of life is expressed repeatedly in Leviticus as, "You shall be holy, for I am holy" (Leviticus 11:45; 19:2; 20:7, 26). Jesus does not speak of imitating God's holiness (God's otherness from the ordinary and the profane); he speaks of the heavenly Father's being "perfect." Behind this word is the Hebrew *tamim*, which means thoroughly consistent, unalloyed, not compromised. That is the criterion of the surpassing righteousness, not an abstract ideal or idea of perfection. Given the meaning of *tamim*, the opposite of the required perfection is hypocrisy.

The word *righteousness*, a favorite word in Matthew, also needs to be understood clearly. Although the Greek word *dikaiosyne* is often translated as justice, its meaning here reflects the Hebrew word (*tsedeq* or *tsedeqah*), which refers to what is right in a particular situation or relationship, even if the act is not good. In the Old Testament, what determines the right thing to do is the character of God in being utterly faithful to the covenant, even though God's action might mean disaster for Israel at the time. Those who "hunger and thirst for righteousness" yearn for rightness, for that state of affairs when every person and everything and every relationship is what it ought to be.

This concern for righteousness was not unique to Jesus, though his understanding of it was different. Not only did the ancient prophets insist on righteousness, but in his own day the leading figure at Qumran (the community where the Dead Sea Scrolls were produced) was called "the teacher of righteousness" (also translatable as "the righteous Teacher") because he taught the law rightly. The Pharisees too had a passion for righteousness, for doing the right thing. Their whole approach to teaching the Torah was animated by the desire to explain in great detail exactly what the Law required or forbade in order to specify the right thing to do (and to avoid doing the wrong thing). The question then is this: How can the disciples' righteousness surpass that of the scribes and Pharisees who also were deeply committed to righteousness? Are Jesus' disciples to be better

Pharisees? Matthew 5:21-47 shows that something else is in view.

Central to 5:21-47 is the sixfold repetition of "You have heard that it was said . . . . But I say." Each time, Jesus quotes the Law and then states God's will. (Sometimes other sayings are added; for example, Matthew 5:29-30 is added to Jesus' saying about looking at the woman with lust because it concerns the eye that triggers sin.) Some of these sayings are found also in Luke, but there none of them is connected with the formula "You have heard . . . . But I say"; so it is reasonable to conclude the formula was created by Matthew in order to emphasize Jesus' distinctive teaching. The question is, What is Matthew telling us when he says that Jesus puts his teaching next to the Law in just this way? Are we to understand that Jesus' own teaching replaces that of Moses? clarifies Moses? goes beyond Moses? What sort of righteousness is this? Such questions can be answered only by looking closely at the text. One thing is clear: Obeying Jesus is not easier than obeying Moses.

Obeying Jesus is not easier than obeying Moses.

Jesus quotes the Law regarding murder, adultery, divorce, oaths, and retaliation and ends by combining what the Law says ("love your neighbor"; Leviticus 19:18) with something the Law does not actually command ("hate your enemy"). In each instance, his own teaching implies that the quoted law is not necessary for those who live as he says. Jesus' words do not say why this is the case, or how it is possible to live the way he envisions, but Matthew gives the clue in the way he leads up to the sermon: "Repent, for the kingdom of heaven has come near." What we are to look for then is how Jesus' teaching in Matthew 5:21-47 makes vivid our Godward turn (repentance) as response to the Kingdom's coming near.

In Matthew Jesus does not begin his mission by reminding people of how wonderful life will be when the Kingdom has actually arrived, or by correcting their understanding of it. Through the various images and expectations of the Kingdom runs one thread—that when God's kingship is real, rightness will prevail. Those who expected the Kingdom (not everyone did) were hungering and thirsting for that rightness. Had Jesus begun his mission by portraying life in the kingdom of God, he would have made people even hungrier for the glorious future, and more impatient with God as well. He did something else instead. He began

meeting that hunger by showing through specific, ordinary, day-to-day situations how believing the news of the Kingdom changes the way a person lives because the believer has been changed. And when the believer has been changed, the relation to the Law has been changed as well. Jesus does not explain such things theologically or philosophically, for he is a prophet and preacher, not a theologian. He does not intellectualize the problem but addresses those who have the problem. By using situations everyone knows, he shows what the Godward life looks like.

Right at the beginning (5:21-22) Jesus shows the difference between law-obedience based on threat of punishment and obedience based on reconciliation, and he does so in a way that offends a basic principle of law—that the punishment must fit the crime. Here the three punishments increase in seriousness—judgment (local justice), the council (the Sanhedrin,* the ruling group in Jerusalem), Gehenna (hell of fire). But the offenses are more or less the same—anger, insult (literally *raka*, a term of abuse), and calling the brother or sister "fool." All these offenses express anger and hostility, but it makes no moral sense to send to the Sanhedrin the one who says *raka* and to Gehenna the one who says "fool." Moreover, because no murder has been committed, the law has been observed, though the purpose of the Law—to limit wrongdoing—has not been achieved, for the anger in view here is not mere irritation but a sign of alienation. The alienated person is "liable to judgment" even if the person has not committed murder. So 5:23-26 calls for reconciliation. Notice that the person addressed is the offender. Jesus does not ask the offended to say, "It doesn't matter." The guilty offender is to seek reconciliation. The sayings in 5:25-26 make clear that the need for reconciliation is urgent, and they rely on the imagery of the debtor's prison to do so. Refraining from murder is one thing; reconciliation is another, for only reconciliation makes the relation right. Those who believe the news of the Kingdom know their own relation to God has been made right by God, the offended one. Therefore they should become obedient by seeking reconciliation with the brother or sister they have offended, and so reflect in the village the moral perfection of the Father in heaven (5:48).

Next comes the command against adultery (5:27). But Jesus recognizes that a person can refrain from adultery in bed while committing adultery in the heart. He has no interest in the legal question, At exactly what point does adultery occur? For him adultery actualizes lust, and the

85

Law cannot prevent lust. Only a changed self, a changed heart, can do that. The added sayings (5:29-30) use the startling image of self-mutilation to make the point: Get rid of the cause and you will be free of the result; that is, get rid of your lust, and you will not need the Law against adultery.

The saying about divorce (5:31-32) comes next because in that society divorce was often linked to adultery. The Law forbids the husband from simply putting the wife out of the house and so requires him to give her "a certificate of divorce" to show that due process has been followed and that she is legally free. Apart from the fact that only men had the right to initiate divorce proceedings, other things must be noted here. (1) Divorce may have been a problem in Matthew's church because in 19:3-9 he reports that Jesus addressed the topic again. In both passages, and only in them, Jesus allows for divorce on the ground of "unchastity" (*porneia* can refer to a whole range of unaccepted sexual activity). (2) In Mark 10:11-12, however, Jesus recognizes that the wife too might divorce her spouse, in accord with Roman but not Jewish law. (3) In Luke 16:18 Jesus forbids divorcing a wife to marry another or marrying a divorced woman. In all of these sayings, the focus is not on the divorce itself but on the adultery with which it is linked. Jesus assumes marriage creates a bond that is sacred. The sayings in Matthew allow for divorce when "unchastity" is involved because the sacred has already been violated.

Jesus then turns to oaths (Matthew 5:33), combining Leviticus 19:12 with a summarizing statement about keeping one's vows to the Lord (as in Numbers 30:2). Oaths and vows were important in antiquity; the former survives today in "oath of office" and in court, the latter in solemn pledges. Because oaths and vows were used to guarantee that contractual obligations were met, great effort was put into determining when and under what circumstances a person might be released from the obligation without being liable to punishment. The more serious the oath, the more necessary the regulations. The Mishnah* (the Talmud's* oldest part) contains a whole section summarizing the various early rabbinic rulings about oaths. As in our "so help me God" formula, ancient oaths appealed to God or to something sacred as the guarantor and expressed the appeal in formulas like "As the LORD lives, he shall not be put to death" (1 Samuel 19:6; 14:44; 1 Kings 19:2). From Jesus' perspective, the issue is not regulating oath-taking or using the right oath to guarantee the truth of what is said or promised, but eliminating oath-taking altogether, for nothing outside the self can guarantee the truthfulness of the self. "Do not swear at all, either by heaven . . . or by the earth . . . or by Jerusalem . . . and do not swear by your head," since we do not have enough control over self or over what may befall us, to guarantee the future. Yes should mean yes, and no should mean no, because if the Kingdom's coming makes everything right, there is no need for an oath. The letter of James says almost the same thing (James 5:12) but does not acknowledge that Jesus said it first.

Next, in Matthew 5:38 Jesus quotes part of the law pertaining to retaliation, "eye for eye, tooth for tooth" (Exodus 21:23-25; Leviticus 24:19-20), and sets over against it, "Do not resist an evildoer." Matthew 5:39 has in view personal insult, for unless one is left-handed, a blow to the right cheek will be given by the back of the hand. By turning the other cheek one refuses to defend one's honor. Nothing is said about turning the cheek to change the offender. What concerns Jesus is the offended person's response to personal aggression. (Compare what Jesus says with 1 Peter 3:16-18.) In Matthew 5:40-41 Jesus teaches that by giving more than is required and by going the second mile, a person refuses to be a victim. In the last saying (5:42) Jesus says we should not *make* a victim, for he urges his followers to refuse neither beggars nor borrowers, but instead to respond positively to human need. Refusal would victimize the needy. Luke's version (Luke 6:30) is shorter and somewhat more severe: "Give to everyone who begs from you [do not victimize them]; and if anyone takes away your goods [if you are victimized], do not ask for them again." The *Gospel of Thomas* has a variation that is less severe, "If you have money, do not lend it at interest, but give [it] to one from whom you will not get it back."

In Luke 6:29-30, Jesus focuses on the disciple, the recipient of the other person's actions; and the consequences of the disciple's response to the other person are of no explicit concern. The disciple might be struck twice, lose the cloak as well as the coat, walk two miles instead of one, and end up somewhat poorer. What does concern Jesus is the disciple's alternative to retaliation and to aggressive behavior returned. Jesus implies that whoever must "get even," protect personal honor, and cling to personal possessions has not yet been transformed by the Kingdom's nearness.

Finally, Jesus contrasts the right attitude toward neighbors and enemies with what has been said, "You shall love your neighbor and hate your enemy." Nowhere does the law of Moses command hatred toward the enemy (Matthew 5:43-47). Leviticus 19:18 says, "You shall love your neighbor as yourself." By dropping "as yourself" Jesus signals he is not interested in giving instructions about *how* we are to love the neighbor, and he sets up the startling reversal in Matthew 5:44: "Love your enemies and pray for those who persecute you." Here too Jesus' eye is on the disciple, not on the effect of right behavior on the opponents. To understand 5:45-46, we must remember that the word in the Greek text is "sons." The New Revised Standard Version uses "children." Here, as elsewhere in the Bible, to be a "son of God" is not to be God's offspring but a Godlike person, one who reflects on earth the character of the One in heaven. "Children" does not convey the biblical idea. So here, by loving the enemy and praying for the persecutor, we replicate the God who sends rain and sun indiscriminately, thereby responding to the evil with the good. Matthew 5:46-47 undergirds the point by noting that there is nothing special (worthy of reward) in loving those who love in return—even tax collectors and Gentiles live by reciprocity. Jesus calls for love of the enemy and prayer for the persecutor because where God rules, people begin acting in Godlike ways.

In Luke's version (Luke 6:27-28), which comes before the saying about turning the cheek, the radical disjunction between what one receives from opponents and what one gives in return is expressed even more sharply: "Love your enemies, do good to those who hate you, bless those who curse you, pray for those who abuse you." According to 23:34, the Jesus who said this did just that while on the cross.

So Then

Three features of Matthew 5 merit attention and invite us to reflect on its content and its importance for our life.

First, the chapter begins with the Beatitudes (see "The Beatitudes," page 89), which express various aspects of the good news by declaring what is the case; none of them is conditional. None of them uses "if" clauses (for example, "if you make your heart pure, you will see God"). The Beatitudes announce God's grace in the face of present conditions. But the Beatitudes are followed by a number of obligations, climaxed by the demand to be perfect as God is perfect. This combination of God's freely given gifts (the Kingdom, comfort, righteousness, vision of God) and obligations is an essential characteristic of the gospel, and of the Bible as a whole. Indeed, the summary of Jesus' preaching says as much: "Repent, for the kingdom of heaven has come near" (Matthew 4:17). In other words, believing the news about the Kingdom obligates us to forge a way of life appropriate to God's reign. Simply put: The disciple's life unites faith and ethics.

Second, we should ponder the relation between the surpassing righteousness required for entering the Kingdom (5:20) and the mandated Godlike perfection (5:48). For one thing, 5:20 implies that the righteousness of the scribes and Pharisees is somehow inadequate, but we are not told how or why this is the case. The sayings that follow in 5:21-47 do go beyond what the Law requires or forbids, but they do not mention scribes and Pharisees; in fact, after 5:20 the Sermon on the Mount never mentions them again. Matthew will show us the flaws in their righteousness as his gospel story moves along, notably in Chapter 23, with its sevenfold denunciation, "Woe to you, scribes and Pharisees, hypocrites." Hypocrisy refers to the difference between appearance and reality—"like whitewashed tombs, which on the outside look beautiful, but inside they are full of . . . all kinds of filth" (23:27). In other words, the disciples' righteousness will surpass that of the scribes and Pharisees when it is free of hypocrisy, when it has integrity, when it is not hollow. That is precisely what the command to be perfect as God is perfect is getting at.

Finally, the Jesus in Matthew 5 is a figure who speaks with astounding authority. He knows God's will and way with such confidence he can quote what the Bible requires and then say what God really requires—and what will happen to those who disregard his own word. At the same time, he does not explain his authority; doing so would deflect attention from his word and invite argument about his explanation. Instead, we are confronted, head-on, with these teachings that are put in such a way we must either shake our head or concede, "Yes, that's got to be right." And to say that is to fall in behind Jesus, whether stumbling or striding. That is how he makes it possible to imitate God's own integrity. Did he say that this imitation would happen all at once?

Do You Want to Become His Disciples, Too?

To be Jesus' disciple is to let him redefine righteousness, blessedness, and perfection. To follow the Jesus who redefines these conditions is to allow him to change the goals of our life, to change life itself.

What picture of Jesus emerges in the Sermon on the Mount and the Sermon on the Plain?

_____

_____

_____

_____

_____

Prayer

By your teachings, Lord, I am warned;
    by obeying them, I am greatly rewarded.
None of us know our faults.
    Forgive me when I sin without knowing it.
Don't let me do wrong on purpose, Lord,
    or let sin have control over my life.
Then I will be innocent,
    and not guilty of some terrible fault.

Let my words and my thoughts
be pleasing to you, LORD,
    because you are my mighty rock and my protector.

(Psalm 19:11-14, CEV)

The Beatitudes

What is a beatitude? Behind the word is the Latin *beatus*, blessed; just as adding *itude* to *exact* to create *exactitude* lets us identify what it is to be exact, so adding *itude* to the root of *beatus* lets us express the state of being blessed. Recall that to bless someone is to confer a favor, to give something good, to grant prosperity (for example, Genesis 24:1; 39:5; Luke 1:42). To call a person "blessed" is to congratulate, to celebrate the person's well-being. Psalms and Proverbs often use "blessed are those who" to encourage or urge a certain type of behavior by congratulating persons who act as desired, as in Proverbs 8:32, where wisdom says, "Blessed are those who keep my ways" (NIV). All such beatitudes acknowledge and praise the person who has met the conditions expressed in the "who" phrases. Without actually saying so, they teach that *if* we do so, we will be in a favorable relation to God. The rich meaning of the Hebrew *'ashre* that stands behind "blessed" is difficult to express; the New Revised Standard Version often uses "happy" (Psalm 1:1), though happiness, in the sense of deep pleasure in one's circumstances, is often not the point. Such is especially the case in the Sermon on the Mount, where the New Revised Standard Version retains "blessed."

11 Counting on God

Strive first for the kingdom of God and his righteousness, and all these things will be given to you as well.

(Matthew 6:33)

They Have No Wine

Anxiety about the future, whether short-term or long-range, is as characteristic of the prosperous (who fear the present will turn sour) as it is of the poor (who fear they will remain near the bottom of the ladder or fall off it altogether). Besides, we sense that the rules, like moral values, keep changing. It's hard to know what to count on.

Beginning With Moses and All the Prophets

This week we study Matthew 6 and related teachings in Luke. The other readings help us see Jesus' teachings in the larger biblical context. Few parts of the Sermon on the Mount make us comfortable; Matthew 6 may actually make us uncomfortable. If so, we should ask why this is the case.

Day 1 Matthew 6; Luke 11:1-13; 12:13-21, 35-38; John 16:16-24

Note that Matthew 6, from beginning to end, is concerned with confidence in God.

Trust God for all you need - (food, clothing etc)
Store up treasures in heaven,
Be ready at all times
There will be pain followed by great joy!

Day 2 Deuteronomy 15:7-11; 24:19-22; Psalm 139:1-18; Proverbs 14:20-21, 31; Isaiah 58:1-12

Today's readings put us in touch with the scriptural roots of Jesus' teachings in Matthew 6.

Share willingly c̄ those in need
How marvelous is our God - He has known us
before our birth - Knows all our needs thoughts + acts

Day 3 1 Kings 3:1-15; 8:22-61; Proverbs 15:8-9; Romans 8:26-27; Philippians 1:3-11

The Lord's Prayer invites us to look also at other biblical teachings about prayer. The passages from First Kings portray Solomon, the wise king, offering exemplary prayers.

Pray for wisdom & a discerning mind
Spirit intercedes for us - God (Knows our heart!
The One who began a good work in 'you' will
bring it to completion.

Day 4 Deuteronomy 6:10-15; Jeremiah 17:5-11; Wisdom of Solomon 1:16–2:11; Tobit 4:5-11

Today's readings relate to Luke 12:13-21, which also is concerned with the seductive power of wealth. Note how the "ungodly" person's arrogance described in the Wisdom of Solomon contrasts with the attitude of both Tobit and Jesus.

God is a jealous God - fear & obey.
Cursed are those who trust in mortals, Blessed are those
who trust in the Lord.

Day 5 Job 31:24-28; Proverbs 13:25; Sirach 29:8-23; 2 Corinthians 12:1-10; Philippians 4:10-13; Colossians 3:1-17; 1 Thessalonians 5:12-22

These readings allow us to compare Jesus' teachings with other parts of the Bible.

Day 6 Read and respond to "Counting on God" and "Do You Want to Become His Disciples, Too?"

Prayer Concerns

Counting on God

To believe the Beatitudes are true, we must count on God to bring to pass what they announce. But their truth is not obvious, for their pronouncements run counter to our everyday assumptions and experience. The Beatitudes also challenge what we think we can count on from God. That's why believing them entails repentance—deliberately turning life Godward so we live by the character of God's reign even though it is not yet fully manifest. The central chapter of the Sermon on the Mount (Matthew 6) helps us see how counting on God affects both religious devotion and secular life in the everyday world.

Matthew 6 consists of two parts, 6:1-18 and 6:19-34. Although some of Jesus' teachings here are found also in Luke, they do not appear in the Sermon on the Plain but at various places in Luke's Gospel.

Counting on God Who Sees

Matthew 6:1 serves as a topic sentence for the first part of Chapter 6; each of the three examples that follow has to do with the contrast between being seen by God and being seen by other people. Moreover, 6:1 links 6:1-18 to 5:20 by repeating the word *righteousness*. The New International Version has "acts of righteousness," which makes this link clear in a way that the New Revised Standard Version ("piety") and Revised English Bible ("religion") do not. While 5:20 requires righteousness that surpasses that of the scribes and Pharisees, here Jesus contrasts two ways of practicing religion, for each way discloses the heart of the person. A hypocrite is one whose external appearance is contradicted by what the person is like on the inside, as 23:27-28 shows.

Matthew 6:1-18 uses sharp, sarcastic contrasts because the subject matter has to do with religious practices, not with beliefs—at least not on the surface. Religious communities, and groups within the same community, often define themselves by contrasting what they do with what others do, especially when they share most beliefs. Further, from biblical times onward, Judaism has emphasized right practice while allowing considerable leeway in ideas. In Matthew's time, and for some time afterward, church and synagogue were distinguishing themselves from each other, sometimes bitterly. We can see this clearly in the way a non-canonical Christian writing from Matthew's time (or a little later), called the *Didache*,* talks about

fasting: "Do not fast with the hypocrites, for they fast on Mondays and Thursdays, but you are to fast on Wednesdays and Fridays. And do not pray like the hypocrites, but as the Lord commanded in the gospel" (the Lord's Prayer follows).

Early Judaism emphasized almsgiving, praying, and fasting; and Matthew 6:1-18 says not a word against the practices themselves. Jesus directs his criticism solely against the ways they are being done; the purpose of the criticism is to highlight the right way of doing these things. The criticism functions the way shadows function in a painting: They make the subject stand out more vividly. Here Jesus relies on caricature to make the point; he is not describing accurately what he sees people doing.

In all three examples, the teaching emphasizes the same theme—the contrast between practicing religion for its public relations value and practicing it secretly. For persons who give alms, pray, and fast in order to enhance their reputation as manifestly devout persons, the acts have achieved their purpose ("they have received their reward"). Persons who give alms, pray, and fast in secret, however, gain nothing in the eyes of the public, do not improve their image in the neighborhood or their standing in the community. Such persons are much more likely to be perceived as irreligious. When we recall that in Jesus' society, reputation (honor) was a central value in village life, we sense the bite of Jesus' criticism, with which the rabbis would not have disagreed.

When Jesus calls for secrecy, he is not urging his followers to hide their religious practices in order to escape ridicule or harassment. That would be putting their light under the bushel basket (Matthew 5:14-16). Nor does Jesus imply religion is strictly a private matter, wholly between me and God. The point of the secrecy lies elsewhere. While praise-oriented doers already have the

> Counting on God, who sees the unseen deed, is nothing other than turning Godward; it is a clear sign that our faith has integrity, that our trust truly is in God.

reward when they are seen approvingly, those who give alms, pray, and fast secretly count on God for the reward that is to come. Jesus does not say it will come a bit later. The point is it will come from God, who sees the doers and responds. Counting on God, who sees the unseen deed, is nothing other than turning Godward; it is a clear sign that our faith has integrity, that our trust truly is in God.

Jesus says not a word about the nature of the reward. Had he done so, had he said that the secret almsgiver's gift would be replaced amply, that the secret prayer would be answered more spectacularly than the seen prayer, that a bounteous table or better health would more than compensate for food given up, he simply would have encouraged people to be fervently religious because it pays—and pays well. Jesus is exposing the heart's motivation, summoning the hearer to cease using God for self-enhancement and public honor. And instead to rely on God, the one who, being the heavenly Father, is not indifferent. By requiring secrecy, Jesus summons his disciples to decide whose approval really matters. By using caricature to portray what is to be avoided, and by relying on vivid imagery to express what is to be done, Jesus' teaching makes the issue clear and the choice unavoidable.

Pondering the Model Prayer

GC 11-1 In assembling the sayings in 6:1-18, Matthew shows he regards prayer to be especially important; for to Jesus' basic point he first adds 6:7-8 and then the Lord's Prayer, and to that he adds 6:14-15 (whose point is similar to Mark 11:25-26). In Matthew 6:7 Matthew uses a rare Greek word that is better translated as "Do not keep on babbling" (NIV, REB) than as the colorless "empty phrases" (RSV, NRSV). The Revised English Bible has Jesus refer to "heathen," the New International Version to "pagans" instead of to Gentiles, perhaps to avoid offending today's Christian readers, most of whom are Gentiles. The Jewish Jesus, however, did not think in terms of heathen or pagans and Christians but in terms of Jews and Gentiles (as did Paul). Matthew 6:8 adds another reason for not praying like Gentiles: They assume they must inform God of their needs. But the Father to whom the disciples pray "knows what you need before you ask him." This truth does not imply the prayer can be omitted. Apparently Jesus assumes prayer is something other than transmitting a list of needs; it is an honest conversation with the parent in heaven during which the needs can be expressed. The model prayer shows quite clearly that in this conversation, God is not

ignorant, waiting to be informed. The heavenly Father knows the disciple needs bread and forgiveness, is vulnerable in the "time of trial," and is exposed to the power of "the evil one." Therefore, prayer is not an occasion to inform God but to express trust in God's goodness.

In Luke Jesus teaches the prayer in response to the disciples' request, "Lord, teach us to pray, as John taught his disciples" (Luke 11:1). That John the Baptist taught his disciples how to pray is said only here. The Lord's Prayer in Matthew is longer than the prayer in Luke because Matthew (or his church) expanded it (Matthew 6:10, 13). The first addition ("Your will be done, / on earth as it is in heaven") restates "Your kingdom come." The second addition ("but rescue us from the evil one") adds a positive note to "And do not bring us to the time of trial." The best-known addition ("For the kingdom and the power and the glory are yours forever. Amen") is omitted by some versions because the best manuscripts do not have it. Those manuscripts that include it do not agree on its wording.

> **Prayer is not an occasion to inform God but to express trust in God's goodness.**

Disciples are to pray first for the hallowing of God's name and the coming of the Kingdom, not for their needs. The status of God in the world comes first. The Greek word behind "hallow" can also be translated as "sanctify," make holy. To sanctify God's name is to make it holy; "hallowed be" means the same as "let your name be made holy." So the prayer asks that God's holiness—God's radical otherness that distinguishes God from everything that is not God—be acknowledged in the world. This otherness does not cut God off from the world, but it does remind us that God is not to be confused with the world. Moreover, "hallowed be" reflects the passive form of the Greek imperative verb and is a polite way of asking God, "Hallow your name." In other words, the disciple is to pray that the Father will make God's Godhood effectively known, a mark of the Kingdom's coming. The three petitions in Matthew 6:9-10 all ask for the same thing—the actualizing of God's will also on earth, the coming of the Kingdom, and the honoring of God as the Holy One.

In the petition for bread, the rare Greek word *epiousios* (pronounced ep-i-OOS-i-os) does not mean every day, as in the daily delivery of a newspaper;

rather it means "for the day," bread being assumed to be the most basic food. In other words, the petition has in view what is essential to sustain life and so acknowledges that continued human existence depends day by day on God the giver.

The petition for forgiveness recognizes we have offended God and believes God will restore the relationship. Matthew's "debts" expresses the idea of sin as an unmet obligation. The word picture is apt because in Jesus' society heavy indebtedness was often unavoidable (especially for the poor tenant farmers); unpaid debts could lead to imprisonment or perhaps even to enslavement. But the one who asks for God's forgiveness must also forgive (as the parable in 18:23-35 makes clear). So important is mutual forgiveness that Matthew underscores it in 6:14-15. Even apart from these verses, Jesus' prayer teaches that only the forgiving can expect to be forgiven by God.

The final petition in 6:13 has in view the perilous nature of human existence and originally may have referred to the distress that, in some thinking, would mark the transition from this age to the age to come (Matthew 24 describes this distress vividly). Indeed, "time of trial" (NRSV) and "the test" (REB) in place of the customary "temptation" (NIV) reflect this interpretation. As we saw in connection with Mark's story of Jesus in the wilderness (Mark 1:12-13), the same word means either temptation or test. Quite likely the Lord's Prayer too refers to a great test when loyalty to Jesus will be on the line. So the prayer asks that the disciples be spared this danger. The addition "but rescue us from the evil one" (not evil in general, as in the accustomed use) implies that in the test Satan himself will be at work.

The prayer is given to the community (*our* Father, *our* bread, *our* debts, as well as lead *us*). True, each person says the prayer; but in praying it together individuals acknowledge their solidarity with the whole community—even when the prayer is said when alone. Ideas and practices often divide, but prayer unites. And it unites in confessing confidence in God.

This prayer, commonly memorized in childhood, triggers a wide range of observations and reflections. First, this prayer, long commonly used in Christian worship, is profoundly Jewish—so much so that were it not for the tragic history of Christians' brutal treatment of Jews, any Jew could easily join us in praying it. The fact is that when Christian Gentiles pray the prayer they not only make Jesus' way of counting on God their own; they also enter into the core of the faith that nourished him.

Second, the simplicity of this prayer should not hinder us from seeing the profound understanding of God and the human condition woven into it. To pray this prayer is to know who we are in relation to one another (forgiven and forgiving sinners), what we are in the presence of God (guilty), and that our existence is vulnerable because it is not in our hands. Yet we are so confident in the goodness of the Holy One that we address him as Father.

Third, we cannot ignore the fact that while calling God "Father" was good news in Jesus' day, in our time many find it hard to say "Our Father," whether because they are offended by the patriarchal character of such language or because memories of their own fathers have ruined the word *Father* when speaking to the Creator who loves and cares. Perhaps they may find it possible to say "Our Father-Mother." Still, the God who is not indifferent to secret almsgiving and who makes the divine name holy in our midst also hears the prayer of those who cannot say "Our Father"; and those who may be offended by those who cannot use this language are forbidden by this prayer to be resentful, for this is the prayer of the forgiven and the forgiving. Jesus' prayer becomes the disciples' prayer when those who say it find their solidarity with all who say it and also with those who are not able to call God Father.

Counting on God Who Cares

GC 11-2 Matthew 6:19-34 calls for realigning our stance toward material goods. The sayings in 6:19-24 alert the disciples to the seductive dangers of wealth; those in 6:25-34 emphasize depending on God for what is needed. Thus 6:19-34 makes clear what is implied in our asking God for "daily bread."

The contrast between heaven and earth in 6:19-21 is basic. Because only in heaven is treasure safe from loss, heavenly treasures are what the disciple is to accumulate. We find this kind of practical wisdom, insight based on experience, in the Wisdom literature.* Similar statements about the transient, insecure status of earthly wealth are found elsewhere in antiquity, including in James 5:2-3. In this part of the sermon (Matthew 6:19-21), Jesus speaks like a sage who gives prudent advice. He sounds a warning that flows from an astute observation: The heart (where one's identity and character are formed) is where the treasure is—that is, because you become what you value, you will also *be* where your values are, secure in heaven (with God) or corruptible on earth. This view is quite different from the conventional wisdom that says you will achieve whatever you set your heart on.

Matthew 6:22-23 changes the subject but continues the warning. It relies on the ancient view that the eye is a light (not a window) that illumines the body's interior. Here the sense of warning is expressed clearly: "The lamp of the body is the eye. If your eyes are sound, you will have light for your whole body; if your eyes are bad, your whole body will be in darkness. If then the only light you have is darkness, how great a darkness that will be" (6:22-23, REB). Nothing is said about how to get, have, or maintain a sound eye. The saying does not offer advice; it sounds a warning: Do not live in darkness. The placement of this saying between 6:21, which warns that we become what we value, and the saying about not serving two masters in 6:24 implies that serving money (*wealth* in NRSV) *is* life in darkness, especially if one regards such life as light.

Having warned that a person must choose between serving God or wealth, the sermon now urges reliance on God instead of anxiety. Again Jesus points to the Gentiles as negative examples to be avoided (6:31-32), though the fact he is speaking to Jews implies he knew they too "strive for all these things." Nor is striving itself wrong. What matters are our priorities. Because God knows our needs, we need not strive to meet them as if we were on our own. Rather, because God is the giver, Jesus can urge his disciples to "strive first for the kingdom of God and his [or *its*] righteousness." Just as the Lord's Prayer asks for today's bread instead of a week's supply, so 6:34 says to live one day at a time: "Today's trouble is enough for today."

That concluding comment in 6:34 makes 6:24-33 quite remarkable. Why? Because it assumes life is precarious, marked by insecurity faced daily by poor Galilean villagers. Precisely to those whose existence is not assured (in today's terms, those who cannot count on an adequate salary but must find a way to live one more day), Jesus addresses his counsel, "Don't be anxious." He knows that people in such circumstances are as anxious about tomorrow as those who have enough and yet want more. Neither the haves nor the have-nots are beyond the danger of storing up for themselves "treasures on earth," though the treasures differ enormously. Neither should think, *What Jesus says doesn't apply to me.*

Important as it is not to overlook to *whom* these words about anxiety over life's necessities are addressed, it is also important to remember *who* said them—the Jesus who had abandoned whatever financial security his craft as a carpenter might have provided in order to count wholly on

God's provision, mediated, to be sure, by those women who shared their resources with him (Luke 8:1-3), or by those who were his hosts at dinners—Levi (5:29), Mary and Martha (10:38-42), various Pharisees (7:36; 11:37; 14:1). He asked others to do as he was doing in relying on God's gracious care made effective through those who shared. His example tells us that the financially secure have no right to say to the poor, "Don't worry; God will take care of you," unless they allow God to do so through their sharing.

The teachings about the treasure determining the heart in Matthew 6:19-21 and about anxiety in 6:25-34 are found also in Luke 12, but in reverse order. As a result, the flow of thought is quite different. Luke first tells the parable of the rich fool who planned to build bigger barns but died before he could do so; the parable ends with the comment, "So it is with those who store up treasures for themselves but are not rich toward God" (Luke 12:13-21). Now comes Jesus' exhortation on not being anxious about food and clothing (12:22-31), ending with "Strive for his kingdom, and these things will be given to you as well." Luke's version is more stringent than Matthew's, where Jesus says, "Strive *first* for the kingdom of God and his [*its*] righteousness, and *all* these things will be given to you as well" (Matthew 6:33). Putting the Kingdom first is the priority of the Lord's Prayer. Here Luke adds a saying not found in Matthew: "Do not be afraid, little flock, for it is your Father's good pleasure to give you the kingdom" (Luke 12:32). This saying makes clear that we do not acquire the Kingdom by striving for it but because God gives it. Yet God does not give it to those to whom it is unimportant or to those who are unwilling to exert themselves to claim it. Now comes Luke's version of Matthew 6:19-21, and it too is more radical: While in Matthew Jesus says not to accumulate treasures on earth, here Jesus says the disciple should get rid of them: "Sell your possessions, and give alms" and acquire "an unfailing treasure in heaven, where no thief comes

> The financially secure have no right to say to the poor, "Don't worry; God will take care of you," unless they allow God to do so through their sharing.

near and no moth destroys. For where your treasure is, there your heart will be also" (Luke 12:33-34).

These sayings in Luke are given a sense of urgency also by the teachings that follow (12:35-48); they emphasize the need to be alert and ready for the coming of the Son of Man, who will arrive "at an unexpected hour." Luke makes clearer than does Matthew that a person's attitude toward wealth and daily needs is to reflect the disciple's counting on God to end soon the present order of things and to begin the new order. And Luke's accompanying volume (Acts) reports that after Pentecost the earliest believers in Jesus did just that: "All who believed were together and had all things in common; they would sell their possessions and goods and distribute the proceeds to all, as any had need" (Acts 2:44-45). The New Testament has no evidence that the practice was repeated elsewhere. Fortunately, there have always been those who conclude that God will give what is needed when they themselves share what they have with those who have less or nothing at all.

So Then

Jesus' words about wealth have disturbed Christian consciences repeatedly, especially his words in Luke. But even in Matthew Jesus urged his disciples to count on God to give them what they need, not to make them prosperous. Yet, most of us are uneasy because we think it prudent to have something not only for tomorrow but also for the day after tomorrow, for "a rainy day"—and especially for retirement. To the prudent who plan ahead, Jesus appears to be a naive romantic, out of touch with reality. He was, however, in touch with another reality—the God whom he trusted as a parent who cared. Jesus' words about wealth were not his prescriptions for the Galilean economy; they were designed to elicit the disciples' trust in the God he trusted.

To be sure, he lived in an economy simpler than ours. For the villagers he knew and taught, life was hard and often precarious. Yet he did not promise that when God's kingdom arrived, they would occupy the villas of the rich or redistribute their land. Not even the great reversal in Luke's Beatitudes and woes promised that. Jesus knew that wealth, whether possessed or desired, has seductive power to diminish trust in God and finally to replace it with false self-security. However vast the differences between our urbanized, technologically-driven economy and his, that insight still holds. What then is today's disciple to do with the temptation to trust wealth rather than God?

We do not acquire the Kingdom by striving for it but because God gives it. Yet God does not give it to those to whom it is unimportant or to those who are unwilling to exert themselves to claim it.

Perhaps, most important, is to assimilate (take into ourselves so it becomes part of our outlook) Jesus' warning that the heart is where the treasure is. To heed that warning is to become inwardly free from the seductive power of "things," so that we are not so attached to them that they own us. Whoever heeds that warning will be freed also from the illusion that the more we have the better we are. And some people will give what they have, not to be better than others, but simply because Jesus' word and example summon them to do so.

Do You Want to Become His Disciples, Too?

To follow Jesus is to let him teach us, by word and example, that counting on God is the daily effect of believing God's kingly rule is at hand. But we cannot count on God unless we also understand what that unseen reality called God is like.

What does the Jesus of Matthew 6 require of you?

_____

_____

_____

_____

_____

Prayer

You are merciful, LORD!
     You are kind and patient and always loving.
You are good to everyone,
     and you take care of all your creation.

All creation will thank you,
     and your loyal people will praise you.
They will tell about
     your marvelous kingdom and your power.
Then everyone will know about
     the mighty things you do and your glorious kingdom.
Your kingdom will never end, and you will rule forever.

(Psalm 145:8-13, CEV)

The Choice

*Not everyone who says to me, "Lord, Lord," will enter
the kingdom of heaven, but only the one who
does the will of my Father in heaven.*

(Matthew 7:21)

They Have No Wine

We live in a time marked both by great tolerance, when being judgmental seems to be a greater sin than the wrong denounced, and by outspoken intolerance of other people's wrongdoing. We cannot be moral beings without making moral judgments; so how do we know when to say no and when to say yes, especially when the consequences are either mixed or unclear? Even "nobody's perfect" implies a judgment about what is right.

Beginning With Moses and All the Prophets

We focus on Matthew 7 and comparable passages in Luke. Like the endings of the other discourses in Matthew (the five discourses: 5–7; 10; 13; 18; 24–25), this chapter emphasizes the coming Judgment in which our accountability will become manifest.

Day 1 Matthew 7; Luke 6:37-49; 11:9-13; 13:22-30

The parable of the two houses confronts us with the theme of choice and its consequences. Look for ways the parable refers to other parts of the sermon.

Judge not - Ask seek knock
Do unto others ---

Day 2 Deuteronomy 11:26-28; 30:15-20; Psalm 1; Tobit 4:5-11, 14-19; Sirach 15:11-20

Today's readings show how deeply rooted in Israel's faith and life are Jesus' teachings. Note how the teachings of Deuteronomy as well as the reading from Sirach are similar to the parable of the two houses in Matthew 7:24-27. What aspects of the passage from Tobit remind you of what Jesus said later? *Delight in the law of the Lord & live*

Day 3 Deuteronomy 18:15-22; Jeremiah 28; Ezekiel 13:1-16; Acts 20:17-38; 1 John 4

Note how persistent the problem of false prophets has been and the different forms it has taken.

Day 4 Romans 2:1-24; 12:14-21; Galatians 6:1-10; 1 Thessalonians 5:1-22

Today's readings, together with Matthew 7:1-5, show that making moral judgments is both necessary and dangerous. Note that sometimes judgment occurs without the word being used and that the word *judge* can also mean condemn.

Day 5 Hebrews 12; 1 Peter 3:8–4:11; 1 John 2

Observe how the exhortations in today's readings assume Christians need explicit help in being faithful. Note what choices are called for.

Day 6 Read and respond to "The Choice" and "Do You Want to Become His Disciples, Too?"

Prayer Concerns

The Choice

The parable of the two houses ends both the Sermon on the Mount (Matthew 5–7) and the Sermon on the Plain (Luke 6:17-49). The title of this lesson applies not only to the ending of each sermon but also to both sermons in their entirety, for each sermon in its own way urges us to make the right choice and to live by it.

Warnings and Promises

GC 12-1 Matthew 7:1-5 contains several sayings about judgment. They belong together, though what unites them is not evident at first glance, for they appear simply to be placed end to end. The first saying forbids judging, but the second assumes we do judge, while the third calls the person a hypocrite who, wanting to be helpful, makes a judgment about someone else. Each saying is intelligible by itself and probably circulated independently before being included here. (Because *you* can be either singular or plural, English translations cannot show that in Greek 7:1-2 addresses the group [plural], while 7:3-5 addresses an individual [singular].) What does Matthew want to achieve when he puts together the sayings in 7:1-5?

According to the conclusion in 7:5, only after we have removed the log from our own eye can we see clearly enough to take the speck out of the other person's eye. But whose eye has the log, and whose the speck? The use of "neighbor" (NRSV) implies that Jesus refers to the fellow human being in general, but the Greek text has "brother" (which includes "sister"). Because "brother" is the fellow disciple, the passage has to do with inner church discipline; the sayings are aimed at the early Christian practice of correcting one another (see Matthew 18). This is why the verbs in 7:1-2 are plural: They address the community. But who is the one with the log in the eye? The "hypocrite" is the fellow disciple who, being unable to see her or his own gross fault, cannot see clearly the lesser fault of the fellow believer. The person is a hypocrite because the person's self-understanding (able to see the speck) is disconnected from reality. Jesus' saying does not prohibit correcting one another; it prohibits doing so without self-correction first. Jesus recognizes that often other people's faults look larger to the corrector than they really are, and that our own faults keep us from seeing this is the case.

Jesus says to the community, "Do not judge, so that you may not be judged" (7:1). Here too the passive form "be judged" refers to God's action at the Great Judgment; consequently, here the word *judge* means to condemn. Jesus does not prohibit making moral judgments about right and wrong, good and bad, but prohibits condemning one another, excluding one another from the Kingdom; that is God's prerogative. (Paul makes much the same point in different language in Romans 12:19.) Nor does Jesus suggest we can avoid God's Great Judgment by not condemning others; for like other faithful Jews, he assumes God will be the judge of everyone (as does Paul; Romans 14:10). Don't condemn lest you be condemned (by God) is the flip side of the petition for forgiveness in the Lord's Prayer:

> Jesus does not prohibit making moral judgments about right and wrong, good and bad, but prohibits condemning one another, excluding one another from the Kingdom; that is God's prerogative.

Those who do not forgive will not be forgiven. Refusing to forgive and condemning are two sides of the same coin.

Matthew 7:2 looks like a proverb, for similar sayings were used in antiquity. When Matthew introduces the saying with "For," he indicates it is the basis on which 7:1 rests. So we can reverse the sequence and say, "As you give, you will get; therefore do not condemn, lest you be condemned."

Luke 6:37 has the same teaching as Matthew 7:1, but in Luke the structure of the saying makes the meaning easier to grasp: "Do not judge, and you will not be judged; do not condemn, and you will not be condemned." The parallelism* shows clearly that the two lines have the same meaning. While the first part of Luke 6:37 says what should not be done, the second part, plus 6:38, states the positive side: "Forgive, and you will be forgiven; give, and it will be given you; A good measure, pressed down, shaken together, running over, will be put into your lap; for the measure you give will be the measure you get back." The saying about forgiveness recalls the Lord's Prayer, which in Luke 11:4 says, "And forgive us our sins, / for we ourselves forgive everyone indebted to us." The saying about the "good measure" is found only in Luke; it is the good news for those who forgive, put in the language of the grainseller's shop.

The prohibition against misuse of holy things, found only in Matthew 7:6, uses the strange image of tossing pearls to pigs. Despite many suggestions, no one knows exactly what Jesus had in mind. A different form of the saying in the *Gospel of Thomas* 93 is more vivid but equally obscure: "Jesus said, 'Do not give what is holy to dogs, lest they throw them on the dung-heap. Do not throw the pearls to swine, lest they grind it [to bits].' " The interpretation in *Didache** 9:5 is improbable: "But do not let anyone eat or drink of your Eucharist, except those who have been baptized in the name of the Lord; for concerning this the Lord has said, 'Do not give what is holy to dogs.' " Clearly, *Didache's* real concern is to make sure the Eucharist is given only to the baptized, and since Jesus had not made this point himself, *Didache* simply uses the saying to support its prohibition.

Matthew 7:7-11 promises that no one asks God in vain to give "good things." A more open-ended promise is hard to imagine. The language of "ask," followed by "give" in response, runs through all three parts of the passage:

(1) Verses 7-8 are phrased carefully—"Ask, and it will be given you [plural]; search, and you will find; knock, and the door will be opened for you. For everyone who asks receives, and everyone who searches finds, and for everyone who knocks, the door will be opened." In 7:8, "For" introduces the reasons that justify what is said in 7:7; here too we can turn it around and paraphrase: "Everyone who asks gets, every seeker finds, and doors are opened to all who knock. Therefore, ask, and it will be given you."

(2) Verses 9-10 consist of a pair of questions that expect no for the answer: No father will give a stone to his child who asks for bread, or a snake to one who asks for a fish. (Luke 11:12 has *egg* and *scorpion* instead of *bread* and *stone*.)

(3) The punch line comes in Matthew 7:11, which gives a surprise twist to 7:9-10. These verses imply that the earthly father is a good man who will not give a stone for requested bread. In 7:11, however, this earthly father who gives good gifts to his children is said to be "evil." Why? Not because he is a bad parent, but in order to bring out the contrast between the earthly father and the "Father in heaven" who is wholly good. The key phrase is "how much more"—a common form of argument (from the lesser to the greater). Jesus is not condemning fathers in Galilee; he is praising the Father in heaven. Even so, he recognizes that even decent fathers are tainted by evil. Jesus did not explain the universality of sin; he assumed it. That's why no one is exempt from his call to repent in response to God's kingly rule.

The effect of God's kingly rule is summed up in Matthew 7:12 (and especially Luke 6:31), probably the best-known and most-quoted of Jesus' sayings. The Golden Rule appears in both sermons, but in different places, and in different wording as well: "In everything do to others as you would have them do to you; for this is the law and the prophets" (Matthew 7:12). Grounding the command in Scripture gives the saying extra bite; perhaps this is the reason Matthew added it (no reference to Scripture in Luke 6:31). Mention of Scripture appears again in Matthew 22:40, where Jesus says that the Law and the Prophets "hang" on two commandments, loving God (the first of the Ten Commandments, Exodus 20:3) and loving the neighbor (Leviticus 19:18). The Golden Rule is really a restatement of Leviticus 19:18.

Various forms of the Golden Rule appear in the biblical, early Jewish, and early Christian texts. (1) "Judge your neighbor's feelings by your own, / and in every matter be thoughtful" (Sirach 31:15). (2) "What you hate, do not do to anyone" (Tobit 4:15)—the oldest negative formulation in the biblical-Jewish tradition. (3) "What is hateful to yourself, do to no other; that is the whole law and the rest is commentary" (Hillel,* a Jewish sage). (4) "Let no man himself do what he hates to have done to him" (Philo,* a Jewish philosopher). (5) "Whatever you wish not be done to you, do not do to another" (*Didache*). In this stream of tradition, the negative form of the teaching is most common and was preserved even in the early Christian *Didache*, while Jesus put the teaching positively. Jesus' way of putting it actually makes doing it harder. These similar teachings suggest that sometimes things are true because Jesus said them (for example, the first beatitude), and at other

> **Jesus did not explain the universality of sin; he assumed it. That's why no one is exempt from his call to repent in response to God's kingly rule.**

101

times Jesus said them because they were recognized as true; to know which is which is important.

The claim that the Golden Rule is the Law and the Prophets is remarkable, for it concentrates everything on the moral aspect of the Law (that which concerns the right way to treat other people) and ignores the vast amount of legislation about rituals, sacred times and objects, and what may and may not be eaten. The Golden Rule does not reject these parts of the Law but regards them as secondary.

Hard Road Ahead

GC 12-2 Matthew 7:13-14 (the narrow gate and hard road) and 7:24-27 (the parable of the two houses) frame the conclusion of the Sermon on the Mount. Each saying in its own way emphasizes choice and its consequences. The saying about the narrow gate and the hard road is found only in Matthew; true, Luke 13:23-24 also uses the image of the narrow door and contrasts the few with the many but makes a quite different point. In Matthew the saying describes a situation, but in Luke it is an exhortation in response to a question: "Someone asked him, 'Lord, will only a few be saved?' He said to them, 'Strive to enter through the narrow door; for many, I tell you, will try to enter and will not be able.'" In Matthew the gate leads to a road, but in Luke the door is part of a house that people want to enter. In Luke the saying prepares for a parable about those who are not admitted, even though they knock and knock and knock (13:25-30). They knock too late.

Matthew 7:13-14 is based on contrasts—gates narrow and wide, roads narrow and hard and wide and easy; endings that are life and death, travelers few and many. No middle way; no shortcut. We must choose. By putting this saying immediately after the Golden Rule, Matthew implies that obeying it requires going through the narrow gate and walking the narrow, difficult path; at the end, however, is life. This life is not already in hand; it is rather the goal of life's walk. Nor is that life found at the end of every narrow street. Jesus does not explain what makes the road to life hard or why the easy road leads to death. He simply says how it is and assumes everyone will recognize he is right. Wisdom teachings are like that. But Jesus' concern is not to say vividly what everyone already knows is true but to urge his hearers to make the right choice. And here the right thing to do is the hard thing. The easy thing has no real future, attractive though it may be now. So the saying begins with a command, "Enter through the narrow gate." The

careful, balanced phrasing of the saying makes it easier to remember (and memorize). Here too the use of "for" (or "because") states the basis for the preceding statement: "Enter through the narrow gate; [why?] for the gate is wide and the road is easy that leads to destruction, and there are many who take it [why?]. For the gate is narrow and the road is hard that leads to life, and there are few who find it."

The image of two contrasting roads leading to contrasting results appears also in various other ancient writings. Jesus' teaching draws on a long, well-established Jewish teaching of "the two ways." This teaching goes back to Deuteronomy 11:26; 30:15, and to Jeremiah 21:8, where in the face of Nebuchadrezzar's threat, Jeremiah speaks God's word: "See, I am setting before you the way of life and the way of death." (That is, if you stay here in Jerusalem, you will be killed; if you leave and surrender, you will live—though as captives.) Some later Jewish texts say God put before Adam the two ways, others that God gave everyone the two ways, of good and of evil. In other texts the idea is present even though they do not mention the two ways explicitly (Psalm 139:24; Sirach 15:14-17). The teaching was taken over by some early Christians as well. The *Didache* begins, "There are two ways, one of life and one of death; and between the two ways there is a great difference." It goes on to explain first the way of life (citing both Jesus' double commandment and the Golden Rule, followed by quotations from the Sermon on the Mount). It also explains the way of death (listing twenty-two vices to start with). So too the second-century writing called the *Epistle of Barnabas** says, "There are two ways of teaching and power, one of light and one of darkness"; over the former are set "the light-bringing angels of God" but over the latter "the angels of Satan." It too spells out the differences in great detail. Built into the whole tradition is the conviction that God gave humanity a clear choice, that we can indeed choose, that we are responsible for the choice, that we can do what is chosen, and that the consequences are clear and certain.

There is a tension between the teaching of the two ways and that of the Beatitudes. The Beatitudes announce God's gracious action without condition; they do not make blessedness depend on our making the right choice, for the initiative is entirely God's. The teaching of the two ways, however, puts the emphasis on our choice and action. By including both, the Sermon on the Mount implies that each accent has its place, depending on the desired response. The Beatitudes intend to elicit joyous response to the good news; the two ways intend to promote the right choice.

Appearance and Reality

Having stated the two ways alternatives in Matthew 7:13-14, the next paragraph (7:15-20) is designed to help the church identify false prophets. False prophets are persons who claim wrongly that their teaching is authorized by God. In the presence of false prophets the matter of choice becomes urgent. How to distinguish the true from the false prophet is an old problem, as Scripture for Day 3 shows. Also, the problem appears to have grown more serious in the early church because the church held that all baptized believers received the Holy Spirit, in whose name the prophet spoke. But if all prophets claim to be inspired by the Spirit but speak "all over the map," how do we know which prophet is to be ignored or rejected? The answer is clear, despite the fact that the language here moves from persons (prophets) to animals (sheep and wolves) to plants (thorns and thistles) to trees. Each shift brings out a new aspect.

Matthew 7:15 assumes the prophets are not members of the local congregation but are traveling teachers "who come to you." The trouble is, they make a good appearance; they look like true prophets. They look like harmless sheep but inwardly (that is, actually) they are "ravenous wolves." But if all sheep (prophets) look alike, how can we identify those who are really wolves? The answer does not lie in comparing one sheep (one prophet's activity) with another, for the prophet's falseness is not visible in things like poor speaking ability or less wonderworking capacity. The sheep metaphor is valuable precisely because it makes this point: All the sheep look alike, though some are not sheep at all. To know which is which, we must look not at their activity but at the results of their activity, at what they produce ("their fruits," a shift in metaphor). Jesus now appeals to what everyone knows is true: Just as each kind of plant produces its own kind of fruit (7:16), so each kind of prophet produces his or her own kind of result. Since like produces like, 7:17-18 goes on to say that the good tree produces good fruit, the bad tree bad fruit, because the good cannot produce the bad, nor can the bad produce the good. The teaching makes no such allowances as, "He may be a scoundrel, but some people have been helped by his ministry."

The teaching in Luke 6:43-45 does not refer specifically to false prophets, as does the teaching in Matthew, but points in the same direction by noting that "it is out of the abundance of the heart that the mouth speaks." Nor does Luke's version threaten the bad tree with destruction, as does Matthew 7:19—a saying that reminds us of John the Baptist's words: "Even now the ax is lying at the root of the trees; every tree therefore that does not bear good fruit is cut down and thrown into the fire" (Matthew 3:10; Luke 3:9). Although Jesus is known as a messenger of God's goodness and grace, he too threatens God's judgment for those who do not repent (Matthew 11:20-24). Choices have consequences. At the same time, 7:19 does not urge the community to cut down the bad tree, for then the church would be doing what is reserved for God. The parable in 13:24-30 makes the same point against those who want to pull the weeds out of the wheat field before the harvest time (the end time). Likewise, 7:15 warns against false prophets but does not say, "Get rid of them!" That will occur at the Judgment, as the next saying shows.

Quite likely the Evangelist thinks of Matthew 7:21-23 as commentary on 7:15-20, for the clear reference to the Judgment ("on that day" is a common way of referring to it) interprets the cutting down of the bad tree, and the reference to prophecy in 7:22 alludes to the "prophets" in 7:15. Here it becomes evident why Jesus says the false prophets are in sheep's clothing: They prophesy, exorcise demons, and work miracles, carrying on the mission of Jesus in Jesus' name. They are clearly and conscientiously believers, for they say, "Lord, Lord." In other words, so far as anyone can *see*, they are model disciples. Yet they will not be allowed to enter the Kingdom, for entrance is granted only to those who on earth do the will of the Father in heaven, who do what is asked for in the Lord's Prayer (Matthew 6:10). Jesus does not deny that confessing him as Lord, prophesying, exorcising demons, and doing wondrous deeds are God's will. He implies, however, that a person can do all these things and *still* not do God's will. Matthew 7:21-23 is probably the harshest teaching in the whole of Matthew; it threatens the self-image of the disciple

> **Although Jesus is known as a messenger of God's goodness and grace, he too threatens God's judgment for those who do not repent.**

103

more than John the Baptist's words threatened the Pharisees and Sadducees who came to him for baptism (3:7-10).

At first glance, Jesus seems less harsh in Luke 6:46, "Why do you call me 'Lord, Lord,' and do not do what I tell you?" But his question is not a request for an explanation; it is a rebuke. In Luke, as in Matthew, Jesus requires more than right words about him. Right deeds rightly done must follow or else disaster lies ahead. That is what the parable of the two houses makes clear (Matthew 7:24-27; Luke 6:47-49).

So Then

Both sermons combine proclamation and obligation, and it is as hard to believe the former as it is to do the latter. The saying about the narrow gate and the hard road implies Jesus was quite aware of this, yet nowhere does he say, "What really matters is that you try"; nor does he counsel what the *Didache* advises: "If you can bear the whole yoke of the Lord, you will be perfect; but if you cannot, do what you can." Instead, both sermons assume the disciple can do as Jesus says; neither sermon wrestles with the dilemma that worried Paul: "I can will what is right, but I cannot do it. For I do not do the good I want, but the evil I do not want is what I do" (Romans 7:18-19). Paul did not have

> In disclosing the truth about God, Jesus also uncovers the truth about us.

the Sermon on the Mount in mind, because it had not yet been written; what he had in mind was the Law, the Torah. But the same sort of despair easily descends on readers of the Sermon on the Mount when we take it out of the setting Matthew gave it and so hear Jesus' demands apart from the news of the Kingdom. Then the sermon does become bad news. But from Matthew's angle, Jesus makes these difficult demands not to produce repentance (in the sense of regret for failure) but to outline the shape of repentance as the Godward turn in response to the news of the Kingdom. To state it more simply: Doing as Jesus says does not bring the Kingdom near; rather, the Kingdom's nearness brings about the Godward turn that these teachings make concrete.

In the Sermon on the Mount, Jesus talks *about* himself and his mission only in Matthew 5:17, though he also refers to himself ("but I say" or "these words of mine"). He does not claim his teachings are unprecedented or unique, nor does he argue his teachings are true. He simply assumes and asserts they are. Each saying is put in such a way that we must say either, "Yes, that's right" or "No, it can't be that way." But even if we say no, we are haunted by these sayings because they go so directly to the heart of the matter—we must decide whether the message is good news or bad. At the same time, we cannot separate the message from the messenger, for he is *in* the message; we cannot concede that what he *says* is right without conceding that *he* is right—and that he is right because he has seen rightly into the human heart and into the nature of God. Therefore, the Sermon on the Mount not only assures us that the heavenly Father knows who we are and what we need but also—and for the same reasons—makes us deeply uncomfortable. For in disclosing the truth about God, Jesus also uncovers the truth about us. Christian teaching has a word to express the identity of the person who reveals both and who does so for our good—Son of God. According to the Synoptics, God too said Jesus was Son of God (Matthew 3:17; Mark 1:11; Luke 3:22), and according to Matthew and Luke, the devil tried to spoil it all by tempting Jesus to be Son of God for his own benefit (Matthew 4:1-11; Luke 4:1-13). But the devil failed because Jesus himself went through the narrow gate and stayed on the hard road that led—and still leads—to life.

Is it surprising that Hebrews calls him the "pioneer" of salvation who was made perfect through sufferings (Hebrews 2:10)? Jesus never said his way would be easy. He did say we must choose—and then do what is chosen.

Do You Want to Become His Disciples, Too?

Being Jesus' disciple means allowing ourselves to be judged by the Teacher before handing out verdicts on others. Building our life on the rock includes that self-discipline.

What is difficult and demanding in the Jesus you hear in Matthew 7?

_____

_____

_____

_____

_____

Prayer

Our LORD, you bless everyone
> who lives right and obeys your Law.
You bless all of those
who follow your commands from deep in their hearts
> and who never do wrong or turn from you.
You have ordered us always to obey your teachings;
> I don't ever want to stray from your laws.
Thinking about your commands
> will keep me from doing some foolish thing.
I will do right and praise you
> by learning to respect your perfect laws.

(Psalm 119:1-7, CEV)

13 Faith as Wonder

Amazement seized all of them,
and they glorified God and were filled with awe, saying,
"We have seen strange things today."

(Luke 5:26)

They Have No Wine

Although we marvel at the dramatic achievements of modern technology and life sciences, our capacity to wonder is diminished in other respects. The earth is round, but our world is flat. It seems that only nature's disasters—hurricanes and tornadoes, earthquakes and floods—remind us how little we control. The sense of awe has departed, and sometimes we miss it.

Beginning With Moses and All the Prophets

This week's study turns to the well-known stories of Jesus' acts commonly called "nature miracles"—Jesus' calming the storm, walking on water, and feeding the multitude. Instead of trying to explain what actually happened, we will look for what these stories can mean for us today.

Day 1 2 Kings 4:42-44; Mark 1:21-28; 4:35-41; **6:30-56; 7:24–8:21**

(1) Note how Mark 6:30 follows 6:13.

(2) **GC 13-1** Locate the similarities and differences between the two stories of the feeding of the crowds. To see the importance of Mark 8:14-21 for Mark as a whole, recall this Evangelist's portrayal of the disciples (see Lesson 7). Note how Mark 8:17 picks up the theme of 6:52.

(3) Observe how the stories of Jesus' feedings surpass the feeding story in Second Kings.

(4) Can you see what Mark 1:21-28 has in common with 4:35-41?

Day 2 Job 9:1-12; 38:1-11; Matthew 8:23-27; 14:13-36; 15:32–16:12

The readings from Job remind us of the biblical sense of God's majesty, and the majesty of what we call "nature," but which the Bible views as creation. Compare Mark 6:51-52 with Matthew 14:32-33, and notice how the difference changes the picture of the disciples.

Day 3 Luke 8:22-25; 9:10-17; Acts 27:1–28:16

Observe that Luke omits everything Mark reports between Mark 6:45 and 8:27 (though the sayings in Mark 8:11-13 appear in other settings in Luke). One way to appreciate the result of this omission is to read Mark again, beginning at 6:30 and omitting 6:45–8:26. How has the picture of Jesus changed?

Day 4 Exodus 16; Isaiah 55; John 6:1-34

Note that nothing in Matthew or Mark is like John 6:14-15. Notice how John 6:14-15 becomes the basis for the exchange between Jesus and the people in 6:25-34.

Day 5 1 Kings 10:1-10; Jonah 1; 3:1-5; Mark 8:11-13; Matthew 12:38-42; 16:1-4; Luke 11:29-32

The theme of this day's readings concerns the request that Jesus provide a "sign" and his replies to the request. Note the difference between his answer in Mark 8:12 and his answer in Matthew 16:1-4. [GC 13-2] Compare Matthew 12:40-42 and Luke 11:30-32 carefully. Note that Matthew 12:40 explains the sign of Jonah in a way Luke does not. Note Jesus' claims about the significance of his mission. Write your understanding of Jesus' claim of being "greater than."

Day 6 Read and respond to "Faith as Wonder" and "Do You Want to Become His Disciples, Too?"

Prayer Concerns

Faith as Wonder

The title of this lesson is deliberately ambiguous. Given the stories in this week's Scriptures, does the title mean faith includes wondering how such things could possibly happen? Or does it mean having faith is not to be taken for granted but is itself something marvelous and beyond explanation? Does it mean faith expresses itself in a sense of awe, of astonishment? Or does the title include all of these meanings?

The paragraph introducing the week's readings says the focus is on what these stories *can* mean today—implying that meaning cannot be required or forced, because it is an occurrence, a discovery. (That old stories, translated ones at that, have meaning or generate meaning today is itself a wonder, something more to be acknowledged than explained.) The meaning of a story depends largely on how it is told and not told, and on the setting in which it is told. This observation is as true of the Gospels as it is of any piece of literature.

Some of these stories are found in only one Gospel, some in two, some in three, and a few in all four Gospels. The more often a story appears, the more meanings it generates. For that reason Jesus in the Gospels cannot be squeezed into one meaning—neither can his teachings and individual sayings nor the stories of his deeds.

Meaning Missed

Mark 8:14-21 reveals that the writer uses the stories of the two feedings (6:30-44 and 8:1-10) to show that the disciples missed the point of these amazing events in their own experience. Mark has already alerted us to the disciples' difficulty in understanding, beginning with Chapter 4, where Jesus explains the parable of the soils and also chides the disciples by asking, "Do you not understand this parable? Then how will you understand all the parables?" (4:13).

Then Mark links the collection of parables in Mark 4 to the story of Jesus' stilling the storm by saying that this event occurred "on that day, when evening had come" (a detail omitted by Matthew and Luke). Several details in this story (Mark 4:35-41) suggest important meanings:

(1) Because Jesus is asleep during the storm, so severe that the boat "was already being swamped," the disciples come close to accusing Jesus of not caring if they were to die (4:38)—already a hint that they do not understand who Jesus is. What follows is his response.

(2) Jesus rebuked the wind and told the raging sea to be quiet (4:39). This twofold action reminds us that in the story of the exorcism in the synagogue (1:21-28), Jesus "rebuked" the unclean spirit. By using the word *rebuked* in 4:39, Mark implies that the wind and waves also are driven by demonic powers. We are not to think that this storm is ordinary, nor that ordinary storms are driven by demonic powers. Rather, if Mark's first readers knew their Greek Bible, they should have seen here an allusion to Psalm 106:8-9, where God "rebuked" the Red Sea at the Exodus:

"Yet he saved them for his name's sake,
    so that he might make known his mighty
      power.

He rebuked the Red Sea, and it became dry."
In Mark the sea did not dry up, but it did become calm. In other words, the story of Jesus' saving action on the Sea of Galilee recalls God's saving deliverance of his people at the Red Sea.

(3) Then, in Mark 4:40, Jesus addresses the disciples, chiding them, "Why are you afraid? Have you still no faith?"

(4) Also, the response of the awed disciples, "Who then is this, that even the wind and the sea obey him?" echoes the response of the congregation in the synagogue, "What is this? ... He commands even the unclean spirits, and they obey him" (1:27). On one level this amazement, this sense of wonder, is appropriate, but on another level it suggests something else: Because the disciples ignore Jesus' question and instead marvel at what he has done, they fail to understand both who Jesus really is and what their fear discloses about themselves.

The word *immediately* (6:45) links the story of the feeding of the five thousand (6:30-44) closely to the story of Jesus' walking on the sea, in which the fear of the disciples is mentioned again (6:45-52). Basic to this sea story is Jesus' word, "Take heart, it is I; do not be afraid" (6:50). Such words of assurance often appear in stories that report the appearing of God or an angel (for example, Tobit 12:15-17; Luke 1:11-13, 26-30; 2:8-10; John 6:19-20; Acts 27:23-25; Revelation 1:17-18), because the appearing of the divine is assumed to be so awesome that those to whom it happens are frightened and need assurance. Jesus' words in Mark 6:47-52 imply he is a terrifying divine presence who comes to them on the water (as Job 9:8 says of God) at dawn, after they had been rowing against the wind. (Is this detail accidental? Don't disciples often row against the wind? Recall what Jesus said about the hard road.) To the end of the story ("and they were utterly astounded," Mark 6:51), the narrator* adds his own explanation, which ties it even more closely to the feeding story: "for they did not understand about the loaves, but their hearts were hardened." What was it about the loaves they did not understand?

After the story of the feeding of the four thousand (8:1-10), the narrator has the Pharisees ask Jesus "for a sign from heaven, to test him." But he flatly refuses: "Truly I tell you, no sign will be given to this generation." And again Jesus departs by boat (8:11-13). Mark uses this boat ride to show how completely the disciples continue to miss the meaning (8:14-21). He uses Jesus' warning against "the yeast of the Pharisees and the yeast of Herod" also to indicate the missed meaning. Here *yeast* is a metaphor for bad influence. The disciples' forgetting the lunch is important to the story. First they respond to Jesus' warning by telling one another that Jesus said this "because we have no bread." Their comment shows how completely they are missing what Jesus is talking about. Next their worrying about having no bread shows that from Jesus' feeding multitudes twice and from their own gathering twelve and seven baskets of leftovers they had learned nothing about Jesus' power to save and provide. If these wondrous events do not disclose the meaning of Jesus, what will?

We can understand the Pharisees' request for a sign. Because they were not present at the feedings, they want an unambiguous sign from heaven, a miracle so clearly from God that it removes any doubt that Jesus is God's agent on earth. The "yeast" against which Jesus warns the disciples is, in this setting, nothing other than the detrimental influence of the Pharisees' way of thinking (still shared by many people today)—that if the miraculous is great enough, doubt will disappear. If the disciples who saw Jesus calm the storm, walk on water, twice feed the multitude with a few loaves and fish still miss the meaning, then it will take something other than a supermiracle to open their eyes.

In Mark the disciples' repeated failure to understand is linked precisely with Jesus' greatest miracles.

But why is Mark so hard on the disciples? By *describing them* he is *addressing readers also*—Christians living three or four decades later and readers today. So too, in reporting Jesus' warning against the Pharisees' yeast, Mark is warning his contemporaries against thinking there is a sign from heaven so stupendous that faith will be replaced by sight, or at least made easier. In Mark the disciples' repeated failure to understand is linked precisely with Jesus' greatest miracles.

Meaning Grasped and Meaning Distorted

Already we have seen that while Matthew's Gospel depends on Mark, it does not emphasize the disciples' failure to understand. To the contrary, near the end of the collection of parables in Matthew 13, only Matthew has Jesus ask, "Have you understood all this?" to which they reply, "Yes" (13:51). However, in Matthew Jesus also charges them with having "little faith." Compare the two accounts of the stilling of the storm: In Mark, once the storm is replaced by "a dead calm," Jesus asks, "Why are you afraid? Have you still no faith?" (Mark 4:40). (Some manuscripts have "Why have you no faith?") But in Matthew, *before* Jesus rebukes the wind and sea he asks, "Why are you afraid, you of little faith?" (Matthew 8:26). The characterization "little faith" appears repeatedly in Matthew, beginning at 6:30 (8:26; 14:31; 16:8; 17:20). Matthew implies that understanding and robust faith do not necessarily go together, for the disciples understand and yet have "little faith."

GC 13-3 Matthew's account of Jesus' walking on the water (14:22-33) differs from Mark's in two respects. First, into Mark's story Matthew inserts a brief story of what happened when Peter asked Jesus, "Lord, if it is you, command me to come to you on the water." Disaster followed when Peter, having started to walk on the water, apparently was more afraid of the wind than he was confident of Jesus, and so began to sink, shouting, "Lord, save me!" Jesus did so but also said, "You of little faith, why did you doubt?" Here strong faith appears to exclude doubt; that is, doubt diminishes and weakens faith, implying that we cannot join Jesus on the water (the abode of dangerous powers) with weak faith. Only with strong faith in Jesus can we escape destruction by evil forces.

The second difference in Matthew's account appears at the end of the story. Mark concludes by writing, "And they were utterly astounded, for they did not understand about the loaves, but their hearts were hardened" (Mark 6:51-52). But in Matthew 14:33 we read that once Jesus and Peter got into the boat, the disciples "worshiped him, saying, 'Truly you are the Son of God.'" Despite Peter's little faith, all the disciples now make the right response. Coming where it does, this confession probably responds both to Jesus' walking on the water and to his saving Peter from the water. Here, wondrous miracles do elicit faith's confession.

Matthew 16:5-12 uses Mark 8:14-21, in which Jesus speaks of yeast but the disciples think he refers to bread. Here Matthew not only adds "you of little faith" (Matthew 16:8) to Jesus' rebuke but also clarifies Jesus' last question in Mark, "Do you not yet understand?" (Mark 8:21). So Matthew 16:11-12 reads this way: "'How could you fail to perceive that I was not speaking about bread? Beware of the yeast of the Pharisees and Sadducees!' Then they understood that he had not told them to beware of the yeast of bread, but of the teaching of the Pharisees and Sadducees." Does understanding strengthen weak faith?

In John as in Mark the story of the feeding of the five thousand (John 6:1-14) is followed by the story of Jesus' walking on the water (6:16-21). But in John the feeding becomes the starting point for Jesus' exchange with those he had fed—which turns into a dispute with "the Jews" on one hand and into a searching discussion with the disciples on the other.

In John it is the fed people who do not understand. After the leftovers had filled twelve baskets, John says, "When the people saw the sign that he had done, they began to say, 'This is indeed the prophet who is to come into the world'" (6:14). They sense that in Jesus God was fulfilling either the expectation that Elijah would return just before the time of salvation, "the great and terrible day of the LORD" (Malachi 4:5-6), or the promise that a prophet like Moses would come (Deuteronomy 18:15). Even if identifying Jesus as the expected prophet falls short of seeing him as the Son of God, the response moves in the right direction.

But then, according to the next verse, they misunderstand Jesus' feeding them, for "they were about to come and take him by force to make him king," causing Jesus to go away from them (John 6:15). Who wouldn't want a king who could feed thousands with only a boy's lunch (6:9)? The people wouldn't give up; they went to Capernaum looking for him (6:22-24). Now Jesus tells them the truth about themselves: "Very truly, I tell you, you are looking for me, not because you saw signs, but because you ate your fill of the loaves"

(6:25-26). If they had seen Jesus' feeding as a sign, as an event that signifies what Jesus really brings (eternal life), they would have acted differently. What they saw in Jesus' act, however, was a sign of what they wanted, not a sign of what he gives.

Signs Denied and Signs Given

John understands Jesus' feeding the multitude as a "sign," the marvelous act that points to some aspect of Jesus' meaning for the human condition. This view of signs is basic to the portrayal of Jesus in John. Here the question is, What is the difference between the view of signs in John and in the Synoptics?

We start with Mark 8:11-13, where the Pharisees ask Jesus "for a sign from heaven, to test him." That is, they challenge Jesus to do something sufficiently "miraculous" that it will demonstrate once and for all that Jesus has the God-given right to speak and do what he says and does. But Jesus rejects the challenge and breaks off the argument without explaining his negative response. He does not say, "I will not give you a sign" but "no sign will be given"—the passive "be given" implying that God will not give it. Jesus' right to speak so confidently about what God will and will not do is precisely what bothers the Pharisees in the first place. But he would not make it easier for them to see that he is God's representative; they must decide whether he is or not. Matthew and Luke, however, prefer another tradition (Matthew 16:4; Luke 11:29), according to which Jesus gives a different response: There will be only *one* sign, the sign of Jonah.

In fact, in Matthew Jesus had already given this same response to the same request, explaining in some detail what he means by the sign of Jonah (Matthew 12:38-42; in Luke 11:29-32 Jesus volunteers the teaching). In fact, he gives two explanations. The first sees in Jonah's three days and nights "in the belly of the sea monster" an analogy to the time the Son of Man will be "in the heart of the earth"—the time between Jesus' death and resurrection. The saying assumes Jesus, like all the dead, will go to the subterranean abode of the dead (*sheol* in Hebrew, *hades* in Greek; this is not "hell" [*gehinnom* in Hebrew], the place of punishment). Understanding this interpretation of the sign of Jonah must await the Resurrection. In other words, after Easter we can see Jonah as an anticipation of Jesus—if we believe Jesus has been resurrected. That is, Jonah is a sign for Christians. Luke does not have this interpretation.

In Matthew's second interpretation Jonah himself is not the sign, but the repentance of the Ninevites that his preaching produced. The saying looks ahead to the Great Judgment when all will be raised. At that time, the Ninevites who repented will condemn Jesus' generation because they did not repent, even though "something greater than Jonah" had occurred among them—Jesus' mission. Jesus is more than a prophet, and precisely this "more" makes their not repenting all the more serious. With this saying goes the comparison with the queen of the South (the queen of Sheba): While she came a great distance to hear Solomon's wisdom, Jesus' contemporaries ignored him. Built into this second interpretation is Jesus' remarkable claim that what is afoot in his mission is greater than both Jonah's call to repentance and Solomon's wisdom. Here the sign of Jonah, instead of helping the Pharisees accept Jesus and his mission, is a word of judgment against them, for they represent "an evil and adulterous generation [that] asks for a sign" (Matthew 12:39). In other words, the sign of Jonah is a warning: Unless you repent, you will be condemned at the Judgment. The sign also implies a promise: If you do repent, you will be spared, as were the Ninevites. But the saying assumes this repentance will not happen.

Now a summary: First, in the Synoptics Jesus refuses to perform a sign (a marvelous act) on demand, one that proves beyond doubt he is God's valid agent. In fact, the sign has already happened—in Jonah's mission and in the queen of Sheba's visit. These past events can be seen as pointing to Jesus, but they do not prove his identity or legitimacy as God's representative. Who Jesus is and what his mission signifies remain, and must remain, a matter of decision, confession, faith. In John, Jesus' wondrous deeds are presented as signs, as events that point to his role as the Redeemer. But only faith understands these events this way. Those without faith miss the real point, as did those who wanted to make Jesus king because he had fed them.

Second, certain details in the Synoptics' telling of the feeding of the five thousand suggest that the writers of these Gospels saw also a symbolic

Who Jesus is and what his mission signifies remain, and must remain, a matter of decision, confession, faith.

meaning of Jesus' deed. In these stories Jesus acts through the disciples, for they are the ones who distribute the food and gather the leftovers. All these feeding stories report that before giving the food to the disciples to distribute, Jesus gave thanks and broke the bread (Matthew 14:19; Mark 6:41; Luke 9:16)—language that reappears in the stories of the Lord's Supper (Matthew 26:26; Mark 14:22; Luke 22:19). The Gospel writers, and perhaps also the Christians who first told the feeding stories, apparently used this language because they saw in those events a foretaste of the Eucharist whose bread the church distributes with Jesus' blessing. The feeding stories do not report the amazement of the disciples. By not commenting on the disciples' reaction, the stories keep the attention riveted solely on Jesus.

So Then

The stories *express* the faith of those who told them. None of these stories reports that someone came to faith in response to Jesus' special deeds. The stories of these events on the sea do tell of the disciples' amazement, for to have neglected such mention would suggest they took Jesus' acts on their behalf for granted—the signature of unbelief. They marveled before they came to understand, and despite the fact they did not understand—at least not before the Resurrection. The Evangelists, fortunately, do not say why they included these stories of fantastic events that most people would say are impossible because they contradict what we know about the world. But since when did Jesus, and the God he represented, fit neatly into reality as we understand it? Are the stories more offensive than the gospel itself? Could the meanings they express really be stated better without stories? By including them, the Gospel writers invite readers to tell the stories themselves—with awe and wonder as expressions of faith.

The relation of story to faith in these stories is not the same as in the stories of Jesus' exorcisms. The latter generated controversy, not about whether Jesus did or did not expel demons but about whether his power came from Beelzebul (Mark 3:22). This controversy shows that anyone could tell a story of Jesus' exorcism as an undoubted event without believing Jesus was acting as "the finger of God" in bringing the Kingdom (Luke 11:20), because the event could be interpreted in quite different ways. Even Jesus' opponents could tell the story without having faith in him. This telling without believing is not the case with the nature miracles discussed here, because faith in Jesus is built into the stories themselves. They are believers' stories.

Many people, however, want to know whether the stories report what really happened. And others conclude that, because the stories do not report that the events generated faith, faith actually generated the stories. Still others have proposed that the stories magnify an unusual event into a miracle; in this way of thinking, a multitude was fed because people shared what they had when they saw the generosity of the boy who offered his lunch, and this sharing was the real miracle. But such an explanation actually destroys the story in order to keep some kind of event as a "historical fact" behind the story. But the alleged "fact" never explains how the story itself came to be told. No Gospel story describes what a video camera might have recorded. Where the nature miracles are concerned, the story is all we have. We should not be disappointed by this. After all, did not Jesus refuse to perform a miracle to generate faith in those who would have seen it happen? Those who today insist on knowing "what really happened" in the nature miracles are in effect asking Jesus to reverse himself, because they think (wrongly) that if they knew the facts, believing would be easier. But the Gospels show repeatedly that many of those who did see did not believe. What reason is there to think we would do better?

Because the stories of the nature miracles express faith, they confront us with an invitation to faith. And the faith they invite us to embrace reflects the conviction that God resurrected Jesus from the dead and that, as a result, the risen Jesus as saving power is present to his disciples and to the world. In short, the nature miracles preach the gospel. Those who believe it respond with awe and wonder.

Do You Want to Become His Disciples, Too?

The disciple trusts the God Jesus trusted—the one whose goodness has power and whose power is for good and so evokes awe and wonder.

When you read the stories of the nature miracles, who is the Jesus you see?

_____

_____

_____

_____

_____

Prayer

In the beginning, LORD, you laid the earth's foundation
    and created the heavens.
They will all disappear and wear out like clothes.
You change them, as you would a coat,
    but you last forever.
You are always the same. Years cannot change you.
Every generation of those who serve you
    will live in your presence.

(Psalm 102:25-28, CEV)

14 Destiny Disclosed

The Son of Man came not to be served but to serve,
and to give his life a ransom for many.

(Mark 10:45)

They Have No Wine

Tomorrow we will harvest mainly what was sowed yesterday and is cultivated today—not only by us. The future brings consequences that sometimes surprise us, and sometimes seem inevitable, because who we are today works its way into who we will be tomorrow. Today's decisions are important even if we cannot foresee their consequences.

Beginning With Moses and All the Prophets

This week's study takes us to the gospel in the Gospels. Here the destiny of Jesus and the destiny of his disciples are disclosed as being intertwined in a way that conveys both good news and awesome demand. We are at the turning point of Mark, where Jesus first speaks of his death (commonly called a "Passion prediction") and what it implies for discipleship. We will look closely at the Transfiguration story, which Mark links to the first Passion prediction; and as in earlier lessons, we will observe how Matthew and Luke used Mark in their portrayals of Jesus. This week's study requires reading many passages, all of which are important for seeing Jesus in the Gospels.

Day 1 Mark 6:14-16; Matthew 14:1-2; Luke 9:7-9; **Mark 8:27-33;** Matthew 16:13-23; Luke 9:18-22

(1) **GC 14-1** Note how Mark 6:14-16 prepares the reader for Mark 8:27-28 (as Matthew 14:1-2; Luke 9:7-9 prepare for Matthew 16:13-14; Luke 9:18-19).

(2) Compare Mark 8:29-30 with Matthew 16:16-20.

(3) Note that Luke omits the exchange between Jesus and Peter in Mark 8:32-33 and Matthew 16:22-23. Why does Jesus call Peter "Satan"?

Day 2 Mark 8:34–9:1; Matthew 16:24-28; Luke 9:23-27

Observe that Mark 8:34–9:1 assembles a number of individual sayings about discipleship.
GC 14-2 Compare carefully what Jesus says in Mark 9:1 with what he says in Matthew 16:28 and Luke 9:27 and note the distinct accent of each Gospel.

Day 3 Deuteronomy 18:15-18; 2 Kings 2:1-12; Sirach 48:1-14; Mark 9:2-29; Luke 9:28-43

(1) Mark 9:2-8 assumes the reader knows the passage from Deuteronomy. Why is Luke 9:28-36 easier to understand than Mark 9:2-8? Notice also how Luke 9:36 explains why there is no further mention of the Transfiguration in the Gospels.

(2) **GC 14-3** Compare what the voice says in the three Transfiguration stories.

(3) Then compare what the voice says at the Transfiguration with what the voice said at Jesus' baptism (Matthew 3:17; Mark 1:11; Luke 3:22).

(4) Compare Mark 9:9-13 with Matthew 17:9-18 and note how Matthew 17:13 explains what Jesus means by "Elijah."

Day 4 Mark 9:30-37; Matthew 17:22-23; Luke 9:43-45; Mark 10:32-45; Matthew 20:17-28; Luke 18:31-34; 22:24-27

GC14-4 Note that the second Passion prediction (Mark 9:30-32; Matthew 17:22-23; Luke 9:43-45) is less detailed than the first. Compare the comments of the Evangelists in Mark 9:32; Matthew 17:23; Luke 9:45. Had you written this story, what would your comment have been?

Day 5 Psalm 118:21-28; Isaiah 5:1-7; Mark 12:1-12; Matthew 21:33-46; Luke 20:9-19

Observe that Mark 12:1-12 (also Matthew 21:33-46; Luke 20:9-19) consists of three parts—the parable (Mark 12:1-9); the quotation of Psalm 118:22-23 (Mark 12:10-11), which in this context implies the resurrection of Jesus, the rejected stone; and the response of the opposition (12:12). Observe that Isaiah 5:1-7 (which sees Israel as God's vineyard) is the unstated image behind the parable.

Day 6 Read and respond to "Destiny Disclosed" and "Do You Want to Become His Disciples, Too?"

Prayer Concerns

Destiny Disclosed

Destiny, like *destination*, sees a person's (or group's) present from the standpoint of the future. But whereas a traveler usually sets the destination at the outset, the future destiny is set by a higher power. The Bible says (or implies) that God sets or "destines" what is in store because God oversees and guides human affairs in accord with the divine purpose. Sometimes destiny is seen as *punishment*, as in Job 15:22 and Jeremiah 15:2 (a wicked person is "destined for the sword"); sometimes it is viewed as *salvation* as in Ephesians 1:5 ("destined . . . for adoption as his children through Jesus Christ"). In Luke 2:34 Jesus himself is "destined" for both, "for the falling and the rising of many in Israel." In the biblical way of thinking, people are responsible for their actions even though God sets their destiny, Judas being a prime example (John 17:12). Talk of destiny is really a way of answering the question, Why? And ultimately the answer points to God's purpose, which is never fully understood.

Jesus' Destiny Stated

In Mark 8:27-33 and Matthew 16:13-23, but not in Luke 9:18-22, the exchange between Jesus and the disciples takes place north of the Sea of Galilee in the area near Caesarea Philippi ("Philip's Caesarea," not the Caesarea on the Mediterranean coast). Mark's story is surprisingly brief: Jesus first asks the disciples who people say he is; then he asks their opinion. Peter's response in Mark is the shortest: "You are the Messiah." In Luke it is "The Messiah of God"; and in Matthew it is the longest: "You are the Messiah, the Son of the living God." (Although the Greek text has *Christos*, "Messiah" [NRSV] translates the Hebrew or Aramaic word behind "Christ," *mashiah*.) Remarkably, instead of congratulating Peter (as in Matthew 16:17), Jesus orders the disciples to say not a word of this to anyone (Mark 8:30; Matthew 16:20; Luke 9:21); but he does not explain why they should remain silent. Instead, he teaches them that the destiny (note the *must*) of the Son of Man is great suffering, rejection, and execution followed by resurrection. (Mark, like Luke, assumes that Jesus is not changing the subject but is talking about himself. Matthew 16:21 avoids any uncertainty about this: "Jesus began to show his disciples that he must go to Jerusalem and undergo great suffering.") (See "The Son of Man," page 123.) This destiny is not driven by human ambition to be the Messiah; it is God-given. To underscore the point, (only) Mark says, "He said all this quite openly" (Mark 8:32).

In Mark Peter rebuked Jesus for his words; and then Jesus rebuked Peter, calling him "Satan." Why this harsh counterattack? Because, Jesus continues, Peter's mind is set "not on divine things but on human things." Peter had the right words about Jesus but got the meaning wrong. Peter is caught in a way of thinking that contrasts so completely with God's (and Jesus') way of thinking that Jesus says Peter speaks for Satan. Those who have been reading Matthew from the beginning remember that Jesus' "Get behind me, Satan" repeats Jesus' rebuff of Satan in the third temptation story (Matthew 4:10). There Satan offered Jesus an alternative destiny (the kingdoms of the world); here Satan uses Peter's rebuke as a "stumbling block" to destroy God's destiny for Jesus (16:23). In each case the alternative is the same, and in both cases Jesus holds firm.

The story of what transpired at Caesarea Philippi is commonly called "Peter's confession" because he rightly identified Jesus as the Messiah-Christ. Matthew clearly understands it so, as 16:17 shows, though Jesus also points out that Peter can say the right thing about Jesus only because God revealed it to him, not because Peter is especially perceptive.

Before faulting Peter for his rebuking Jesus, we should bear in mind that while Jewish hopes for the Messiah took many forms in Jesus' day, they did not include the idea that the Messiah *must* undergo what Jesus foresees for himself. That was—and is—offensive, an absurd idea of "Messiah." Suddenly then, Jesus' question, "Who do you say that I am?" confronts us as well. Putting the right label (Messiah) on Jesus is not enough because, as in Peter's case, it is possible to miss the point most profoundly just when we are using the right words.

Using the right words to identify Jesus properly is important. More important still is seeing how Jesus puts his own meaning into the right words. For Christians, Jesus is the one who defines "Messiah"; otherwise, he doesn't fit most traditional meanings of Messiah. That is why the vast majority of Jews refused to see Jesus as the Messiah.

The Disciples' Destiny

This passage combines a number of sayings in which the thought moves from *invitation* (Mark 8:34) to *warning* to those who decline it (8:35-38) to the *destiny* promised to those who accept it (9:1).

Jesus' words of invitation are identical in all three Synoptics (Mark 8:34; Matthew 16:24; Luke 9:23), except for the word "daily" that Luke has inserted: "If any want to become my followers, let them deny themselves and take up their cross daily and follow me." The invitation implies that Jesus has taken up his cross first. The first Passion prediction (Mark 8:31), however, did not mention his cross (the word appears here for the first time). In fact, neither of the other two Passion predictions in Mark (9:30-32; 10:33-34) or in Luke (9:44; 18:31-33) says that Jesus will be crucified; this detail appears only in Matthew 20:19. These observations imply that the wording of the invitation is a Christian formulation that expresses, quite correctly, what following Jesus the crucified actually means. The first three Gospels are unanimous here in insisting that self-denial and cross-bearing characterize the kind of life to which Jesus invites. Matthew 10:37-39 and Luke 14:26-27 make the same point; also in these two passages Jesus says nothing about his own cross, for that is assumed throughout. In all these passages about the disciples' cross-bearing, we hear the voice of the crucified and now living Jesus, for true discipleship means following the whole Jesus, not only heeding his words. In other words, to follow a Jesus without his cross is to follow a partial Jesus, one whose mission lacks its consummation.

> To follow a Jesus without his cross is to follow a partial Jesus, one whose mission lacks its consummation.

The warnings in Mark 8:35-38 reinforce the invitation by emphasizing the negative destiny of those who avoid the self-denial of discipleship and instead insist on their self-acquired security. According to these verses, they are the real losers, not those who deny themselves.

Mark 8:35 combines warning and promise. The force of 8:35 emerges more clearly if we first look at two similar sayings in Luke, the first at Luke 17:33:

"Those who try to make their life secure will lose it, but those who lose their life will keep it."

This saying expresses an observation that is generally valid, as is usually the case with proverbs. The second is Luke's version of Mark 8:35, in which this general observation is tied specifically to Jesus (Luke 9:24):

"For those who want to save their life will lose it, and those who lose their life for my sake will save it."

Mark 8:35 adds another phrase—"and for the sake of the gospel"—in order to include explicitly all post-resurrection believers for whom accepting the gospel proves costly.

The two sayings in Mark 8:36-38 refer to those who do not "deny themselves," but who instead "want to save their life." The first saying (8:36-37) in effect asks, "What's the point of gaining everything if you lose yourself? When that happens, what does the loser have to buy back the life already lost?" In other words, this "saver" is really a loser, not the one whose self-denial includes cross-bearing. The second saying (8:38) has in view the Last Judgment when the Son of Man (here assumed to be the resurrected, exalted Jesus) will arrive (an event commonly called the Second Coming, a phrase not used in the New Testament). In this context, the saying implies that those who want to "save their life" in the present by being "ashamed" of Jesus and his teachings, by not acknowledging him, will lose everything at the end. Matthew 16:27 makes this point explicit by adding, "Then he [the Son of Man] will repay everyone for what has been done." (The parable of the Last Judgment in Matthew 25:31-46 spells this out.) This emphasis on the end underscores the importance of making the right decision in the present. Choices do have consequences, ultimate ones in fact.

Mark 9:1 returns to the promise: Some of Jesus' hearers will live to "see that the kingdom of God has come with power." (Whereas Luke 9:27 reads simply "see the kingdom of God," Matthew 16:28 reads "see the Son of Man coming in his kingdom.") Because we are studying Jesus in the Gospels (just now focusing on Mark), we must look for the meaning of the promise in Mark. We need not read far, because the next story discloses what Mark had in mind.

Jesus' Destiny Confirms His Identity

Like the nature miracles discussed earlier, the story of Jesus' transfiguration in Mark 9:2-8 (found also in Matthew 17:1-8 and Luke 9:28-36) challenges us first to understand the story itself, then to believe what it conveys about Jesus. We need to be alert to the details that allude to Moses and Elijah in the Old Testament and may also reflect early Jewish traditions, especially about Moses. The story does not actually quote Scripture; it assumes the reader will take the hint. We look first at the story itself and then at its relation to 9:1.

The story moves through three phases—the setting and the Transfiguration itself (9:2-4), what Peter said (9:5-6), and what the heavenly voice said in response (9:7). (Only Luke reports the Transfiguration occurred while Jesus was praying [Luke 9:29]—a detail consistent with other parts of this Gospel in which Jesus prays just before especially important events; see Luke 3:21; 6:12; 9:18; 11:1, and what follows in each case.)

Important details in the story recall similar details in the story of Moses in Exodus 24. Just as Moses took three men with him when he went up Mount Sinai, so Jesus takes three disciples. Just as God spoke out of the cloud that had "settled" on that mountain, so here the heavenly voice speaks out of the cloud that had "overshadowed" Jesus and the three disciples. As the description of God's glory ("like a devouring fire") indicates that God's presence was visible, so the description of Jesus' clothing ("dazzling white, such as no one on earth could bleach them") is a physical sign Jesus was now transfigured (transformed) into his resurrected state (as are the saints in Revelation 3:4-5). Luke 9:29 adds that Jesus' face "changed," and Matthew 17:2 says it "shone like the sun"; these details allude to Exodus 34:29, which says that when Moses came down from Sinai he "did not know that the skin of his face shone because he had been talking with God." The allusions to Moses indicate that this story is about the manifestation of heavenly reality, confirmed by God's voice from the cloud. That Jesus was changed in the presence of the disciples means they saw (in advance) what Jesus had promised in the first Passion prediction—that he would "rise again" (Mark 8:31). (In Philippians 3:21 Paul uses a similar word—"transform"—to say that at Christ's coming our lowly bodies will become like his "glorious body" [RSV].)

Then Moses and Elijah appeared, also heavenly figures (Mark 9:4). Elijah, according to 2 Kings 2:11, had been taken to heaven by the fiery chariot. Though Moses had died, no one knew where he was buried (Deuteronomy 34:5-6). That Moses and Elijah appeared together may also suggest that they represent "the law and the prophets" (that is Scripture, as in Matthew 5:17; 7:12). Mark and Matthew report that the two figures were talking with Jesus, but Luke says they were talking *to* him about his coming death (Luke 9:31). In this way Luke prepares the reader for his report of Jesus' conversation with the two persons whom he met on Easter afternoon: "Beginning with Moses and all the prophets, he interpreted to them the things about himself in all the scriptures" (24:27).

What Peter said (Mark 9:5-6) was inappropriate, beginning with calling Jesus "Rabbi" in this situation. Exactly what he wanted to build is not entirely clear. The Greek word, rendered as "dwellings," (NRSV) and "shelters," (NIV) literally means "tents" and in the Septuagint is used also for the booths erected at the Feast of Tabernacles (Sukkoth). Mark explains that Peter made this foolish suggestion because the disciples "were terrified" (an appropriate reaction when the divine manifests itself). Luke implies that Peter wanted to extend the experience, for in this Gospel Peter made his proposal "just as they [Moses and Elijah] were leaving him" (Luke 9:33). Luke also replaces Mark's reference to the disciples' terror with a different explanation: They were sleepy but awake enough to see "his glory and the two men" beside Jesus (Luke 9:32). While Mark says Peter "did not know what *to say*" (Mark 9:6), Luke says Peter did not know "what he *said*" (Luke 9:33). Matthew apparently assumes no explanation is needed, and so gives none.

From the overshadowing cloud came the voice (of God), which first confirms Jesus' identity as God's Son with words that almost repeat what the voice had said at Jesus' baptism (Matthew 3:17; Mark 1:11; Luke 3:22), and then adds a command, "Listen to him!" (This command virtually quotes Deuteronomy 18:15, where Moses says, "The LORD your God will raise up for you a prophet like me from among your own people; you shall heed such a prophet," (literally, "Listen to him" in the Septuagint).

We can now see how the Transfiguration story fulfills Jesus' promise in Mark 9:1—some of his hearers will live to see that "the kingdom of God has come with power." The next verse sets the stage for this fulfillment: A mere six days later "some" did see, namely the three disciples.

What they saw and experienced was a preview of the risen, glorified Jesus. What they heard was God's voice commanding them to "listen to him!"—indicating that Jesus' teaching about his destiny and that of his followers was authoritative; that is, God's kingship was to become evident in their obedience to Jesus. Because the Transfiguration previewed the future, Jesus ordered the disciples to tell no one about it "until after the Son of Man had risen from the dead"—and they obeyed (Mark 9:9-10). This order carries forward the similar command to remain silent about what Peter had said at Caesarea Philippi (8:30).

When we look at Mark 8:27–9:8 as a whole, we can see what Mark has told us about Jesus' identity: He is the Messiah (though Peter does not yet understand what sort of Messiah); the expected Moseslike prophet; the Son of God, the Beloved; the Son of Man

> **Jesus was less than people hoped for because he was more than they expected.**

who "must" suffer greatly, be rejected, be killed, and then "rise again." In bringing together these various ways of identifying Jesus, Mark also implies that it is Jesus' destiny that defines, and so redefines, what it means to be Son of God, Son of Man, Moseslike prophet. To define these titles first and then apply them to Jesus (as if he fit the expectations and ideas already held) is not appropriate because his God-given destiny is what tells us who he is and who he is for us. In other words, Jesus does not fit the expected redeemer figures, because his way to the cross ruptures those expectations. Jesus was less than people hoped for because he was more than they expected. Isn't that still true?

Importance of Jesus' Identity

Along with the second Passion prediction in Mark 9:30-32 (which the disciples did not understand) and the third in 10:32-34, Mark reports several incidents that show that the disciples' failure to understand continued (9:30-37; 10:35-45).

Right after the second Passion prediction Jesus responds to their argument over which of them is the greatest; and after the third prediction James and John ask for special honor, thereby angering the other disciples. In 10:43-44 Jesus responds,

"Whoever wishes to become great among you
        must be your servant, and
whoever wishes to be first among you
        must be slave of all."

Now comes the well-known saying that links what is required of the disciples to what is required of Jesus: "For the Son of Man came not to be served but to serve, and to give his life a ransom for many" (10:45). Even though Jesus has spoken three times of his impending destiny, he has not mentioned its purpose. Now he does.

First, although suffering, rejection, and death are his God-given destiny (true also of John the Baptist, implied in Mark 9:11-13 and made explicit in Matthew 17:10-13), Jesus will "*give* his life." God's will for him and what he wills for God coincide. This congruence of his will with God's will shows Jesus to be God's Son, for the Son represents the Father.

Second, in saying that he gives his life as "a ransom for many," Jesus points out that he is not doing this for his own benefit, that his death is not the price he is willing to pay in order to remain consistent no matter what (though it was that too). Rather, his death is for the benefit of "many"—a Semitic way of saying "a multitude," a group whose size is open-ended. A ransom is what is paid to liberate others, especially captives. Jesus did not explain exactly what he had in view; the metaphor *ransom* was sufficient. Later, Christian theologians tried to explain the metaphor, and so got to asking to whom the ransom was paid (the devil?) and so forth. The saying also became important for the doctrine of Atonement; *Atonement*, however, is a metaphor that images something else—not release but the removal of the sin that keeps persons alienated from God. Although Jesus did not elaborate or explain in which sense his death would "ransom" others, or from whom or from what, Christian doctrine has consistently held that Jesus' death liberates from the power of sin those persons who believe the gospel, and has used what Jesus said here to support that teaching.

If we look again at Mark 10:45, we see that the word *for* (because) introduces Jesus' ransom saying as the reason for what he said in Mark 10:43-44—that whoever wants to be great must be the servant. In other words, Jesus' own self-giving for others is the basis for this unexpected way to be "great" or "first" (10:43-44). The basis for this trait of discipleship

> **Jesus' death made the ransom free, but it did not make it cheap.**

(self-giving) could hardly be stated more clearly. (Matthew 20:26-28 makes the connection explicit—"just as the Son of Man came." Luke 22:24-27 makes the same point in different words used at the Lord's Supper. The ransom saying is not found in Luke.) This connection between Jesus' self-giving into death for others and the disciples' way of living restates what Jesus had said before about the disciples' self-denial and cross-bearing in Mark 8:34-35. In other words, the ransomed are to live in accord with the life of the one who ransomed them; otherwise they are still in bondage to the drive to "gain the whole world." Jesus' death made the ransom free, but it did not make it cheap.

So Then

Jesus' words about self-denial and cross-bearing as marks of discipleship are especially hard to accept today, for we have absorbed the notion that real life is characterized by self-assertion. All too often we have reduced cross-bearing to putting up with an insoluble difficulty or unavoidable pain. But for Jesus, cross-bearing was not a way of talking about endurance; it was a metaphor for being willing to forgo, for the sake of others, the primacy of self-enhancement and self-assertion, and if necessary being willing to suffer—whether abuse, pain, or even death—because of loyalty to him. But in the mystery of God's ways, this way of living is not loss but gain. Jesus had the right to say such things because he lived what he said.

We should be neither surprised nor dismayed if the Transfiguration story leaves us perplexed, wondering what it all means. What finally matters is whether we believe that the Transfiguration conveys an important truth about Jesus and his destiny—and here *believing* means letting the story shape our own grasp of his significance and our response to it. Nor should we be surprised or dismayed if the story does not "open up" just now; that well may occur later, perhaps when we least expect it. The same is true of Jesus himself. What he and the deathward life he lived mean for us, and his significance for what we count on, usually unfold piecemeal because our lives are neither complete nor completely coherent. Like the first disciples, we miss the point until Jesus reminds us what following Jesus' way all comes down to— allowing Jesus' destiny to shape our own. Becoming malleable to the impact of Jesus' destiny does not occur without struggle. But those who persist and prevail will indeed "not taste death until they see that the kingdom of God has come with power" in their own lives.

Do You Want to Become His Disciples, Too?

Fear of the future does not control the disciple who has learned from Jesus that the future is in God's hands. The disciple's confidence in the future flows from relying on the God on whom Jesus relied, come what may. When this reliance on God characterizes our life day by day, we are "ransomed" from bondage to our compulsion to make our future secure by our own efforts.

How do you answer Jesus' question, "Who do you say that I am?"

Jesus is the the way, the truth and the life. When I suffer it helps to know He suffered, died & resurrected. He gives me strength He is my strength & my hope -

Prayer

You, LORD, are all I want!
　　You are my choice, and you keep me safe.
You make my life pleasant, and my future is bright.

I praise you, LORD, for being my guide.
Even in the darkest night,
　　your teachings fill my mind.
I will always look to you,
　　as you stand beside me and protect me from fear.
With all my heart, I will celebrate,
　　and I can safely rest.

(Psalm 16:5-9, CEV)

Day 3 Matthew 18:21-35; Luke 17:1-4; 1 Corinthians 6.1-8, 2 Corinthians 2:1-11; Deuteronomy 19:15-21; Proverbs 24:29; Ecclesiastes 7:5; Sirach 28:1-7

(1) Note that the obligation to forgive is followed by a warning to those who refuse to forgive (Matthew 18:21-22, 23-35).

(2) Observe that Luke 17:4 requires repentance, but Matthew 18:21-22 does not.

(3) Deuteronomy 19:15-21 is the biblical basis for the requirement of two witnesses.

(4) Note that 1 Corinthians 6:1-8 insists that Christians should settle conflicts within the church.

(5) Does Proverbs 24:29 imply forgiveness?

Day 4 Matthew 19:1-15; Mark 10:1-16; Luke 18:15-17; 1 Corinthians 7; Genesis 2:18-25; Deuteronomy 24:1-5

(1) Matthew 19:1-15 (Mark 10:1-16; Luke 18:15-17) is included here because it concerns the church's self-discipline. GC 15-2 Compare what Jesus says here about divorce with Matthew 5:32 and Luke 16:18.

(2) Notice how Matthew 19:13-15; Mark 10:13-16; and Luke 18:15-17 again focus on the child.

(3) Observe how Paul's teaching about divorce and marriage in 1 Corinthians 7:10-16 is similar to and different from the teaching of Jesus.

Day 5 1 Corinthians 12:12-26; Titus 3:1-11; Hebrews 6:1-8; James 5:19-20; Proverbs 15:1-5, 10; 17:9-10; 19:20

(1) Consider why the passages from Proverbs are appropriate here.

(2) First Corinthians 12:12-26 reminds us why one person's problems affect the whole community of faith. Compare Titus 3:10 with Matthew 18:17. Note that Hebrews 6:4-8 concerns apostasy (deliberately renouncing the faith), not moral lapse. In James 5:19-20 note the high value on restoring the wayward person to the community.

Day 6 Read and respond to "Merciful Discipline" and "Do You Want to Become His Disciples, Too?"

Prayer Concerns

Merciful Discipline

Many of Jesus' teachings assembled in Matthew 18 are found only in this chapter. Those that appear also in Mark and Luke are found in different contexts and often are worded somewhat differently. Seeing these differences reminds us that the Gospel writers often wrote down Jesus' teachings in ways that let them address the problems faced by Christians, many living outside Palestine, three to six decades after Jesus.

The Starting Point

By beginning the discourse with the story of Jesus and the children, Matthew lets Jesus point out that a proper attitude is essential for any discussion of the internal life of the church. In Matthew Jesus does not respond to the disciples' argument over who of them is the greatest (as in Mark 9:33-34 and Luke 9:46) but answers a different question, "Who is the greatest in the kingdom of heaven?" Even so, what looks like an innocent request for information may well conceal the real question, How can I get to the top? Seasoned teachers and counselors know how often the stated question is a way of asking something else. In other words, in his use of Mark, Matthew softened the disciples' real concern without doing away with it. But before saying who would be the greatest *in* the Kingdom, Jesus points out what is required to *get into* the Kingdom in the first place. To do so, he calls a child "whom he put among them." By putting the child in their midst Jesus makes it impossible for them to miss the point.

Now Jesus challenges them, "Unless you change and become like children, you will never enter the kingdom of heaven" (Matthew 18:3). (The word *change* translates a Greek term that means "turn," a synonym for "repent"; "unless you turn around," REB.) Here the change or turnaround Jesus calls for does not focus on sin but on a change of attitude, which can be much harder. But what does it mean to "become like children"? Children, after all, are often exuberant, sometimes unruly, not yet fully responsible, and sometimes cruel. The next saying (18:4) reveals what Jesus has in mind—humility. This answer to the disciples' question is remarkable, whether they asked the question out of curiosity or to find out what they must do to get to the top. (For similar sayings, see Matthew 20:26-27; 23:11-12; Mark 10:43-44; Luke 14:11; 18:14; 22:26.) Jesus is not advocating what is commonly called low esteem or any other

form of denying one's self-worth. Nor does he say, "Become humble in order to become great," for humility is not a roundabout way to achieve status.

The saying in Mark 10:15 (also Luke 18:17) makes a somewhat different point: "Whoever does not receive the kingdom of God as a little child will never enter it." Here entering the Kingdom requires being receptive, accepting the Kingdom as sheer gift. The custom of rewarding children for good behavior must not mislead us into thinking our entering the Kingdom is God's reward for a good life; rather, such a life reflects having received the Kingdom the way a child receives a gift—with joy and gratitude.

Matthew 18:5 makes another point with the child Jesus placed among the disciples: "Whoever welcomes one such child in my name welcomes me" (Mark 9:37; Luke 9:48). Here Jesus identifies with the child, just as he identified himself with the disciples on their mission: "Whoever welcomes you welcomes me, and whoever welcomes me welcomes the one who sent me" (Matthew 10:40; similarly Luke 10:16). In Matthew 25:35-36 Jesus speaks of his identification with the hungry and thirsty, the stranger, the naked, the sick, and the imprisoned. Jesus' concern for children is reported also in Matthew 19:13-15 (and Mark 10:13-16; Luke 18:15-17). When those who brought children to be touched by Jesus were turned away by the disciples, he rebuked them, saying, "Let the little children come to me, and do not stop them; for it is to such as these that the kingdom of heaven belongs"—as it does to "the poor in spirit" (Matthew 5:3). In welcoming children, the church does as Jesus did. Jesus' attitude toward children was unique for teachers of the time.

Matthew 18:6-10 assembles various sayings about "stumbling" (causing harm to someone). The first warns any disciple who might "put a stumbling block before one of these little ones who believe in me" (18:6) and who might "despise" one of them. The warning reminds the disciples that "in heaven their [the children's] angels continually see the face of my Father in heaven"(18:10). Matthew 18:7 recognizes that although "occasions for stumbling are bound to come," the person by whom they come is still responsible for the stumbling that results. Matthew 18:8-9 shifts the focus to the disciples' own stumbling (more or less repeating 5:29-30). By inserting here these sayings about the hand, foot, or eye that may cause stumbling, Matthew implies that the disciples' own stumbling is the stumbling block for "these little ones."

Despising "one of these little ones" is a serious offense because "their angels continually see" God. The phrase probably expresses the old idea that each of us has a heavenly counterpart. If so, then whoever despises the earthly little one also despises the angelic counterpart who has the privilege of seeing God. The purpose of mentioning "their angels" is not to provide information about the angels but to underscore that the "little ones" are important in the eyes of God. This purpose might be reflected by those manuscripts that add 18:11: "For the Son of Man came to save the lost."

Notice how 18:1-10 carries out the saying in 7:3-5 about taking the log out of one's own eye before removing the speck in the neighbor's eye: Before giving directions for disciplining someone else, an offender in the church, Matthew 18 first insists that the disciples must have the right attitude themselves and so are not the cause of someone else's "stumbling."

When Trouble Comes

Also, the way Matthew 18:12-20 is put together is worth careful attention. Matthew 18:12-14 points in two directions. On one hand, after the parable of the good shepherd who rejoices when he finds the stray sheep, Jesus' comment ("So it is not the will of your Father in heaven that one of these little ones should be lost") links the parable backward to 18:10 ("do not despise one of these little ones").

Now the "little ones" takes on another or an additional meaning—the stray sheep, the wayward Christian. On the other hand, the parable also points ahead to 18:15-17, the procedures to be used when one "member of the church" (literally "your brother") offends another. The comment in 18:15, that if the procedure is successful, "you have regained that one" clearly is like the shepherd's retrieving the stray sheep. In other words, by putting these sayings side by side, Matthew makes an important point: It is God's will that offenders in the church be restored, not excluded. (Luke 15:4-7 tells the parable in a different setting.)

> It is God's will that offenders in the church be restored, not excluded.

The disciplinary procedures (Matthew 18:15-20), found only here, are stated clearly. First, the offended person is to go privately to the offender in order to resolve the problem. If that does not work, a second attempt should follow, this time with two witnesses so that the dispute is not a matter of "my word against his or her word." If that doesn't work, the whole congregation is to take up the matter; and if then the offender "refuses to listen even to the church," that person is to be treated as an outsider ("as a Gentile and a tax collector"). The stray sheep who refuses to be restored to the flock remains outside the fold; the shepherd has done his best.

> The stray sheep who refuses to be restored to the flock remains outside the fold; the shepherd has done his best.

Because the church takes the last step, 18:18-20 goes on to explain the authority of the church to exclude the stubborn offender. Here too the passage places side by side sayings that can be understood separately. In fact, the *first* (18:18) is a variation of what Jesus had said to Peter at Caesarea Philippi: "Whatever you bind on earth will be bound in heaven, and whatever you loose on earth will be loosed in heaven" (16:19). There the authority was given to Peter (*you* is singular); here the church has it (*you* is plural in 18:18). The *second* (18:19-20), found only here, promises that God will grant the prayer shared by two or three disciples because Jesus is among them when they pray. In this setting, the promise assumes that the church's "binding" and "loosing" will include prayer asking God to confirm the congregation's action.

We return now to 16:17-19, which reports Jesus' response to Peter's words, "You are the Messiah, the Son of the living God" (only in Matthew does Peter say "the Son of the living God"; the disciples had already said, "Truly, you are the Son of God" in 14:33). Recall that in Mark and Luke Jesus responds by ordering the disciples "not to tell anyone" about him. In Matthew, however, Jesus congratulates Peter: "Blessed are you, Simon son of Jonah! For flesh and blood [human beings] has not revealed this to you, but my Father in heaven" (Matthew 16:17). That is, rightly identifying Jesus is not a matter of shrewd human insight but the result of God's disclosure. Paul makes the same point in different language: "No one can say 'Jesus is Lord' except by the Holy Spirit" (1 Corinthians 12:3).

Jesus continues: "And I tell you, you are Peter [Greek: *Petros*, rock], and on this rock [*petra*] I will build my church, and the gates of Hades will not prevail against it"—that is, death will not have the power to limit what Jesus will build; those in the church will defeat death. (See "Renaming Simon," page 131.) Although Protestants often have claimed that the "rock" on which Jesus will build his church is Peter's confession, today most scholars agree that the "rock" is Peter himself. However, Protestants continue to point out that nothing is said here about Peter's handing on the keys to his successors, as the Roman Catholic Church maintains. However, Protestant and Catholic scholars agree that the "binding" and "loosing" is an expression referring to the forgiveness of sins. That is, at Caesarea Philippi Peter has the authority to forgive ("loose") or withhold forgiveness ("bind"); in Matthew 18:18 the church has this authority, as it does in John 20:23, where the resurrected Jesus tells the disciples, "If you forgive the sins of any, they are forgiven them; if you retain the sins of any, they are retained" (here too *you* is plural). In none of these passages is forgiveness of sins a general amnesty announced by the church "to whom it may concern."

The Evangelist who wrote Matthew appears to have been quite aware that this authority to forgive or withhold forgiveness brings an awesome responsibility; for now in Matthew 18:21-22 he reports Peter's question, "Lord, if another member of the church [literally 'my brother'] sins against me [picking up 18:15], how often should I forgive? As many as seven times?" Jesus' answer is astounding: There is no limit! In Luke this teaching has a different setting—and is put differently as well: "If the same person sins against you seven times a day, and turns back to you seven times and says, 'I repent,' you must forgive" (Luke 17:4). The obligation to forgive repeatedly puts a certain bite into the disciples' own prayer for forgiveness: "Forgive us our debts, / as we also have forgiven our debtors" (Matthew 6:12), especially in light of 6:15: "If you do not forgive others, neither will your Father forgive your trespasses."

The parable of the forgiven debtor makes the same point. The unusual length and amount of detail in this parable, found only in Matthew 18:23-35, underscore its importance. The plot takes for granted the custom of putting into prison those who cannot repay their loans. Both the repeated use of "fellow slaves" (18:28, 31, 33) and

the reference to "your brother or sister" in 18:35 connect this parable with Peter's question in 18:21, showing that what is in view in Matthew 18 as a whole is the internal life of the church.

On Community Discipline

Matthew's paragraph about church discipline is simple and brief compared with the rules of the community at Qumran. One of the first Dead Sea Scrolls found is a document called *The Community Rule* that states the rules for admission to the community and for remaining a member in good standing. One passage is somewhat like Matthew 18:15-17. The *Rule* says that members should rebuke one another in truth, humility, and charity, not with anger. It also says that the rebuke should occur on the same day as the offense and adds, "Let no man accuse his companion before the Congregation without having admonished him in the presence of witnesses." In the *Rule* specific offenses get specific punishments: for example, six months penance for deliberately lying, deceiving, or taking revenge; thirty days for whoever has "guffawed foolishly"; ten days for interrupting. Matthew 18 differs from the *Rule* by the concern for the "little ones" and by the emphasis on forgiveness. The *Rule* expresses the community's insistence on being pure; in Matthew Jesus desires that no one be excluded except as a last resort. Moreover, Matthew 5:21-47, in contrast with *The Community Rule*, specifies no punishment for the person who does not do as Jesus says.

Even though the Gospel of Matthew was written a generation after Paul, seeing how the apostle handled problems within the church is useful in putting the whole phenomenon of early church discipline in broader perspective. To be sure, Paul's letters addressed problems that arose in congregations that had come into existence only recently through his own mission. Matthew, on the other hand, was written for a church with a much longer history, whose beginnings were not the result of the Evangelist's preaching. Paul wrote out of a sense of responsibility for maintaining the faithfulness of his new churches in a way that Matthew did not. Indeed, Paul could write, "I am not writing this to make you ashamed, but to admonish you as my beloved children . . . . Indeed, in Christ Jesus I became your father through the gospel" (1 Corinthians 4:14-15). Paul, however, nowhere provides a set of procedures for handling problems in his churches (in 6:1-6 he simply insists that grievances should be settled within the church, not taken to court).

What he wrote are various counsels for treating specific problems whose character and causes we can only surmise, such as 1 Corinthians 7, which concerns questions of marriage and divorce. So too, in 2 Corinthians 2:1-11, exactly what caused the painful conflict between Paul and an unnamed person (during the apostle's visit to the church in Corinth) is obscure. Of interest here, however, is Paul's emphasis on forgiveness; without forgiveness the church would remain polarized and Satan would be the winner.

In 1 Corinthians 5, however, we find no talk of forgiveness, apparently because the problem is not strained personal relations but an immoral action (a man is cohabiting with his stepmother; that is, incest). Apparently, some church members approve, perhaps because they see the man's action demonstrating the idea that salvation is for the soul but not for the body. This inference is precisely what Paul rejects because Christ's resurrection implies the resurrection of our bodies, so that "the Lord [is] for the body" (6:13). What Paul calls for now is not forgiveness (presumably the man insists on keeping this relationship) but expulsion. He uses the imagery of the yeast to say what we might say about the "bad apple"—get rid of it before all the apples are spoiled. A person who deliberately violates the truth of the gospel forfeits his or her place in the church, as Paul sees matters. So too Hebrews 6:4-8 denies forgiveness to apostates, those who renounce Christ. What to do with those who because of persecution renounced Christ but repented later would become a major problem for the church, not only in the third century when the North African church was torn apart by this question but also in our own day. In this light we are aware that while Matthew 10:21 expects betrayal in time of persecution, nothing is said about what to do about the betrayer. Matthew 18, on the other hand, apparently has in view personal conflicts and moral lapses (the stray sheep) and so emphasizes restoration and forgiveness, in ordinary times.

So Then

The procedures on discipline outlined in Matthew 18:15-17 are useful reminders that a perfect church is hard to find— though some people go from church to church looking for one. In fact, there has never been a church or congregation that is 100 percent pure. Even the book of Acts, which celebrates the harmony of the earliest church in Jerusalem (Acts 4:32-35), goes on to report that a couple, Ananias and Sapphira, withheld some of the money they got from selling their property while implying that they gave it all to the common fund (5:1-11), just as it reports that the Greek-speaking believers grumbled because they thought their poor widows did not get a fair share of the fund (6:1). Until the Kingdom has fully come or we are in heaven, Christians remain flawed, sometimes with devastating consequences. The common expression, "Nobody's perfect," is a fact, not a justification for doing wrong.

The procedures in Matthew 18:15-17 also remind us that unless personal conflicts are resolved, they eventually affect the larger community, the congregation. Many church conflicts could be avoided if personal conflicts were resolved early on, even following the procedures in Matthew.

The unusual passage about discipline procedures should not overshadow the rest of the chapter, beginning with the concern lest "these little ones" stumble over the behavior of the adults. The text does not spell out what might cause them to take offense; this silence leaves it up to us to identify the stumbling blocks.

Especially important in this chapter is forgiveness—not simply because forgiveness is often difficult. Jesus' teaching is hard to appropriate properly because 18:21-22 seems to ask the offended person to forgive endlessly even if the offender does not ask for forgiveness, though Luke 17:4 avoids this by making forgiveness depend on repentance.

The parable that concludes Matthew 18 makes another point that we must keep in mind: The Christian who has been forgiven so much by God must surely forgive lesser offenses by others. Otherwise, we nullify God's forgiveness.

By having these sayings of Jesus follow one another, each with its own accent, Matthew created a body of teachings that invites—indeed, requires—careful thought and pastoral care for one another that is both prudent and wise. Neither "binding" nor "loosing" should be done rashly, for God's will is the restoration of the stray to the community that looks to Jesus.

Do You Want to Become His Disciples, Too?

The way of Jesus requires letting go as well as holding firmly. It requires letting go of grudges (forgiveness means letting go), of the pride that keeps us from saying, "I was wrong," or the urge to say, "None of your business" to the person who wants to be helpful. The way of Jesus also requires holding firmly to the conviction that God has let go of whatever has come between us and the Eternal so that we can let go of whatever has come between us and other people and make a fresh start. That conviction is rooted in the good news. To accept God's forgiveness is to accept the obligation to forgive—and to accept forgiveness.

What surprises you or shocks you about the Jesus who comes through this week's readings?

_____

_____

_____

_____

_____

Prayer

I am your servant, LORD, and you have kept your promise
  to treat me with kindness.
Give me wisdom and good sense. I trust your commands.
Once you corrected me for not obeying you,
  but now I obey.
You are kindhearted, and you do good things,
  so teach me your laws . . . .
When you corrected me, it did me good
  because it taught me to study your laws.
I would rather obey you
  than to have a thousand pieces of silver and gold.

(Psalm 119:65-68, 71-72, CEV)

Renaming Simon

Although the New Testament indicates, in various places, that Jonah's son Simon was renamed Peter, it provides no uniform account of the circumstances in which this renaming occurred. "Peter" is based on a pun also in Aramaic (*kepha'*, meaning rock). Sometimes the Aramaic word was transliterated into Greek (and then into English) as "Cephas" (as in the early tradition quoted by Paul in 1 Corinthians 15:5: The risen Christ "appeared to Cephas"); at other times, Paul uses the Greek translation "Peter" (as in Galatians 2:7-8). Once in Luke (5:8) and often in John (for example, 1:40; 6:68; 13:6; 18:15), he is called Simon Peter, but never so by Paul. In John, Jesus renamed Simon when they first met: " 'So you are Simon the son of John? You shall be called Cephas' (which means Peter, [*rock* in Aramaic and Greek])." Mark and Luke point out that Jesus renamed Simon (Mark 3:16; Luke 6:14) but do not say when he did so. Only Matthew 16:18 reports that Jesus renamed him in response to his confession, "You are the Messiah, the Son of the living God." According to Mark 3:17 Jesus also gave the sons of Zebedee a new name, "Boanerges, that is, Sons of Thunder," apparently a nickname that recognized their forceful disposition. *Peter,* on the other hand, expresses his role, first as leader of the disciples, later as leader of the earliest church.

16 The Journey Is the Way

Blessed . . . are those who hear the word of God
and obey it!
(Luke 11:28)

They Have No Wine

"Nothing ventured, nothing gained" reminds us that life without risk becomes dull. On the other hand, "Look before you leap" warns against impulsive action. We get lots of advice, but whose advice is sound? And how do we acquire the wisdom to make the right choice? We are often told, "You learn by experience." True enough. But whose experience? The experience of the hesitant usually reinforces hesitation, but that of the adventurous encourages our own venturing.

Beginning With Moses and All the Prophets

We focus on a distinctive part of Luke, specifically Luke 9:51–18:14. Up to 9:50 the story in Luke generally follows Mark and beginning at 18:15 will do so again. This section reports a variety of Jesus' teachings, some of which appear in different settings in Matthew and Mark, but many of which are found only here. (See "Stories and Teachings of Jesus Only in Luke 9:51–18:14," page 141.) Because the section is rather long, about as long as all of Mark 1–9, we will attend to those passages found only in Luke, while looking occasionally also at similar passages in Matthew and Mark.

Day 1 **Luke 9:51–10:42;** Leviticus 19:1-18; Deuteronomy 6:1-9; 2 Kings 1

(1) Note that Luke 9:51 introduces the whole narrative that follows by referring to the Ascension (stated in 24:51 and reported in Acts 1:9-11). James and John's question in Luke 9:54 might reflect the story in Second Kings.

(2) Luke 9:1-2 reports that Jesus sent the twelve disciples on a mission (like Matthew 10:5 and Mark 6:7), but only Luke 10:1-20 reports a mission by seventy (some manuscripts say seventy-two) and their return. Note that in 10:17-18 Jesus interprets the emissaries' exorcisms as Satan's "fall."

(3) In 10:25-28, note how Jesus answers the lawyer's question by combining Deuteronomy 6:5 and Leviticus 19:18. Compare the lawyer's question in Luke with that of the scribes in Mark 12:28. Note also how the lawyer's second question, in Luke 10:29, leads into the parable of the good Samaritan.

(4) Observe how 10:42 emphasizes the importance of Jesus' teaching in 10:39.

Day 2 Luke 11–12; 1 Timothy 6:17-19; 2 Chronicles 24:17-27; Ecclesiastes 8:14-15; Micah 7:2-7; Sirach 5:1-13; 11:14-19

(1) Notice how Luke 11:5-8, which emphasizes persistence in asking, leads into 11:9-13, which is almost identical with Matthew 7:7-11.

(2) Observe how in Luke 11:27-28 Jesus shifts the focus away from himself (expressed in the woman's word about his mother) and toward his teaching.

(3) Observe that 12:13-34 assembles Jesus' various teachings that contrast trust in God with trust in wealth.

(4) Note that 12:35-59 places together different sayings, but that each of them contains a warning.

Day 3 Luke 13–14; Psalm 118:19-29; Proverbs 25:6-7; Sirach 31:12-22

(1) In Luke 13:1-9, notice how the parable of the fig tree implies that God has granted time for repentance before the disaster comes (according to 13:1-5).

(2) Note who warns Jesus in 13:31; note also that Jesus' reply is a veiled Passion prediction, followed by the lament over Jerusalem (13:34-35), which in Matthew appears at the end of the seven woes against the Pharisees (Matthew 23:37-39).

(3) Observe that in Luke 14:1-24 Jesus' teachings are given at the Pharisee's dinner. Compare 14:1-6 with 13:15 and Matthew 12:11.

(4) Observe that Sirach 31:12-22 is more concerned with manners than is Jesus in Luke 14:7-14.

(5) In 14:25-35, note that Jesus' words about discipleship are addressed to those who already were "traveling with him."

Day 4 **Luke 15–16;** Psalms 51; 139:1-18; Isaiah 58:6-12; Sirach 4:1-10

(1) Note that the theme of "lost and found" ties together the three parables in Luke 15, and that the stray sheep in Matthew 18:12 is the lost sheep in Luke. Note also that each parable ends on the same theme—joy.

(2) Observe how the use of money connects the parable in 16:1-9 and the saying in 16:10-13.

(3) Note that the parable in 16:19-31 makes two related points, one in verses 25-26, the other in verses 27-31.

Day 5 **Luke 17:1–18:14;** Genesis 19:15-29; Ezekiel 33:10-20

(1) Note that in Luke 17:7-10 Jesus does not tell a parable but makes a comparison that could have been given as a parable; note also that the comparison requires the master to have one slave.

(2) Do not miss the fact that in 17:11-19 the one grateful man is a Samaritan.

(3) Note the similarity between the persistent widow in 18:1-8 and the persistent friend in 11:5-8; but note also the differences.

(4) Note how 18:9 becomes a setting for the parable in the same way that 16:14 does. Note that the Pharisee and the tax collector represent types of persons and how the conclusion expands the point of the parable itself.

Day 6 Read and respond to "The Journey Is the Way" and "Do You Want to Become His Disciples, Too?"

Prayer Concerns

134

The Journey Is the Way

Luke 9:51 marks a turning point in Luke's story of Jesus. While Luke, like Matthew and Mark, has reported that Jesus twice foretold his death (Luke 9:22, 44), only Luke says that from this point on Jesus was determined to go to Jerusalem. Later, when Luke's account again follows Mark's, Jesus brings together his words about the suffering Son of Man and the outcome of this journey: "See, we are going up to Jerusalem, and everything that is written about the Son of Man by the prophets will be accomplished" (Luke 18:31). What will happen to Jesus there is not to be understood as a series of unfortunate circumstances or the result of miscalculation; rather, he will seize his destiny—a point 9:51 clearly implies but does not need to say. Everything Luke reports between 9:51 and 18:31 occurs on the way to Jerusalem. Luke reminds us of this journey repeatedly (10:38; 13:22; 14:25; 17:11), though we never learn exactly where Jesus went. Luke implies that the names of the stopovers are unimportant. What is important is that the journey to Jerusalem is really the way of Jesus. (Recall that in Acts Luke refers to the early believers as those of "the Way.")

During the journey the disciples learn Jesus' way, often by what he says to them (Luke 10:1-2, 23; 11:1-2, 5; 12:1, 4, 8, 22, 42; 16:1; 17:1, 5-6, 22; 18:1, 16, 28-29); otherwise, by overhearing Jesus when he speaks to others. Luke suggests that discipleship *is* a journey in Jesus' way.

The Journey as Jesus' Way

Luke 9:51-62 shows that Jesus, not the disciple, determines the shape of discipleship. The Gospel shows this by putting side by side the story of the Samaritans' lack of welcome in 9:51-56 and three sayings of Jesus to would-be disciples in 9:57-62 (the first two sayings are found also in Matthew 8:19-22).

> **Jesus, not the disciple, determines the shape of discipleship.**

According to the first Passion prediction Jesus will "be rejected" by religious leaders. So the story of Jesus' journey to Jerusalem begins with rejection (Luke 9:51-56)—hardly accidental, for according to Luke, Jesus' ministry in Galilee also began with rejection, in Nazareth (4:16-30). Now the next phase of the story also begins with rejection, this time in Samaria. It is Luke's way of anticipating what lies ahead.

A glance at a map shows that the most direct route from Galilee to Jerusalem takes the traveler through Samaria, unfriendly territory. Perhaps because of the long-standing ill will between Jews and Samaritans (John 4:9), Jesus sent emissaries ahead "to make ready for him"—to find lodging and perhaps gather an audience. But the Samaritans refused when they sensed that Jesus' determination to go to Jerusalem implied rejection of their own religion, centered on their rival temple on Mount Gerizim. Upon hearing of this rejection, James and John wanted to call fire from heaven to punish the inhospitable Samaritans, as Elijah had done (2 Kings 1:10-16); in fact, many manuscripts add "as Elijah did" at the end of Luke 9:54. But Jesus rebuked them; a number of manuscripts add, "and said, 'You do not know what spirit you are of, for the Son of Man has not come to destroy the lives of human beings but to save them' " at 9:55-56. But Jesus is not another "Elijah," and so he responded differently—"They went on to another village." Jesus and his followers do what he tells his emissaries to do in 10:10-11: When people reject you, move on. (Matthew 10:14 is more explicit.)

In 9:57-62 Luke has assembled three incidents whose outcomes are not recorded in order to focus on Jesus' words. In the first and third, someone volunteers to follow Jesus; but in the second, Jesus invites someone to follow. In response to the first person's eagerness to follow wherever Jesus goes, Jesus points out that he (as the Son of Man) has no space of his own, implying that the volunteer must be ready to be on the move constantly and that the man's "wherever you go" will cost more than he may have thought. In response to the man who wants to fulfill his family duties first, Jesus replies harshly, "Let the dead [the spiritually dead] bury their own dead [the deceased]." Matthew 8:22 has the same reply, but in Luke Jesus goes on to tell the man to proclaim the Kingdom. To the third, who recognizes that following Jesus means leaving family and so wants to say good-bye first, Jesus says, "No one who puts a hand to the plow and looks back is fit for the kingdom of God" (Luke 9:62). Following Jesus trumps even family obligations.

Later, in 12:51-53, Jesus says he did not come to bring peace "but rather division" in households. In 14:25-33 he is even clearer: "Whoever comes to me and does not hate father and mother, wife and children, brothers and sisters, yes, and even life itself, cannot be my disciple." (Here *hate* is a deliberate exaggeration designed to emphasize the difference from its opposite, *love*—devotion or attachment as in 16:13.) Jesus continues (14:27), "Whoever does not carry the cross and follow me cannot be my disciple." A similar form of these sayings is found in Matthew 10:37-38, but only in Luke does Jesus go on to warn against starting something a person cannot finish (Luke 14:28-32), adding the most severe demand of all: "So therefore, none of you can become my disciple if you do not give up all your possessions" (14:33). The would-be disciple should indeed count the cost before identifying with this Jesus who had left both his family and his trade.

Sell, Give, Follow

More than any other Gospel, Luke contains sayings in which Jesus is alert to the dangers of wealth. He did not regard it as a neutral thing, as an inert possession, because he saw its power over those who possessed it, or who insisted on acquiring it, as shown in Luke 12:13-21. The passage begins with a request from someone in a crowd, "Teacher, tell my brother to divide the family inheritance with me." Instead of inquiring about the dispute between the heirs, Jesus flatly refuses to get involved. Rather, he uses the request to address the crowd, "Take care! Be on your guard against all kinds of greed; for one's life does not consist in the abundance of possessions." Then he tells the parable of the rich man who planned to become even richer but whose sudden death put an end to his plans to "relax, eat, drink, be merry." The last line expresses the alternative Jesus saw: "So it is with those who store up treasures for themselves but are not rich toward God." Those whose wealth is for themselves are poor with respect to God.

> The would-be disciple should indeed count the cost before identifying with this Jesus who had left both his family and his trade.

Nowhere do the Gospels report that Jesus urges tithing as a way to keep control over wealth. Not that he opposed tithing in principle. Rather, he saw that giving ten percent does not necessarily get at the real issue, so he criticized those who tithe even herbs while neglecting more important matters of the Law—justice and love of God (Luke 11:42; Matthew 23:23 has "justice and mercy and faith"). As Jesus sees it, the way to end the power of wealth over a person is to get rid of it altogether (Luke 14:33).

Luke is not the only Gospel in which Jesus insists that the power of wealth over a person must be broken if a person is to follow him, for Matthew and Luke report Mark's story of Jesus' exchange with the rich man and Jesus' exchange with Peter that follows (Mark 10:17-31; Matthew 19:16-30; Luke 18:18-30). In all three accounts, the man asks what he must do "to inherit eternal life." The question is appropriate, and the man is not rebuked for asking it. And what is the answer? Jesus quotes from the Ten Commandments. This answer disappoints the man who claims he has been obeying them all his adult life. So Jesus says there is one thing he has not done, though Jesus does not say what it is. But what he goes on to say implies the man has not really obeyed the first commandment ("You shall have no other gods before me"; Exodus 20:3), for Jesus tells him, "Sell all that you own and distribute the money to the poor, and you will have treasure in heaven; then come, follow me" (Luke 18:22). Jesus sees that this answer is even more disappointing, and so tells the man that it is indeed hard for those with wealth to enter the Kingdom—harder in fact than getting a camel through a needle's eye.

Mark and Matthew say the man went away when he heard Jesus tell him to sell everything, so these Gospels have Jesus make the same emphasis to the disciples. Understandably, they now ask, "Then who can be saved?" Jesus' reply points to the power of God: "What is impossible for mortals is possible for God"—implying that severing personal reliance on wealth too is a miracle, because this detachment from wealth is not achieved by determination alone or by repudiating wealth and the status that goes with it. The self-impoverishment Jesus has in view entails more than selling: It entails also giving the proceeds to the poor and then joining Jesus. The three steps of selling, giving, and following are one act in which having no other gods becomes concrete. And that act is as miraculous as the paralyzed man's obeying Jesus' command to get up, pick up his bed, and go home (Luke 5:24)—maybe more so.

Somewhat like the man who said he has already obeyed the commandments, Peter now says, "Look, we *have* left our homes and followed you" (18:28). Jesus' response restates what he said to the rich man and goes beyond it as well: "Truly I tell you, there is no one who has left house or wife or brothers or parents or children, for the sake of the kingdom of God who will not get back very much more in this age, and in the age to come eternal life" (18:29-30). With this the scene ends where it began (18:18)—eternal life. Luke does not spell out what the "very much more" includes but leaves it open so that each person will discover what it is. In Mark, Jesus' form of the promise is extravagant (perhaps because it mocks the disciples' concern): "a hundredfold now in this age—houses, brothers and sisters, mothers and children, and fields, [and so includes a bite] *with persecutions*—and in the age to come eternal life" (Mark 10:30). The new family is made up of all Jesus' followers, in accord with what Jesus said in Mark 3:35, "Whoever does the will of God is my brother and sister and mother."

On the Use and Misuse of Money

The two parables in Luke 16 (found only here) illustrate how money can be used shrewdly or callously. The first (16:1-8) bristles with so many problems that scholars continue to debate not only what it means but even where it ends. The interpretation offered here is plausible but not certain. The interpretation depends especially on how the reader understands the situation that the story takes for granted, and on what the reader makes of the first part of 16:8 ("And his master commended the dishonest manager because he had acted shrewdly"); the rest of 16:8 is a comment on the story.

The story assumes that the manager has the right to make loans, perhaps to tenant farmers, in the name of the owner of the estate. The story may also assume that the IOU to the owner included the amount taken by the manager who made the loan; that is, his own percentage or "cut"—a practice attested elsewhere in antiquity. If this practice is assumed here, then we no longer need be perplexed that Jesus seems to be commending dishonesty. In fact, 16:8 does not say the manager is commended because he was dishonest; it says the dishonest manager (who had already been squandering the owner's property) was shrewd in changing the IOU's.

The parable is about an irresponsible manager who, hearing that he is being fired, looks out for his future by forfeiting that part of the debt repayment that he expected to get for himself, in one case 100 percent interest, in the other 25 percent. As a result, the owner would lose nothing, but the manager might be welcomed into the homes of those whose debt has been reduced. He still lost his job, but even so, the owner commended him "because he had acted shrewdly."

To this parable are attached various sayings, beginning with the comment at the end of 16:8, which observes that such people as the dishonest manager show more shrewdness in looking out for themselves than those who are enlightened by Jesus' message but do not act with similar shrewdness because they fail to see that his message creates an urgent situation. The next saying (16:9) urges the disciples to "use your worldly wealth [Greek: 'mammon of unrighteousness' or 'unrighteous mammon'] to win friends for yourselves, so that when money is a thing of the past you may be received into an eternal home" (REB). This saying uses the parable to say, in effect, act now to secure your future with God. It might also suggest that we do this by giving our wealth to the poor.

The parable of the rich man and Lazarus (16:19-31) illustrates the great reversal expressed in Luke's form of the first beatitude: "Blessed are you who are poor, / for yours is the kingdom of God," as well as its counterpart, "But woe to you who are rich, / for you have received your consolation (Luke 6:20, 24). In the parable the poor, sore-covered, and scavenging Lazarus goes to Abraham (in heaven); but the rich man goes to Hades, where his torment is worsened by seeing where Lazarus now is. It's both too late and impossible to ease the rich man's agony now. Then the parable makes another point: If the rich man's brothers would be merciful to the poor (as a result of listening to Moses and the prophets), they could avoid ending up where he now is—so he thinks. But in fact, they will not listen, "even if someone rises from the dead" to tell them to change their ways. In other words, despite Jesus' resurrection and the gospel message, some people simply refuse to listen because they are too enslaved by the power of self-indulgent wealth and the accompanying disregard of the poor at their door (16:19-21). By placing this parable near Jesus' words in 16:9, Luke implies that had the rich man used his *mammon* to befriend Lazarus, he too would have been received into an eternal home.

Good News and Bad News

The great reversal expressed in the beatitude and woe in Luke 6:20 and 24 rests on the conviction that God will make right the plight of the poor. The same conviction is expressed in the parable of the unjust judge "who neither feared God nor had respect for people" (18:2-8). Nonetheless, a widow kept pestering him with her plea for justice, for what we might call "judicial relief." After refusing repeatedly, he finally concluded that he would grant her request rather than be worn out by her persistence. Jesus now points out, reasoning from the lesser to the greater, that if this scoundrel finally grants justice, God will surely grant justice to his chosen ones who cry to him day and night; moreover, God will not "delay" because the Kingdom is at hand. While the parable has in view those deprived of justice, Luke applies it to the disciples, for he introduces it by writing, "Then Jesus told them a parable about their need to pray always and not to lose heart" (18:1). The journey is arduous, and even the disciples are vulnerable to despair. They too need to hear the promise of the great turnaround, lest the good news become old news with less and less capacity to effect change.

Despite Jesus' resurrection and the gospel message, some people simply refuse to listen because they are too enslaved by the power of self-indulgent wealth and the accompanying disregard of the poor at their door.

In Luke 12:1-12 there is good news for the disciples. In fact, Luke points out that despite the opportunity to address thousands, Jesus spoke first to the disciples (12:1). He began with a warning against the bad influence of the Pharisees' hypocrisy (this saying has a different setting in Mark 8:15 and Matthew 16:6), to which Luke has added other sayings, most of which appear in Jesus' second discourse in Matthew 10 (the mission charge to the twelve disciples). Of special interest is the way Jesus' words to the disciples end in Luke 12:11-12. Jesus says, "When they bring you before the synagogues, the rulers, and the authorities, do not worry about how you are to defend yourselves or what you are to say; for the Holy Spirit will teach you at that very hour what you ought to say." And according to Acts, so it was. In Acts 4, which reports that Peter and John were brought to trial before the authorities, the narrator introduced Peter's words this way: "Then Peter, filled with the Holy Spirit, said" (4:8; also Stephen in 7:54-56).

Jesus, having addressed others (Luke 12:13-21), again speaks to the disciples (12:22-34), using words that we find in the Sermon on the Mount concerning freedom from worry about life's necessities (Matthew 6:25-33, 19-21). Tucked into this collection of teachings is Luke 12:32, found only in Luke: "Do not be afraid, little flock, for it is your Father's good pleasure to give you the kingdom." Luke seems to sense that on the journey the disciples too needed to hear good news. They still do.

To others, however, Jesus brings bad news. Luke 13:1-9 begins with the report that someone told Jesus "about Galileans whose blood Pilate had mingled with their sacrifices." (Josephus does not mention this.) That is, the Roman troops massacred some Galileans, presumably pilgrims, while they presented their animal sacrifices at the Temple. We can only surmise why this bad news was brought to Jesus. Perhaps the informers hoped that he, being a Galilean, would loose a tirade against Pilate, known for his cruelty. In any case, Jesus makes a shocking two-part response, first referring to the massacred Galileans, then to those who were killed by a falling tower. Neither group was killed for being worse sinners than others. God doesn't work that way. Then Jesus brought his bad news: "Unless you repent, you will all perish just as they did." The threat of destruction hangs over everyone's head; only repentance—a moral U-turn—can avert it. The parable of the fruitless fig tree follows (13:6-9) and makes the same point: Unless the tree bears fruit, it will be cut down. (The "fruit" alludes to the expression "fruits worthy of repentance" as in 3:8.) In this context, the parable also suggests that one cannot evade repenting by talking about the "just deserts" that other people got for their sins; to the contrary, since everyone needs to repent, those who are alive still have time to do so—a hint of good news even in bad news.

The parable in Luke 18:9-14 (only in Luke) contains both bad news and good news, depending on which of the two persons represents us. Jesus uses the Pharisee and tax collector as representatives of two kinds of religiosity: The former thinks he does not need to repent because he is already righteous; the latter knows he must repent, for in asking for God's mercy he admits he has done wrong. Jesus does not imply the Pharisee is wrong in what he says about himself. The trouble is that in praying he positions himself before God as a good, devout

138

person who even fasts and tithes and so assumes he does not need God's mercy—that's for sinners. And so he is blind to his need to repent of being so proud of his moral and religious achievements. Luke did not err in introducing this parable as Jesus' word "to some who trusted in themselves that they were righteous and regarded others with contempt." This Pharisee is bad news for all religious people with such attitudes, but the guilty tax collector is good news for all those who are not ashamed to admit to God that they are not righteous, and so ask for God's mercy.

That there is good news for the sinner who repents is emphasized in the three "lost and found" parables in Luke 15. Here too, Luke tells us how he wants us to understand these parables: They are Jesus' response to those who grumbled because he "welcomes sinners and eats with them" (15:1-2). As the shepherd rejoices because he found the hundredth sheep, "Just so, I tell you, there will be more joy in heaven over one sinner who repents than over ninety-nine righteous persons who need no repentance" (15:7). (The last phrase does not mean that 99 percent of the people are righteous; nor are we to infer that Jesus means "who think they need no repentance." Rather, because the lost sheep is the sinner who is retrieved by repentance, the logic of the parable requires that the ninety-nine need no repentance because they are not lost.) Also the parable of the lost and found coin emphasizes joy in heaven "over one sinner who repents"—even though neither parable mentioned repentance (who ever heard of a repenting sheep or a repenting coin?).

The parable of the two sons (15:11-32), however, emphasizes precisely the repentance of the younger brother (15:17-19, 21). Moreover, the rejoicing that was only mentioned in the first two parables is sketched in the third, which concludes with the father's explanation to the angry older brother, "This brother of yours was dead and has come to life; he was lost and has been found"— actually he was not "found" but returned (turned back, repented).

So Then

Luke's travel account gives us much to ponder, beginning with the figure of Jesus. The Jesus we see in this part of Luke as a whole is both a many-sided person and a man who knows who he is and what he is to do. Sometimes he warns; sometimes he assures. Both beatitudes and woes are on his lips. He tells parables, even long ones, and at other times he makes his point with terse, memorable statements. He prays and gives a prayer to the disciples. At times he addresses the crowds he attracted; at other times he speaks privately to his disciples. He accepts a Pharisee's invitation to dinner but criticizes his host. Some Pharisees try to provoke him to say something they can use against him; other Pharisees warn him that Herod Antipas wants to kill him. Not only does he speak often of the way wealth perverts one's relation to God, but he also says a person must choose God or mammon, calling would-be followers to sell what they own and give the money to the poor. He has a way of knowing what each person or group needs to hear; this sense of specific need lies at the root of his many-sidedness, for again and again we see him trying to get through to people so they will change their ways, make a U-turn, repent. The more attached they are to what they are, the more he requires in order to free them. He wants people to heed him, not primarily to think well of him. When someone calls him "Good Teacher," he refuses to claim goodness for himself, saying that only God is good (Luke 18:18-19). He seems determined to leave no one as found. The readers of this part of Luke know themselves addressed by this fascinating, sometimes frustrating Jesus who tells them what they *need* to hear more often than what they *want* to hear.

> The readers of this part of Luke know themselves addressed by this fascinating, sometimes frustrating Jesus who tells them what they *need* to hear more often than what they *want* to hear.

Following such a person is not easy. He knows it and does not hesitate to say so. Although Luke helps his readers understand why Jesus said what he did, they, like Jesus' hearers, still have many questions. But the important questions do not request more information about Jesus; they rather concern the resistance to what he says about turning life around so that it is lived Godward. These questions also include the reluctance to believe his assurances.

Do You Want to Become His Disciples, Too?

The disciple knows that following Jesus is a journey, a continuing process. In this life, no one has arrived. Nor does the disciple always follow closely or walk confidently; sometimes we tag along and occasionally stumble. Still the journey continues. We fall in behind him, not because we have really understood him but because we sense that he was right. Journeying with Jesus may not always be an adventure, but it is a venture. Always. Those who venture with him know they will never be the same again.

Who is this Jesus who determines the shape of your discipleship?

_____

_____

_____

_____

_____

Prayer

Your teachings are wonderful, and I respect them all.
Understanding your word brings light
    to the minds of ordinary people.
I honestly want to know everything you teach.
Think about me and be kind,
    just as you are to everyone who loves your name.
Keep your promise and don't let me stumble
    or let sin control my life.
Protect me from abuse, so I can obey your laws.
    Smile on me, your servant, and teach me your laws.

(Psalm 119:129-135, CEV)

Stories and Teachings of Jesus Only in Luke 9:51–18:14

(Jesus' Journey to Jerusalem)

9:51-56	Refused by Samaritans
10:1, 17-20	Sending and return of the seventy
10:29-37	*Parable:* the good Samaritan
10:38-42	Martha and Mary's dinner for Jesus
11:5-8	Friend who responds at midnight
11:27-28	True blessedness
12:13-21	*Parable:* the rich fool
12:47-48	The beaten slaves
13:1-5	Two tragedies and repentance
13:6-9	*Parable:* fruitless fig tree's one more chance
13:10-17	Sabbath healing of crippled woman
13:31-33	Pharisees warn about Herod
14:1-6	Healing man with dropsy
14:7-14	On humility: an illustration
15:1-7	*Parable:* the lost sheep
15:8-10	*Parable:* the lost coin
15:11-32	*Parable:* the lost (prodigal) son
16:1-13	*Parable:* the dishonest manager
16:14-15	On the hypocrisy of the Pharisees
16:19-31	*Parable:* the rich man and Lazarus
17:7-10	Analogy of the obedient slaves
17:11-19	Healing ten lepers
17:20-21	The kingdom of God is "among you"
18:1-8	*Parable:* the widow and the unjust judge
18:9-14	*Parable:* the Pharisee and the tax collector

17 Destiny Symbolized

He was teaching and saying, "Is it not written,
'My house shall be called a house of prayer
for all the nations'?
But you have made it a den of robbers."
(Mark 11:17)

They Have No Wine

Religions, including Christianity, generate an amazing amount of business. Equipping a new church requires pews and carpets, lighting and sound equipment, organ and pianos, kitchen equipment, heating and air conditioning, and perhaps athletic facilities as well (all of which provide jobs); and the church program requires all sorts of things, from candles to buses. Large churches have complex budgets, investments, camps, houses—all requiring astute secular skills in management and finance. As we think about it, we wonder whether the heart of the matter—the life of the Spirit—has gotten lost. And what happened to the sense of the sacred when the sanctuary is a "multiuse, flexible space"? When we lose our sense of the Holy One, we have indeed run out of wine.

Beginning With Moses and All the Prophets

We resume using Mark as the starting point, picking up at Mark 11, which begins with the story of Jesus' arrival in Jerusalem, celebrated by all churches as Palm Sunday (though palms are mentioned only in John). The Gospels do not actually say that Jesus entered Jerusalem on a Sunday; the day has been inferred by reckoning back from the Crucifixion on Friday. Some of the Old Testament passages pertain directly to the Gospel accounts; others are relevant to the general theme of true worship.

Day 1 Mark 11:1-25 (26); Psalm 118:21-28; Isaiah 56:1-8; Jeremiah 7:1-15

(1) See how Mark 11 is put together: First, by having Jesus' action in the Temple occur the next day, the entry into the city becomes an event in its own right; second, the action in the Temple is framed by the story of the fig tree; third, sayings are added to the narrative (some manuscripts add 11:26; the saying about forgiveness is like Matthew 6:14).

(2) Note how the story of Jesus' entry into the city is designed to evoke a sense of wonder—getting the colt, riding a colt never ridden before, the words of the crowd.

(3) See that Mark implies that the fig tree interprets Jesus' words in the Temple. Note that 11:17 combines Isaiah 56:7 and Jeremiah 7:11 (Jeremiah 7:1-15 repays careful reading here).

Day 2 Matthew 21:1-22; 17:20; Luke 17:6; Leviticus 21:16-24; Zechariah 9:9-10

(1) Note that in Matthew Jesus' action in the Temple is the climax of his entry into the city.

(2) Note that Matthew 21:4-5 points out that Jesus' arrival fulfills Zechariah 9:9.

(3) Compare the words of the crowd in Matthew with those in Mark 11:9-10. What is significant about the differences? Observe also that only Matthew reports what the crowds in Jerusalem were saying about Jesus.

(4) Note that only in Matthew does Jesus heal "the blind and the lame" in the Temple, thereby overcoming the prohibition in Leviticus 21:18. Observe that only in this Gospel do the children in the Temple repeat, "Hosanna to the Son of David," and that Jesus regards this as fulfilling the Septuagint (Greek) version of Psalm 8:2 (which differs from the Hebrew).

(5) Note how Matthew 21:20-22 changes Mark 11:21-23.

Day 3 Luke 19:28-48; Jeremiah 6:6-8

(1) Note that also in Luke Jesus' action in the Temple climaxes his entry into the city. Note that only Luke points out that Jesus was teaching in the Temple "every day" (19:47) and that this detail leads naturally into 20:1.

(2) Observe that only in Luke 19:39-44 do some Pharisees object to what the crowd was saying when Jesus arrived in the city and that only here does Jesus predict what actually occurred when the Romans laid siege to Jerusalem.

Day 4 John 2:13-25; 12:9-19; Psalm 69:6-12

    (1) Note that in John, Jesus explicitly objects to the buying and selling (2:16). Note how the disciples, remembering Psalm 69:9, understood Jesus' act and word. Observe that in John 2:21 the narrator explains what Jesus meant by his response to the request for a "sign."

    (2) Note that in John, Jesus' entry to Jerusalem has a quite different setting (John 12:9-12), that here Jesus takes the initiative, and that Zechariah 9:9 is important here too.

Day 5 Psalm 24; Isaiah 1:10-20; Amos 5:21-24

These Old Testament passages, especially Amos 5:21-24, remind us that valid worship must be of a piece with morality and justice. Does Psalm 24:3-4 imply that only the "pure in heart" are welcome?

Day 6 Read and respond to "Destiny Symbolized" and "Do You Want to Become His Disciples, Too?"

Prayer Concerns

Destiny Symbolized

In going to Jerusalem Jesus seized his destiny and did so voluntarily. He did not go because he had been summoned by religious or political authority that sought to interrogate him. Nor was he talked into the journey by some followers who saw in the Passover crowds an opportunity to reach more people than in the Galilean villages. He did not go on a sudden impulse either. He went because he knew he had to—a "had to" that was rooted so deeply in his mission that the journey was avoidable only if he defaulted out of fear. Now we see what began to happen when he got there.

Mark

The careful reader of Mark 11:1-25 may well end with more questions than answers. Two basic reasons account for this puzzlement. The first pertains to Mark. The stories of Jesus' arrival and of his action in the Temple combine significant details with a striking absence of detail. In the story of the entry, for example, Mark tells us more about how Jesus acquired the colt (six verses) than about what happened when he got it (five verses). Nor does the Gospel explain what Jesus thought he was doing or what he thought of what the crowd said and did. Mark neither explains why Jesus entered the Temple nor why he left. Nor does Mark tell us why Jesus hoped to find figs on the tree when it was not fig season. Mark tells us of Jesus' disruptive action in the Temple but says not a word about any response by the authorities.

The second reason we're puzzled pertains to ourselves: We want the missing details so we can know the whole story of what actually happened. Our curiosity is aroused but not satisfied; evidently Mark's interests and ours are not the same. Rather than conclude that Mark wrote carelessly, we should infer that Mark may have told us everything he thinks we need to know in order to get the point for ourselves.

Mark's story of Jesus' arrival in Jerusalem (the arrival itself appears only at the beginning of 11:11) has two parts—the acquisition of the colt (11:1-7) and the action of the crowd (11:8-10). Together the parts of the story convey the image of Jesus determined to come to Jerusalem as a kingly figure where he elicits appropriate acclamation. With authority he dispatches two disciples to requisition a colt (whose owner does not appear), telling them how to justify their taking it away:

"The *Lord* [not simply Jesus] needs it and will send it back immediately." (To ask when it was sent back or whether Jesus had made an unreported prior arrangement with the owner is to ask precisely the wrong sort of question, Mark implies.) Leaving the "need" unexplained underlines the sovereign claim of Jesus and lends a degree of mystery to the story, not resolved until the second part of the story: Jesus rides not because he is tired but because he comes as a kingly figure signaling "the coming kingdom of our ancestor [Greek: 'father'] David." Having arranged for the colt, Jesus remains silent for the rest of the story. Now it is those who surround him (and the disciples?) who speak; in fact, they shout, turning the event into a festal procession like that of a king (as was done centuries before when Jehu was proclaimed king, according to 2 Kings 9:13). Putting their cloaks and the branches on the road was their way of rolling out the red carpet.

The acclamation in Mark 11:9-10 invites close examination. The first word, *Hosanna*, uses English letters to spell two Hebrew words meaning, "Save us, we pray." Here, however, the word appears to be used more generally as a shout of jubilation or praise, like "Hallelujah!" "Blessed is the one who comes in the name of the Lord" quotes Psalm 118:26. This psalm was sung at the Feast of Tabernacles (or Booths) held in the fall. The next line is remarkable because nowhere else is David called "our father." According to Mark, in celebrating Jesus' arrival the crowd expresses its hope for the restored Davidic kingdom. The last line too is unexpected, for strictly speaking, the crowd would not ask God to "Save us [Hosanna] in the highest heaven" but on earth. Mark may have taken the line to call for jubilation in heaven. Exactly how Mark expects the reader to understand the crowd's hope that Jesus will restore David's kingdom is by no means clear. Are we to think the crowd understood rightly that Jesus, as Messiah, would restore David's kingdom? Or are we to think the crowd misunderstood the nature of Jesus' kingship?

With the acclamation the crowd fulfills its role and disappears from the stage. (Again, asking whether they accompanied Jesus to the city and then scattered, like asking whether they were Passover pilgrims who joined Jesus, is to introduce matters that take us away from what Mark wants us to see.) Mark 11:11, a quiet ending of a noisy day, deliberately separates Jesus' entry from his action the next day. This separation allows each day to have its own claim to our attention. Within this Gospel, Mark 11:1-11 functions as the lens through which the rest of the Gospel is to be viewed: Jesus arrives as king but later is mocked and executed as "King of the Jews." Mark implies that Jesus did not come to Jerusalem as a Passover pilgrim but as one who, in his own way, claimed to be Israel's king and who was killed because his kingship was misunderstood. In this story Jesus' destiny is symbolized.

> **Jesus did not come to Jerusalem as a Passover pilgrim but as one who, in his own way, claimed to be Israel's king and who was killed because his kingship was misunderstood.**

What happens the next two days (11:12-25) also symbolizes destiny, this time the destiny of the Temple. Mark implies this by framing the story of Jesus' action in the Temple with the story of the fig tree. Those who read this story as an accurate account of what really happened usually are baffled by it, wondering why Jesus would punish the tree for not bearing fruit out of season. If Jesus is going to do something miraculous with the tree, why didn't he have it produce figs by the next morning? Again, the wrong kind of question. We do better by regarding the story as we regard the story of Jonah—as a truth symbolized as a story. The event did not produce the meaning; rather, the meaning produced the story, so that the story *is* the meaning.

Old Testament prophets used the fig tree to symbolize some aspect of their understanding of Israel. For example, in Hosea 9:10 God says,

"Like grapes in the wilderness,
I found Israel.
Like the first fruit on the fig tree,
in its first season,
I saw your ancestors [the patriarchs],"

that is, with hope and joy. In Jeremiah 8:13, on the other hand, God expresses disappointment over Israel by saying,

"there are no grapes on the vine,
nor figs on the fig tree;
even the leaves are withered."

Likewise, Micah 7:1-2 begins a lament about Israel's moral corruption by saying,

"Woe is me! For I have become like one who . . . finds no cluster to eat;
there is no first-ripe fig for which I hunger.
The faithful have disappeared from the land."

In Mark a fig tree with no figs but only leaves is used to symbolize the Temple, and the tree's fate expresses the fate of the Temple. It was, in fact, destroyed by the Romans during the war (A.D. 66-70)—the time when Mark was written. Jesus' response to the fig tree's fruitlessness interprets Jesus' response to what he found in the Temple—lots of leaves.

The story of Jesus in the Temple commonly is called "the cleansing" of the Temple. The story of the fig tree, however, suggests that Mark did not understand it this way. Jesus too may not have understood his action as a "cleansing," for this word implies that he cleaned it up so it would function more properly. That he intended to restore its proper, God-willed purpose, however, is not clear.

Giving attention to what was going on and where it was happening is essential for our understanding of the story. Here "the Temple" refers to the whole Temple precinct, not the sanctuary alone. In this area, priests (or their agents) set up shop where people could buy the animals or birds that met the specifications for sacrifices and where they could change their money into acceptable Temple coins before giving it. In other words, the traders provided a necessary service. We must visualize the scene—noisy cattle, sheep, and birds being delivered, inspected, and sold; people arguing over exchange rates; groups of people coming and going. Jesus' words, "You have made it a den of robbers" often have been taken to mean that the merchants were overcharging or cheating, but the Gospel does not say so. Rather, as Mark tells it, the offense was deeper than that.

According to Mark 11:17, Jesus "was teaching and saying"—that is, the words that follow were the "texts" for Jesus' extended teaching. The theme of the teaching is the contradiction between the first part of the verse and the second part, which is introduced by "But." The first part quotes Isaiah 56:7, which concludes the promise that the offerings of law-obeying Gentiles will be accepted in the Temple,

"for my house shall be called a house of prayer
for all peoples."

In the second part, that promise is contradicted by what Jesus sees:

"But you have made it a den of robbers."

These words paraphrase Jeremiah 7:11, part of the prophet's sermon at the Temple gate (Jeremiah 7:1-15). There the prophet denounces the people for falsely assuming that no disaster will befall Judah because God would protect the Temple: Do you say, "We are safe!"—only to go on doing all these abominations [theft, murder, adultery, idolatry were just mentioned]? Has this house ... become a den of robbers in your sight?" The sermon ends with a prediction of the Temple's destruction. Perhaps Mark suggests that Jesus had Jeremiah's whole sermon in mind when he followed Isaiah's words of promise with, "But you have made it a den of robbers." If so, Jesus turned the question in Jeremiah into an outright accusation that interprets what he sees—thriving religious activities based on the assumption that they assure God's protection of Judah. That would indeed contradict God's intent for the Temple—a house of prayer for everyone, Gentiles included.

Mark then comments that the chief priests and scribes, who sought a way to kill Jesus, "were afraid of him, because the whole crowd was spellbound by his teaching" (11:18). Mark does not actually say that Jesus predicted the destruction of the Temple. He didn't need to, for he probably assumed the readers would see that Jesus was applying Jeremiah's sermon to the present situation. Jesus' action and teaching were not, therefore, his way of repudiating the Temple (and the sacrificial system) itself. To the contrary, deed and word expressed his concern for its integrity, as does the detail (only in Mark) that "he would not allow anyone to carry anything through the temple" (precincts). Since the Temple was God's house, it must not be used as a shortcut. The whole passage, framed by the story of the fig tree, implies that God's judgment would come on the Temple, not because it was wrong but because it was being misused (in ways not specified). Even though John tells the story differently, he agrees, for he reports that the disciples remembered Psalm 69:9: "Zeal for your house will consume me" (John 2:17). In both Gospels, then, Jesus acted out of zeal *for* the Temple, and thus against abuses, not out of zealous hostility against it.

> Jesus acted out of zeal *for* the Temple, and thus against abuses, not out of zealous hostility against it.

Matthew

GC 17-1 Although Matthew 21:1-22 is similar to Mark 11:1-25, the changes Matthew made in Mark show that his Gospel has other emphases; consequently, we will focus on the distinctive elements of the passage.

First of all, Matthew points out that the way Jesus came to Jerusalem makes actual (fulfills) Zechariah 9:9, and to make this point Matthew virtually repeats the formula used often in Matthew: "This took place to fulfill ...." In fact, he took this fulfillment so literally that Jesus, instead of asking the disciples to fetch a colt, now asks them to bring two animals, a donkey and a colt. Zechariah 9:9 says,

> "Rejoice greatly, O daughter Zion! ...
> Lo, your king comes to you;
>   triumphant and victorious is he,
> humble and riding on a donkey,
>   on a colt, the foal of a donkey."

In Hebrew poetry the line about the donkey and the line about the colt are an instance of synonymous parallelism*—two lines say the same thing in different words. In other words, in Hebrew, "on a colt, the foal of a donkey" simply rephrases "on a donkey." The quotation in Matthew 21:5, however, is closer to the Septuagint which reads "mounted on a donkey and a young colt" (the Greek word for "and" can also mean "even"). So Matthew inferred that Jesus asked for two animals; in fact, in Matthew 21:7 "them" can refer to the two animals, but "he sat on them" can refer either to the animals or to the cloaks. (Some copyists saw the problem and in 21:7 changed "them" to "it," while others changed the text to read "on the colt.") The Evangelist did not see this event as the "triumphal entry," as it sometimes is called today, but as the humble arrival of the king.

The most significant changes Matthew makes in Mark's account appear in 21:10-17. (1) By having Jesus go into the Temple immediately, Matthew makes Jesus' actions there the climax of the entry. In fact, what occurred in the Temple appears as the goal of his coming to the city. (2) If we might infer from Mark 11:11 that Jesus and his disciples entered the city and the Temple unnoticed, such an inference is excluded by Matthew 21:10-11, according to which "the whole city was in turmoil" over Jesus. Reading that the crowds said, "This is the prophet Jesus from Nazareth in Galilee" prepares us for Jesus' prophetic act and word when he arrives at the Temple. (3) While in Mark, Jesus does no healing at all in Jerusalem, according to Matthew 21:14 he "cured" the blind and the lame people who came to him. According to Leviticus 21:18-21 these and other physically impaired people are forbidden to offer sacrifices or come into the sanctuary itself. Here in Jerusalem

Jesus makes it possible for the excluded to participate, as in Galilee he had healed a leper, a Gentile, and a woman (Matthew 8:1-15). (4) Likewise unique to Matthew is the report that children in the Temple were shouting, "Hosanna to the Son of David"—the only ones there to recognize his royal, messianic status. Understandably, the chief priests and scribes protested, "Do you hear what these are saying?" implying that Jesus should tell them to be quiet (Matthew 21:15-16). (5) Of course Jesus hears them! But he also defends them by putting his own question to the priests and scribes. The question is derived from the Greek version of Psalm 8:2. The New Revised Standard Version renders the Hebrew text this way:

> "Out of the mouths of babes and infants
>   you have founded a bulwark because of your foes,
>   to silence the enemy and the avenger."

The Septuagint, however, can be translated this way:

> "Out of the mouth of babes and nursing babies
> I will prepare praise for the sake of your foes
>   to destroy the enemy and the avenger."

Jesus' words agree with neither:

> "Out of the mouths of infants and nursing
>   babies
>   *you have prepared* praise *for yourself.*"

Apparently Matthew adjusted the wording of the psalm, as writers of the time often did, in order to convey his point. God has caused himself to be praised by this marvel: Infants too young to speak hail Jesus as the Son of David. Of course Jesus would not tell them to be quiet. And so the first day in Jerusalem ends where it began: Jesus is celebrated as the Son of David (Matthew 21:9, 15).

Matthew makes two changes in the story of the fig tree (21:18-19)—first, by omitting "it was not the season for figs," Jesus' response to its fruitlessness is less offensive. Matthew also makes it clearer that Jesus' word, "May no fruit ever come from you again" was a powerful curse, for "the fig tree withered at once." The disciples are curious: "How did the fig tree wither at once?" Jesus' reply, however, turns attention toward what the disciples too might do: "Truly I tell you, if you have faith and do not doubt, not only will you do what has been done to the fig tree, but even if you say to this mountain, 'Be lifted up and thrown into the sea,' it will be done"—a promise similar to that in 17:20. This reply turns the mountain into a metaphor for difficulty; we still speak of faith that moves mountains. By adding Jesus' reply, Matthew uses the story to urge strong faith.

Luke

Luke's story of Jesus' coming to Jerusalem (Luke 19:28-38) begins very much as Mark's does but then makes significant changes. The reader of Mark (and Matthew) may wonder what prompted the crowd to hail Jesus as it did, for neither Gospel explains why people, who presumably had not seen Jesus before, said what they did. The reader of Luke, however, is not left with this question, for in this Gospel "the whole multitude of the disciples began to praise God joyfully with a loud voice for all the deeds of power that they had seen" (19:37). Their action is a response to Jesus' miraculous deeds in his mission up to this point. Also what they shouted is peculiar to this Gospel. Whereas Mark's story implied that Jesus was coming as a kingly figure, and Matthew relied on Zechariah to tell the reader that Jesus is the king, in Luke the jubilant disciples actually call him king:

> "Blessed is the king
>   who comes in the name of the Lord!"

They also shout,

> "Peace in heaven,
>   and glory in the highest heaven!"

These last words remind the reader that in Luke the angels praised God in similar words when Jesus arrived in the world as a baby:

> "Glory to God in the highest heaven,
>   and on earth peace among those whom he favors!" (2:14).

But why did the disciples not shout about peace on earth?

A clue to the answer may well be found in the next two paragraphs, occurring only in Luke (19:39-44). When some Pharisees asked Jesus to tell the disciples to stop this shouting, Jesus said, in effect, that they cannot be repressed: "If these were silent, the stones would shout out." The word cannot be silenced because this is the God-set time for

In Luke, Jesus' mission began in the Nazareth synagogue, his accustomed place, and ends in the Temple, his rig tful place.

the king of Israel to bring heaven's peace to earth. But it will not be so, for as Jesus neared the city he lamented its blindness: "If you, even you, had only recognized on this day the things that make for peace! But now they are hidden from your eyes."

Jerusalem does not know who Jesus really is and so does not welcome its king; instead, the leaders will persist in looking for ways to kill him (19:47, repeating part of Mark 11:18). (Later, the crucified Jesus would repeat this theme of ignorance [Luke 23:34], as would Peter [Acts 3:17] and Paul [Acts 13:27].) Instead, the city will be besieged and destroyed because it "did not recognize the time of your visitation from God" (Luke 19:43-44). Thus the disciples do not shout "Peace on earth" because Luke knows what really happened was war. Luke could omit the story of the fig tree because his prediction of Jerusalem's fate in the war against Rome was more specific.

Luke's report of Jesus' action in the Temple (the climax of his arrival in the city, as in Matthew) is short, saying only that Jesus expelled the merchants. As in Matthew, in Luke Jesus says the Temple is to be a house of prayer, but both Gospels omit "for all the nations"—perhaps because when these Gospels were written, the Temple had already been destroyed. Only Luke notes, "Every day he was teaching in the temple" (19:47). In Luke Jesus' mission began in the Nazareth synagogue (4:16-30), his accustomed place, and ends in the Temple, his rightful place, where he is about his Father's business, as he pointed out when only twelve years old (2:49).

John

This Gospel gives a quite different picture (John 12:12-19). Not only is the entry to Jerusalem separated completely from Jesus' act in the Temple, but also here the inhabitants of the city "took branches of palm trees and went out to meet him." (In antiquity it was common practice for city residents to meet kings, governors, and high officials and to escort them into the city.) Appropriately, the crowd hails Jesus as "the King of Israel." In response Jesus himself "found a young donkey and sat on it." We are left wondering. Did his actions signal that he accepted the honor; or did he at the same time criticize it by riding on a donkey, not on a horse as kings were expected to do?

GC 17-2 When we compare John's account of Jesus' action in the Temple (John 2:13-22) with the Synoptic accounts, several distinct features stand out. (1) The deed itself is told in more detail (2:14-15). (2) Jesus quotes neither Isaiah 56 nor Jeremiah 7 but simply gives an order: "Take these things out of here! Stop making my Father's house a marketplace!" Does he not realize (or care) that the Temple could not function without the market and money-changing? (3) Whereas in the

Synoptics the priests express consternation over Jesus' action, here they ask for a sign that authorizes his deed. His response is characteristic of Jesus in this Gospel—his words are absurd for those who take them literally but profound for those who understand. So Jesus says, "Destroy this temple, and in three days I will raise it up." The retort is understandable: It took forty-six years to build this temple, and you will raise it up in three days? How could they know "he was speaking of the temple of his body"? Even the writer must point out, lest also the reader miss the point: The authorizing sign is Jesus' death and resurrection. Indeed after that the Temple will be irrelevant for believers, for as Jesus told the Samaritan woman, "The hour is coming, and is now here, when the true worshipers will worship the Father in spirit and truth" (John 4:23), and that will occur neither in her temple on Mount Gerizim nor in Jerusalem (4:21).

So Then

Although we know that the cross lies ahead, on Palm Sunday we celebrate Jesus' coming to Jerusalem because in light of Easter we believe that Jesus, for one brief moment, was hailed rightly. And so we identify with those on the road. Indeed, churches that distribute palm fronds encourage us to do so. Appropriate as this practice may be, we should bear in mind that this kingly figure does not come as a proud conqueror but as a silent humble one on a lowly donkey. If we still want to call his

> **On Palm Sunday we celebrate Jesus' coming to Jerusalem because in light of Easter we believe that Jesus, for one brief moment, was hailed rightly.**

arrival "the triumphal entry," we must remember that it is the anticipatory triumph of humility and self-giving that we celebrate, not the proud displays of power that go with triumphal arrivals. Otherwise the Jesus of Palm Sunday is out of character with the Jesus who chided the two disciples who wanted him to promise them the perks of their discipleship (Mark 10:35-37). He went on to say, "Whoever wishes to become great among you must be your servant" (10:43). In other words, if we identify with the crowd that hails Jesus, we obligate ourselves to identify with him as well. If we identify with neither, we are merely watching a local parade.

Some of us may find it easier to identify with Jesus in the Temple. Indeed, the more anger against institutionalized religion, including the church, we have bottled up inside, the quicker we are to cheer as Jesus sends the traders fleeing and the coins rolling, perhaps wishing that the Gospels had described the people's cheers, "Hosanna! Right on, Jesus!" While the Gospels do not say Jesus acted in anger, we have no reason to deny him this emotion. But what angered him? Was it not his sense that the business of the Temple was overshadowing its purpose? To denounce rummage sales, Christmas fairs, and similar efforts to raise money for the church's budget as today's form of what Jesus saw in the Temple might shield the critic from seeing other ways the purpose of the church may be obscured by all its activities. Sometimes people use more energy to keep the church going than to keep the church going to the people. The real business of the church is more than busyness.

Sometimes those who have perceived wrongs in the church have even disrupted worship. But even they would not regard such action as normal but as an extreme measure evoked by wrongdoing that must be stopped. In recent decades many Christians have understood their discipleship to require them to engage in protests beyond the church building. For them, emphasizing the humble Jesus leads all too easily to acquiescence in wrong by doing nothing to change it. They follow the active Jesus who challenges wrong. Determining what discipleship requires (or allows) is not always easy.

Do You Want to Become His Disciples, Too?

This week's Scripture has presented two differing images of Jesus—the humble, silent man riding into Jerusalem and the assertive figure striding into the Temple. Disciples might therefore conclude that they may choose which Jesus to regard as the model to be followed. But in choosing either image, we would—unwittingly—replace following a whole Jesus with following that aspect of Jesus that confirms what we prefer. But is not the whole point of following Jesus that we should be more challenged than reinforced? And that includes being challenged by his zeal for the holy.

Describe the Jesus who confronts you both by riding into Jerusalem on a donkey and overturning tables in the Temple.

_____

_____

_____

_____

_____

150

Prayer

Our God, you deserve praise in Zion,
    where we keep our promises to you.
Everyone will come to you because you answer prayer.
    Our terrible sins get us down, but you forgive us. . . .

Our God, you save us, and your fearsome deeds
    answer our prayers for justice!
You give hope to people everywhere on earth,
    even those across the sea.

(Psalm 65:1-3, 5, CEV)

18 Sharp Words in the Temple

Jesus said, "Pay Caesar what belongs to Caesar,
and God what belongs to God."
His reply left them completely taken aback.
(Mark 12:17, REB)

They Have No Wine

We have so many questions. More than we can answer. Despite our questions—persistent questions—we somehow find an answer we can live with. And then something happens or someone enters our lives (or leaves), and suddenly the questions return: Why? What for? What's the use? So what? Sometimes we don't even know what to ask—not because we're stupid but because life questions *us*. And what would we do if someone gave us an answer—an answer that goes to the heart of the problem? Would we question that too?

Beginning With Moses and All the Prophets

In this week's lesson various people put questions to Jesus, some designed to put Jesus on the defensive or to lure him into an argument. In Mark these exchanges between Jesus and his questioners occur in the Temple; sometimes Luke has Jesus say these things in different settings. (See "Questions in the Temple," page 163.) Read Mark 11:27–12:44 as a unit first to see Mark's portrayal of Jesus' Temple teaching as a whole. John has no equivalent account of Jesus' last week.

Day 1 Mark 11:27–12:12; Matthew 21:23-46; Luke 20:1-19; 7:29-30; Isaiah 5:1-7

(1) Note that the narrator's explanation in Mark 11:32 continues the explanation in 11:18. Note that in Matthew 21:26 the questioners themselves admit their fear, and Luke 20:6 tells the reader what they fear.

(2) Observe that in Matthew 21:28-32, found only here, Jesus turns the parable of the two sons into an accusation of the questioners.

(3) **GC 18-1** Note how the parable in Mark 12:1-11 uses the image of Israel as a vineyard found in Isaiah 5. Note also that the Evangelist's comment in Mark 12:12 ties the parable to 11:18. Note also that Matthew 21:45 reads "parables" (not "this parable" as in Mark) in order to refer to both Matthew 21:28-31 and 21:33-41. The quotation about the rejected stone (Mark 12:10-11, Matthew 21:42; shortened in Luke 20:17) is taken from Psalm 118:22-23. Observe that the saying in Matthew 21:43, found only here, interprets 21:41. According to 21:43, who is deprived of the kingdom, and who receives it? Notice also that the parable in Matthew 22:1-14 has two stages, 22:1-10 and 22:11-13, and ends with a general comment in 22:14.

Day 2 Mark 12:13-17; Matthew 22:1-22; Luke 14:16-24; 20:20-26; Romans 13:1-7; 1 Peter 2:11-17

(1) Note how Mark 12:13 continues the story from 12:12; observe also how Luke 20:20 elaborates what Mark has said. Notice how Luke 20:26 expands the concluding comment in Mark 12:17.

(2) Note that whereas Jesus does not actually say whether the tax should be paid or not, Paul is explicit in Romans 13:1-7. Note how 1 Peter 2:11-17 agrees with Paul.

Day 3 Mark 12:18-27; Matthew 22:23-33; Luke 20:27-40; Acts 23:1-10; Exodus 3:1-6; Deuteronomy 25:5-10

(1) **GC 18-2** Note that each Gospel introduces the question about the resurrection in the same way (Mark 12:18; Matthew 22:23; Luke 20:27). Note how Paul, when before the council (Sanhedrin*), exploited the differences between the Sadducees and Pharisees (Acts 23:6-10).

(2) Observe that the hypothetical case presented in Mark 12:19-23 is based on Deuteronomy 25:5-10.

(3) Read the first part of Jesus' reply in Mark 12:24-25 and then see that Luke 20:34-36 omits Jesus' accusation in Mark 12:24 but makes an important addition. Note that the second part of Jesus' answer (Luke 20:37-38) appeals to Exodus 3:1-6. Note that Jesus' use of this passage turns on "I am" (the text does not say, "I was").

Day 4 Mark 12:28-37, 41-44; Luke 10:25-28; 21:1-4; Leviticus 19:11-18; Deuteronomy 6:4-9; Psalm 110

(1) **GC 18-3** Note that in Mark 12:28 there is no suggestion that the scribe aims to test Jesus as in Matthew 22:34. Notice that in Mark 12:29-31 Jesus combines Deuteronomy 6:4-5 and Leviticus 19:18. Observe what the scribe says about "all whole burnt offerings and sacrifices" in Mark 12:33 and Jesus' response in 12:34.

(2) Note that in Luke the story of the lawyer's question appears in an earlier setting (10:25-28), and that there the question is about eternal life. Note also that Jesus asks him what the Torah says, and that the lawyer quotes Deuteronomy 6:5 and Leviticus 19:18. Note Jesus' response, the lawyer's next question and its motivation (Luke 10:29), and the way Jesus answers it.

Day 5 Mark 12:38-40; Matthew 23; Luke 20:45-47; Exodus 13:9, 16; Numbers 15:37-41; Deuteronomy 11:18; 2 Chronicles 24:20-22

(1) Note that in Mark 12:35-37 Jesus takes the initiative and asks his own question, whose wording in Matthew 22:42 differs from that in Mark 12:35 and Luke 20:41.

(2) Observe that in Mark 12:36 "the Lord" refers to God, and that Jesus questions the scribes' view that "my Lord" refers to the messiah. That is, if David calls the messiah "my Lord," how can the messiah be David's son? Note that Matthew 22:46 spells out what Mark and Luke, who report no response, assume.

(3) Observe that in all three Gospels Jesus, having called into question the scribes' interpretation of Scripture, now makes accusations against them (Mark 12:37-40; Luke 20:45-47), which Matthew expands into a whole discourse (Matthew 23). Note also that according to Matthew 24:1, this entire discourse is given in the Temple; some of the sayings occur in different settings in Luke.

(4) Note that while Jesus does not use the word *hypocrisy* or *hypocrite* in Matthew 23:1-3, his accusation shows what these words mean when they appear in 23:13, 15, 23, 25, 27, 29.

(5) Note that Jesus rejects neither phylacteries (small black boxes containing Scripture, one tied to the upper left arm, the other above the forehead, according to Exodus 13:9, 16) nor fringes (based in Numbers 15:37-41) but their ostentatious use.

(6) In Matthew 23:29-32, note how Jesus denies that the current generation is better than its forebears.

(7) Note that in Matthew 23:33 Jesus talks like John the Baptist in 3:7.

(8) Note that in Luke 11:49-51 Jesus quotes "the Wisdom of God" (probably a writing now lost), according to which God's wisdom is the sender, but in Matthew 23:34 Jesus speaks of himself as the sender of messengers, perhaps thereby implying that he is God's wisdom. Note also that "this generation" (23:36) will pay for the whole history of martyrdom, from A to Z (Abel to Zechariah, whose death is reported in 2 Chronicles 24:20-22).

Day 6 Read and respond to "Sharp Words in the Temple" and "Do You Want to Become His Disciples, Too?"

Prayer Concerns

Sharp Words in the Temple

Jesus was a more complex person than most of our images of him allow for. In our mind's eye we see him being compassionate and caring, blessing children, welcoming a despised tax collector to his circle, healing the sick, and being such a convivial guest that people said he was a "glutton and a drunkard." None of these traits appears in this week's Scripture passages. Also the Gospels' earlier chapters report occasions when Jesus could be sharp. The Sermon on the Mount contains the warning that on Judgment Day he will dismiss as evildoers those who did not do God's will even though they had done good in Jesus' name (Matthew 7:21-23). He pronounced doom on two towns that refused his message (Matthew 11:20-24) and accused Pharisees of abandoning God's command in order to cling to human tradition (Mark 7:9)—to cite a few instances. But in Jerusalem the opposition hardens, and Jesus sounds more and more harsh and less and less generous. Indeed, in our Scripture readings Jesus seldom speaks positively. Beginning with his action in the Temple, he is repeatedly critical of those he meets and of what he sees. Somehow we must absorb this aspect of Jesus into our thinking about him and devotion to him. Otherwise, our reading of the Gospels will be selective and our allegiance will be to a simplified Jesus.

In all three Synoptics the question of Jesus' authority is raised at the beginning of his Temple teaching (Mark 11:27-33, repeated by Matthew 21:23-27 and Luke 20:1-8). The question had been raised earlier (for example, Mark 1:27; 2:10-11; 6:1-3; Matthew 12:38-39), and then too Jesus had refused to explain the source of his conviction that he was authorized by God and the coming of God's reign. But in the Temple he also does something else: He puts the questioners on the spot by asking whether John's baptism (which stands for John's mission as a whole) was authorized by God ("from heaven") or not. According to Mark 11:31-33 they saw the trap in Jesus' counter-question and so pled ignorance. Although Jesus had recognized the difference between John's mission and his own (Luke 7:24-35), he nonetheless thought that God authorized both of them. So by confronting the questioners with the issue of John's authority, he implied that if they did not acknowledge John's authority, they would not acknowledge his, even if he explained it. In both cases, acknowledging authority entailed responding positively to their

mission. Moreover, Jesus knew that in their asking him to account for his authority, the questioners showed that they did not and would not heed him. In addition, Jesus probably sensed that they would contest any answer he gave. We may assume that the early Christians valued this story, before and after it was written down, because they recognized its truth: A person cannot acknowledge Jesus' authorization by God and yet refuse to heed what he says.

Jesus on the Attack

According to Matthew 21:28-32 (which Matthew adds to what he took from Mark 11:27-33), Jesus goes on the attack, using the parable of the two sons, in which one son said he would obey but did not, and the other said he would not obey but changed his mind and did. In asking which son was obedient, Jesus set a trap that could not be avoided this time, for the answer is obvious. Jesus' inference is a

> **A person cannot acknowledge Jesus' authorization by God and yet refuse to heed what he says.**

harsh judgment: The questioners say they obey God's will but do not; but the despised tax collectors and prostitutes, whose lives show they do not obey, nonetheless did become obedient by believing John. To make matters worse, even seeing the tax collectors and prostitutes become obedient did not prompt the scribes and priests to "change [their] minds" (repent) and do likewise. (Interestingly, some manuscripts omit "not" so that now the text says they did repent afterward.) Jesus' application of this parable to the questioners rests on his conviction that what counts is doing and that saying without doing is fatal. He had already said as much in 7:21.

Jesus' response to the religious leaders' question about his authority shows that he knows they have rejected him. In the parable of the wicked tenants and the sayings attached to it (Mark 12:1-12; Matthew 21:33-46; Luke 20:9-19), he sees this rejection as the climax of Israel's history of rejecting God's emissaries. Although not every detail in the story refers to something in Israel's history, the story's plot clearly implies that the tenants (the religious leaders) in charge of the vineyard (God's people) have repeatedly disobeyed by mistreating the slaves (the prophets) sent to collect the income, and cap their rebellion by finally killing the son (Jesus). The point of the parable comes at the end: The tenants will be destroyed (an allusion to the destruction of Jerusalem in the war against Rome), and the vineyard will be given to other tenants (for Mark, probably the increasingly Gentile church). So the parable makes the same point as the fate of the fruitless fig tree yet goes beyond it by saying what will happen to the vineyard after the wicked tenants are destroyed.

The parable is consistent also with the conclusion of the woes against "scribes and Pharisees, hypocrites" in Matthew 23:34-36: This generation's treatment of God's emissaries completes the history of rejection from Abel onward. In this harsh parable Jesus sounds like those Old Testament prophets who often declared that the nation would be destroyed because it rejected God's will (for example, Isaiah 3:16-26; Jeremiah 4:5-8; 15:6-7; Amos 2:4-5). In fact, he is even more negative, for unlike the prophets, he promised no restoration.

Jesus' doom-saying differs from that of the prophets in another respect: They usually pronounced God's judgment because of the sins of the people, but Jesus' words are directed mostly against the religious leadership, not against the people. Mark concludes the scene by reporting, "When they [the chief priests, scribes, and elders, 11:27] realized that he had told this parable against them, they wanted to arrest him, but they feared the crowd" (12:12; Matthew adds "because they regarded him as a prophet"; see also Mark 11:18 and 12:37). Also Matthew 23 says not a word against the people's misuse of their religion but is directed explicitly against "scribes and Pharisees, hypocrites." Indeed, in this chapter the Jewish people are the victims of scribal and Pharisaic practices: The people are locked out of the Kingdom (23:13); the proselytes are worse off than the Pharisees who converted them (23:15).

Just as a careful reading of Matthew 23 discloses no criticism of the Jewish religion of Jesus' day, so it reveals no denunciation of Pharisaism as such. Indeed, Jesus teaches, "The scribes and Pharisees sit on Moses' seat [that is, in interpreting the Torah, they function in Moses' place]; therefore, do whatever they teach you and follow it." A stronger affirmation of scribal and Pharisaic teaching is hard to imagine. But because their deeds do not match their words, hearers should follow their words but not their deeds. The subsequently repeated name-calling, "scribes and Pharisees, hypocrites" does not annul what Jesus says at the beginning of the chapter. Rather, calling them hypocrites locates their flaw in the disparity between word and deed; nowhere do the Gospels report that Jesus said that all scribes and Pharisees are hypocrites. In fact, the Pharisees were as sensitive about hypocrisy as was Jesus. Indeed, *Pirke Aboth*, the oldest tractate in the Mishnah*, reports that a sage said, "Not the study of the Law but the carrying out of it is the essential thing" (1:17).

Although Matthew 21:23-46 concerns "the chief priests and the elders," the next parable, the wedding banquet in 22:1-14, does concern the people's response to Jesus as the emissary of the kingdom of God. (Just as the parable of the tenants assumes everyone knows that the vineyard represents Israel, so this parable assumes the reader knows that the king's banquet is an image of the messianic banquet that celebrates the arrival of God's reign.) According to this story, the people twice refuse the invitation, perhaps an allusion to John the Baptist and Jesus. Consequently, the king "sent his troops, destroyed those murderers [of his slaves], and burned their city"—a response that probably reminded Matthew's first readers of the destruction of Jerusalem. Nonetheless, "the wedding is ready"; so the king tried once more, this time filling the hall with "good and bad" whom his slaves found in the streets—perhaps an allusion to the Gentile Christians. Had the parable ended here, it would end on the same note as the parable of the wicked tenants: There the wicked are replaced by tenants who will "give . . . the produce at the harvest time"; here they are replaced by the good and bad at the feast. But the parable continues: The king discovered a guest without "a wedding robe" (in Revelation 19:7-8 the bride's [the church's] wedding garment is "the righteous deeds of the saints"). In other words, the king's graciousness in inviting the good and the bad in no way eliminates their need for righteousness—a theme emphasized repeatedly by Matthew (Matthew 5:20; 23:27-28). So Matthew's ending of the parable reminds the increasingly Gentile church that without requisite righteousness their fate will be like that of Israel.

Jesus the Astute Interpreter

The stories in Mark 12:13-37 (also in Matthew 22:15-46; Luke 20:20-44) show Jesus as an astute interpreter not only of Scripture but also of the people who used questions to trick him into giving answers that would expose him as dangerous (the question about taxes), foolish (the question about resurrection), or incompetent (the first commandment). In each instance, however, the efforts failed, partly because he saw through the questions to the questioners, and partly because his astute grasp of the issues allowed him to give responses that were not debatable. When Jesus, having silenced the questioners with his answers, reversed the pattern by asking *them* a question (about the messiah), he again left them speechless (Mark 12:35-37). And in all three Gospels the questioning ceased. We look closely now at each story. We will attend primarily to Mark, since the variations in Matthew and Luke here are minor.

According to Mark 12:13, the authorities, unwilling to arrest Jesus because of his popularity (12:12), "sent to him some Pharisees and some Herodians to trap him in what he said." Little is known about the Herodians (mentioned also in 3:6 as plotting with the Pharisees "how to destroy him"); probably they were people loyal to Herod Antipas, whose jurisdiction included Galilee but not Judea, which now was governed directly by the prefect appointed by Rome. In any case, they with certain Pharisees agreed to be the agents of the others. In other words, except for the Sadducees who are not mentioned, Jesus is questioned on behalf of "the establishment." Since the people responded positively to Jesus, his opponents had a problem—how to drive a wedge between Jesus and the people. The question about taxes offered a possibility to achieve this purpose (12:13-17).

The taxes in question are neither property taxes nor duties on goods, but the *kensos*, the head tax imposed on residents of Judea, Samaria, and Idumea (west of the Dead Sea) in A.D. 6 as part of the arrangement by which the area was now governed directly by a Roman-appointed prefect (sometimes called procurator). The Jews hated this tax because it symbolized their subservience to Rome. The question, "Is it lawful to pay taxes [the *kensos*] to the emperor, or not?" obviously does not refer to the Roman law but to God's law. This question too is a trap: If Jesus says yes, he risks alienating himself from the people because he compromises the authority of God's law; if he says no, he challenges Rome's authority. Instead of responding immediately, Jesus asks for a denarius ("the coin used for the tax," Matthew 22:19). Coin in hand, he asked, "Whose head is this, and whose title?" The answer was obvious—Caesar's. It's his coin. So, "Give [literally, 'give back'] to the emperor [Greek: Caesar] the things that are the emperor's, and to God the things that are God's" (Mark 12:14-17). Now the ball was in their court.

The *Gospel of Thomas* 100 has an interesting variant: "They showed Jesus a gold (coin) and said to him, 'Caesar's officers demand taxes from us.' Jesus said to them, 'Give to Caesar what belongs to Caesar, give to God what belongs to God, and give to me what is mine.' "

Exactly what Jesus was conveying has generated much discussion, because his pronouncement can be interpreted in various ways. Some say Jesus implicitly acknowledges that "the things that are the emperor's" should not be withheld, a view akin to Romans 13:1-7, and so infer that for Jesus a person need not choose Caesar or God because the choice concerns who gets what. Others point out that when Jesus rebuked Peter at Caesarea Philippi (Matthew 16:23), he used the same phrase ("the things of God," NIV) to express a radical alternative ("divine things . . . human things," NRSV). So they infer that in both places Jesus insists on the alternative—God or Caesar—an alternative that is consistent with "No one can serve two masters" (Matthew 6:24). However, if Jesus had been forcing a radical choice between God and Caesar, the point seems not to have registered, for apart from Luke, Jesus' answer is not mentioned again, not even at his trial before Pilate. Only Luke reports that the Sanhedrin told Pilate, "We found this man perverting our nation, forbidding us to pay taxes to the emperor, and saying that he himself is the Messiah, a king." Luke evidently reports this to show that Jesus was falsely accused and implies that Pilate saw this too; for when Jesus answered his question, "Are you the king of the Jews?" with "You say so," Pilate declared, "I find no basis

> Jesus' pronouncement regarding God and Caesar does not express the idea of the separation of church and state. It rather becomes a question, What is Caesar's, and what is God's?

for an accusation against this man" (Luke 23:2-4). Many historians, however, doubt the accuracy of Luke's report of this scene. After all, none of the disciples was there to report what was said. But if Luke's report is not to be trusted, we are left with the fact that in neither Matthew nor Mark is Jesus' word about taxes used as evidence that he had challenged Caesar's rights. In any case Jesus' pronouncement regarding God and Caesar does not express the idea of the separation of church and state. It rather becomes a question: What is Caesar's, and what is God's? Christians, and others, have been pondering that question ever since.

The Sadducees' question is more clever than profound (Mark 12:18-27). They take for granted that Jesus, like the Pharisees, believes there will be resurrection, while they themselves deny it. Their question, however, is based on Deuteronomy 25:5-6, which requires a childless widow to marry the deceased husband's brother, lest there be no heirs and the widow have no support, though the latter point is not made explicit. The book of Ruth is based on this law. To point out the absurdity of resurrection, the Sadducees confront Jesus with a hypothetical case in which the widow of the first brother becomes the wife of the second, upon whose death she marries the third, and so on until she has married all seven brothers. Finally, the woman dies. Now comes the question: "In the resurrection whose wife will she be?"

But Jesus rejects the question, for it reflects ignorance of both Scripture and God's power. In Mark 12:25-27 he addresses the twofold ignorance in reverse order. Had they understood God's power (that is, that resurrection is not restoration to *status quo ante* [situation before death] but transformation as a result of God's power), they would know that there will be no marriage for those who rise from the dead, because they will be like the angels. Jesus, knowing that the Sadducees accept only the Pentateuch as Scripture, does not try to establish the truth of resurrection by appealing to Daniel 12:2: "Many of those who sleep in the dust of the earth shall awake, some to everlasting life, and some to shame and everlasting contempt." Instead he confronts them with a key text in a book they do accept as Scripture, Exodus 3:6. Here God declares to Moses, long after the patriarchs are dead, "I am ... the God of Abraham, the God of Isaac, and the God of Jacob." Since this announcement implies the present tense (though *am* is absent from the Greek and Hebrew, for it is not needed in such statements), Jesus infers that God "is God not of the dead, but of the living." So then, "You are quite wrong." But why? What has Jesus' inference from Exodus got to do with the Sadducees' question or for that matter, with resurrection itself? Aren't the patriarchs dead? Not according to Jesus' last word in Luke: To God "all of them are alive" (Luke 20:38). This conclusion simply spells out what Jesus implies in Mark.

To see how Jesus could use the aliveness of the patriarchs as an argument for resurrection, we need to bear in mind two ideas Jesus probably assumed here. First, according to long-standing Hebrew thought, the dead are in the abode of the dead, Sheol, a gloomy place in the underworld. Psalm 6:5 says, "For in death there is no remembrance of you; / in Sheol who can give you praise?" Likewise, Psalm 115:17 says, "The dead do not praise the LORD, / nor do any that go down into silence." Second, the Hebrews believed that the person does not exist without a body of some sort. Therefore, if God is the God of the patriarchs, who are alive, they must have bodies; that is, they must have been resurrected. We do not know whether Jesus reasoned this way, but such considerations may help us understand the logic of his response.

Although Jesus' teaching about the Law, in which he ties together love of God and love of neighbor, appears in all three Synoptics, the settings differ because in each Gospel the teaching serves a different purpose. In Luke 10:25-28 it is part of Jesus' teaching on the way to Jerusalem. Moreover, it sets the stage for the parable of the good Samaritan. But Mark and Matthew agree that this teaching on the Law is Jesus' reply to the third question put to him in the Temple, though they disagree on why the question was asked (Mark 12:28-34; Matthew 22:34-40). In Matthew the expert in the Law asks it "to test" Jesus, but in Mark it is a scribe's honest question. Furthermore, the scribe not only approves of Jesus' answer (which in Mark begins with the Shema, "Hear, O Israel: the Lord our God, the Lord is one"), but adds, "This is much more important than all whole burnt offerings and sacrifices." Jesus in turn observes that this man is "not far from the kingdom of God"—implying, perhaps, that he can close the remaining distance by doing what he himself said was most important.

From time to time the sages sought to identify the command that either was the most important or expressed the heart of the 613 commandments in the Pentateuch. Most famous is the formulation of Hillel,* who lived a few years before Jesus began his ministry. When a Gentile promised to convert if Hillel could teach him the whole Torah while standing on one foot, Hillel replied, "What is hateful to yourself, do not do to your neighbor; this is the whole Law, the rest is commentary. Go and learn." Whether Jesus was the first to *combine* love of God and love of neighbor is not clear; nor does it matter, for the truth of Jesus' teaching does not require evidence that he said it first. Nor did he claim to. After all, he quoted Scripture!

What holds these two commandments together is the word *love*. Love of God and love of neighbor are inseparably joined here; love of neighbor is not secondary. True, in Leviticus the neighbor is the fellow Hebrew. But when Jesus, replying to the question, "Who is my neighbor?" tells the story of the good Samaritan, he clearly and decisively broadens the inherited understanding without repudiating it. And he expanded it even more when, in another setting, he commanded love of enemies (Matthew 5:43-44).

When Jesus takes the role of the questioner (Mark 12:35-37; Matthew 22:41-46; Luke 20:41-44), he challenges the widely held view that the messiah will be the son of David (and thus legal heir to the throne in the restored monarchy). Jesus questions this identification by appealing to Psalm 110:1: "The Lord [God] said to my Lord,

'Sit at my right hand

until I put your enemies under your feet.' "
By what reasoning does Jesus conclude that this verse does not teach that the messiah is David's son? (1) David is the author of the psalm. (2) Here David reports what the Lord (God) said to someone whom David calls "my Lord." (3) In a patriarchal society (here assumed) the father (the superior) does not use *Lord* to speak to the son (the inferior). (4) So if David himself, inspired by the Holy Spirit as Jesus points out, uses "Lord" to refer to the one addressed by God, this figure cannot be David's son; he must be David's superior. Although only the first line ("The Lord said to my Lord") figures explicitly in Jesus' punch line, the other lines of the psalm underscore his argument, for they refer to a status far greater than that of a Davidic king.

When Jesus, replying to the question, "Who is my neighbor?" tells the story of the good Samaritan, he clearly and decisively broadens the inherited understanding without repudiating it.

What God says to this unidentified figure enthrones him in heaven as "God's right-hand man," exercising God's power in God's name, until God subdues the regent's enemies. If this be the exalted status of the messiah, how can he be David's offspring? Jesus does not answer his own question. Asking it is enough to require serious, fresh thinking. Mark's concluding comment—"And the large crowd was listening to him with delight"—does not mean they knew the answer to his question; rather, the comment suggests they were pleased that once again Jesus had bested his opponents. They had not succeeded in driving a wedge between him and the people.

We may assume that Mark knows the answer to Jesus' question. Only in Mark's Gospel does Jesus admit, during his trial before the high priest, that he is "the Messiah, the Son of the Blessed One." Moreover, Jesus continues, " 'You will see the Son of Man / seated at the right hand of the Power,' / and 'coming with the clouds of heaven' " (citing Daniel 7:13). Here Jesus the Messiah, God's Son, is seated at God's right hand (as Psalm 110:1 said). What is not said is how he got there. But Mark and his readers know: God exalted him to this position at the Resurrection.

Did Mark, in telling the story of Jesus' question as he did, imply that Jesus was not the Son of David (here capitalized to indicate that the phrase is being used as a title of office)? That is quite unlikely, since in Mark 10:46-52 the blind beggar Bartimaeus twice hails Jesus as Son of David and is not rebuked for doing so. Furthermore, he became one of Jesus' followers on the way to Jerusalem. Also, only Mark reports that as Jesus approached Jerusalem the crowd's shout included the line, "Blessed is the coming kingdom of our ancestor David" (11:10).

But how can Mark appear to affirm that Jesus is the Son of David and yet have Jesus himself point out that what God says in Psalm 110 does not refer to David's son? Mark does not explain, largely because he is writing a Gospel narrative, not a theological essay. It is possible, however, that Mark assumed what Paul wrote in Romans 1:3-4—the gospel concerns God's "Son, who was descended from David according to the flesh and was declared to be Son of God with power ... by resurrection from the dead." In other words, as a human person, Jesus was indeed David's descendant whom the Resurrection declared to be God's Son with power. "Son of God with power" describes rather well the status of the one seated at God's right hand. In other words, in Mark Jesus challenges the scribes' view of the messiah because he knows that the messiah's real identity is Son of God and that the Resurrection will disclose this.

So Then

The relevance of this week's Scripture passages for our own faith and discipleship may not be apparent at first, for most of the questions raised here, including the one Jesus asked (Mark 12:35-37), concern matters that seem remote to us. A second look, however, indicates that our initial view may be too hasty, especially when we examine closely Mark 11:27–12:37 as a whole, which highlights the following questions:

1. What is Jesus' authority?   Mark 11:27-33
2. Is the tax to Caesar to be paid?   Mark 12:13-17
3. Is resurrection belief credible?   Mark 12:18-27
4. What is the most important obligation?   Mark 12:28-34
5. Who is the Messiah, really?   Mark 12:35-37

Each of these questions is understandable as an issue in Jesus' day. At the same time, each contains a basic theological issue that believers still face. The Evangelist put the incidents, each focused on a question, in a deliberate sequence, so that questions 1 and 5 reinforce each other, as do 2 and 4.

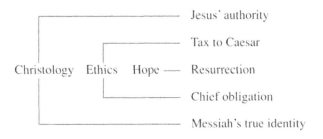

By using this way of reporting Jesus' treatment of these issues back then, Mark allows Jesus to confront us *now* with the same questions:

Why is Jesus decisive? (Christology);

Whom must we obey above all? (ethics);

What can one hope for beyond this life? (hope).

Since we too have these questions, we need to see what we can learn from the ways they are answered here. However, in the first and last stories, no answer is given! In the first, Jesus refuses to account for his authority; and the last story ends abruptly with Jesus' own unanswered question. In both cases, the stories silently require the reader to answer the Christological question, Why is Jesus decisive? Reliable historical information about what Jesus said and did, as well as about the fit between his mission and the ways of God in Scripture, may well be useful in coming to faith and remaining there. But at the end of the day, one's own decision remains unavoidable. Jesus' evocative silence in these two stories reminds us of that.

Jesus' answer to the question about paying the tax and his answer to the question about the Great Commandment fit together like a hand in a glove. What else is giving to God what is God's than the complete love of God coupled with love of neighbor? Together, the answers Jesus gives provide the North Star by which we find our way when otherwise we do not know the right thing to do. Jesus

did not spell out in detail just what obedience requires or does not allow, whether with respect to Caesar or neighbor. Sometimes we make mistakes—perhaps because we presume to know what our obedience requires, but then discover that we got it wrong (our past century was plagued by horrible errors made in the name of doing right). Still, the central ethical question is, Whom shall we obey? And we need to answer it again and again, beginning with Jesus' replies.

Jesus' reply to the question about resurrection (at the center of the five stories) addresses the question at the heart of all our questions, What may we hope for beyond this life? Perhaps, like the Sadducees, we rely on our own clever questions to justify our skepticism about resurrection (for instance, How can a person who has been blown to bits by a bomb be resurrected?). Such questions do not, however, dissolve the unavoidable one, What may we hope for? We may ignore or evade this question, but it too has a way of coming back, often when we least expect. Like the other questions put to Jesus in Mark, it may come to us even in the "temple." In any case,

> **Jesus challenges the scribes' view of the messiah because he knows that the messiah's real identity is Son of God and that the Resurrection will disclose this.**

Jesus' reply was appropriate and profoundly simple, and so remains pertinent— especially to the impertinent. What addresses our doubts and denials is his straightforward observation: "You do not know God's power" (Mark 12:24, at the beginning), and "You are quite wrong" (12:27, at the end). The two verdicts are as inseparable as the two sides of Caesar's denarius: Whenever we do not acknowledge the character and power of God, we do not know what to hope for, because we start from the wrong premise. Jesus' answer reminds us that ultimately, and decisively, a valid answer to that question depends not on what we can or cannot imagine about life after death (as in the Sadducees' case) but on what is possible for the One who, being the living God, is the God of the living. What we can hope for depends not on our own potential but on the potency of God.

Do You Want to Become His Disciples, Too?

In a life of discipleship the answers we give today need to be renewed and realigned again and again, because even the same questions take on a different form and acquire a different urgency as we live from year to year. So we turn to what Jesus did and said, and to what he refused to say. The answers he gave, like the answer he is, often spark new questions, so that we turn again and again to his words and his actions to find a clue that will see us through the day or week. We question because he promised, "Ask, and it will be given you." The disciple learns by asking questions—and by valuing them.

Why is this Jesus decisive for you?

_____

_____

_____

_____

_____

Prayer

Your love is faithful, LORD,
> and even the clouds in the sky can depend on you.
Your decisions are always fair.
They are firm like mountains, deep like the sea,
> and all people and animals are under your care.

Your love is a treasure, and everyone finds shelter
> in the shadow of your wings.
You give your guests a feast in your house,
> and you serve a tasty drink that flows like a river.
The life-giving fountain belongs to you,
> and your light gives light to each of us.

(Psalm 36:5-9, CEV)

Questions in the Temple

	Matthew	Mark	Luke
Jesus' authority	21:23-27	11:27-33	20:1-8
Parable of two sons	21:28-32		
Parable of the wicked tenants	21:33-46	12:1-12	20:9-19
Parable of wedding feast	22:1-14		*(14:16-24)**
Taxes	22:15-22	12:13-17	20:20-26
Resurrection	22:23-33	12:18-27	20:27-40
Great Commandment	22:34-40	12:28-34	*(10:25-28)*
David's son	22:41-46	12:35-37	20:41-44
Woes against hypocrites	23:1-36	12:38-40	20:45-47
Lament over Jerusalem	23:37-39		*(13:34-35)*
Widow's gift		12:41-44	21:1-4

*Italic indicates different placement

163

19 Signs of Danger and Dangerous Signs

Be alert at all times, praying that you may have the
strength to escape all these things that will take place,
and to stand before the Son of Man.

(Luke 21:36)

They Have No Wine

The fear business is thriving. While the future has always had its uncertainties, nowadays fear is being promoted. Night after night the evening news tells us that research suggests that all sorts of disasters are possible. Publishers have learned that "the end of the world" is profitable. The more we fear the future, the more susceptible we become to promises that turn out to be false.

Beginning With Moses and All the Prophets

This week's readings present an aspect of Jesus' teachings that is a significant part of Jesus in the Gospels. In some places these passages are ignored, while in others they are emphasized more than the Sermon on the Mount. For the first four days, our starting point will be Mark 13, which Matthew and Luke adopted and modified. On Day 5, we focus on Matthew 24:37–25:46, which Matthew added to what he took from Mark 13. Matthew 24–25 constitutes the last of the five discourses in this Gospel (the others being Chapters 5–7, 10, 13, 18). Each of these discourses ends on the theme of the coming judgment; Chapters 24–25 concentrate on this theme.

Day 1 Mark 13:1-8; Matthew 24:1-8; Luke 21:5-11; Amos 5:18-20; Isaiah 13:6-16; 34:1-4; Ezekiel 7

(1) Note that the teachings in Mark 13 and Matthew 24–25 are given on the Mount of Olives, while in Luke Jesus says these things in the Temple. **GC 19-1** Note also that in Mark and Matthew Jesus' teachings respond to the questions disciples put to Jesus privately, implying that this teaching is not for the public.

(2) Observe that the questions in Mark 13:4; Matthew 24:3; and Luke 21:7 concern both the time when the Temple will be destroyed and the clues for the beginning of the drama; note that Jesus answers the questions in reverse order (the "signs" in Mark 13:5-31; the "time" in 13:32, omitted by Luke).

(3) Note that Jesus warns, more clearly in Luke 21:8-11 than in Mark 13:5-8 and Matthew 24:4-8, against those who misread "the signs of the times." Note the difference between the warning against false prophets in Matthew 7:15-20 and the one in 24:23-25.

(4) The readings from Amos, Isaiah, and Ezekiel are but a sample of the many passages in the prophets that speak of the future as disastrous punishment.

Day 2 Mark 13:9-13; Matthew 10:17-21; 24:9-14; Luke 12:49-53; 21:12-19; Micah 7:1-7

(1) Note that the persecution foreseen in Mark 13:9-13 appears at Matthew 10:17-21 (part of Jesus' discourse on mission).

(2) Note that some of the language of Micah 7:1-7 (which describes Israel's condition that God will punish) appears in Mark 13:12 as a prediction of what Christians will endure.

(3) Observe that Jesus' promise in Mark 13:10 (expanded in Matthew 24:14) is omitted by Luke and replaced by 21:13. Note also how Luke 21:15 is like Mark 13:11, yet omits the Holy Spirit, perhaps because Luke 12:11-12 has already stated this promise.

(4) Observe that Luke 21:18 promises more than the assurance in Luke 12:7.

Day 3 Mark 13:14-23; Matthew 24:15-28; Luke 17:20-37; 21:20-24; 2 Thessalonians 2:1-12; Daniel 8:11-14; 9:27; 11:31; 12:11; 1 Maccabees 1:41-64

(1) Note that Matthew 24:15 makes clear what Mark 13:14 assumes—that the "desolating sacrilege" to be set up in the Temple will repeat what Daniel wrote about (Daniel 8:13 ["the transgression that makes desolate"]; 9:27; 11:31; 12:11), namely the pagan altar put in the Temple by Antiochus in 167 B.C. (described more fully in 1 Maccabees* 1:41-64). Note also that centuries before, Ezekiel 7:22 expected the Temple to be profaned. Note that 2 Thessalonians 2:3-4 expects a person to profane the Temple.

(2) Note that Luke 21:20-24 expects the destruction of Jerusalem.

(3) Note that Matthew adds 24:26-28 to what he took over from Mark 13:21-23.

Day 4 Mark 13:24-37; Matthew 24:29-36; Luke 21:25-36; 1 Thessalonians 4:13–5:11; Daniel 7:13-18

(1) **GC 19-2** Note that the disasters in the heavens predicted in Mark 13:24-25; Matthew 24:29; and Luke 21:25 rely on Isaiah 13:10. Note that these events will be a "sign" that the Son of Man's coming is at hand, whereas in Mark 13:7-8 they are signs of coming earthly disasters. Observe that only Luke sees these events as the occasion for hope (Luke 21:28).

(2) Observe that the "one like a son of man" (NIV), "human being" (NRSV) in Daniel 7:13, is called "the Son of Man" in Mark 13:26 because here this is a title of office for Jesus. Observe that 1 Thessalonians 4:13-18 describes the Lord's coming in a somewhat similar way.

(3) Note that the insistence that only God knows *when* these events will occur (Mark 13:32) is Jesus' answer to the disciples' question in 13:4.

(4) Note how each Gospel urges its readers to be "awake" (Mark 13:37; Matthew 24:42; 25:13; Luke 21:34-36), and that in Matthew and Luke this word is Jesus' last word about the future. Note that Paul, using different language, makes a similar point in 1 Thessalonians 5:1-11.

Day 5 Matthew 24:37–25:46; Luke 12:35-48; 19:11-27; 1 Corinthians 3:10-15; 4:1-5

    (1) Note that the sayings in Matthew 24:37-51 reinforce 24:36. Note what Matthew 24:38-39 infers from the story of Noah in Genesis 6:1–7:16. Observe that these sayings appear earlier in Luke (12:39-40; 17:26-27).

    (2) Note that the point of the parable of the bridesmaids is stated at the end (Matthew 25:1-13). Note also that the rejection of the unprepared (25:12) is like 7:21-23.

    (3) Observe how vividly the parable of the talents (25:14-30) portrays the theme of accountability and so prepares the reader for the portrayal of the Last Judgment that follows (25:31-46) as the climax of the discourse.

    (4) Note how the judgment scene agrees with Matthew 7:21-23, recalls 5:20, and fits 5:43-48.

Day 6 Read and respond to "Signs of Danger and Dangerous Signs" and "Do You Want to Become His Disciples, Too?"

Prayer Concerns

Signs of Danger and Dangerous Signs

Mark 13 contains Jesus' long, uninterrupted discourse (13:5-37), given to disciples on the Mount of Olives, which, being separated from Jerusalem by the Kidron Valley and being higher than the city, affords a striking view of the city to the west. The Temple, with its white stone and gold leaf, dominated the view then, as does the Dome of the Rock today. Mark prepares the reader for the subject matter by reporting that as Jesus and the disciples left the Temple, the disciples marveled at the large buildings in the Temple complex and at the large stones, thereby prompting Jesus to predict that the whole place will be leveled (13:2). Neither the magnificence of the Temple, with its gold ornamentation, nor the size of the stones assures its permanence. Now with the whole city spread before them, the disciples (in Mark, the four whom Jesus first called; 1:16-20) ask, "When will this be?" and what will indicate that "all these things" are about to happen (13:4). In Luke 21:7 they ask only about the Temple, but in Matthew 24:3 they ask also about the sign of Jesus' coming at the end of the age. In all three Gospels, however, Jesus does more than satisfy their curiosity about the future; he also warns them lest they misunderstand what will befall them. Indeed, the whole discourse, including its expanded form in Matthew, is devoted to the distinction between signs of danger and dangerous signs.

When Signs of Danger Become Dangerous Signs

Jesus' teachings in Mark 13:5-23 begin and end on the same note—a warning against dangerous figures (so also Matthew 24:4-5; in Luke Jesus issued the warning before, in 17:20-23). However, in none of the Gospels does Jesus say who *they* are, when they will come, where they will come from, or where they will show up. Unfortunately, a number of them succeed in leading many astray by who they claim to be: "I am he" (specified in Matthew as "I am the Messiah"). Even if the "many" who will be misled may be the general public, the warning is clearly addressed to the believers: "Beware that no one leads you astray." Why they should need this warning is not explained. Will some followers, for whatever reasons, come to doubt that Jesus is the Messiah and instead believe those who claim to be? Or will they believe those who claim to be Jesus returned? Luke implicitly underscores the danger these

people create, for according to 21:8 they will announce, "The time [of the end? of redemption?] is near," which is virtually what Jesus wants the future church to believe when certain things occur: "Stand up and raise your heads, because your redemption is drawing near" (21:28), and "When you see these things taking place, you know that the kingdom of God is near" (21:31). Like Mark and Matthew, Luke implies that if the readers attend carefully to what Jesus says in these passages, they will know why those who make messianic claims for themselves are wrong, for here Jesus outlines what will happen before the end—including the appearance of precisely such deceivers.

Jesus first insists that "wars and rumors of wars" are not evidence that the end is here (Mark 13:7) or even approaching (Luke 21:9). Mark 13:8 elaborates: In addition to wars there will be earthquakes and famine (Luke 21:11 adds "plagues" and "dreadful portents and great signs from heaven," spelled out later in 21:25-26). These disasters are "but the beginning of the birth pangs," the first contractions, which, though unavoidable, are not to be confused with the delivery itself. Knowing this, the readers should not get overexcited when they hear of such things.

The first warning concerns the danger of being misled by the misinterpretations advanced by others; but the second (Mark 13:9-13) addresses the danger that Christians might abandon their faith because they will experience persecution, betrayal by family, martyrdom, and general hatred "because of my name" (that is, because they are known as Christ-people). Nonetheless, those who remain faithful "will be saved." Most of what we read in 13:9-13 is found in Jesus' mission discourse in Matthew (Matthew 10:17-21). So at this point Matthew, instead of repeating, has Jesus predict what else can be expected—torture, false prophets, increase of lawlessness causing "the love of many" to "grow cold" (24:9-13). Flogging in the synagogue was punishment for blasphemy; Paul said he endured this five times (2 Corinthians 11:24). In Acts 26:9-11 he admits that while persecuting the church he punished them "often in all the synagogues" and "tried to force them to blaspheme." That Christian Jews would experience the hostility of the synagogue is promised also in Luke's Sermon on the Plain: "Blessed are you when people hate you, and when they exclude you [from the synagogue], revile you, and defame you"—literally, "cast out your name as evil" (Luke 6:22). In John 16:2 Jesus says, "They will put you out of the synagogues. Indeed, an hour is coming when those who kill you will think that by doing so they are offering worship to God." Believers will also be brought to trial before Gentile governors and kings, yet they are not to worry about what to say there, for the Holy Spirit will tell them what to say (Mark 13:9-11; Matthew 10:19-20). Although Luke 12:11-12 also promises the Holy Spirit's role in the courtroom, in Luke 21:14-15 Jesus himself will be at work in the court: "I will give you words and a wisdom that none of your opponents will be able to withstand or contradict."

But even the persecution and martyrdom of believers is not evidence that the end is here, because before that will occur "the good news must first be proclaimed to all nations [or Gentiles]" (Mark 13:10). What in Mark is a divinely set necessity ("must") is a promise in Matthew 24:14: "And this good news of the kingdom will be proclaimed throughout the world, as a testimony to all the nations; and then the end will come." Neither passage, however, promises that the nations will believe the gospel. What is foreseen is not the Christianization of the world but its evangelization.

Jesus' third warning returns to the danger of misreading a disaster. The "desolating sacrilege" will be erected "where it ought not to be." Curiously, while Mark reports no explanatory words from Jesus, he inserts a parenthesis: "Let the reader understand." Since Mark assumes we will get the point concerning this sacrilege, he goes on to report Jesus' counsel to "those in Judea": "Flee!" (Mark 13:14-20; Matthew 24:15-22; Luke 21:20-24).

Matthew helps the reader understand the "desolating sacrilege" by replacing Mark's "where it ought not to be" with "in the holy place"—that is, the sanctuary of the Temple complex—and by pointing to the words in the book of Daniel, though he does not say which words (Matthew 24:15-16). Scholars agree that in Daniel 8:11-14 "the transgression that makes desolate" refers to the profaning of the Jerusalem Temple by Antiochus Epiphanes, who forbade the continuing of Jewish sacrifices (spelled out more fully in Daniel 9:27: "He shall make sacrifice and offering cease; and in their place shall be an abomination that desolates"—repeated in 11:31 and 12:11). According to the account in 1 Maccabees 1:41-64, after "a desolating sacrilege" had been erected on the altar, pagan sacrifice was offered on the twenty-fifth day of December, 167 B.C., part of the effort to stamp out the Jewish religion. This outrage led to the Maccabean revolt, whose success was celebrated by the rededication of the Temple and the renewal of sacrifice exactly three years later; it is still celebrated by the Feast of Hanukkah.

Mark's warning about the desolating sacrilege implies that the Temple will be profaned again as it was two centuries before. (Mark and his readers might have thought Jesus' words had almost come to pass in A.D. 40 when the emperor Caligula ordered a statue of himself to be placed in the

What is foreseen is not the Christianization of the world but its evangelization.

the Temple; he died, however, before the order was carried out.) When that happens, the Judeans (Judean Christians) are to flee to the mountains, apparently to avoid God's wrath, whose coming would unleash unprecedented suffering (Mark 13:19). The desolating sacrilege is to be the sign of the ultimate danger.

Luke's readers are spared puzzling over the offensive thing in the Temple. In this Gospel the Judean Christians are to flee when they see "Jerusalem surrounded by armies," for this siege means "its desolation has come near" (Luke 21:20). Those in the city must leave, and those in the country must not enter it; "for these are days of vengeance, as a fulfillment of all that is written" (21:21-22). The verses that follow clearly refer to the fate of Jerusalem and its inhabitants when Titus captured the city in A.D. 70. In Mark and Matthew Jesus insists (not clearly alluding to Jerusalem) that the coming suffering will be greater than any in the past or future (Mark 13:19; Matthew 24:21). In such a time some will claim to have found the Messiah, but they are not to be believed. The "false messiahs and false prophets" are dangerous signs, for they might lead astray "the elect," the otherwise faithful Christians.

Ignorance and Vigilance

According to Mark 13:24-25, also Matthew 24:29, the terrible suffering on earth will be followed by strange happenings in the sky:

"The sun will be darkened,
    and the moon will not give its light,
and the stars will be falling from heaven,

and the powers in the heavens will be
  shaken."
These celestial events too are signs of disaster, not to be confused with an eclipse or the "falling stars" that we can see from time to time. In fact Luke edits Mark to make this clear: "There will be signs in the sun, the moon, and the stars, and on the earth distress among nations confused by the roaring of the sea and the waves"—no ordinary storms. "People will faint from fear and foreboding of what is coming upon the world, for the powers of the heavens will be shaken" (Luke 21:25-26). It will seem that the cosmos is coming apart, that creation is returning to chaos. The strange behavior of sun, moon, and stars is a common motif in the prophets' oracles about the coming wrath of God. To Isaiah 13:10 we could add 34:4; Ezekiel 32:7-8; Joel 2:10-11, 30-31; 3:14-16; Amos 8:9. Some Jewish apocalyptic texts elaborate the strange behavior of the cosmos. For example 2 Esdras* (also called 4 Ezra) 5:4-5 predicts,

> "The sun shall suddenly begin to shine at night
>   and the moon during the day....
> the peoples shall be troubled,
>   and the stars shall fall."

The Christian apocalypse, the Revelation to John, draws from the same stock of celestial signs. When the sixth seal was opened, the earth quaked, "the sun became black as sackcloth, the full moon became like blood, and the stars of the sky fell to the earth as the fig tree drops its winter fruit when shaken by a gale, the sky vanished like a scroll rolling itself up, and every mountain and island was removed from its place" (Revelation 6:12-14).

Mark 13, as well as Matthew 24 and Luke 21, calls attention to the sequence of future events—wars, earthquake and famine, "the beginning of the birth pangs" (during which Christians will be persecuted and killed?), *then* the desolating sacrilege, *then* unprecedented suffering (during which the Judeans are to flee), *then* "after that suffering" there will be confusion in the cosmos, and "*then* [not before] they [not specified] will see 'the Son of Man coming in clouds' with great power and glory. *Then* he will send out the angels and gather his elect" (Mark 13:26-27). In Matthew 24:30-31 the scenario is slightly different: After the powers in the heavens are shaken, "then the *sign* of the Son of Man will appear in heaven, and then all the tribes of the earth will mourn, and [then?] they will see 'the Son of Man coming on the clouds of heaven' with power and great glory. And he will send out his angels." None of the Gospels, however, says a word about how long will be the time

of suffering or the time span during which celestial disturbances will occur. Only Matthew 24:29 says that the heavenly events will occur "immediately after the suffering." In all three Gospels Jesus now points to the fig tree: Just as its leafing out indicates summer is near (not yet here), "so also, when you see these things [probably everything mentioned since the beginning of the discourse] taking place, you know that he [the Son of Man] is near, at the very gates" (Mark 13:28-29; Matthew 24:32-33; Luke 21:29-31; in Luke, however, it is the kingdom of God that is near).

> **The exact moment when the Son of Man will come is God's secret, and he keeps it. So Jesus closes the door to all calculations and timetables about "the end of the world."**

To our surprise Jesus now says in all three Gospels, "This generation will not pass away until all these things have taken place" (Mark 13:30; Matthew 24:34; Luke 21:32). Moreover, Jesus proceeds with the assurance, "Heaven and earth will pass away, but my words will not pass away." Nonetheless, he continues (though not in Luke), "But about that day or hour no one knows, neither the angels in heaven, nor the Son, but only the Father." The exact moment when the Son of Man will come is God's secret, and he keeps it. So Jesus closes the door to all calculations and timetables about "the end of the world." Readers know what to expect and the sequence of events; but they remain ignorant of the timing because God wants it that way.

Also surprising is the conclusion Jesus draws from this unremovable ignorance (Mark 13:33-37). Instead of saying, "Since you do not know the time, don't worry about it," he commands the opposite: "Beware; keep alert." Using the analogy of a man going on a journey who assigns each slave his task and commands "the doorkeeper to be on the watch," he urges, "Therefore, keep awake—for you do not know when the master of the house will come [back], in the evening, or at midnight, or at cockcrow, or at dawn, or else he may find you asleep when he comes suddenly. And what I say to you I say to all: Keep awake." In Mark this word is Jesus' last on the subject of the future. Clearly,

Mark understands the man who goes and returns suddenly to symbolize Jesus' sudden coming as the Son of Man. Luke 21:34-36 restates the point: "Be on guard so that your hearts are not weighed down with dissipation and drunkenness and the worries of this life, and that day does not catch you unexpectedly, like a trap. For it will come upon all who live on the face of the whole earth. Be alert at all times, praying that you may have the strength to escape all these things that will take place, and to stand before the Son of Man" (the judge). With this the discourse ends in Luke.

Years before (around A.D. 51), Paul made the same point Mark and Luke make. In 1 Thessalonians 5:1-11 he too insists that "the day of the Lord" will come unexpectedly, "like a thief in the night." But Paul does not write about preceding sufferings; to the contrary, he writes, "When they say, 'There is peace and security,' then suddenly destruction will come upon them, as labor pains come upon a pregnant woman, and there will be no escape!" But he goes on to assure his readers that since we Christians are day people and not night people (that is, we can see what is going on), we should not fall asleep but keep awake. He also urges vigilance. In the previous chapter (1 Thessalonians 4:13-18) Paul explains that on that day, "the dead in Christ will rise first. Then we who are alive . . . will be caught up in the . . . air; and so we will be with the Lord forever" (4:16-17). Our Gospel passages, on the other hand, say nothing about the resurrection and merely allude to the rapture in passing. They are more interested in creation's rupture than in the Christians' rapture.

Warning: You are Accountable!

Matthew 24:37-51 continues the instruction about the coming of the Son of Man; but instead of elaborating the brief description of the event in 24:30-31, the passage indicates how his coming affects those who are not prepared for it. According to 24:37-39, his coming will find people going about their lives without any premonition that every-thing will end abruptly—as it was in Noah's day: "They knew nothing until the flood came and swept them all away"—a point made also in 1 Thessalonians 5:2-3. The next saying (Matthew 24:40-41) uses different imagery to continue the thought: Of two in the field, and of two women at the grinding wheel, one will be taken and the other left. This being "taken" probably alludes to the rapture, as does the gathering of his elect in 24:31. Still, the rapture itself is not described because what matters here are the consequences.

The note on which Mark 13 ended ("Keep awake") is the theme of Matthew 24:42-44. Indeed, it provides the positive exhortation that frames the negative example of the man who did not stay awake: Had he done so, he "would not have let his house be broken into" because the thief would not have caught him off guard, asleep. The exact time of the Son of Man's coming is what the disciples do not know, as 24:36 has already pointed out. But this ignorance is no excuse; to the contrary, precisely *because* they do not know the time, they must stay awake constantly. The saying also implies that whoever is not awake either does not care or thinks he or she knows when the thief will come and so can sleep until the last minute.

Matthew 24:45-51 at first looks like a more elaborate version of what Jesus said in Mark 13:33-37; but while both passages concern the slave who is surprised by the unexpected return of the master, the allegorical parable in Matthew has different concerns. (This two-part parable does not say clearly whether there are two slaves, one "faithful and wise," the other "wicked," or whether we should think of one slave who makes the wrong choice, as in Luke 12:42-46). In any case the master entrusts

> His coming will find people going about their lives without any premonition that everything will end abruptly—as it was in Noah's day.

his household to a slave, who is thereby responsible for the well-being of other slaves. When the returning master finds the slave "at work" (that is, doing what he was told to do), he will be rewarded with even greater responsibilities. The slave, however, uses the master's delay to abuse the other slaves and to carouse. But will he be surprised when the master arrives unexpectedly! He will be punished with the hypocrites ("cut . . . in pieces," an apt metaphor for total destruction). The basic structure of the plot suggests that the parable is allegorical; that is, the master (Jesus) puts a slave in charge of his house-hold (a leader or leadership responsible for the well-being of the church) while he is gone (after the Ascension). If all goes well, the slave is rewarded when the master (Jesus as the Son of Man) returns. But if the slave takes advantage of the master's delay (the Son of Man's coming has been postponed) and acts wickedly (the leadership becomes corrupt), the master who returns will punish resolutely. In this reading of the parable the emphasis falls on what the slave does during the master's absence and what he is found doing when the master arrives. To be "faithful and wise" is to be obedient, and to be found "at work," to be "ready" (Matthew 24:44), to be "awake" (24:42). Being ready for the coming of the Son of Man is not idle waiting but being at work. Expect a reckoning.

The parable of the ten bridesmaids makes a similar point (25:1-13). When the delayed bridegroom suddenly arrives, only the wise women (who have oil for their lamps) join the groom at the wedding banquet. The foolish find themselves excluded because they are not prepared. Because the parable emphasizes preparedness, we should not allegorize all the details (the lamps, the oil, the sleeping, the buying from dealers, the shut door); these details are necessary to make the story vivid. Matthew's concluding line clearly discloses his point: "Keep awake therefore, for you know neither the day nor the hour" (25:13).

Next comes the parable of the talents (a talent was a great sum of money), whose plot concerns the slaves' accountability for what has been entrusted to them during the master's long absence (25:14-30). Here too the returning master (the coming Son of Man) rewards the faithful slave (who enriches the master) and punishes the faithless one who does nothing with what he received, being afraid to fail a harsh master. Knowing that he must give an account of the one talent, he ventures nothing and wants only to survive by not losing it. As it turns out, however, he loses everything.

GC 19-3 Luke's version (Luke 19:12-27) introduces a subplot into the parable, which otherwise resembles Matthew 25:14-30. In the added plot a "nobleman" went to a distant country to get royal power for himself and return (Luke 19:12)—an allegorical way of referring to Jesus' ascension to heaven where he will receive power at God's right hand and then return as the Son of Man. In Luke the nobleman gives each of ten slaves one "pound" with which to "do business" in his absence. While he was gone, the citizens of his country "hated him and sent a delegation after him, saying, 'We do not want this man to rule over us' " (19:14), an allegorical way of referring to the Jews' refusal of Jesus' messiahship proclaimed in the gospel. Nothing more is said about the citizens until the end of the parable. In the meantime, the parable reports what happens when the nobleman returns, "having

received royal power." Now he learns that one slave turned his one "pound" into ten pounds, the next turned his into five, and so makes the first a ruler over ten cities and the next over five cities. But the slave who simply returned the pound he had been given finds that he now loses even that. The stewardship of the other seven and their reward is ignored, for the point has already been made: The reward matches the achievement. Finally, the returned nobleman deals with his enemies who refused his kingship: He orders them slaughtered while he looks on (19:27)—perhaps an allusion to the slaughter that occurred when the Romans sacked Jerusalem. By inserting the subplot, Luke implies that both the nobleman's slaves (believers) and his enemies will be held accountable when the Son of Man comes.

In Matthew, Jesus' discourse concludes with the portrayal of the Last Judgment (Matthew 25:31-46), which occurs when the Son of Man has been enthroned (in 25:34 he is called the king) and so has the right to be the judge of "all the nations" (*ethnē*, also means Gentiles) now gathered in his presence. Interpreters continue to disagree over the identity of the *ethnē*. Are they all humanity? all Gentiles? all Christians, Jewish as well as Gentile? Probably the latter is preferable. A striking feature of the passage is the repetition of the criteria that determine whether persons are among the sheep (the righteous or blessed) on the right or among the goats (the accursed) on the left—feeding the hungry, giving drink to the thirsty, welcoming the stranger, clothing the naked, caring for the sick, and visiting prisoners. Noticeably absent from the list is any reference to miracle-working or to confessing Jesus as Lord—the very things to which the rejected appeal in 7:21-23. That deeds of mercy are rewarded is not surprising. What is surprising is that the needy recipient is the judge, and his explanation of how this was the case: "Just as you did it to one of the least of these who are members of my family, you did it to me" (25:40). Nowhere else in the Gospels does Jesus identify himself so fully with the vulnerable and the needy.

> **Being ready for the coming of the Son of Man is not idle waiting but being at work. Expect a reckoning.**

The fact that the doers are surprised to learn that what they did for the needy they actually did for Christ indicates that they did not *use* the needy, did not regard service to them as a way of earning Christ's approval. Here we recall that when Matthew 1:22-23 quotes Isaiah 7:14,

"Look, the virgin shall . . . bear a son,
and they shall name him Emmanuel,"
the Evangelist explains that this name means "God is with us." The judgment scene discloses that the *us* is particularly the hungry and thirsty, the stranger, the naked, the sick, and the imprisoned. Because this teaching dominates the picture of the judgment, Matthew's readers—today's church included—now know what they are accountable for.

So Then

When we reflect on these teachings in Mark 13, Matthew 24–25, and Luke 21 as a whole, we discover that what the chapters emphasize diverges significantly from the interests of many readers today, who want to know exactly what will happen at "the end of the world" or at "the Second Coming" (a phrase not used until the second century). These chapters do contain brief descriptions of what is to come; but two observations should be pondered.

First, even if we were to organize all the predictions in these passages into a single scenario and then fill in the gaps by using 1 Thessalonians 4–5 and 1 Corinthians 15, the information still would be incomplete. And would not such an effort show that we think that what any one Gospel, or Paul, has to say is not adequate for us? Second, the more preoccupied we are with constructing the scenario of the end, the more we bypass what the Gospels, and Paul, are more concerned with—the way to live now.

Just as observing what is advertised on the evening news reveals significant aspects of the audience, so looking at the various warnings, prohibitions, and commands, as well as the words of encouragement, discloses how the Evangelists "read" their readers' situation. They see their readers as exposed to a combination of external dangers they cannot avoid and various developments within the community, some of which threaten to split the churches (Mark 13:6, 21-23; Matthew 24:11-12), others of which are eroding the believers' confidence (Mark 13:13). In short, the readers are vulnerable to moral and spiritual consequences of various *mis*-interpretations of horrible experiences. The Evangelists wrote what they did in order to let Jesus steer the church through the rough waters in the coming narrows—the same Jesus whose name provokes hatred, flogging, and trials before governors and kings; the same Jesus who had rebuked the demonic of the deep and then asked, "Why are you afraid?" (Mark 4:39-40).

> The fact that the doers are surprised to learn that what they did for the needy they actually did for Christ indicates that they did not *use* the needy, did not regard service to them as a way of earning Christ's approval.

Comfortable Christians may be relieved that these chapters were addressed to Christians in the distant first century or may become uncomfortable because the figure of Jesus these chapters portray seems to be stern, harsh, and without compassion. Both responses merit thoughtful attention. Perhaps it is enough here to observe two things: (1) In the past two millennia Christians often have found these chapters germane to their situations; also today conflicts and corruption, persecution, and martyrdom are a significant part of the worldwide church's daily experience. (2) If the Jesus of these chapters seems foreign to us, it may be because we have filtered out his stern side to make him more attractive. But the whole Jesus of the Gospels is the Jesus we need.

Do You Want to Become His Disciples, Too?

Of the many implications of these chapters for our discipleship, three can be singled out as of enduring significance. First, discipleship means persistent faithfulness, steady adherence to Jesus, especially in rough times. The more difficult the circumstances, the easier it becomes to begin to follow someone else—especially those who promise to explain the future by combining scattered biblical passages with the morning paper and so turn faith into reliance on a blueprint of their own making. We need not fall for it.

Second, when it comes to the "when" of the Second Coming, the disciple should avoid speculation because the Jesus of these chapters has both insisted that only God knows the time and told us how to live with our not knowing: We are to be ready by being faithful and at work. The conscientious worker does not need to know when the inspector will arrive before doing what is expected. Nor does the faithful disciple need to know the day of the Son of Man. Besides, if the disciple did know it, what would the disciple do with that knowledge?

Third, as followers of Jesus, we know that we are accountable for the quality of our own discipleship, for our own obedience and righteousness (the foolish bridesmaids could not borrow from the wise); that everyone has received something for whose use every person will have to give an account. Moreover, on that day, the judge will not reward us for our opinions and ideas, not even for the right ones, but for the way we treated the least of his siblings, our neighbors.

What is it about Jesus as judge that calls you to be obedient in the present and unafraid of the future?

174

Prayer

Send your light and your truth to guide me.
Let them lead me to your house
    on your sacred mountain.
Then I will worship at your altar
    because you make me joyful.
You are my God, and I will praise you.
    Yes, I will praise you as I play my harp.

Why am I discouraged? Why am I restless?
I trust you! And I will praise you again
    because you help me, and you are my God.

(Psalm 43:3-5, CEV)

20 Destiny Seized

He said, "Abba, Father, for you all things are possible;
remove this cup from me; yet, not what I want,
but what you want."

(Mark 14:36)

They Have No Wine

No one likes to accept the inevitable, because we want to determine—or at least shape—our future. Even if we sense that it's all for the best in the long run, we struggle to find an alternative we can manage. We do not want to be seen—including by ourselves—as failures. When our sense of self-worth is threatened by the inevitable, we find it hard to avoid resentment. Life shouldn't turn out this way.

Beginning With Moses and All the Prophets

This week and next, we study the Passion story* as told in each of the Synoptic Gospels. Reading John's account helps us see the Synoptics more clearly. Matthew and Luke did not change the sequence of events in Mark (as they sometimes had done before), though Luke did insert two passages (Luke 22:24-30; 22:35-38) into Mark's story (see chart below). We recall that in the first Passion prediction Jesus had said that "the Son of Man *must* undergo great suffering" (Mark 8:31); this *must* means that what will occur in the Passion story carries out God's will. The Passion story's perspective is as important as its plot.

	Matthew	Mark	Luke	John
The plotting	26:1-5	14:1-2	22:1-2	11:57
The anointing	26:6-13	14:3-9		12:1-8
The betrayal	26:14-16	14:10-11	22:3-6	
Passover preparation	26:17-19	14:12-16	22:7-13	
The supper	26:20-29	14:17-25	22:14-23	13–17
Dispute over greatness			22:24-27	
Kingdom conferred			22:28-30	
Denial predicted	26:30-35	14:26-31	22:31-34	13:21-38
"Buy a sword"			22:35-38	
Gethsemane	26:36-46	14:32-42	22:39-46	
The arrest	26:47-56	14:43-52	22:47-53	18:1-12
Before Caiaphas and Peter's denial	26:57-75	14:53-72	22:54-71	18:13-27

Day 1 **Mark 14;** 1 Corinthians 11:23-26; Exodus 12:14-28; 24:3-8; Leviticus 24:13-16; Daniel 7:13-14; Zechariah 13:7-9

Some suggestions here require looking ahead to Matthew 26 and Luke 22.

(1) Don't miss the artistry in Mark 14. Note, for instance, how 14:1-11 sets the stage with a sense of tragedy and foreboding. Note also that the brief statements at the ends of sections function like a change of scene in a drama (14:11, 42, 72).

(2) **GC 20-1** Note that although both Mark 14:2 and Matthew 26:5 say that the intent was to avoid arresting Jesus during Passover, neither Gospel explains why he was in fact arrested then. Note also that Luke 22:1-2 avoids this problem.

(3) Note that there are three meanings of the woman's act in Bethany—the woman's, the disciples', and Jesus' (Mark 14:3-9; Matthew 26:6-13).

(4) Observe that Mark 14:17; Matthew 26:20; and Luke 22:21 clearly imply that Judas shared the supper, and that none of the Synoptics says when he left, but that John 13:30 does mention the departure. (John does not report what Mark 14:10-11 says.)

(5) Observe that the "false teaching" reported in Mark 14:57-58 distorts what Jesus had said at 13:2.

(6) Note the high priest's question and Jesus' answer (Mark 14:61-62). Note that Jesus alludes to Daniel 7:13-14 and Psalm 110:1. Note that this answer is construed as blasphemy.

(7) Note that Exodus 12:14-28 helps us understand what is involved in Mark 14:12-16, that Exodus 24:3-8 uses "the blood of the covenant" taken up by Jesus in Mark 14:24, that Jesus cites Zechariah 13:7-9 in Mark 14:27, that Leviticus 24:13-16 lies behind Mark 14:63.

1 Corth: 23-26 - Institution of Lord's supper.   Exodus 12: 14-28 First Passover
Zechariah 13: 7-9 - Shepherd struck / flock scatters
Deut 19:21 ---- eye for an eye etc.
Matt 26:28 --- adds "for forgiveness of sins"
Isaiah 50:5-6 - Prophesy of Jesus's torture

Day 2 Matthew 26; Deuteronomy 15:7-11; 17:6-7; 19:15-21; Isaiah 50:5-6

Today we focus on Matthew 26.

(1) Note that 26:2 is a Passion prediction found only here and that Jesus foretells *how* he will be killed (as in 20:19).

(2) Observe that in 26:15 Judas asks to be paid and is paid on the spot—details found only here.

(3) Observe what Matthew 26:28 adds to Jesus' words taken from Mark 14:24.

(4) Note that in Matthew's and Mark's accounts of Jesus in Gethsemane, Jesus prays three times (once in Luke).

(5) Note how Matthew 26:64 (and Luke 22:70) change Jesus' reply in Mark 14:62.

Day 3 Luke 22; Exodus 34:18; Isaiah 52:13–53:12; Jeremiah 31:27-34; Ezekiel 45:21

Luke 22 is the center of attention today.

(1) Note how 22:3 accounts for Judas's action, and that in John 13:27 this occurs at the Last Supper.

(2) Note that in Luke's account of the supper (Luke 22:15-20) there are two cups. Observe that only in Luke does Jesus ask for repetition "in remembrance of me," and that this detail is found also in 1 Corinthians 11:25. Note also that in Luke, as in 1 Corinthians 11:25, Jesus speaks of the "new covenant," alluding to Jeremiah 31:27-34. Many manuscripts of Mark and Matthew also have "my blood of the new covenant."

(3) Observe that in Luke the question about the identity of the betrayer (22:23) leads into its opposite: Who will be the greatest? See also Mark 10:42-45; Matthew 20:25-28.

(4) Observe that only Luke has Jesus transfer the Kingdom to the disciples (22:29-30).

(5) Note that many manuscripts omit 22:43-44. Compare Mark's explanation of why the disciples slept (14:40) with Luke's explanation (22:45).

(6) Observe that in Luke 22:49 the disciples ask whether they should defend Jesus with the sword. Note that only in Luke does Jesus heal the slave's ear (22:51). Notice especially Jesus' last word at his arrest (22:53).

(7) Note that Jesus' reply to the high priest not only adds a rebuke (22:67-68) but omits referring to the Son of Man's "coming with the clouds of heaven," and so ends with an allusion to the Ascension.

Luke 22:3 - Satan entered Judas

Last Word - power of darkness

Day 4 John 11:4-57; 12:1-8; 13; Psalm 41:4-10

(1) Note that John 11:55-57 assumes that Jesus' action in the Temple had not taken place a few days before, as in the Synoptics.

(2) Observe that also in John there is an anointing of Jesus in Bethany (12:1-8) and that here it is Judas who complains about the wasted money.

(3) Note that John 13, like the Synoptics, reports a meal at which Jesus identifies his betrayer and predicts Peter's denial. Note also that in John Jesus does not institute the Lord's Supper, that this is not a Passover meal, and that only here does Jesus wash the disciples' feet.

Day 5 John 18:1-27; 1 John 4:7-12

    (1) Notice that John 18:2 says that Jesus had met often in the garden (not named). Note also that 18:18 gives more details than the Synoptics. Observe that in 18:9 John calls attention to the way Jesus' own word is fulfilled (17:12). Observe also that John does not include the story of Jesus' agony in Gethsemane.

    (2) Observe that in 18:14 John explains who Caiaphas is by the cross-reference to 11:45-33.

    (3) Note that in 18:15 "another disciple" who was known to the high priest is never named (probably he is "the one whom Jesus loved," 13:23, often thought to be John).

    (4) Observe how the story of Jesus before Annas (18:19-24) differs noticeably from Mark 14:55-65.

[handwritten notes: M. Mr. L. = Lord's Supper / John → Last Supper / Paul → Eucharist (the Thanksgiving)]

Day 6 Read and respond to "Destiny Seized" and "Do You Want to Become His Disciples, Too?"

Prayer Concerns

The Names of the Last Meal

    Jesus' last meal with his disciples is sometimes called the Lord's Supper, sometimes the Last Supper, and sometimes the Eucharist (beginning with *Didache*). (1) The earliest reference to "the Lord's supper" appears in 1 Corinthians 11:20, where, in chiding the Corinthians for the way they misuse the meal, Paul says they do not really eat "the Lord's supper." Although the Synoptics do not use this phrase but say instead that it was a Passover meal (as Paul does not), in both First Corinthians and the Synoptics Jesus solemnly interprets the bread and wine as his body and blood. What Jesus said is known as "the words of institution" because in both 1 Corinthians 11:24-25 and Luke 22:19 Jesus "institutes" a ritual by saying, "Do this in remembrance of me." Paul's phrase "the Lord's supper" is applied to all three Synoptics even though "Do this in remembrance" is not found in Mark and Matthew. (2) Because John's Gospel lacks the words of institution, this account is known as the Last Supper. (3) *Didache* 9, like Paul, assumes the churches celebrate this meal and calls it "the Eucharist" (the Thanksgiving) in keeping with the prayers it prescribes, each of which begins with a word of thanks for the cup and for the wine. (Paul too says that Jesus gave thanks for the bread before he broke it.) *Didache* also insists that only "those who have been baptized in the Lord's name" may eat or drink the Eucharist and cites Jesus in support: "Give not what is holy to the dogs" (Matthew 7:6).

Destiny Seized

Each Evangelist wrote the Passion story with special care (Matthew 26–27; Mark 14–15; Luke 22–23; John 18–19). Each in his own way lets us see certain contrasts, particular highlights next to dark dimensions, partly by the way he tells the individual episodes, and partly by where he places them in the whole story. By this means each Gospel writer invites the readers to do more than see what happened, to "see into" what happened. While this feature characterizes each Gospel as a whole, it is especially important in each Passion story.

Each Gospel has its own way of telling us Jesus was not caught off guard by what happened that Passover time; John does this by the frequent references to the "hour" to come, the Synoptics by the three "Passion predictions" (Mark 8:31; Matthew 16:21; Luke 9:22). Lest the readers forget that Jesus has foreseen what lies ahead, Matthew's Passion story begins with Jesus' saying, "The Son of Man will be handed over to be crucified" (Matthew 26:2). To catch the force of this remarkable statement, we need to remember that "Son of Man" is a title for Jesus' exalted office as God's representative (Matthew had just ended Jesus' last discourse in Matthew 25 with the parable of the Great Judgment in which Jesus, the Son of Man, sits "on the throne of his glory" (25:31). Who then can miss the strangeness built into Jesus' word that "the Son of Man will be handed over to be crucified"? To miss the strangeness of what follows, not only in Matthew, is to miss the moral shudder and awe that the Passion stories evoke.

> **Each Gospel has its own way of telling us Jesus was not caught off guard by what happened that Passover time.**

From Bethany to Gethsemane

The story of Jesus' anointing in Matthew 26:6-13 and Mark 14:3-9 differs from that in John 12:1-8. Luke does not have the story, perhaps because Luke 7:36-50 reports another story of Jesus' anointing. Here we focus on Mark 14:3-9.

The remarkable story has an unusual setting—a dinner "in the house of Simon the leper." Since lepers were excluded from society, was the host known as "Simon the leper" even after being cured? In any case, this detail alerts the reader to expect something unusual. During the meal, an unnamed woman appears with "an alabaster jar of very costly ointment of nard" which she breaks and empties on Jesus' head. Breaking the jar shows that she kept nothing back for another occasion. Though her motivation is not reported, the act expressed unreserved devotion. Her motivation was not what was criticized, however, but the "waste." On the market this ointment could have brought a whole year's wages for a laborer and been given to the poor. Many would agree also today. After all, hadn't Jesus told the rich man to sell what he had and give the money to the poor (Mark 10:21)?

But Jesus objects to the objection. "Let her alone . . . . She has performed a good service for me. For you always have the poor with you, and you can show kindness to them whenever you wish [alluding to Deuteronomy 15:11], but you will not always have me." Instead of ending with this rebuke, Jesus goes on to interpret her deed: "She has anointed my body beforehand for its burial." He was right: This anointing was the only one his body would receive, for Jesus' body was not anointed before burial, but simply wrapped in a linen shroud; on Easter morning the women came to the tomb to do what should have been done (Mark 15:46–16:1); by then anointing was irrelevant. The Bethany story ends with Jesus' promise, "Wherever the good news is proclaimed in the whole world, what she has done will be told in remembrance of her" (14:9). Mark saw to it that Jesus' promise would come true. The whole scene, however, was more than Judas could take; so he left the dinner to betray the anointed.

Judas too is remembered, but as the betrayer. To this day to call someone "Judas" is to denounce the person as a traitor who succeeds by deception, for the kiss concealed his ill will (Mark 14:44-46; Matthew 26:48-50; Luke 22:47-48; but not in John).

Attempts to understand Judas keep returning to three questions because none of them has been answered convincingly to everyone. (1) What did Judas betray? According to Mark 14:44 the kiss was the prearranged sign by which Judas would identify Jesus. In John no such identification is necessary because Jesus identifies himself, twice in fact (John 18:4-8). John implies Judas knew that also on this night Jesus would lead his disciples to the garden. So he might have betrayed Jesus by disclosing where he could be caught. On the other hand, the Synoptics assume that at night the chief priests would not have known for sure which man was Jesus, despite the fact they had met and questioned him in the Temple. By kissing Jesus, Judas made sure the authorities would arrest the right man. Probably the word *betrayed* is used in a general way to refer to the means by which the authorities could find, identify, and capture Jesus.

(2) Why did Judas turn traitor? According to Luke 22:3, Judas decided to betray Jesus when "Satan entered into" him, thereby making him Satan's agent. John has the same view, though John's Gospel places Satan's act at the Last Supper. That Satan was the hidden actor is also implied in John 6:70-71, where Jesus asks, "Did I not choose you, the twelve? Yet one of you is a devil." The narrator explains that Jesus was speaking of Judas. Still, Satan's role does not tell us what was in Judas's mind. Was he disillusioned by Jesus? What had Jesus said or done (or not said or not done) that disappointed Judas so deeply that instead of simply drifting away he became a traitor? The answer remains his secret. The Gospels' answer— Satan's act—puts Judas's action in the framework of a cosmic struggle between God and Satan.

(3) How did Jesus come to know that his betrayer would be Judas? According to John 6:64 Jesus recognized that "among you are some who do not believe," which the narrator explains as follows: "For Jesus knew from the first who were the ones that did not believe, and who was the one that would betray him." Even so, the fact remains that in all the Gospels the only time Jesus says a single critical word about Judas or to him is in John's account of the anointing in Bethany,

The cost of salvation includes Judas's infidelity as well as Jesus' faithfulness.

where Judas is the one who complains. At no point had Jesus rebuked Judas as he had Peter (Mark 8:32-33) or John (Mark 9:38-40) or James and John (Mark 10:35-40; Luke 9:51-55). Perhaps the most we can say historically is that Jesus came to see into Judas's heart.

Judas remains a mystery, a tragic figure. His role at the climax of Jesus' mission is clear enough even though his mindset is not. On the historical level, the Synoptics imply that if Judas had not volunteered to betray Jesus, he would have been arrested *after* Passover, for the authorities did not want to take action against a popular figure. But Judas's decision presented them with an opportunity they seized. Theologically, he is as essential to Jesus' destiny as Pharaoh was to that of Moses. Judas too had a destiny, dark though it was. Jesus recognized this and did not condemn him, but instead said, "The Son of Man goes as it is written of him, but woe to that one by whom the Son of Man is betrayed! It would have been better for that one not to have been born" (Mark 14:21). The cost of salvation includes Judas's infidelity as well as Jesus' faithfulness.

The one we remember most, of course, is Jesus, the self-giver. His well-known saying in Mark 10:45 interprets the purpose of his mission as service, giving his life "a ransom for many." Not until his last meal does he restate the meaning of his death. In the Synoptics this meal is a Passover meal; in John it occurs the day before Passover. None of the efforts to harmonize this difference has been successful. Here we concentrate on the Synoptic reports of the meal that has come to be known by three names. (See "The Names of the Last Meal," page 179.)

By including the strange story of how the disciples found the place where the Passover meal would be eaten (Mark 14:12-16; Matthew 26:17-19; Luke 22:7-13), the Synoptics show that Jesus is in charge of this whole event, just as he had been of his arrival in Jerusalem. These Gospels also assume the readers need no explanation of what the disciples did to prepare the meal or what the meal commemorates—the Exodus of the Hebrew slaves from Egypt. The Gospels, however, show no interest in describing the meal; they simply allude to certain details of the Passover as they concentrate on what was distinctive and decisive in what Jesus said and did.

In all three Synoptic Gospels Jesus looks beyond his impending death to the time when he will again share the cup of wine with his disciples in the kingdom of God: "Truly I tell you, I will never again drink of the fruit of the vine until that day when I drink it new in the kingdom of God" (Mark 14:25; also Matthew 26:29; Luke 22:18). He does not mention his resurrection explicitly. The saying appears to be a pledge of abstinence but is really a solemn promise that Jesus' impending self-giving will not be in vain, for the establishment of God's reign is certain. If this future drinking refers to the messianic banquet (a common image for the celebratory character of God's future reign) as many interpreters hold, then this promise in effect makes this Passover meal an anticipation of the future celebration, the *hors d'oeuvre* for the banquet to come, presumably soon. This future horizon appears also in 1 Corinthians 11:26, Paul's comment on the Lord's Supper: "For as often as you eat this bread and drink the cup, you proclaim the Lord's death until he comes."

Especially important are the words of institution. Their wording varies not only from Gospel to Gospel but also in the manuscripts of each Gospel, as well as of First Corinthians. While these differences make it difficult to know exactly what Jesus said that night (besides, the texts are in Greek; he probably used Aramaic), they should not be overemphasized either. The main formulations are as follows, with manuscript variations in brackets. (See also "Luke's Account of the Supper," page 187.)

The Bread

Paul:		This is my body that is [broken] for you
Mark:	Take;	this is my body
Matthew:	Take, eat;	this is my body
Luke:		This is my body, which is given for you

Cup of Wine

Paul:	This cup is the new covenant in my blood
Luke:	This cup that is poured out for you is the new covenant in my blood
Mark:	This is my blood of the [new] covenant which is poured out for many
Matthew:	This is my blood of the [new] covenant which is poured out for many for the forgiveness of sins

The words of institution must not be separated from the action to which they are linked, for the meaning is conveyed by the combined word and deed. In every case the bread saying is preceded by a report of what Jesus did: He blessed the bread (so Mark and Matthew; in Paul and Luke he gave thanks) and *broke* it. Those manuscripts which at 1 Corinthians 11:24 read "my body that is broken" make clear that it is the broken bread that represents Jesus, not the bread itself. Likewise, when the tradition used by Paul and Luke adds "for you" it makes explicit what is implied when Mark and Matthew report that Jesus gave the pieces of bread to the disciples (they did not help themselves): In distributing the broken bread while saying, "Take, this is my body," Jesus enacts the meaning of his death as his self-giving for them.

Likewise, each Gospel in its own way emphasizes that all the disciples *drank* from the cup of wine, explicitly making them thereby participants in its meaning. (Although Paul's tradition does not include this detail, his own understanding of the eating and drinking in 1 Corinthians 10:16 agrees with the Gospels at this point: The cup is "a sharing in the blood of Christ," and the bread is "a sharing in the body of Christ.")

While all forms of the cup saying refer to the covenant, they do so somewhat differently; they also assume that the readers are familiar with basic elements of the Old Testament understanding of covenant-making. Although the Bible records covenants (agreements) between individuals (for example, Genesis 31:44-54), the most important covenant was between God and Israel, reported in Exodus 24:3-8.

The words of institution must not be separated from the action to which they are linked, for the meaning is conveyed by the combined word and deed.

While covenants between individuals normally expressed terms mutually agreed upon, in the covenant between God and Israel (like those between a king and his vassals) only God stipulates the terms even though both have obligations as a result. To state it more precisely, the covenant with Israel was a unilaterally initiated compact with bilateral obligations (God would be faithful, and Israel would obey the Law). Covenant-making being a sacred act, it was accompanied by the sacrifice of animals whose life-bearing blood sealed the agreement. In Exodus 24, half of the blood is dashed on the altar, half on the people. Moses calls this "the blood of the covenant" (24:8)—the words Jesus used in Mark 14:24 and Matthew 26:28. By using these words with the cup, of which they all drank, Jesus interpreted his own lifeblood as the sacrifice that sealed the covenant between the disciples and God. (This made Judas's treachery all the more reprehensible.) Since Jesus linked this cup to the coming Kingdom, he indicated that this covenant is the final, definitive compact between God and humans. Understandably, Paul's tradition, Luke, and some manuscripts of Mark and Matthew saw this as the "new covenant" foreseen by Jeremiah 31:27-34.

In Mark and Matthew the cup saying continues "which is poured out." The phrase does not refer to profuse bleeding; rather, to pour out blood is a common biblical way of referring to violent death, as in Matthew 23:35 and Acts 22:20 ("shed," NRSV). The phrase may also allude to the death of the servant of God in Isaiah 53. If so, it is to the Hebrew text of Isaiah 53:12 ("poured out his life unto death . . . bore the sin of many"); for the Greek text reads, "his soul [life] was given over to death . . . and he bore the sins of many." In biblical usage, *many* is not restrictive (as if the alternative were *all*) but inclusive (a great, unlimited number). How Jesus' violent death is "for" many is not indicated here. Later, Christian doctrines of the Atonement will offer explanations.

The Disgraced Denier

The dignity with which Jesus accepts and interprets his destiny is enhanced, negatively, by Judas's betrayal and by Peter's denial. Although the details vary, this enhancement is evident also in John. Since Matthew 26:30-35 differs only slightly from Mark 14:26-31, we will focus on Mark and Luke 22:31-34.

The hymn Mark mentions (Mark 14:26) probably was from the Hallel psalms sung at the end of the Passover meal (Psalms 115–118). The subsequent exchange between Jesus and the disciples, particularly Peter, marks the transition from "the upper room" (the phrase is based on Mark 14:15) to Gethsemane. Abruptly, Jesus tells the disciples, "You will all become deserters," and he backs up this disconcerting prediction by alluding to Zechariah 13:7 ("Strike the shepherd, that the sheep may be scattered"), which he turns into a prediction: "I [God] will strike the shepherd, / and the sheep will be scattered." He then adds a promise that will be important on Easter: "But after I am raised up, I will go before you to Galilee" (Mark 14:28; 16:7). The disciples ignore the promise, however. Instead, Peter insists that while others may desert Jesus, he will not. Jesus now punctures this overinflated self-confidence by declaring, "This very night, before the cock crows twice, you will deny me three times." But Peter is adamant, "Even though I must die with you, I will not deny you." The others will not allow Peter to be more loyal than they, so "all of them said the same." The stage is set for the humiliation that occurs before sunrise.

In Luke 22:28-30, before Jesus predicts Peter's denial, he makes a noteworthy statement that has no place for the disciples' desertion: "You are those who have stood by me in my trials; and I confer on you, just as my Father has conferred on me, a kingdom, so that you may eat and drink at my table in my kingdom, and you will sit on thrones judging the twelve tribes of Israel." In Luke the disciples do not abandon Jesus. Indeed, Luke omits Mark 14:50, "All of them deserted him and fled" when Jesus was arrested. (The disciples simply disappear from the story until Easter.)

What follows (Luke 22:31-34) looks like a combination of originally separate sayings, for not only does Jesus begin by addressing Simon (22:31) and end by calling him Peter (22:34), but after his initial words to Peter Jesus addresses all the disciples ("Satan has demanded to sift all of you like wheat"), then speaks again to Simon, "but I have prayed for you [singular]." As a result of this odd back-and-forth, Simon hears what Jesus says to the group—that they will undergo a Satan-driven experience that will separate the faithful (wheat) from the unfaithful (chaff). But Jesus continues: He has already prayed for Peter, lest his faith fail totally; in fact, when he (Peter) has "turned" (repented), he is to strengthen the others—a hint of Peter's leading role in the Jerusalem church. Now Peter declares his unswerving loyalty: "Lord, I am ready to go with you to prison and to death!" (In Acts 5:17-26; 12:1-11 Peter is imprisoned.) *At this point* Jesus emphatically predicts Peter's triple denial: "I tell you, Peter, the cock will not crow this day, until you have denied three times that you know me." And so it was.

> Jesus interpreted his own lifeblood as the sacrifice that sealed the covenant between the disciples and God.

The awesome strangeness of what transpired in connection with that Passover meal merits reflection. Jesus interprets his ultimate act of self-giving for the sake of others and enacts it by giving all the disciples bread and wine. Yet he knows that one will betray him and another deny him. And the denier claims to know himself better than Jesus knows him. The most solemn moment in the whole Jesus story up to now is marred by Judas's deception and Peter's self-deception. Yet Jesus is undeterred by what he knows these men will do. Their acts are part of his destiny that he has seized.

While the accounts of the denial are quite similar, Luke omits Peter's curse and the oath that he does not know Jesus (Mark 14:71) but inserts a detail that makes the scene all the more poignant: When the cock crowed, "the Lord turned and looked at Peter" (Luke 22:61). Then the confident ex-fisherman remembered. Disgraced and humiliated, he slipped away (so Matthew and Luke) and wept bitterly. It must have been a long night. Not until Easter would Peter see daylight.

The Arrested Deliverer

The words of institution, like the earlier Passion predictions, refer unemotionally to Jesus' death and disclose neither ambivalence nor resistance to that grim destiny. And while a degree of pathos is present in the predictions that he will be betrayed, deserted, and denied, not until the last moments of freedom in Gethsemane do the Gospels disclose that only with agony did Jesus accept his destiny. The physical suffering that Jesus would endure shortly (Mark 14:65; 15:15, 17) was preceded by the mental and spiritual suffering in Gethsemane. Whereas in Mark and Matthew Jesus "threw himself on the ground," in Luke he "knelt down"; most art portrays the Jesus of Luke. The disciples' sleepiness underscores the agony of Jesus' aloneness.

Many people treasure the Gethsemane story because here Jesus seems most real, most truly human; here they find it easier to identify with him—and with the disciples, for that matter. Those who use the Lord's Prayer heed Jesus' admonition, "Pray that you may not come into the time of trial" (Mark 14:38; see Matthew 6:13). They know all too well that Jesus was right when he added, "the spirit indeed is willing, but the flesh is weak." And since the Lord's Prayer asks that God's will be done, the disciple who uses this prayer identifies with Jesus, who in Gethsemane wrestled with his destiny until he could pray the same.

Often what the text says gives us so much to think about that we fail to see the importance of what it does *not* say. This is the case here, for we easily overlook a significant silence—the silence of God. Now the heavenly voice that spoke at Jesus' baptism and transfiguration remains silent (the addition to Luke partly makes up for this: An angel strengthened Jesus; Luke 22:43). The story in Mark, however, implies that Jesus knows that God's silence means no: The cup will not be removed.

Jesus will not flee it while he still has a chance. Instead, he accepts his destiny; indeed he now seizes it boldly: "The hour has come; the Son of Man is betrayed into the hands of sinners. Get up, let us be going. See, my betrayer is at hand" (Mark 14:41-42).

Why Mark's report of Jesus' arrest (14:43-52) includes 14:47 (the attack on the slave) and 14:51-52 (the naked young man who fled) is far from clear; only Mark has the latter. Only in Luke does Jesus heal the ear after a stern "No more of this!" (Luke 22:51). In Matthew Jesus not only repudiates armed resistance but also asserts that if resistance were in order, he could summon angels to intervene—but adds that then the Scripture would not be fulfilled. According to John, when Peter cut off

> **Jesus interprets his ultimate act of self-giving for the sake of others and enacts it by giving all the disciples bread and wine. Yet he knows that one will betray him and another deny him.**

the right ear of the slave Malchus, Jesus told Peter to sheath the sword and asked, "Am I not to drink the cup that the Father has given me?" In all three Synoptic Gospels Jesus rebukes those who came to arrest him "with swords and clubs," as if he were a dangerous bandit, and also points out that they could have arrested him while he was teaching in the Temple. The Gospels have already informed us why the religious leaders had not done so: They feared the people (Mark 12:12; Matthew 21:46; Luke 20:19). Jesus' concluding comment in Luke is apt: "But this is your time, and darkness is in control" (Luke 22:53, CEV).

A careful reading of Mark 14:53–15:1; Matthew 26:57–27:2; Luke 22:54–23:1 shows that these Gospels agree on the following: (1) After his arrest, Jesus was taken directly to the house of the high priest, in whose courtyard Peter's denial occurred while Jesus faced the chief priests, elders, scribes, and even "the whole council" (Sanhedrin). (2) At some point that night, Jesus' guards blindfolded, taunted, and beat him. (3) In the morning, the Sanhedrin met (again), bound Jesus, and handed him to Pilate.

A careful reading also discloses a significant difference: While in Luke the all-important exchange between the high priest and Jesus occurs in the morning before the Sanhedrin, in Mark and Matthew it occurs at night, implying that this nocturnal meeting served as a preliminary hearing intended to produce the charge against Jesus that would be brought before the official meeting of the Sanhedrin in the morning. In other words, only in Luke did Jesus have a trial before the duly assembled Sanhedrin; in Mark and Matthew, his fate was decided by a mock court assembled the night before. We must note, however, that historians question whether such a night meeting would have occurred (because it was contrary to law, although written down later), especially during the night of Passover. Suffice it to say we can either assume that the Sanhedrin and the high priests would have obeyed the law (and so discount the Gospels) or argue that the Gospels are right and that the Sanhedrin and the high priests were so eager to get rid of Jesus that they violated their own rules.

According to Mark 14:55-59 and Matthew 26:59-61, the night session began with efforts to find evidence against Jesus that would justify his execution. Such evidence required the agreement of two witnesses. But because the allegations that Jesus had claimed he would destroy the Temple did not agree, and because Jesus did not refute them either, the high priest questioned Jesus directly. He asked, "Are you the Messiah, the Son of the Blessed One?" (Mark 14:61). In Matthew, the high priest, after putting Jesus "under oath before the living God," turns Peter's confession at Caesarea Philippi into a demand: "Tell us if you are the Messiah, the Son of God." Jesus' first reply seems evasive, "You have said so," but this can also be taken as a tacit yes. In Mark, however, the answer is startlingly forthright: "I am." The reader has known this from the first line of this Gospel, and Jesus has known it since he heard the voice at the baptism, and three disciples have known it since the Transfiguration; but not until now has Jesus himself asserted his identity. In Galilee he had tried—often in vain —to keep it secret (see Mark 1:34, 44-45; 3:11-12; 8:29-30).

In Luke when Jesus is commanded to say whether he is the Messiah, he first replies curtly, "If I tell you, you will not believe; and if I question you, you will not answer" (Luke 22:67-68). When an accused man answers this way, he reverses roles, so that now the Sanhedrin is accused by Jesus the judge. This reversal becomes evident if we identify the unspoken logic of Jesus' double reply. The first part reflects his perception that even if he did say he was the Messiah, they would

not believe it because they already knew he wasn't. But if he said he was not the Messiah, they wouldn't believe that either because if they did, their case against him would collapse. They could not accuse him of claiming to be what he said he wasn't. In the second part of his reply the accused Jesus accuses the Sanhedrin of disobeying. Neither the setting nor the office of the high priest overawe this Jesus; he remains his own man. Only Luke has Jesus respond this way.

All the Synoptics, however, report that Jesus went on to speak of the Son of Man enthroned at God's right hand, but they differ in the words he used.

Mark: "You will see the Son of Man
                        seated at the right hand of the Power"
Matthew: "From now on you will see the Son of Man
                        seated at the right hand of Power"
Luke: "From now on the Son of Man will be
                        seated at the right hand of the power of God"

Mark: "and 'coming with the clouds of heaven'"
Matthew: "and coming on the clouds of heaven"
Luke: (omits this line)

In Mark the New Revised Standard Version puts "coming with the clouds of heaven" in quotation marks because this phrase quotes Daniel 7:13 but does not use the quotation marks in Matthew because by changing "with the clouds" to "on the clouds" the line ceases to be a quotation and becomes an allusion. Luke, by omitting the whole last line, shifts the reader's attention away from the Second Coming and keeps the focus on Jesus' post-Resurrection status that results from the Ascension, which only Luke reports. Luke also eliminates "You will see" because the enthroned Son of Man is not visible to the Sanhedrin. Jesus can, however, predict it. To Jesus' prediction, the whole Sanhedrin now asks, "Are you, then, the Son of God?" (They realize that only God's Son would be at God's right hand.) Now comes Jesus' answer, "You say

The transition from Jesus the actor to Jesus the acted upon does not imply God's purposes are being frustrated but the opposite—they are being fulfilled.

that I am," which the Sanhedrin, like the high priest in Mark and Matthew, takes as a yes. The high priest calls this blasphemy, for which the penalty is stoning according to Leviticus 24:13-16. According to the Mishnah, a person must actually pronounce the sacred name of God (Yahweh) in order to be guilty of blasphemy. But Jesus' indirect language ("the Power") avoids the name itself, so how can he be guilty? The high priest, however, sees that Jesus' words about the enthroned Son of Man refer to himself, and this is enough for the high priest to charge Jesus with blasphemy. No witnesses are needed now, for Jesus has condemned himself. As the Gospel writers see it, Jesus has accepted, seized, and proclaimed his destiny. As the high priest sees it, however, Jesus is a blasphemer. His fate is sealed.

So Then

Now we step back in order to call attention to several characteristics of these chapters as a whole.

To begin with, we notice the stark contrasts between how these chapters (Mark 14; Matthew 26; Luke 22) begin with how they end. At the outset Jesus is honored by the ointment poured lavishly on his head by a devoted woman, but at the end he is taunted by guards who make fun of him. After Jesus bonds himself to the disciples by giving them the bread and the cup, the disciples desert him, one betrays him, and another denies him. Thus the solidarity with his followers at the table is replaced by the solitary Jesus before his enemies. And the changes occur swiftly, relentlessly, once they are set in motion by that enigmatic figure, Judas. In short, these chapters portray the transition in the way Jesus occupies center stage—namely, the transition from Jesus the actor to Jesus the one acted upon. Once he is arrested, others take him from place to place; others

decide what will happen to him. He who healed the sick and promised the Kingdom to the poor is now beaten and accused of blasphemy. The repeated prayer in Gethsemane replaces, without warning, the determination with which he led his disciples to Jerusalem, the confidence with which he challenged others to take up their cross and follow him, and the boldness with which he acted in the Temple. The Jesus story seems to have turned into its opposite. Has something gone wrong?

Not really. Not according to the Gospels anyway. For one thing, the Passion predictions prepare us to read the Passion story as the working out of what Jesus had foreseen. Jesus is the recipient of other people's actions, but he is not portrayed as a helpless victim, or as a villager who is no match for the wily urban powerful. In fact, although the Gospel writers cannot say so without spoiling the story itself, they clearly understand that though God is silent as Jesus says less and less, God is in fact at work in this strange story. We find no hint whatever that they thought God stayed out of it until the Resurrection. So the Passion story is about Jesus *and* about God at the same time. Whoever wants to read the Passion stories "with the grain" must read them theologically, which is to say, with an eye for what they disclose about God when Jesus gives his life as "a ransom for many" (Mark 10:45).

In other words, the transition from Jesus the actor to Jesus the acted upon does not imply God's purposes are being frustrated but the opposite—they are being fulfilled. The high priest, savoring his success, probably thought so too, assuming that the divine purpose was being fulfilled through his treatment of Jesus. Not until Easter's dawn would it become clear whether Caiaphas or Mark got it right—and then only if the Easter message is believed.

Do You Want to Become His Disciples, Too?

Jesus is not a flat, one-dimensional figure but a many-sided one. Some people are attracted to his way of life, others to his teaching; still others to the way he did not compromise his integrity despite being abandoned, betrayed, denied, wrongly accused, taunted, and beaten. Whatever may prompt us to become Jesus' followers, we are finally confronted by the need to see him whole, and that means, among other things, being willing to adopt and adapt his Gethsemane prayer—"not what I want [including what I want from Jesus], but what you want," not despite Jesus but because of Jesus. That is, the disciple need not conceal his or her deepest resistance to God's will, for Jesus' agony sanctified this struggle for everyone. And then he moved forward. The disciple knows there are no shortcuts.

Picture Jesus at each event in the Passion story and then describe the whole Jesus you see.

_____

_____

_____

_____

_____

Prayer

I praise you, LORD, for answering my prayers.

    You are my strong shield, and I trust you completely.

You have helped me,

    and I will celebrate and thank you in song.

You give strength to your people, LORD,

    and you save and protect your chosen ones.

Come save us and bless us.

    Be our shepherd and always carry us in your arms.

(Psalm 28:6-9, CEV)

Luke's Account of the Supper

Luke 22:15-30 differs from Mark 14:17-25 and Matthew 26:20-29 in two important respects. (1) Whereas Mark and Matthew report that Jesus spoke of his betrayer before he instituted the Lord's Supper, in Luke Jesus does so afterward. Moreover, Luke has assembled a number of Jesus' sayings about various things, so that his account of what was said at the supper is much longer than accounts in Mark and Matthew. (2) Luke 22:15-20 presents scholars with a famous problem, for here Jesus offers the cup, then the bread, then "after supper" another cup; hence the "long text" found in most manuscripts. But a number of good manuscripts avoid the problem of the two cups by eliminating part of 22:19 and all of 22:20, namely: "which is given for you. Do this in remembrance of me. And he did the same with the cup after supper, saying, 'This cup that is poured out for you is the new covenant in my blood.'" While this solves the problem of the second cup, it also eliminates the interpretation of the bread and wine. Some interpreters prefer the short text (REB); others prefer the long text (NRSV, NIV).

21 Destiny Achieved

At three o'clock Jesus cried out with a loud voice,
"Eloi, Eloi, lema sabachthani?" which means,
"My God, my God, why have you forsaken me?"

(Mark 15:34)

They Have No Wine

Some people feel guilty for things they did not do. But feeling guilty and being guilty are not the same. (In fact, sometimes the guilty do not *feel* guilty.) Still, both imagined guilt and real guilt warp life until expunged, until I am released from it. My suffering will not bring release, even if I think I am being punished. Where do I look next?

Beginning With Moses and All the Prophets

In all the Gospels, the Passion story takes a decisive turn when Jesus is handed over to Pilate. Pilate's role in the story creates problems for historians, however, because he is portrayed as being so sympathetic to Jesus that he would have released him had not the Jews insisted on his execution. (See "Pontius Pilate," page 192.) Here too, our task is not to ferret out what really happened but to understand what the Gospels, primarily the Synoptics, say about Jesus' last hours. The chart shows where individual elements of the Passion story are found. GC 21-1

	Matthew	Mark	Luke	John
Sent to Pilate	27:1-2	15:1	23:1	18:28-32
Judas's suicide	27:3-10			
Before Pilate	27:11-14	15:2-5	23:2-5	18:33-38
Sent to Herod			23:6-16 (17)	
Pilate consents	27:15-26	15:6-15	23:18-25	18:38–19:16
The mocking	27:27-31	15:16-20		19:2-3
Simon of Cyrene	27:32	15:21	23:26	
Jesus' last oracle			23:27-31	
The Crucifixion	27:33-44	15:22-32	23:32-38	19:17-24
Penitent criminal			23:39-43	
Jesus' mother				19:25-27
Jesus' death	27:45-56	15:33-41	23:44-49	19:28-30
Pierced side				19:31-37
Burial	27:57-61	15:42-47	23:50-56	19:38-42
Guard posted	27:62-66			

Day 1 Mark 15; 13:1-2; Exodus 26:31-35; Psalms 22:1-18; 69:19-21; Amos 8:9-10

(1) Note how the title "King of the Jews" runs through Mark 15 and how Pilate taunts the Jews in 15:12 ("*you* call . . .").

(2) Note that in 15:23 Jesus refuses a sedative. Observe that the Crucifixion is not described. Note also that some manuscripts add 15:28, which refers to Isaiah 53:12. Observe how Mark 15:24 alludes to Psalm 22:18 and how John 19:23-25 emphasizes this detail.

(3) Note that the charge that Jesus would destroy and rebuild the Temple, made before the Sanhedrin (Mark 14:57-58), reappears in 15:29. Note also that nowhere in Mark does Jesus say anything that could be taken as the basis for this charge.

(4) Observe that in 15:34 Jesus quotes Psalm 22:1 but is misunderstood, and that in Mark 15:36 he accepts a sedative. Note how Jesus' life ends (15:37).

(5) Note that the only person in Mark who calls Jesus "God's Son" is a Gentile (15:39).

(6) Note which of Jesus' followers witnessed the Crucifixion (15:40-41) and compare this passage with Luke 8:2-3.

Mark 15:28 Scripture fulfilled - "He was counted amg. the lawless"
Isaiah 53:12 - "He was counted avg the transgressers
Exodus: Curtain made & hung to separate th Holy of Holys from the holy
Psalm 22 - My God why have you forsaken me - etc
Cast lots for my clothing.
Psalm 69 - Vinegar to drink

Day 2 Matthew 27; Acts 1:15-20; Jeremiah 32:6-15; Zechariah 11:7-14; Wisdom of Solomon 2:12-24

(1) Note that Matthew 27:12-14 emphasizes Jesus' silence more than Mark 15:4-5, and that this detail accords with Isaiah 53:7, though neither Gospel points this out.

(2) Observe that only in Matthew does Pilate offer a choice between two men named "Jesus" (27:16-17).

(3) Note that in 27:19 Pilate's wife intervenes ("that innocent man," NRSV, obscures the Greek "that righteous man"), and that at 27:24 in some manuscripts Pilate too says Jesus is "righteous." Recall the role of interventions by dream in 1:20; 2:12, 13, 19.

(4) Note that Matthew 27:39 (like Mark 15:29) alludes to Psalm 22:7 without saying so. Observe how Matthew 27:40 reminds the reader of Jesus' temptations in 4:3-6. See also how 27:43 alludes to Psalm 22:8. Observe that the taunt in Matthew 27:43 ("I am God's Son") picks up Jesus' reply to the high priest in 26:63-64.

(5) Note that in 27:50-54 Jesus' death is accompanied by wondrous signs beyond the tearing of the Temple curtain, and note the role they play in the centurion's comment.

(6) Note that 27:62-63 assumes the priests and Pharisees know that Jesus' Passion predictions promised his resurrection (16:21; 17:23; 20:19).

Math: Judas returns the money & hangs himself -
Jesus is silent - ~~But~~ Pilate washes hands - Crown of thorns & robe

Day 3 Luke 23; 9:7-9; 13:31-33; 20:19-26; Acts 4:23-28; Psalm 22:16-18

    (1) Note the charges against Jesus and that Pilate's question picks up the last item (Luke 23:2-3). Note that according to 23:13-15 Herod and Pilate now are two witnesses to Jesus' innocence, and in 23:16 Pilate has Jesus flogged anyway. Note how Acts 4:23-27 uses this story.

    (2) Note that some manuscripts add Luke 23:17; notice also that Pilate, instead of offering a choice, wants to release Jesus (23:20).

    (3) Observe that Jesus' last public word (23:28-31) foresees disaster for Jerusalem.

    (4) Note that only in Luke does Jesus forgive his crucifiers (23:34), though some manuscripts omit 23:34. Think about how the omission of that verse affects your understanding of Jesus.

    (5) Observe that Luke's version of the mockery (23:25) is the shortest and does not address Jesus.

    (6) Note that only in Luke does one of the crucified "criminals" acknowledge Jesus' innocence (23:41). Notice also that in most manuscripts the criminal asks Jesus to remember him when Jesus comes "into" his kingdom (at his enthronement), but in others he asks that Jesus remember him when he comes "in" his kingdom (or "kingship," referring to the Second Coming).

    (7) Note that Luke omits Jesus' cry of abandonment (Mark 15:34) and last loud cry (Mark 15:37); instead Jesus dies devoutly (Luke 23:46).

    (8) Note also that in 23:47 the centurion does not call Jesus "God's Son" but instead acknowledges his innocence.

    (9) Observe that 23:50-51 exempts Joseph from the hostile action of the Sanhedrin; notice also that the unused tomb (23:53) corresponds to the colt not yet ridden (19:30).

Luke 23; 34 " Father forgive them ---
42 -- "Remember me when you come into Kingdom
Women followed & were present

Day 4 Acts 2:22-24; 3:11-21; 7:51-60; 8:26-35; 10:34-43; 13:23-31; 1 Timothy 6:11-16

Since Luke and Acts have the same author, we note how some of the sermons in Acts refer to the Passion story. First Timothy 6:13 also refers to Jesus before Pilate.

    (1) Note how Acts 2:22-24 characterizes Jesus' mission and that here the Romans are seen as the crucifying agents of the Jews.

    (2) Note how the climax of Stephen's speech (Acts 7:51-56) alludes to what Jesus said in Luke 11:47-51; observe that Stephen sees the Son of Man at God's right hand, as in Luke 22:69.

    (3) Note that Peter's sermon to the Roman centurion and those with him (Acts 10:34-43) ignores Pilate's role in Jesus' death and in 10:39 blames the Jews.

    (4) Observe how Paul's sermon to Diaspora* Jews (13:16-41) speaks of Jesus' death in 13:26-31. Note also the explanation for the action against Jesus (13:27).

Day 5 John 18:28–19:42; Exodus 12:43-46; Deuteronomy 21:22-23; Psalms 22:15; 69:1-2; Zechariah 12:10

   (1) Note that in John 18:29-30 Pilate asks for the charge against Jesus and that the reply assumes his guilt.
   (2) Observe that 18:31 explains why Jesus is brought to Pilate, a detail not found in the Synoptics.
   (3) Note that despite Jesus' claim to be a king, Pilate finds "no case against him" (18:38; repeated in 19:4, 6). Also observe how the chief priests use Jesus' claim to kingship to sway Pilate (19:12-16). Notice that in 19:19-22 Pilate has the last word after all.
   (4) Note that 19:17 contradicts what the Synoptics say about Simon of Cyrene (Mark 15:21).
   (5) Note how John 19:23 accords with the first line of Psalm 22:18 and John 19:24 accords with the second line.
   (6) Note that 19:28 assumes the reader recognizes the allusion to Psalm 22:15.
   (7) Note that Jesus' last word (John 19:30) has in view his entire mission and that 19:28 prepares the reader for this perspective.
   (8) Observe carefully the circumstances that account for Jesus' pierced side (19:30-34), how the truth of this detail is assured (19:35), and that the two biblical quotations (19:36-37) provide additional witnesses (the first refers to the Passover lamb [Exodus 12:46]; the second modifies Zechariah 12:10).
   (9) Note that only in John does Nicodemus (John 3:1-15) join Joseph in burying Jesus (19:38-42). Note what the enormous amount of spices implies about what Nicodemus expected (that is, did not expect).

Day 6 Read and respond to "Destiny Achieved" and "Do You Want to Become His Disciples, Too?"

Prayer Concerns

Pontius Pilate

The little that is known about Pontius Pilate, the fifth Roman governor of Judea, exceeds what is known of his predecessors and successors. Most of what is known comes from Josephus, Philo*, and the Gospels. An inscription found at Caesarea in 1961 calls him *Pontius Pilatus Praefectus Iudaeae*. As prefect he was responsible for the Roman administration of Judea. His tenure began in A.D. 26 (or 19, as has been argued recently) and lasted until 36/37, when he was deposed because of his ruthless suppression of the Samaritans. Philo refers to "the briberies, the insults, the robberies, the outrages and wanton injuries; executions without trial constantly repeated, the ceaseless and supremely grievous cruelty" that marked his administration. Philo may have exaggerated, however, for Rome left Pontius Pilate in office longer than any other prefect. Moreover, whereas his predecessor Valerius Gratus appointed and deposed a new high priest virtually every year—a sign of tension between Rome and Jerusalem—Pilate kept Gratus's last appointment, Caiaphas, in office, indicating a more stable relationship.

On at least two occasions, however, he clashed with his Jewish subjects. In the one incident he brought to Jerusalem, by night, images of Caesar attached to the army's standards, prompting a massive protest in which the Jews, "threw themselves upon the ground, and laid their necks bare, and said they would take their death very willingly" rather than tolerate this violation of the prohibition against images. Pilate backed down (Josephus, *Antiquities* 18.3.1). The other incident occurred when he appropriated Temple funds to build an aqueduct; this time he did not back down but repressed the opposition bloodily (*Antiquities* 18.3.2). Whether Luke 13:1 refers to this event is not clear. After Pilate was deposed, he disappears from history but thrives in legend. By the end of the second century, there circulated a work called the *Acts of Pilate*, long lost but whose later versions amplify his defense of Jesus. At the beginning of the third century, the North African theologian Tertullian thought that Pilate became a Christian. Later the Coptic and Ethiopic churches came to regard him as a saint.

Destiny Achieved

The four Gospels agree that everything from the time Jesus is taken to Pilate to the time he is placed in the tomb occurred between dawn and dusk of the same day, Friday. Mark reports that Jesus was crucified at 9:00 A.M., died at 3:00 P.M., and was buried by sundown. According to this timetable, a remarkable amount of activity occurred before 9:00 A.M.

Jesus in the Hands of Pilate

Jesus was not handed over to Pilate out of courtesy to the emperor's representative who happened to be in Jerusalem. According to John 18:31 this transfer was necessary because the Sanhedrin was "not permitted to put anyone to death." While the Sanhedrin had already agreed that Jesus is to be executed, Pilate must carry out the verdict. Though this rationale is clear, historians continue to debate whether the statement in 18:31 is correct; they point out that the Sanhedrin did have authority to stone to death those who seriously violated Jewish law. Since the high priest declared, and the Sanhedrin agreed, that Jesus was guilty of blasphemy (Mark 14:64), the Jewish authorities would not have exceeded their authority by stoning Jesus. Unfortunately, the Synoptics do not say why Jesus was nevertheless taken to Pilate. We can surmise that, given Jesus' popularity with the people (11:18; 12:12; 14:1-2), the Sanhedrin did not want to be responsible for Jesus' death and so was determined to make the Romans take the blame. To achieve this, the charge of blasphemy had to be replaced with charges of anti-Roman activity.

Luke 23:2-5 reports the Sanhedrin's charges against Jesus. By beginning with "perverting our nation," the Sanhedrin implies that the nation is, and would remain, loyal to Rome unless Jesus persuaded it to do otherwise. By accusing Jesus of "forbidding us to pay taxes to the emperor," they achieve the aim in their raising the question with Jesus a few days before, even if they had to distort his answer to do so (20:20-25). By reporting Jesus' claim to be "the Messiah, a king," they distort also his response to the Sanhedrin (22:67-71) but thereby characterize Jesus as a threat to Roman rule. Since this charge is the most serious of the three, Pilate asks if Jesus is indeed "the king of the Jews." Jesus gives him the same answer he gave to the Sanhedrin—"You say so." But whereas they took it as a yes, Pilate takes it as a no, and ignoring the allegation about the tax, says, "I find no basis

for an accusation against this man"—hardly a positive portrayal of Pilate's political astuteness. Frustrated by this reply, the leaders then accuse Jesus of causing unrest among the people, from Galilee to Jerusalem—turning his popularity into evidence against him.

Learning that as a Galilean Jesus comes from the jurisdiction of Herod Antipas (one of the sons of Herod the Great), Pilate uses this legal point to get Jesus off his hands and sends him to Herod. (Luke has already reported Herod's desire to see Jesus [9:7-9], repeated now at 23:8, but ignores that he had written that some Pharisees had warned Jesus, "Herod wants to kill you," 13:31.) But Jesus is as uncooperative with Herod as with Pilate. So Herod returns Jesus to Pilate, who concludes that Herod too found Jesus not guilty of the charges and so declares, "He has done nothing to deserve death." Before Jesus is released, however, a flogging might teach him a lesson. ("Flog" [NRSV] renders a Greek word that means instruct, educate, chasten.) The flogging itself is not reported in Luke as it is in Mark 15:15 and Matthew 27:26.

As Luke tells it, when the crowd heard Pilate say he would release Jesus, it demanded the release of Barabbas, in prison for insurrection and murder (Luke 23:18-19). Although Pilate wanted to release Jesus, he finally capitulated to the shouting crowd whose "voices prevailed" (23:23). Luke's comments at the end of the scene portray Pilate as a weak man who yields to the crowd despite his own better judgment, just as they portray the crowd as so perverse that it insisted that a murderer be released and that Jesus, who had restored life, be crucified instead. So Pilate gave in. "He released the man they asked for" and "handed Jesus over as they wished" (23:24-25).

While Mark 15:15 simply says that Pilate released Barabbas, "wishing to satisfy the crowd," Matthew says, "When Pilate saw that he could do nothing, but rather that a riot was beginning," he washed his hands and said that he was not responsible for this innocent man's death and so put the responsibility on the crowd. Now comes the fateful sentence: "Then the people as a whole answered, 'His blood be on us and on our children!'" So Barabbas was released; Jesus was flogged and handed over to the soldiers for crucifixion (Matthew 27:24-26). Since the author of Matthew was probably a Jew himself, he would have viewed the crowd's words as referring to the current and next generation. Later Gentile Christians, however, saw in these words the Jewish people's volunteered responsibility for Jesus' death and so held the Jewish people continuously responsible for his execution. Fortunately, in recent years Christians have rejected this use of the text and its horrible legacy and have come to see that Pilate's hand-washing was a futile gesture: Crucifixion was, after all, a common Roman form of execution.

Luke's account of the Barabbas factor is shorter than Mark's and Matthew's, in which Pilate offered a choice—Jesus or Barabbas (Mark 15:6-15; Matthew 27:15-26). Some Bibles use those manuscripts that give the latter's name as "Jesus Barabbas" (NRSV and REB); these versions probably reason that Matthew wrote "Jesus Barabbas" and that copyists were more likely to have eliminated "Jesus" as Barabbas's first name than to have added it. Nothing else is known of Barabbas or of the custom of freeing a prisoner during Passover.

In the Hands of the Soldiers

Before crucifying Jesus, however, the soldiers must have some fun with the prisoner. They dress him like a king; crown him with thorns; give him a reed as scepter; kneel before him (in Matthew); and mock him, "Hail, King of the Jews!" Then they show their contempt by spitting on him and hitting him on the head with the reed. Finally, they replace the royal garb with his own clothes and lead him to the Skull (Mark 15:16-20; Matthew 27:27-31). The *Gospel of Peter** tells it differently: "And having taken the Lord, they pushed him as they ran and said, 'Let us drag away the Son of God now that we have power over him.' And they put a purple robe on him, and made him sit on the seat of judgment, saying, 'Judge justly, king of Israel.' And one of them brought a crown of thorns and put it on the Lord's head; and others stood and spat in his eyes and still others slapped his cheeks; others pricked him with a reed, and some of them scourged him, saying, 'With this honor let us honor the Son of God' "(*Gospel of Peter* 3:6-9).

The Gospels do not emphasize Jesus' suffering. Because he is the one acted upon, they concentrate on others' actions. Still, what the Gospels do say justifies the assumption that Jesus, beaten at night and flogged in the morning, was now so weakened that the soldiers saw he could not carry the crossbeam of the cross, as was customary, all the way. So they commandeered a passer-by and made him carry it (Mark 15:21; Matthew 27:32; Luke 23:26). "Simon of Cyrene" probably was a Jew from that

part of North Africa known today as Libya, where there was a sizable Jewish community. We can only speculate why he was "coming in from the country" before 9:00 A.M. We may, however, surmise that later he became a Christian, for Mark records that he was "the father of Alexander and Rufus," brothers so well-known to Mark's readers that this identification suffices. Imagine the story he told his sons when he got home!

In Mark and Matthew the next thing we are told is that the soldiers, Jesus, and Simon are at Skull Place. Luke slows the action, so to speak, by inserting Luke 23:27-32, which adds three details that suggest a procession—the crowd that followed, including wailing women (23:27); the addition of two "criminals" who were to be crucified as well (23:32); and most important, Jesus' words to the wailers (23:28-31). Even if these words combine originally separate sayings, as has been suggested, the several elements now form one important comment from Jesus. His basic point is stated first: "Do not weep for me, but weep for yourselves and for your children." The *for* at the beginning of 23:29 states why they should do so: Far worse things will happen to them and the next generation. These events will be so wretched that people will regard the childless as blessed (not cursed, as common opinion held). Those times will be so bad that people will ask that Hosea 10:8 come true:

> "They shall say to the mountains, Cover us,
> and to the hills, Fall on us."

Death will be preferable to life. The *for* that introduces Luke 23:31 states the perspective of the whole passage: "For if they do this [crucify me] when the wood is green [when it will make but a small fire], what will happen when it is dry [when it will start a great conflagration]?" The allusion to the destruction of Jerusalem and to the burning of the Temple was probably clear to Luke's readers.

The Crucifixion is stated as simply as possible, not described. We are not told how Jesus was fastened to the crossbeam. From Thomas's demand to touch "the mark of the nails in his hands" (John 20:25), we learn that he was nailed, not tied, to the cross (the *Gospel of Peter* 6:21 says that when they took Jesus' body off the cross, "they drew out the nails from the hands of the Lord"). Similarly, had John not written that Jesus' clothes were divided into four parts, one for each soldier, we would not know how many soldiers were involved. Even so, we should not assume that John makes explicit what the Synoptics assume.

Some details are found in all four Gospels, some only in the Synoptics, and some only in one Gospel, as the following list shows:

1. Details found in all four New Testament Gospels
   - crucified between two others
   - clothes divided
   - charge posted (wording varies)
   - Jesus takes sour wine
   - women at the cross (names vary)
   - Joseph buries Jesus
2. Details found only in the three Synoptic Gospels
   - mocked by priests and scribes
   - darkness at noon
   - Temple curtain torn in two
   - centurion's comment (wording varies)
3. Details found only in Mark and Matthew
   - Jesus refuses sedation
   - mocked by passers-by
   - mocked by both bandits
   - cry of abandonment
4. Detail found only in Mark
   - crucified at 9:00 A.M.
5. Details found only in Luke
   - Jesus forgives the crucifiers
   - soldiers mock
   - penitent criminal and Jesus' response
6. Details found only in Matthew
   - crucifiers watch the crucified
   - earthquake and dead raised
   - guard at the tomb
7. Details found only in John
   - four items of clothing plus seamless robe
   - Mary and the beloved disciple
   - Jesus thirsts
   - side pierced by soldiers
   - Nicodemus joins Joseph
   - garden as location of the new tomb

While John has no mocking of the crucified, the taunting of Jesus is an important feature in all the Synoptics, though they do not portray it the same way. Having distinguished the people who "stood by, watching" (silently) from the leaders who "scoffed" at Jesus (Luke 23:35), Luke reports that the soldiers too mocked Jesus, as did one of the "criminals" crucified with him. In this Gospel, then, Jesus is mocked three times but not by the people. In Luke the other man crucified with Jesus asserts the injustice of the situation—"we are getting what we deserve . . . but this man has done nothing wrong"—and asks Jesus to remember him, either when Jesus comes "into" his kingship (*basileia* can mean either kingship or kingdom), that is, when Jesus is enthroned or when he comes "in" his kingship at the Second Coming, depending on the manuscripts used. But Jesus promises that today they will be together "in Paradise" (23:43), the blessed abode of the dead. (*Paradise*, from Old Persian where it meant an enclosed space, came to mean a park or garden in Greek and Hebrew.)

In all three Synoptics, the taunting includes some form of "Save yourself, you Messiah/King of Israel," but only in Mark and Matthew do those who pass by taunt him with his words about destroying the Temple and rebuilding it—the false charge made the night before in the high priest's house (Mark 14:57-59; Matthew 26:60-61).

The Gospels report Jesus' crucifixion as simply and as starkly as they do because the writers saw nothing unusual in the act itself; Jesus was crucified as others had been and along with two other prisoners as well. At the same time the Gospel writers were convinced that Jesus' crucifixion was unique because both Jesus and his mission were decisive, as shown by the heavenly voice

> **The Gospel writers were convinced that Jesus' crucifixion was unique because both Jesus and his mission were decisive.**

at the baptism and Transfiguration, the Passion predictions, his words of institution, and his response to the high priest's question. We should not be surprised, then, that the Synoptic Gospels (though not John) report that strange events occurred when Jesus died. The Synoptics first mention the darkness from noon to 3:00 P.M.—implying that what was occurring was God's judgment as foretold in Amos 8:9:

"On that day. . .
   I will make the sun go down at noon,
   and darken the earth in broad daylight."

No one who recalls that Passover occurs at full moon will try to explain this darkness by calling it a solar eclipse. The darkness is symbolic. The *Gospel of Peter*, however, takes it literally: "And many went about with lamps, supposing it was night, and they went to bed" (*Gospel of Peter* 5:19)—utterly missing the point.

Another marvel is reported by all the Synoptics: The Temple curtain was torn (in Matthew, at the very moment Jesus died). The torn curtain (presumably the one separating the innermost part of the sanctuary, the Holy of Holies, from the rest of the sacred space) may symbolize both the coming destruction of the Temple and thus part of God's judgment, and the conviction that through Jesus' death access to God is open to all, not just to the high priest, who alone had the right to enter the Holy of Holies. The destruction of the Temple was understood by the lost *Gospel of the Nazaraeans,** of which Jerome* wrote, "In the Gospel that is written in Hebrew letters we read, not that the curtain of the temple was torn, but that the astonishingly large lintel of the temple collapsed."

Other marvels appear only in Matthew 27:51-53: "The earth shook, and the rocks were split. The tombs also were opened, and many bodies of the saints who had fallen asleep [that is, died] were raised. After his [Jesus'] resurrection they came out of the tombs and entered the holy city and appeared to many." Apparently this is Matthew's way of expressing the belief that Jesus' resurrection signals the general resurrection of the dead.

All the Synoptics report that the Roman centurion was so impressed by what he saw that he declared Jesus to be innocent (Luke) or acknowledged, "Truly this man was God's Son!" (or "a son of God"; the Greek can be translated either way). In Mark the centurion responds to the way Jesus died, but in Matthew 27:54 his words express his terror in response to the earthquake and the opening of the tombs.

What was the last thing Jesus said? The so-called "Seven Last Words of Christ" that are the basis of many Good Friday meditations are really a collection of everything Jesus said at Golgotha and put into a sequence found in no Gospel. Strictly speaking there can be only one last word. Yet here too the Gospels are not unanimous, for in each case Jesus' last word discloses how each Gospel writer wants the reader to view Jesus in his dying. In John Jesus apparently has his whole mission in view when he declares triumphantly, "It is finished" (John 19:30). In Luke Jesus dies devoutly, saying loudly so that all may hear, "Father, into your hands I commend my spirit," and then stops breathing (Luke 23:46), for he has given back the breath of life; it was not taken from him. He who had said that the Son of Man would be "handed over to the Gentiles" now hands himself into the hands of God.

In Mark and Matthew, however, events are quite different. At 3:00 P.M. Jesus cries out loudly the opening line of Psalm 22, which these Gospels regard as so important that they use Hebrew, which they then translate, "My God, my God, why have you forsaken me?" Some bystanders, however, think that in his calling out "Eli" or "Eloi" Jesus was calling for Elijah to come to his aid; others offer Jesus "sour wine" to relieve his pain while they wait to see whether the prophet will indeed appear. Jesus might not be able to save himself (as the priests and scribes mockingly told one another in Mark 15:31-32), but maybe, just maybe, Elijah will do it for him. Instead, "Jesus gave a loud cry and breathed his last."

Some interpreters want to relieve Jesus of such a horrid end and, perhaps influenced by Luke, point out that Jesus quoted only the beginning of Psalm 22, and then assume that he ran through the rest of it silently until he reached at least 22:24, which says that God

> "did not hide his face from me,
>   but heard when I cried to him."

We have no way to prove or disprove what someone claims was in Jesus' mind but not on his lips. But also, we have no evidence that Mark and Matthew thought Jesus had the rest of the psalm in mind. Their theology is far too profound for such an interpretation, for they understood that the "ransom" was not cheap.

What the *Gospel of Peter* says is somewhat puzzling: "And the Lord cried out, 'My power, my power, you have forsaken me!'" (*Gospel of Peter* 5:19). Here, as in Mark 14:62 and Matthew 26:64, "power" might be indirect language for God. What is remarkable, however, is that here Jesus does not ask Why? but accuses God of forsaking him. But when this gospel continues, "And saying this, Jesus was taken up" (to heaven), it suggests that by the Ascension God showed that Jesus was wrong in his accusation. We can understand why a second-century bishop wrote that a person may read this gospel at home but not in church worship.

Luke, who had distinguished "the people" from "the leaders" (Luke 23:35), brings the scene to a close that is both ominous and dignified. Ominous because he reports that "when all the crowds who had gathered there for this spectacle saw what had taken place, they returned home, beating their breasts"—a sign that they knew great wrong had been done and there would be consequences. Dignified because Luke adds, "All his acquaintances, including the women who had followed him from Galilee, stood at a distance, watching these things." That's too good an ending to mar by listing their names. Luke will disclose them later (24:10).

> Jesus' last word discloses how each Gospel writer wants the reader to view Jesus in his dying.

In the Hands of Joseph

Compared with most men left to die suspended between earth and sky, Jesus had to endure the horror of crucifixion for but six hours, not for days. Mark's account of Jesus' burial, apart from the detail of Pilate's ascertaining whether Jesus was already dead "for some time," is as simple and unadorned as his account of the Crucifixion. Only the essential matters are reported; not a word is said about grief or of any hesitation about asking for Jesus' corpse. Joseph from Arimathea (a town not far from Jerusalem) appears abruptly at this point in all the Gospels and then disappears from the story. Only in John is he joined by Nicodemus (John 19:39-40). We are left to wonder how Jesus' body was taken off the cross. Here the *Gospel of Peter* says, "And then they drew out the nails from the hands of the Lord, and laid the body upon the earth. And the whole earth was shaken, and a great fear arose. Then the sun shone and it was found to be the ninth hour [3:00 P.M.]. . . . And Joseph took the body of the Lord, and washed it, and wrapped it in a linen shroud, and brought it to his own tomb, called the garden of Joseph" (*Gospel of Peter* 6:21-24). Mark does not say whose tomb was used; John and Luke say it had not been used before; only Matthew says it was Joseph's "own new tomb," and only John says it was convenient to use it "because it was the Jewish day of Preparation [the sabbath was imminent, as Luke also notes], and the tomb was nearby." All the Gospels agree that this burial was to be an interim arrangement until after the sabbath, when the body would be buried properly, with spices.

The women who had observed Jesus' crucifixion and death also noted where Jesus' body was placed, for they intended to give it the proper burial. According to Luke 23:55-56, these women, among them Mary from Magdala and another Mary, had accompanied Jesus all the way from Galilee. Mark and Matthew agree, though apart from Mary Magdalene they give different names. Although Mary Magdalene is mentioned in all the Gospels, only in Luke 8:2 do we learn that "seven demons had gone out" of her, presumably because Jesus had exorcised them; the Gospels have no story of this. (Nor is there any evidence that she had been a prostitute, or that she was the "sinner" who in 7:37-38 bathed Jesus' feet with her tears, wiped them with her hair, and then anointed them.)

While Luke says Jesus' women friends observed the sabbath (23:56), Matthew says his male enemies did not; for "the chief priests and the Pharisees," remembering that Jesus had predicted his resurrection "after three days," went to Pilate on the sabbath ("the next day" after the Crucifixion on Friday) and asked him to post a guard lest the disciples steal the body and then announce that Jesus had been raised from the dead (27:62-66). Amazingly, Pilate complied, and the soldiers sealed the tomb and as we will learn later stayed to guard it. This story, and its sequel in Matthew 28:11-15, defies historical probability. The *Gospel of Peter* is even less believable. Here we learn that a centurion named Petronius accompanied the soldiers and that "the elders and scribes came with them to the tomb." Matthew's story is designed to refute a wrong interpretation of the empty tomb. It reminds us that the empty tomb does not prove the Resurrection; it proves only that Jesus was not there.

So Then

We leave the Passion stories with many questions, partly because key players, like Caiaphas and Joseph, appear and disappear abruptly; partly because each story moves swiftly, giving only essential details and allowing each person to ask one question or give one brief reply; and partly because the narrator frequently condenses extended action or words into a simple phrase. At every point we want to know more. This desire is understandable. At the same time this desire well may conceal an illusion—that if we did have more information about Jesus, we would find it easier to become his followers. But the Gospel writers were wiser. By not giving us all the details, their accounts are

> **Matthew's story is designed to refute a wrong interpretation of the empty tomb. It reminds us that the empty tomb does not prove the Resurrection; it proves only that Jesus was not there.**

> **We are confronted by a story whose very starkness makes our response to it unavoidable.**

lean, focused on the sequence of events, so that we are not distracted by matters that satisfy our curiosity; instead, we are confronted by a story whose very starkness makes our response to it unavoidable. The nature of that response now invites attention.

No one can prescribe or proscribe another person's response to the Passion story because each person brings personal life experience to the reading of this story. Nor does the same person respond to it the same way at different times of life. Sometimes we see more clearly, understand more fully—and sometimes less fully—than at other times. Still, a few observations may help us come to terms with the Passion story in ways that fit its character.

To begin with, although the Gospels report Jesus' call to take up our cross and follow him, they do not imply we are to duplicate the way he got to his cross or his way of dying on it. His way was his alone; that particular history cannot be repeated. It is one thing for Christians who find themselves victimized by unjust government procedures, tortured, and murdered because of their loyalty to Jesus to find that their agony parallels his. In some circumstances, they too may sense that their cruel death is their destiny that they must seize as he did his. But they do not set out to duplicate Jesus; rather, they find this the price of being faithful to him.

Nowhere do the Gospels, or the New Testament as a whole, suggest that the disciple should strive to die as Jesus did; for his was not the model death. And while Jesus' suffering before and on the cross clearly had its heroic dignity, free of self-pity and recriminating remarks, the Gospels do not portray it as the hero's death that elicits — or should elicit—our admiration. Rather, the Gospels assume that if the readers remember that at the supper Jesus said his death was to be "for you," they will read this story as those who are beneficiaries of that life and death. The Gospels may also assume we have been alerted to the uncomfortable fact that the same realities that animated those hostile to Jesus also animate us. So we cannot claim we would have acted differently. In other words, we are to read with the sort of deepened, clearer self-knowledge that is expressed in the prayer of the week.

The Passion stories can, and should, do more than elicit our confession of sin; for they are written out of the conviction that God was at work precisely in what befell Jesus, and that the deepest levels of the human condition are addressed and overcome definitively at the cross. In other words, the Passion stories are narrated atonement. They do not use the word *atonement*, for it belongs to a different form of discourse— Christian doctrine. The Gospels do not offer a doctrine or theory of the Atonement; rather, they make the development of such doctrines and theories inevitable. What the Gospels offer us are four accounts of a singular life and death in which salvation is promised to those who accept it as the new covenant. So we find ourselves where we began this study—noting that "Christ died for our sins in accordance with the scriptures."

> **The Gospels offer us four accounts of a singular life and death in which salvation is promised to those who accept it as the new covenant.**

Do You Want to Become His Disciples, Too?

How does any one of us become and remain a disciple of a man who was executed because he was condemned to death by a corrupt justice system? Do we not become disciples by looking, in light of the Resurrection, through the cross to the life of uncoerced self-giving for the benefit of others; by seeing ourselves as the beneficiaries of his death; and by letting that life and death reshape our own life as a grateful response? The crucified does not want our admiration; he wants our obedience.

Why is this crucified Jesus the one you look for and want to follow?

_____

_____

_____

_____

_____

Prayer

You are kind, God! Please have pity on me.
> You are always merciful! Please wipe away my sins.
Wash me clean from all of my sin and guilt.
I know about my sins,
> and I cannot forget my terrible guilt.
You are really the one I have sinned against;
> I have disobeyed you and have done wrong.
So it is right and fair for you
> to correct and punish me.
I have sinned and done wrong since the day I was born.
But you want complete honesty,
> so teach me true wisdom.
Wash me with hyssop
> until I am clean and whiter than snow.

(Psalm 51:1-7, CEV)

22 This Jesus God Raised Up

> We know that Christ, being raised from the dead, will
> never die again; death no longer has dominion over him.
>
> (Romans 6:9)

They Have No Wine

The prospect of facing those we have wronged makes us uneasy. They might not have forgotten what we did. They might be waiting for a chance to get even. If only we could think of something good we can do for them to make up for what we have done. Or maybe we should simply avoid them. But then it gets harder and harder to face them. The trouble is, only the wronged can free us from this growing alienation we have set in motion. But can we count on their goodwill, their graciousness?

Beginning With Moses and All the Prophets

This week we conclude our study of the Synoptic Gospels by examining their last chapters, each of which begins with a story of the discovery of the empty tomb and the news that Jesus has been resurrected. The earliest references to Jesus' resurrection, however, are in Paul's letters, written about twenty years *after* the Easter event but nearly twenty years *before* Mark's Gospel. Beginning with Paul allows us to clarify first the concept of resurrection and the language used to express it; then we turn to the Gospels.

Day 1 1 Thessalonians 1:2-10; 4:13-18; 1 Corinthians 15:1-28; Philippians 2:1-13; 3:20-21; Romans 6:5-11

    (1) Note that Paul's first letter refers to Jesus' resurrection as central in the gospel (1 Thessalonians 1:10; 4:14).

(2) Note that in 1 Corinthians 15:3, Paul says he handed on the tradition regarding Jesus' resurrection that he had received (presumably when he became a believer, no later than A.D. 35). Note that the James in 15:7 is Jesus' brother mentioned in Mark 6:3 and Galatians 1:19; observe also that in 1 Corinthians 15:8 Paul includes himself in the list. Note that in 15:20, 23, Christ is "the first fruits" of the resurrected. Observe how 15:25-28 interprets Psalm 110:1 as referring to Christ's reign at God's right hand, resulting from his resurrection.
(3) Observe that Philippians 2:9 refers to Jesus' resurrection as God's exalting him; note how Philippians 3:20, like 1 Thessalonians 1:10, refers to Christ's coming, and how Philippians 3:21 says more fully what 1 Thessalonians 4:16 assumes.
(4) Note how Romans 6:4-11 restates the connection between Christ's resurrection and the Christian.

Day 2 Mark 16:1-8; Acts 2:22-36; 1 Peter 3:17-22; 1 Kings 17:17-24; Daniel 12:1-3

(1) Note that the "young man" interprets the absence of Jesus' body (Mark 16:6-7); note that he singles out Peter. Note also the cross-reference to Mark 14:28. Note that the women disobey; why were they afraid?
(2) Note that the story in 1 Kings 17:17-24 reports a resuscitation, not a resurrection; note also that the only clear expression of resurrection in the Old Testament, Daniel 12:1-3, includes the theme of judgment.
(3) Note that in 1 Peter 3:17-20 Jesus preached to the dead in "prison," that is in Hades (the realm of the dead), and that this act is in tension with Jesus' promise to the penitent criminal in Luke 23:43 on one hand, but on the other hand is the basis for the line in the creed, "He descended into hell [Hades]."

Day 3 Matthew 28; Daniel 7:13-14

    (1) [GC 22-1] Observe that the women's question in Mark 16:3 is answered in Matthew 28:2 (but not in Mark). Observe the similarity between Mark 16:6-7 and Matthew 28:5-7.

    (2) Note that in Matthew the women obey the angel (28:8), and that the risen Jesus repeats the command to go to Galilee (28:7, 10).

    (3) Observe how 28:11-15 is designed to explain away a story that itself was designed to explain away Jesus' resurrection.

    (4) Observe the influence of Daniel 7:13-14 on Matthew 28:18. Note the contrast between Matthew 10:5-6 and 28:19; hear also the echo of 1:23 in 28:20.

Day 4 Luke 24; Acts 1:1-11

    (1) Observe that in Luke 24:6-7 the women are not reminded of Jesus' promise to meet the disciples in Galilee but rather of his Passion prediction made *in* Galilee (Luke 9:22).

    (2) Note that whereas Matthew 28:16 implies that the disciples believed the women (Luke 24:10), Luke 24:11 says they did not believe them. Observe how this prepares the reader for 24:36-43. Note also that some manuscripts add 24:12. Note that no story recounts the appearance to Simon (24:34; see also 1 Corinthians 15:5).

    (3) Observe how fully Luke 24:13-35 reports this incident; note how the author emphasizes Jesus' interpretation of Scripture (24:25-27, 32, 44-46), and the new theme added in 24:47.

    (4) Note the tension between the command to stay (Luke 24:49) and the command to go (Matthew 28:7, 10; Mark 16:7).

    (5) Notice that some Bibles translate those manuscripts that explicitly mention the Ascension in Luke 24:51 (NRSV and NIV) and as a result relate the Ascension twice—once on Easter (note the "then" in 24:50) and then six weeks later (Acts 1:3-11). Other Bibles (RSV and REB) translate manuscripts that omit "and was carried up to heaven."

    (6) Observe that Luke ends the Jesus story (24:52-53) where it began, in the Temple (Luke 1:5-8).

Day 5 John 20–21; Mark 16:9-20; Luke 5:1-11

    (1) Observe carefully the role of Mary Magdalene in John 20:1-18; note also that Jesus speaks of his impending Ascension in 20:17.

    (2) Note that in 20:19-20, as in Luke 24:36-40, Jesus points to his body in order to remove doubt about his identity. Note that only John 20:20 mentions his "side," for only John reports the spear wound in 19:34.

    (3) Observe that the commissioning of the disciples, which in Matthew occurs later in Galilee, here occurs in Jerusalem on Easter night (John 20:21-23), as in Luke 24:36-40.

    (4) Note how the story of "doubting Thomas" leads up to Jesus' pronouncement in 20:29.

    (5) Note the similarity between the story in John 21:1-8 and Luke 5:1-11.

    (6) Finally, read the additions to Mark, noting

- that one manuscript expands 16:8, correcting the same verse's earlier statement that the women disobeyed the young man.
- that Mark 16:9 takes account of Luke 24:10-11, and that Mark 16:12-13 alludes to Luke 24:13-35 and summarizes Luke 24:36-41 as "but they did not believe them."
- that in Mark 16:14 Jesus chides the disciples for not believing Mary Magdalene and the two men on the road, and that some manuscripts add an exchange between the disciples and Jesus.
- that Mark 16:15-16 not only paraphrases the Great Commission in Matthew 28:19-20 but also adds that baptism is required.
- that snake-handling is one of the signs that will characterize the church's mission (16:18).
- that Mark 16:19 combines the Ascension with the interpretation of Psalm 110:1 found in Paul (Philippians 2:9-11).

Day 6 Read and respond to "This Jesus God Raised Up" and "Do You Want to Become His Disciples, Too?"

Prayer Concerns

This Jesus God Raised Up

If there were no Resurrection, there would be no Christian faith. In fact, had the disciples, and through them many others as well, not believed that God resurrected Jesus, we would not know there ever had been this Jesus of Nazareth. Those who had seen and heard him would have remembered him and for some years would have told others about him, but we have no reason to think that what they remembered would have come to the attention of people beyond Galilee and Judea. The memory of Jesus endured and took root in the lives of those who had not known him because they were convinced the disciples and others were right in claiming that the cross was not the end of the story, for God had countersigned Jesus' life by resurrecting him from the realm of the dead. Easter is the most challenging day of the Christian year, for it celebrates an event that has neither precedent nor parallel but whose consequences rearrange the lives of those who believe it occurred. If we are to understand such an event, we must begin by grasping what those who first announced Jesus' resurrection were talking about.

> **If there were no Resurrection, there would be no Christian faith.**

Resurrection Logic

The English word *resurrect* is traceable to the Latin *resurgere*, to rise, or to raise again. When used of the dead and buried, the word pictures bringing the dead back to life by causing them to rise again, to stand up again. The Greek noun for resurrection is *anastasis*, and the verb is *anistēmi*, to raise, erect, cause to stand, stand up. Its ordinary literal sense is evident in Luke 4:16, where Jesus "stood up [*anestē*] to read." Understandably then, the person who spoke of bringing the dead back to life could say that they "rose up" (or "rose up again"), as if from lying down in sleep. In fact, Daniel 12:2 refers to the resurrection in that way: "Many of those who sleep in the dust of the earth shall awake, some to everlasting life, and some to shame and everlasting contempt."

At just this point we see that the meaning of *resurrection* comes to depend heavily on other beliefs with which the concept came to be associated, for here Daniel envisions a future when accounts will be settled, when persons are rewarded or punished. From around 165 B.C., the resurrection of the dead is always part of the scenario of the end time and the beginning of the age of salvation when all the problems of "this age" are overcome. Not all visions of this salvation time included resurrection, but those that did expressed the belief in various ways. Sometimes only the righteous would be raised (as a reward, especially for those who had suffered and died because they were faithful). Thus in Luke 14:13-14, Jesus urges that instead of inviting guests who can return the favor we should invite "the poor, the crippled, the lame, and the blind. And you will be blessed, because they cannot repay you, for you will be repaid at the resurrection of the righteous." The book of Revelation promises two resurrections—the first is for martyrs only, who get to reign with Christ for a thousand years as their reward (Revelation 20:4-6); the second includes all the dead, so that they can be judged (20:11-15).

Now we can see the decisive point: Because resurrection was always understood to be an event of the end time, when God would make everything right (including doing right by the righteous and punishing the wicked), resurrection was never thought of as mere restoration to life but always as transformation of the person into a new mode of existence. This transformation is precisely what the Sadducees missed when they asked Jesus about the resurrection (Mark 12:18-27); for their question assumed that the resurrected woman and the seven brothers to whom she had been married in this life would simply be restored to *status quo ante* (life as before) in the

> **Easter is the most challenging day of the Christian year, for it celebrates an event that has neither precedent nor parallel but whose consequences rearrange the lives of those who believe it occurred.**

next life. Jesus, however, points out that resurrection means transformation into a different mode of being ("like angels" was his way of putting it). We cannot overemphasize the difference between resurrection and resuscitation or reanimation, a resumption of life as it was.

One important assumption runs through all ways of talking about resurrection in the New Testament: Because Hebrew and early Jewish thought viewed the person as an animated body, a body with life-breath, resurrection concerns the whole person, never part of the person. That is, resurrection was always understood to involve some sort of body, never the release of an eternal soul from the body (an idea found in ancient Greek thought). Those who believed in resurrection assumed the resurrection body no longer would be subject to death; that is, the *person* would become immortal at resurrection. Paul expresses this concisely in Romans 6:9: "We know that Christ, being raised from the dead, will never die again; death no longer has dominion over him."

One more assumption: Since resurrection is neither resumed life nor released eternal soul but transformation of the body-self, the resurrection event is always understood to be an act of God, not a natural process. For this reason Paul normally says either that God "raised" Jesus (as in 1 Corinthians 6:14) or Christ "was raised" by God (as in 15:4). What is really at stake in resurrection is the nature and power of God, as Jesus pointed out to the Sadducees. Because resurrection is really about God, the New Testament says little about the transformed existence. Paul writes of a "spiritual body" (15:44) but never describes it. In Philippians 3:20-21 he writes of Christ's coming when "He will transform the body of our humiliation ['lowly bodies,' NIV; 'humble bodies,' REB; 'these poor bodies,' CEV] that it may be conformed to the body of his glory" [or, glorious body]." What matters is the transformation, the event by which the believer shares a mode of existence already enjoyed by the resurrected Jesus Christ. As we will see, the assumption that resurrection entails a transformed body-self underlies the stories of the Easter appearances.

Finally, we can now bring these preparatory paragraphs to bear on the resurrection of Jesus by noting that in 1 Corinthians 15:20, 23 Paul refers to the resurrected Christ as "the first fruits of those who have died" (literally, "fallen asleep"). "First fruits" refers to the first sheaf of the grain harvest that the ancient Israelite was to deliver to the priest (Leviticus 23:9-14); by giving this sheaf, the worshiper acknowledged that the whole harvest belongs to God. Paul, however, uses "first fruits" as a metaphor to express the solidarity between Christ's resurrection and the resurrection of believers. He could do this because he saw that the sheaf could represent the harvest because it was part of the harvest. What is Paul getting at?

In postbiblical Jewish and early Christian thought, resurrection always involved groups of people, never single individuals. But on the first Easter, only one person was resurrected. Logically this fact created a problem, for one could argue that since the dead are still in their graves (or in *Sheol*, the subterranean abode of the dead), Christ was not raised. (Paul may have argued this way against the Christians before encountering the risen Christ, though he does not say so.) So Paul must find a way to acknowledge that all the dead are still dead while at the same time insist that "in fact Christ has been raised from the dead" (1 Corinthians 15:20). That is, he can give up neither the conviction that resurrection is a group experience nor the conviction that only one person, Christ, has been raised. Calling the resurrected Christ "the first fruits of those who have died" is a way of solving this problem, for by definition the first fruit clearly implies that the rest of the crop, of which the sheaf is a part, is ripening. (An analogy: The first ripe strawberry means that strawberry season is at hand.) In other words, by using "first fruits" as a metaphor for the risen Christ, Paul allows for the difference in time between Christ's resurrection and the coming resurrection of believers while maintaining the solidarity between the one and the many. Further, if Christ is the "first fruits," the fact that the dead are still dead does not count against the claim that *Christ* has been raised. To the contrary, if *he* has been raised, then the resurrection of the rest of the dead is assured, for the resurrection of Christ and the resurrection of Christians stand or fall together; they cannot be split apart, though they are separated in time. If they were split apart, the resurrection of Jesus would not touch us at all. It simply would be an ancient miracle.

> The resurrection of Christ and the resurrection of Christians stand or fall together; they cannot be split apart, though they are separated in time.

Appearance Logic

Except for Mark, all the New Testament Gospels conclude with stories in which the resurrected Jesus appears. Similarly, the tradition Paul quotes in 1 Corinthians 15:3-7 emphasizes Christ's appearances. Our examination of each Gospel's conclusion will be helped if we look first at the appearance stories and Paul's tradition as a whole. By noting five things we do *not* find, we can appreciate better what we do find.

First, despite the fact that in the Passion predictions Jesus had spoken repeatedly of his resurrection (Mark 8:31; 9:31; 10:34), none of the Gospels reports that the disciples recalled what Jesus had said and therefore waited for the Resurrection to occur. No one seems to have expected Jesus' resurrection. In Mark and Luke the women "bought spices so that they might go and anoint him," since there had not been time to give him a proper burial. We might conclude that the women did not hear or hear of the Passion predictions. But none of the Gospels attributes the desire to bury Jesus properly to ignorance of the Passion predictions. The reason is not hard to discern: For the Gospel writers, the resurrection of Jesus was an awesome surprise not because the women or Joseph and Nicodemus had not been informed of the Passion predictions but because resurrection is an awesome, surprise-generating event by definition. In other words, far from being a case of wish fulfillment, the appearances evoked doubt, fear, and disbelief as well as joy.

Second, Peter became the first leader of the Jerusalem church and was succeeded by James, Jesus' brother who had not been a disciple; yet the New Testament contains no story of Jesus' appearance to them. Interestingly, 1 Corinthians 15:5, 7 distinguishes the appearances to these two men from those to the apostles—"to Cephas, then to the twelve"; and "to James, then to all the apostles." Luke 24:34 mentions an appearance to Simon (Peter) but none to James. In other words, although these appearances to individuals were remembered, these men's roles in the church were nowhere given legitimacy by stories that made them special recipients of the risen Jesus' authorization. Instead, the Gospels agree that women were the *first* to see the risen Christ, and the Gospels also agree that one of the women was Mary of Magdala. In other words, the Gospels imply that the privilege of seeing the resurrected Christ first was given not to those who would have power and authority but to those who would not.

Third, the Jesus who appeared was not resuscitated, for he had a resurrection body. The appearance stories show the unusual nature of that body: Those to whom he appeared do not recognize him at first; he suddenly appears in a room without using the door (explicitly noted in John 20:19, and probably assumed in Luke 24:36). In all four appearance stories we find continuity (it's really Jesus) and discontinuity (he's different now). In other words, what these appearance stories express in narrative form is the basic meaning of resurrection—a transformed body-self. We have no evidence that Paul knew or did not know these stories, for he never mentions them, and silence is not always a sign of ignorance. But if he had, he might well have called the body of the resurrected Jesus his "spiritual body" or his "glorious body."

Fourth, never do any of the persons who find the tomb empty conclude, "He has been resurrected." The empty tomb (which Paul never mentions but probably took for granted) is consistent with the Resurrection but in no way proves it, as Mary Magdalene's complaint shows: "They have taken away my Lord, and I do not know where they have

> **The privilege of seeing the resurrected Christ first was given not to those who would have power and authority but to those who would not.**

laid him" (John 20:13). In John Jesus corrects her interpretation of the empty tomb by disclosing himself as the resurrected but not yet ascended Christ. In the Synoptics the Resurrection is proclaimed by the figure or figures in the tomb. (When Matthew 28:2 says the figure was an angel, he probably makes explicit what Mark 16:5 and Luke 24:4 imply.) When the empty tomb stories report that the news of Jesus' resurrection is delivered by angelic beings, they express exactly what, according to Matthew, Jesus said in response to Peter's confession at Caesarea Philippi: "Flesh and blood has not revealed this to you, but my Father in heaven" (Matthew 16:17).

Fifth, the New Testament Gospels have no story of the Resurrection itself. No narrative tells us what happened or how it happened. The appearance stories tell us only the results of what happened to Jesus. For a hint of what happened, we can go to the *Gospel of Peter** 9–10. There we read that the soldiers guarding the tomb "saw the skies open up

206

and two men come down . . . and approach the tomb. The stone . . . began to roll by itself and moved away to one side; then both men went inside . . . . They [the soldiers] see three men leaving the tomb, the two supporting the third, and a cross was following them. The heads of the two reached up to the sky, while the head of the third . . . reached beyond the skies. And they heard a voice from the skies that said, 'Have you preached to those who sleep [the dead]?' And an answer was heard from the cross, 'Yes!' " In the *Gospel of Peter* the soldiers saw and reported what happened but did not become believers. In the New Testament, however, only believers report the Resurrection (emphasized in Acts 10:40-41). Why? Because to affirm Jesus' resurrection is to affirm his vindication by God. And no one can affirm that and remain a neutral or indifferent observer. A person can say as fact that some people believed God raised Jesus from the dead, but the person who says, "God raised Jesus from the dead" is doing more than reporting a fact; he or she is acknowledging that Jesus is the act of God and therefore of decisive and definitive significance for the person making this acknowledgment.

The Synoptics' Concluding Logic

Although the Gospels use the logic of the appearance stories, each Evangelist makes his own emphasis by the way he tells the story.

Mark's unexpected ending at 16:8 continues to intrigue interpreters. Scholars agree that everything after "for they were afraid" was not part of the original text; it is missing from most of the best Greek manuscripts as well as from those in Latin, Syriac, and Coptic (used in Egypt, alongside Greek). Conceivably Mark's Gospel might have gone on to report Jesus' meeting the disciples in Galilee, as they were instructed in 16:7; but if it did so, that ending was lost almost from the start. Instead of guessing what it might have said, most interpreters assume that this Gospel ends where the best manuscripts end it, and then ponder the meaning of such an ending.

In 16:7 the women are commanded to tell the disciples and Peter that the risen Christ is going (present tense) ahead of them to Galilee, where they will rendezvous with him as he had said (14:28). No reason is given in either passage for this meeting in Galilee, thereby leaving the reader wondering why it must take place there. Nor are we told why Peter is mentioned separately, though we may surmise this mention is a hint that he is forgiven for his denial, as are the disciples for fleeing into the night.

That "terror and amazement" seized the women (16:8) is an understandable reaction, especially in light of what they had already seen that weekend: the Crucifixion, noonday darkness, Jesus' loud last cry and burial in a tomb behind a large stone, and now a youth in white who made them bearers of a strange message. What is not so easy to understand is why their fear caused them to disobey the command. We can make our own addition to Mark, saying "but when they got hold of themselves, they did convey the message." That reasoning might make a more satisfying ending to the whole story, and it might even be correct. But that sort of conclusion is precisely what Mark refused to write. So this Gospel ends with fear-driven disobedience, quite the opposite of the faith and obedience we expect.

The more puzzled we are by this ending, the more it may dawn on us that the Evangelist may have been wiser and more theologically alert than most of us readers—especially when we allow our historical and psychological questions to eclipse what his terse conclusion asks of us. At least several considerations can nudge our thinking into different channels. First, the clear emphasis on Galilee should start our recalling where it all began, yet the youth does not speak of Jesus' going back but of his "going ahead" of the disciples, using the same word as in 10:32: "They were on the road, going up to Jerusalem, and Jesus was walking ahead [going ahead] of them; and they were amazed, and those who followed were afraid." When we read that the youth says that the risen Christ "is going ahead of you to Galilee," are we not to hear a hint—that Jesus still goes ahead of the disciples, despite their fear? that the disciples in Mark's time (and in ours) are to read this Gospel's story of Jesus in Galilee in such a way that the risen One meets them in those stories and sayings? And does not Mark imply that this "going ahead" is the meaning of Jesus' resurrection? The writer alerted us to this perspective, for his opening line says that the story that follows is "the beginning of the gospel." So Mark ends his Gospel by inviting us to start reading again, this time seeing and hearing the risen Christ in the stories of Jesus.

In Matthew the women do not come to the tomb to anoint Jesus' body properly, as in Mark and Luke, but "to see the tomb"; so they do not worry about who will roll away the stone either. Yet Matthew explains (to the reader) how the tomb came to be open: An angel "rolled back the stone and sat on it." His appearance so terrified the guards that they "became like dead men." But the angel ignored them and instead addressed the women, slightly modifying what the young man in Mark said. But in Matthew the women do as they are told: "They left the tomb quickly with fear and great joy, and ran to tell his disciples" (Matthew 28:8). Before they reached them, however, Jesus met them, and in response they "took hold of his feet, and worshiped him." Then Jesus spoke to them, paraphrasing and abbreviating what the angel had already told them to do. Because the women obeyed, "the eleven disciples went to Galilee, to the mountain to which Jesus had directed them" (28:16)—a new detail. (In Matthew pivotal events occur on mountains—Jesus' climactic temptation, the inaugural sermon, the Transfiguration, the predictions of the end, and now the concluding scene.) And like the women whom Jesus met, the disciples worshiped Jesus when they saw him—though the Gospel immediately qualifies this by saying "but some doubted" (28:17, which can also be translated "but they doubted"). Their doubt, Matthew implies, was removed by the risen Jesus' words, with which the Gospel ends.

What Jesus says falls into three parts. (1) In a self-proclamation (28:18) he declares that God has given him "all authority in heaven and on earth." This goes beyond what he had claimed during his lifetime: "All things have been handed over to me by my Father; and no one knows . . . the Father except the Son and anyone to whom the Son chooses to reveal him" (11:27), implying that because of his resurrection he now has the same authority as God. This declaration may allude to what Daniel 7:13-14 says about the heavenly figure ("one like a son of man") and to what Psalm 110:1 says about the one at God's right hand.

(2) This cosmic authority is the basis of the commission to "make disciples of all nations" (Matthew 28:19). This disciple-making is to have two aspects—baptism and instruction. Here is the first appearance of the baptismal formula, "in the name of the Father and of the Son and of the Holy Spirit"; probably it was used in Matthew's church. (Earlier baptism had been "in the name of Jesus Christ" alone, as Acts 2:38; 8:16; 10:48; 19:5; 1 Corinthians 1:13-15 show.) The emphasis on "teaching . . . everything that I have commanded you" helps us understand why Matthew has compiled many of Jesus' teachings into the five discourses, each with its own theme. Such compilations are easier to teach and remember. We should not, however, conclude that Matthew 28:20 has in view only the words of Jesus that are in the form of a commandment, for the exemplary deeds and demeanor of Jesus are included as well, as the

invitations to "follow" Jesus show. Here then we find the passage that largely accounts for the character and content of Matthew's Gospel.

(3) Jesus' last word is a *promise* of his continuing presence "to the end of the age"—that is, until his coming. Earlier Jesus had promised his presence with the church assembled: "Where two or three are gathered in my name, I am there among them" (18:20). Here he promises his presence with the church dispersed in mission. Additionally, according to 1:23, Mary's child is to be called "Emmanuel," explained as "God is with us." Now, at the end of this Gospel, the Resurrection makes that promise come true and remain true "to the end of the age."

Luke's concluding chapter is the longest by far. Also, from a literary point of view it has the most effective ending: Jesus is taken up to heaven (though some manuscripts omit "and was carried up into heaven"), and the joyous disciples "were continually in the temple blessing God" (24:51-53). This Gospel too ends where it began—in the Jerusalem Temple (Luke 1). From Jerusalem the gospel is to spread to "Judea and Samaria, and to the ends of the earth" (Acts 1:8). In Luke's second volume, Acts, Jerusalem retains its central importance even as the gospel is taken to Asia Minor, Greece, and Rome. Accordingly, in Luke the angelic messengers at the tomb do not remind the women that Jesus had promised to meet the disciples in Galilee; instead the angels say, "Remember how he told you, while he was still in Galilee, that the Son of Man must be handed over to sinners," and so forth (Luke 24:6). And only in Luke does Jesus himself say that "repentance and forgiveness of sins is to be proclaimed . . . to all nations, beginning from Jerusalem" (24:47), as well as command the disciples to "stay here in the city" until they are empowered by the Spirit (24:49). And the disciples obey: They do not go to Galilee.

Luke is also the only Gospel that reports how the disciples responded to the women's news: "These words seemed to them an idle tale, and they did not believe them" (24:11). Not even Peter, who went to see the empty tomb for himself, got beyond amazement (24:12). Later, when Cleopas and his companion returned to Jerusalem, the disciples told them, "The Lord has risen indeed, and he has appeared to Simon [Peter]" (24:34); but we do not learn where this occurred. Apart from these two responses, Peter plays no role whatever in Luke 24. Not until Acts 1:15 does he begin to fulfill Jesus' word to him at the supper: "When once you have turned back, strengthen your brothers" (Luke 22:32). The turning itself, though implicitly the result of the risen Jesus' appearing to him, is not reported.

The centerpiece of Luke's concluding chapter is the story of the risen Jesus' joining Cleopas and his companion on their way to Emmaus and their recognizing him "in the breaking of the bread." To this story is joined the story of Jesus' demonstrating to the disciples, plus the two companions who had returned to Jerusalem, that the one they suddenly saw among them was not a ghost, for he showed them that he had a real body and ate a piece of fish as well. Thereby

> **In the appearance stories the transformed Jesus changes those he meets into bold witnesses; in doing so, he preserves and reveals his true identity and continuing vocation.**

Luke insists that Jesus was really resurrected, that the disciples really saw *him*, and therefore the Resurrection is something that happened to Jesus and is not to be confused with a visionary experience of the disciples; rather, the resurrected Jesus changed them because resurrection changed Jesus.

The dominant theme in Luke 24, however, is that the whole Jesus event accords with Scripture. Jesus himself insists on this to Cleopas and his associate (24:27), and they acknowledge that his interpretation of Scripture was right because their hearts were "burning" as he "was opening the scriptures" (24:32). Later that same night Jesus makes the same point to the assembled group, adding that "repentance and forgiveness of sins is to be proclaimed in his [the Messiah's] name to all nations" (24:44-47). Finally, the disciples are to be witnesses empowered by the Spirit, whom Jesus will send. Here too the Jesus event ends with a forward look.

So Then

A few theological reflections are in order, beginning with the stories we have examined. While each Gospel ends somewhat differently, the concluding chapters nonetheless have a common trait that sets them apart from the chapters that precede them: The reader is in a world where the familiar has become strange, the uncanny is the norm, and explanations mystify. The previous chapters are characterized by the stark realism of Jesus' dread of death, Judas's betrayal, Peter's denial, capped by the lean accounts of the Crucifixion and burial.

But these concluding chapters (when seen together) pile wonder on wonder and mix belief with unbelief, sameness with difference. Earth's places—Jerusalem, Emmaus, Galilee—are the same, but the world of those we see there has changed—forever—because one of those executed on Friday was resurrected. In the appearance stories the transformed Jesus changes those he meets into bold witnesses; in doing so, he preserves and reveals his true identity and continuing vocation.

The Gospels say that Jesus appeared to the disciples. This way of putting it is useful because it identifies them for the reader. Strictly speaking, however, they *had been* his disciples, for they abandoned him and fled into the night (except in Luke). So it was to deserters and to the denier that the resurrected Jesus appeared. Yet the Gospels report not a single rebuke, not even a caustic reminder, from the lips of Jesus. Instead, he has absorbed their deed into his and so freed them from it. That is, he forgave them, reconciled them to himself, rectified the wronged relationship, and so gave them a new future. Christian theology has a word for such an act—*grace*.

But there is more. According to the Gospels and Paul, the resurrected Jesus made himself known also to those who had been disappointed in him (Cleopas and friend), to his brother James who had ignored him, and to Paul who was persecuting Jesus' followers. Put theologically, these appearances express the initiative of grace, for in them the resurrected Christ does more than heal broken relationships; by intruding into these people's lives, he reaches out to create new relationships. The logic built into these appearance stories goes counter to the common view that Christ always waits for people to turn to him. Christian theology has a phrase also for this—*prevenient grace*.

Finally, those to whom he appeared became his emissaries. (Since Cleopas and his companion were among the disciples when Jesus said, "You are witnesses of these things" in Luke 24:48, we may assume that they too became his emissaries, even though we know nothing more about them.) Those who had fled are now sent, commissioned to make disciples throughout the world; James becomes a leading figure in the Jerusalem church, and Paul becomes the apostle to the Gentiles. Indeed, he says that this was God's purpose in revealing his Son to him (Galatians 1:16). In other words, the transformed Jesus continues to change the lives of people through those whom he has already changed. Resurrection does that sort of thing too.

Do You Want to Become His Disciples, Too?

To be a disciple of the transformed Jesus who changes people calls for a willingness to accept his forgiveness for the ways we have ignored, hidden, abandoned, or even denied our commitment to him. Accepting his forgiveness is not easy because doing so means facing up to what we did (or did not do), but accepting forgiveness is still easier than carrying the burden of our unforgiven past because that only gets heavier. But the forgiven are freed from that piece of their history, though not free of Christ, for he goes before them—and they follow.

How does this resurrected Jesus reveal to you the purpose and power of God?

_____

_____

_____

_____

_____

Prayer

You are kind, LORD, so good and merciful.
You protect ordinary people,
    and when I was helpless, you saved me
and treated me so kindly
    that I don't need to worry anymore.

You, LORD, have saved my life from death,
    my eyes from tears, my feet from stumbling.
Now I will walk at your side in this land of the living.
I was faithful to you when I was suffering,
    though in my confusion I said, "I can't trust anyone!"

What must I give you, LORD, for being so good to me? ...
I will keep my promise to you when your people meet.

(Psalm 116:5-12, 14, CEV)

Turning Now to John

We have been reading only those passages in John that are similar to the Synoptics. Now we reverse the pattern: John becomes the centerpiece, and we read passages in the Synoptics that are similar to John (and sometimes different from John). When we do look at the Synoptic Gospels, our purpose is to highlight what is distinctive about John. The lessons take us through John from beginning to end, keeping the flow of the story before us. (Reading the whole Gospel through, without stopping if possible, is a good way to get a sense of the whole story before we start.)

Because we are studying Jesus *in* the Gospels, the focus is on what this Gospel tells us about Jesus that is unique and what makes it unique. John invites us to see Jesus from another angle.

23 In the Beginning Was the Word

The Word became flesh and lived among us, and we have seen his glory, the glory as of a father's only son, full of grace and truth.

(John 1:14)

They Have No Wine

Sometimes we don't know what we're looking for. In simple situations, we may find ourselves at the pantry or at the desk, wondering what we came to get. We knew what we were looking for when we started out and may soon recall it. But when it comes to the big goals in life, we sometimes keep looking and looking. Is it because we don't remember what we should be looking for? Or are we looking in the wrong places? Some people claim that looking is more interesting than finding, but most of us are not satisfied with a life of seeking without finding. To spend our whole life looking for something to live by and live for, yet never finding it, is well . . . .

Beginning With Moses and All the Prophets

This week we examine the first chapter of John because it allows us to see the perspective from which this Gospel tells the story of Jesus. The Prologue (John 1:1-18) is especially important; we will be referring to it repeatedly. The other readings help us understand both the background and the foreground of the Prologue.

Day 1 John 1:1-18; 1 Corinthians 8:4-6; Colossians 1:15-20; Hebrews 1:1-4

Today's readings celebrate the relation of Christ to Creation, emphasized in the first verses of John.

(1) Note that John 1 consists of three parts—the Prologue (1:1-18), the testimony of John the Baptist (1:19-34), and stories that report how Jesus acquired his first followers (1: 35-51). Note also that John the Baptist is the link among these three parts.

(2) Note carefully what is said about the Word in 1:1-5 and how carefully 1:8-9 distinguishes John from Jesus.

(3) Note that 1:10-13 contrasts the refusing of the light with the receiving of it.

(4) Note that 1:14 states the Incarnation (the word means "enfleshment"); note the contrast between what is said of the Word in 1:1-4 and what is implied by *flesh* in 1:14.

(5) In 1 Corinthians 8:6, note that by using "through whom" of Christ but not of God, the statement says that Christ is the mediator of Creation, which John 1:3, 10 says in different words. See how Hebrews 1:1-4 makes the same point. In Colossians 1:15-20, note how important the phrase "all things" is.

Day 2 Genesis 1:1–2:3; 28:10-17; Proverbs 8:1-31; Wisdom of Solomon 7:22–8:1; Sirach 24:1-29

These readings bring to our attention the biblical background of yesterday's reading about Christ and Creation. Especially important are the passages that celebrate wisdom's role in Creation. (In both Hebrew and Greek the word *wisdom* [Greek: *sophia*] is a feminine noun, making it easy to visualize wisdom as a woman.)

(1) Note that in Proverbs 8:22-31 she is present at Creation.

(2) Observe that some of what Wisdom of Solomon says about wisdom is said of Christ in Colossians 1:15-17 and Hebrews 1:1-4.

(3) Note that in Sirach*, wisdom, having come from God's mouth (at Creation, Sirach 24:3), rules the world (as God's agent, 24:6), makes Jerusalem her home (24:8-12), and is finally identified with the law of Moses (24:23).

Day 3 **John 1:6-8, 15, 19-34;** 3:22-30; 4:1-3; 5:31-36; 10:40-42; Mark 1:1-11

Today we read everything this Gospel says about John the Baptist.

(1) In John 1 note that 1:6-8 insists that John's role is to bear witness (the same word can be translated "testify"), that his first testimony is a riddlelike statement about his relation to Jesus (1:15), and that his witness reaches its climax in 1:34. Notice that this Gospel does not report Jesus' baptism, yet John the Baptist seems to know what Mark 1:1-11 reports.

(2) In John 1:29, 35-37 note what prompted John's disciples to follow Jesus.

(3) Only in John 3:22-24 and 4:1 do we read that Jesus too was baptizing and that his mission overlapped with John's (compare Matthew 4:12; Mark 1:14). Note how the story about potential rivalry ends in John 3:30. Observe that if we put quotation marks at the end of 3:30 (as in the New Revised Standard Version), then 3:31-36 are the Gospel writer's comment; but if we put them at the end of 3:36, then 3:31-36 continues what John the Baptist said (as in the New International Version).

(4) Note that in 5:31-33 John's witness to Jesus is acknowledged as true by Jesus, and in 10:40-42 by the people.

Day 4 John 1:35-51; Matthew 4:18-22; Luke 5:1-11; Job 38:4-15; Isaiah 40; 42:5-8

(1) Observe that in John 1:51 Jesus uses Genesis 28:12 to express the significance of his mission.

(2) **GC 23-1** Note how differently John accounts for Jesus' first disciples (John 1:29-51) from Matthew 4:18-22; Luke 5:1-11.

(3) Observe that the Old Testament readings celebrate God as Creator and that Isaiah insists that the Redeemer is the Creator; note that this insistence appears in the Prologue of John.

Day 5 1 John 1:5-10; 3:1-3; 4:1-6; 5:1-5; 2 John

The passages from First John show that what John 1:14 asserts was being denied by some Christians. Note how vehemently the author of First John responds.

Day 6 Read and respond to "In the Beginning Was the Word" and "Do You Want to Become His Disciples, Too?"

Prayer Concerns

In the Beginning Was the Word

We need not read far into John's Gospel before realizing we are in a world that differs from that of the Synoptics, even though some of the places and some of the people are the same. The opening line itself alerts us to expect something different: "In the beginning was the Word." Beginning of what? Mark's Gospel too starts by referring to "the beginning," but there it is "the beginning of the good news of Jesus Christ, the Son of God." But in John Jesus is not even mentioned until 1:17. John's Gospel takes us back to the absolute beginning, to the "when" before anything had a beginning, to before Creation. Already then there was "the Word" and there was God. John is not talking about God's word, for "in the beginning" the Word *was* God and was *with* God. Any story that starts there, especially a story about Jesus, is bound to be different.

The first eighteen verses (the Prologue) tell us whom the story of Jesus is really about, alert us to what to expect in that story, and point out why Jesus is so important. The words in the Prologue are simple; but the sentences and the thought they express are not.

The Prologue (John 1:1-18)

Although the Prologue is chiefly about the Word, it is also about John the Baptist (in this Gospel he always is called simply "John"). The text begins with the Word (1:1-5), shifts to John (1:6-8), returns to the Word (1:9-14), then switches back to John (1:15) before ending where it began—with the Word, now called God's Son, in God's presence (1:16-18).

The first five verses announce the identity of the Word without explaining what "the Word" refers to. The author assumes his readers will recognize what he is writing about since "the Word" was a well-known idea at the time (see "What John Meant by "the Word," p. 221). These initial five verses have struck many interpreters as poetry, and some have thought they are an early Christian hymn that the Gospel writer used. The poetic character of 1:1-5 becomes apparent when the lines are printed as follows (one of several possibilities):

"In the beginning was the Word,
And the Word was with God,
And the Word was God.
He was in the beginning with God.

All things came into being through him,
And without him not one thing came into being.

What has come into being in him was life,
And the life was the light of all people.
The light shines in the darkness,
And the darkness did not overcome it."

Clearly, the Word is the one through whom God created everything, so that everything (including humans) owes its existence to the Word. What the poem emphasizes, however, is that the Word is the source of life, which is everyone's light. We will see that *life* and *light* are words loaded with meaning in Jesus' teaching. What makes *light* so significant is that it "shines [present tense] in the darkness." The text does not say where this darkness came from, but it implies something happened to Creation (readers are expected to assume it was "the Fall" in Genesis 3). As a result, there is a struggle between light and darkness in which light prevails—"the darkness did not overcome it." Here the translation "has never mastered it" (REB) captures better the double meaning of the Greek—"overcome" (NRSV) as well as "understood" (NIV). Right from the start, we are introduced to a feature of John—the use of words that have more than one meaning. So, with this rather abstract language, the Prologue signals what John's Gospel is about—the Word-Creator-light in the darkness. The signal is both ominous and assuring.

> The Word is the one through whom God created everything, so that everything (including humans) owes its existence to the Word.

John 1:9 connects the lines about the Word in the world to 1:5 by referring to the Word as "the true light that . . . was coming into the world." John 1:11 states in a general way the Gospel's overarching theme: The Word came to "what was his own [literally, 'his own things,' what rightly belongs to him because he created them] and his own people did not accept him." But some of his own people did accept him by believing in his name (1:12). Here *name* refers not to the name Jesus but to that which reveals a person's true identity; the same understanding of *name* occurs when Jesus speaks of revealing God's name: "I have

215

made your name known to those whom you gave me from the world" (17:6). The Prologue explains that becoming God's children by believing entails nothing less than the new birth—not an ordinary human birth but one that is "of God" (1:13), that has its origin in God's act. (John 3 picks up this theme when Jesus talks to one of his own people, Nicodemus.) Seen as a whole, 1:9-13 develops what 1:5 implies about the light in the darkness: "The light shines in the darkness, and the darkness did not overcome it."

We would exaggerate only slightly in saying that John's whole Gospel rests on the astounding declaration in 1:14: "And the Word became flesh

In becoming flesh the Creator became creature "and lived among us."

and lived among us, and we have seen his glory, the glory as of the Father's only son, full of grace and truth." (The New Revised Standard Version's alternative translation, used here, is much closer to John's overall theology.) Strictly speaking, this verse is the only New Testament statement of the Incarnation, though such passages as Romans 8:3-4 and Hebrews 2:14-18 assume it. The later controversies over the nature of Christ repeatedly emphasized the first part of John 1:14 in order to insist that Jesus was a real human being, but the two assertions go together— (1) "The Word became flesh" and (2) "we have seen his glory." When the two assertions are seen together, the whole declaration is doubly challenging because it uses the word *flesh*.

Here *flesh* stands not simply for what is physical and touchable but also for what is weak, vulnerable, transient. In becoming flesh the Creator became creature "and lived among us." No halo made Jesus so evidently different from other men of his age that people could look at him and say, "He must be a god" or "There goes the embodied *Logos*." The Incarnation made the Creator one of us, a real human, not a humanoid (a being that only resembled a human). At the same time, becoming flesh did not make him just another human, for in this Gospel the enfleshed *Logos* remembers he was not always a human, and Jesus knows that his prehuman status will be restored (John 16:28). He knows that as the Word enfleshed he is the heavenly sojourner who is "not of this world" (8:23). Ever since John's Gospel was written, Christian theology has struggled to understand and express this paradox (truly God, truly human).

The enfleshed *Logos* was "full of grace and truth" (1:14); indeed, from that abundance "we have all received, grace upon grace" (1:16). These words, like "and we have seen his glory," make a confession, the confession of "all who received him, who believed in his name." These confessional statements express the gratitude of the recipients, the beneficiaries of the Incarnation. John 1:17 explains why they are beneficiaries: "The law indeed was given through Moses; grace and truth came through Jesus Christ." We must resist the temptation to insert the word *but* between the two halves of this remarkable sentence, for that would make the contrast greater than it is. The statement is not a putdown of the Law (after all, "was given" implies God was the giver); rather, it points out that in Jesus Christ grace and truth became an event. That is, what makes Jesus decisively different from the Law is not that he explained grace and truth better but that grace and truth were embodied in him. Grace and truth are those qualities on which our relation to God depends, for without grace there would be only judgment, and without truth there would be only guesses and illusions. (The translation "came" in some English Bibles does not do justice to the Greek word, which really means "became.") Later, Jesus speaks of his "coming" (John 14–17) but the Prologue speaks of grace and truth as *becoming* a historical event called Jesus Christ. Here the point is not arrival but actualization.

> Grace and truth are those qualities on which our relation to God depends, for without grace there would be only judgment, and without truth there would be only guesses and illusions.

Also the Prologue's ending points ahead: The Son makes the Father known (1:18). He can do this because he is close to the Father (literally, "in the Father's bosom").

Since the Prologue in John discloses the Gospel's perspective—the story of Jesus is the story of the enfleshed Word in the world he created—we may be surprised to find that while Jesus speaks repeatedly about himself, he never claims to be the Word enfleshed. Instead, Jesus uses other language to express the same idea. For instance, he says, "I am the bread of life .... I have come down from heaven" (6:35, 38). In this Gospel, the more explicitly Jesus speaks of his identity and mission, the more he offends his hearers. Only the readers of the Prologue know why he talks this way. That is, the readers *of* the story know what no one (except Jesus) *in* the story knows.

To sum up, the Prologue makes the enfleshment of the *Logos*—the Word becoming flesh—the lens through which readers are to read the story that follows. The writer of John's Gospel says, in effect, unless you read this story as the account of the Word enfleshed, you will not understand anything that matters; in fact, you will misunderstand everything. But if you believe the Prologue, you will both grasp what is going on and know that you too are confronted with Jesus' claims, for the Prologue does not say that years ago the light "shone" in the darkness but that it "shines." And if you let this light shine on you, you too will receive "grace upon grace."

The Baptizer's Witness

The Fourth Gospel has a distinctive perspective also on John the Baptist. Here John's mission is focused solely on being a witness who proclaims the significance of Jesus "so that all might believe" (John 1:7). This Gospel assumes that John baptized Jesus but does not actually say so. The Fourth Gospel knows that when Jesus was baptized a voice was heard, but this Gospel does not report what it said to Jesus ("You are my Son," Mark 1:11; Luke 3:22); instead, it implies that the voice spoke to John, telling him, "He on whom you see the Spirit descend and remain is the one who baptizes with the Holy Spirit." In this way the Fourth Gospel uses the events at Jesus' baptism to account for John's witness. While Mark's readers learn from the descent of the Spirit and the voice who Jesus is, John's readers know this from the Prologue and the Baptizer's witness.

GC 23-2 In keeping with the Prologue's insistence that John is not the light but the witness to the light (John 1:7-8), this Gospel subordinates the Baptizer to Jesus more strongly than do the Synoptics (Mark 1:7-8; Matthew 3:11-12). John's first witness (John 1:15, partly repeated in 1:30) reads like a riddle because it makes sense only if we know how to read the double meanings. "He who comes after me ranks ahead of me" seems to contradict itself for "he who comes after me" refers to a follower, a disciple. But can the follower come "ahead of me"? Yes, "because he *was* before me" to start with. Have they changed places? Not at all.

The readers of the Prologue know the answer to the riddle: Because the Word, who was in the beginning with God, became incarnate as Jesus, he indeed "was" before John was born; even though now in Galilee Jesus comes "after" John (later than John), he still "ranks ahead" of John.

Repeatedly the Baptizer points out that his role is subordinate to that of Jesus. He insists he is not the Messiah or Elijah or "the prophet" (the expected Moses-like figure; Deuteronomy 18:15, 18); he is rather the "voice ... in the wilderness" (John 1:23; Isaiah 40:3). John himself recognizes why Jesus is his superior: Jesus is "the Lamb of God who takes away the sin of the world" (John 1:29). The Fourth Gospel no more explains how John knew this than Matthew explains how the Baptizer came to realize

> **John's Gospel says, in effect, unless you read this story as the account of the Word enfleshed, you will not understand anything that matters.**

that Jesus should be baptizing him instead of his baptizing Jesus (Matthew 3:14). **GC 23-3** According to John 3:25-30, not even news of Jesus' surprising popularity provokes John to jealousy, for Jesus' ascendancy is in accord with God's will for both men. In fact, "he must increase, but I must decrease." The Synoptics report John the Baptist's uncertainty about Jesus: "Are you he who is to come, or are we to wait for another?" (Matthew 11:2-3; Luke 7:18-19). In the Fourth Gospel John is completely confident that he knows who Jesus is and why he is decisive.

Later Jesus speaks positively about John and at the same time claims his own message surpasses John's (John 5:33-36): "He was a burning and shining lamp [not the light], and you were willing to rejoice for a while in his light. But I have a testimony greater than John's." The final word about John, the judgment of the people who came to Jesus, confirms both his lesser status and the truth of his witness: "John performed no sign, but everything that John said about this man [Jesus] was true." The last comment "And many believed in him [Jesus] there" (10:41-42) rounds out and fulfills what was said about John in the Prologue: "He came as a witness to testify to the light, so that all might believe through him" (1:7).

The Promise of Jesus

John's word that he must decrease while Jesus increases begins to come true even before John says so, for John's circle of disciples is diminished when two of them leave John to follow Jesus instead. And they do so because of John's witness when he sees Jesus "walk by": "Look, here is the Lamb of God!" (1:35-37). By calling Jesus "the Lamb of God," John points ahead to the Crucifixion, which in this Gospel occurs at the very time the Passover lambs are being slaughtered. The rest of John 1, however, reports how certain other persons came to be Jesus' disciples. These reports too help us understand noticeable features of John's perspective.

One feature appears in the first report, beginning at 1:38—specifically, the Gospel's reliance on "loaded words," words that imply more than they mean literally. Thus Jesus' question to John's former disciples, "What are you looking for?" is more than an offer to be helpful; the question also suggests that Jesus is aware they are seeking something that was not satisfied when they followed John. The author, being a skillful narrator, builds suspense into the story by delaying the real answer, which appears in what Andrew tells his brother, "We have found the Messiah" (1:41). In the meantime, the two men respond to Jesus' question with their own, also suggestive, "Rabbi, . . . where are you staying?" Only on the surface might it appear that they want him to recommend an inn for the night (as the literal-minded reader might infer also from the time of day mentioned in 1:39). Rather, the repeated use of "staying" suggests either that they want an enduring relation with Jesus or that they want to know if he is only a passing phenomenon.

Mark and Matthew also report that Jesus' first disciples were the brothers Andrew and Simon (Mark 1:16-20; Matthew 4:18-20). If we try to combine the reports of John and the Synoptics, we miss the point of both. We get the same result if we try to combine John's account of Jesus' renaming Simon (John 1:42) with Matthew's account (Matthew 16:13-19). While Matthew's story implies that Simon got his new name because Jesus approved of his confession, in John Jesus' renaming Simon when they first met implies that Simon got a new name solely because of Jesus' word. In this Gospel the initiative is always with Jesus.

John ignores many details in order to let his interests stand out clearly. We are not told why Jesus found Philip, who is the only one of the four that Jesus summoned to discipleship, or why the Galileans, Andrew and Peter, were in Judea, where Jesus appears to be (see John 1:43). Likewise, we can ask how, at this point, Philip could tell Nathanael that "Jesus son of Joseph from Nazareth" is the one about whom Moses and the prophets wrote (1:45). We can imagine plausible answers to such questions, but doing so here would turn our attention away from what John wants us to see.

John 1:45-51 carries forward the theme of 1:14: "The Word became flesh . . . , and we have seen his glory." Here, the "flesh" is concrete: Jesus is from Nazareth, so insignificant a village that Nathanael doubts anything good can come from there. Instead of arguing the point, Philip simply says, "Come and see" (1:46). Philip and Nathanael "saw" Jesus' glory in the fact that he declared Nathanael to be "an Israelite in whom there is no deceit" before they met, and then said, "I saw you under the fig tree before Philip called you." Jesus promises Nathanael he will see "greater things than these" (what he had seen Jesus able to do)—specifically, "heaven opened and the angels of God ascending and descending upon the Son of Man" (1:50-51). Jesus' promise refers to Jacob's dream at Bethel, to which the patriarch responded by saying, "Surely the LORD is in this place—and I did not know it! . . . This is none other than the house of God, and this is the gate of heaven" (Genesis 28:10-17). In other words, Jesus' promise interprets his whole mission as the event in which there is access to God. Whoever sees Jesus that way sees his glory, and the glory is to be seen in this man from insignificant Nazareth. So Jesus' promise is at the same time a challenge to see the glory of the *Logos* enfleshed. Indeed, the promise of Jesus is kept when we, like Nathanael, see him for what he truly is.

> **John intentionally wrote this Gospel as he did so that the readers *of* the story confront the same claims Jesus makes *in* the story.**

So Then

Now that we focus on John, the distinctive character of this Fourth Gospel is becoming ever more evident. Important as it is to see *how* and *where* John differs from the Synoptics, more important is understanding *what* makes it so different—the astounding claim that Jesus from insignificant Nazareth is really the *Logos* enfleshed, the incarnate Son of God. The other three Gospels also see Jesus as God's Son, yet they understand "Son of God" somewhat differently. In Matthew and Luke Jesus is God's "Son" because of the virgin birth. In John, however, the Son of God is Jesus because the Son (another way of referring to the *Logos*) *became* Jesus. (Although Christian theology has often combined these views by inferring that the Incarnation occurred when Mary became pregnant by the Spirit, John does not find it necessary to say when the Word became flesh.) Any author who is convinced that the Word made flesh is the real truth about Jesus' identity will tell the Jesus story differently, even when telling the same particular incident as the other Gospels.

Does it make any difference whether or not we believe that Jesus is the *Logos* enfleshed? John certainly is convinced that it does, and his reason for doing so is not obscure, for in one way or another it appears again and again in this Gospel: Because Jesus is the enfleshed Word, the one through whom life came into being, he can impart life to those who receive him, to those who believe in his name, who allow themselves to be changed by believing that he is who he claims to be and really does what he claims to do. And in John the result of this change is called "eternal life."

One more thing: John's perspective accounts for the fact that he wrote this Gospel in the first place. Whereas Luke wrote so that Theophilus "may know the truth concerning the things about which you have been instructed" (Luke 1:4)—that is, to set the record straight—John wrote so "that through believing [that Jesus is the Christ, the Son of God] you may have life in his name" (John 20:31). That is, John intentionally wrote this Gospel as he did so that the readers *of* the story confront the same claims Jesus makes *in* the story.

Do You Want to Become His Disciples, Too?

John 1 contains important clues about becoming a disciple and about what Jesus promises to a follower. Both remain significant today. First, in John 1 Jesus finds and summons to his circle only one person, Philip. Each of the others becomes a disciple either because of John the Baptist's witness or because a disciple brings him to Jesus (Simon) or told him about Jesus (Nathanael). Often that is still how a person becomes a disciple. Second, would-be disciples who have questions are not turned back as unlikely prospects; instead, they are told to "come and see." They are given space in which to see for themselves who Jesus is. And what will they see if they really see? They will see "heaven opened and the angels of God" going up and down on the ladder that leads to God; they will know that Jesus is the way to God. So the disciple is one who sees who Jesus is and accepts what he gives. And that is more than we are looking for. The disciple is first of all one who receives. And sometimes being a receiver is harder than trying to be a doer. Why is that?

How does Jesus as the Word broaden, challenge, or confirm your understanding of who Jesus is?

_____

_____

_____

_____

_____

Prayer

Treat me with kindness, LORD,
>   so that I may live and do what you say.
Open my mind
>   and let me discover the wonders of your Law.
I live here as a stranger.
>   Don't keep me from knowing your commands.
What I want most of all and at all times
>   is to honor your laws . . . .
I am eager to learn all that you want me to do;
>   help me to understand more and more.

(Psalm 119:17-20, 32, CEV)

What John Meant by "the Word"

John's understanding of "the Word" is the key to this Gospel. That's why "the Word" appears before the story of Jesus begins.

In creating the Prologue, especially the first five verses, the writer tapped into a way of thinking about God's relation to the world that had roots in both biblical and ancient Greek philosophy. While the opening line echoes the beginning of Genesis, the writer of John was probably influenced more by the way the Old Testament understanding of wisdom was developed in the Wisdom of Solomon* and Sirach,* in which certain aspects of Greek thought were taken up. So we begin with the Greek inheritance concerning the Word, or the *Logos* (pronounced lawgoss not lowgoss). The term had a wide range of meanings—word, content of an argument or speech, reason, explanation. Several centuries before Christ, some strands of Greek philosophy (especially as developed by the Stoics), emphasized the *Logos* as reason, holding that the whole universe operates according to the *Logos/Reason*, because it permeates everything. Consequently, the universe is reasonable and can be understood by reasoning. Furthermore, Stoics thought that a sliver of the *Logos* is found in humans, making it possible for humans to understand the universe in order to live in accord with it.

What the Jewish writers of the Wisdom of Solomon and Sirach, as well as Philo,* found useful in Greek thought on *Logos* was the role of the *Logos* in governing the world. They saw that this role or *Logos* could be harmonized with what Proverbs 8 says about wisdom (*sophia*), though they did not say that wisdom *is* God. Rather, they saw wisdom as the self-expression of God; and since the Torah expressed God's will for the world, it was not difficult to regard wisdom, Torah, and *Logos* as various ways of understanding how God is related to creation. By the time John was written, in circles open to Greek thought, the theology of wisdom and the theology of the *Logos* were almost interchangeable (even though *sophia* is a feminine noun and *Logos* is a masculine noun), for in both cases, wisdom or *Logos* was the Reality through which God created and governs the world. John's first readers would not have been surprised to read that "all things came into being through him, and without him not one thing came into being" (John 1:3).

They might have been somewhat surprised, however, to read that "the *Logos* was God." This does not mean that "*Logos*" and "God" are simply two names for one being, for John also implies that the *Logos* was a being distinct from God, for "in the beginning" he was "*with* God." At the same time, John did not think this concept compromised the oneness of God. We find this way of thinking hard to follow because we are not at home in Greek ways of thinking, much of which wrestled with the problem of how the invisible eternal God is related to the visible transient world. Strange as it may seem to us, in antiquity *Logos* theology supported the oneness of God (monotheism) by insisting that the world was not created by some deity or power other than the one God. We can say that in John the *Logos* is God activated, God at work, God self-expressed toward the world, as distinguished from God as absolute Origin.

What readers in John's day were not prepared for, however, is the declaration that "the *Logos* became flesh." No one had said such a thing before. The "flesh" that the *Logos* "became" was a person with a name, Jesus. Here it is essential to be precise: For John, the one "through" whom all things came to be is not Jesus of Nazareth, but the *Logos* who became Jesus by Incarnation. As the *Logos-become-Jesus,* and *only* on this basis, does he make known the unseen God (1:18; also Colossians 1:15: "He is the image of the invisible God"). So it is not surprising that in John Jesus says, "Whoever has seen me has seen the Father" (John 14:9).

Now we see why John's Gospel is so different. It has to be, for it is the story of the *Logos* enfleshed as Jesus of Nazareth.

24 We Have Seen His Glory

Jesus said to him, "Have you believed because you have seen me? Blessed are those who have not seen and yet have come to believe."

(John 20:29)

They Have No Wine

Most of us are uncomfortable when we are the only one who doesn't get the joke or the one who fails to see what everyone else on the tour sees in a painting at the museum. Sometimes, in self-defense, we think, "There's not *that* much there to see." Misunderstanding troubles us even more when others have misunderstood us, or we have misunderstood them. In fact, sometimes people misunderstand each other because they are talking past each other. Come to think of it, it's hard to understand what understanding really is.

Beginning With Moses and All the Prophets

By reading John 2–4 as a unit we see how John introduces Jesus' mission. The unit begins and ends in Cana, a village in Galilee. In between, Jesus has been to Capernaum, to Jerusalem where he talked to Nicodemus, to the Judean countryside near the Jordan River, and to a town in Samaria. References to the first and second signs hold the unit together like bookends (2:11; 4:54).

Day 1 John 2–4

(1) We now concentrate on John 2:1-12. Note that Jesus' mother is not named here (or in 19:25-27) and that despite Jesus' harsh word to her in 2:4, she senses he will do something to save the situation (2:5).

(2) Observe that the wonder is not described, only the result (2:9); note also that the steward's rebuke (2:10) implies that the good wine (as much as 180 gallons) is wasted by being served late instead of at the beginning of the party. This detail suggests that readers should watch for strange reversals in the rest of John's Gospel.

(3) See how 2:11 links this event to the Prologue (1:14); note also the disciples' response to the sign.

Day 2 John 2:13-25; Mark 11:15-19; 8:11-13; Matthew 12:38-42; 1 Corinthians 1:18-25; Psalm 69:6-12

(1) Reading again Mark 11:15-19 helps us see the distinctive features of John's story of Jesus in the Temple. Note that whereas Mark says nothing about the disciples' response, John 2:17 does.

(2) **GC 24-1** Compare the request for a sign in 2:18 with Mark 8:11-13 and Matthew 12:38-42. Note also that Paul knows of the interest in "signs" (1 Corinthians 1:18-25).

(3) Note that the meaning of Jesus' response in John 2:19 turns on the double meaning of "this temple" and that the Jews' response (2:20) is fully understandable because the narrator's explanation is for the readers. Note that 2:22 implies that not even the disciples understood Jesus at the time.

(4) Note the narrator's comment in 2:23-25. "Entrust" in 2:24 translates the same word as "believed" in 2:23.

Day 3 John 3:1-21, 31-36; Numbers 21:4-9

(1) Note that for Nicodemus, Jesus' signs are evidence that Jesus is a "teacher ... from God," not a teacher "of God."

(2) Note that Jesus does not respond positively to Nicodemus but changes the subject. He also uses words with two meanings: *anōthen* means both "all over again, from the beginning" and "from above." So too, *pneuma* means both "wind" and "spirit."

(3) Note that being born of Spirit is the same as being born "of God" in John 1:12-13.

(4) Observe that in 3:7, 11, 12 the word *you* is plural, showing that these words are not addressed to Nicodemus alone but also to the readers.

(5) Note that 3:11 alludes to 1:11, as does 3:19-20.

(6) Observe that 3:14-15 sees a similarity between Jesus on the cross and the serpent on the pole in Numbers 21:4-9.

223

Day 4 John 4:1-42; 2 Kings 17:24-41; Isaiah 2:2-4

    (1) Notice how much John 4:7-15 depends on the double meaning of water, drink, and thirst.

    (2) Observe the tension between 4:21 (which foresees that also the Jerusalem Temple will be replaced) and 4:22 (that nonetheless, salvation is "from the Jews"). Note how differently Jesus speaks of Jerusalem worship compared with Isaiah 2:2-4.

Day 5 John 4:43-54; 20:24-31; Matthew 8:5-13; Acts 2:22; Romans 15:14-21; Hebrews 2:1-4

    (1) **GC 24-2** Note that the story in John 4:46-53 has certain similarities to the story in Matthew 8:5-13 ("royal official" suggests the father was a Gentile).

    (2) Note that Jesus' comment in John 4:48 can be taken either as a simple observation or as a complaint. Notice that the same theme (seeing and believing) returns in 20:24-31.

    (3) Observe that Acts 2:22; Romans 15:14-21; and Hebrews 2:1-4 all assume that gospel preaching was accompanied by signs and wonders.

Day 6 Read and respond to "We Have Seen His Glory" and "Do You Want to Become His Disciples, Too?"

Prayer Concerns

We Have Seen His Glory

Ordinarily, signs do not need to be interpreted because their words (or symbols) inform (Amity Road), warn (Slippery When Wet), or tell us what to do (Stop) or not to do (No Parking). But sometimes the word *sign* is itself an interpretation as in "This is a sign of." Such an expression acknowledges that we are interpreting in a specific way what we are seeing or hearing, as in "That's a sign of neglect." When we interpret what we see, we assume we are recognizing the true meaning. For example, we would not look at a well-kept house and yard and say, "That's a sign of neglect." Of course, we also misinterpret what we see. The constant, restless activity of a child is not always a sign of poor upbringing but may be a symptom of attention deficit disorder. So too, what may look like a sign of laziness may actually be evidence of depression. Snap judgments, prejudice, and sheer ignorance are among the many reasons we sometimes err in saying, "That's a sign of . . . ."

Except for the reference to road signs, everything in the previous paragraph fits some part of the Gospel According to John. In this Gospel the story of Jesus' public mission begins with an event that is identified as "the first of his signs"—turning water into wine—and virtually ends with the observation, "Although he had performed so many signs in their presence, they did not believe in him" (12:37). John 2–12 reports Jesus' public mission (it's more of a mission than a ministry); John 13–17, his mission to the disciples; the Passion story begins at John 18. The "signs" Jesus did are found only in John 2–12; some scholars have called this part of John "The Book of Signs." Some also have proposed that the writer of the Gospel used an already written account of Jesus' signs. In any case, the stories of Jesus' signs are now part of the Gospel, and with these signs we are here concerned.

John's Understanding of Jesus' Signs

What we often call Jesus' "miracles" John calls "signs." Although general references to Jesus' signs appear at various places (such as John 2:23; 3:2; 6:2; 7:31; 20:30), the Gospel reports only seven "sign" events:

- changing water into wine (2:1-11)
- healing the official's son (4:46-54)
- healing a lame man in Jerusalem (5:1-18)
- feeding the multitude (6:1-15)
- walking on the sea (6:16-21)
- healing the man born blind (9:1-12)
- raising Lazarus (11:38-44)

Of this list, only the feeding of the crowd is reported in all the Synoptics, though the story of the healing of the official's son may be John's version of Matthew's story of the healing of the centurion's servant (Matthew 8:5-13). None of these seven signs is an exorcism. While these signs occurred during Jesus' public mission, John 20:30 implies that Jesus did many signs after the Resurrection, though only the catch of fish is reported in John 21.

One other feature of the stories in John needs to be noted: Beginning with the third sign (healing the lame man in 5:1-18), each sign produces a controversy about Jesus or more often a controversy *with* him. The controversies with Jesus concern themes central to Jesus' identity and mission. In other words, these controversies point us to the meaning of Jesus' deed—*if* we can see how the deed points to the meaning of Jesus for some aspect of the human condition.

John's Gospel does not explain why it regards Jesus' wondrous deeds as "signs," and so invites us to detect the reason. By regarding Jesus' wondrous deeds as "signs," this Gospel challenges us to see what they signify about Jesus. And to see this, we must believe what Jesus says about himself in the controversies. Also, the very fact that Jesus' deeds provoke controversy shows

> Jesus' wondrous deeds are called signs in order to present readers of this Gospel with the same challenge the deeds presented to those who observed them—the challenge to see Jesus as more than a miracleworker, to see Jesus as the one whose deeds signify that he is the one who heals the human condition.

225

that we can acknowledge the wondrous character of the deed and still not see it as a sign that signifies the meaning of Jesus. According to 12:28-29, even God's voice from heaven was taken to be thunder, or at best the voice of an angel. At one point Jesus himself rebukes the crowd that was looking for him after he had fed them, "Very truly, I tell you, you are looking for me, not because you saw signs, but because you ate your fill of the loaves" (6:26). We cannot have the sign without the deed; they, however, had the deed without seeing the sign.

Jesus' wondrous deeds, then, are called signs in order to present readers of this Gospel with the same challenge the deeds presented to those who observed them—the challenge to see Jesus as more than a miracle-worker, to see Jesus as the one whose deeds signify that he is the one who heals the human condition. That the signs are as important for the readers of the stories as for the observers of the events—if not more so—is clearly implied at the end of John 20. After Thomas believes Jesus is truly resurrected because he has seen his wounded side and hands, Jesus asks, "Have you believed because you have seen me? Blessed are those who have not seen and yet have come to believe" (20:29). To this the narrator adds, "Jesus did many other signs in the presence of his disciples, which are not written in this book. But these are written so that you may come to believe [or, 'may continue to believe,' as other manuscripts have it] that Jesus is the Messiah, the Son of God, and that through believing you may have life in his name." So this Gospel challenges us as Jesus once challenged those who saw him: Can you see the sign in the deed? If you can, you too have seen "his glory."

Signs Done and Signs Spoken

John 2–4 constitutes a clear unit that begins and ends in Cana and so is framed by the first and second signs (2:11; 4:54). Between the first and second signs are reports of Jesus' conversations with two quite different persons—Nicodemus, a respected "teacher of Israel" who fails to understand Jesus, and the disrespected Samaritan woman who seems to understand him—or does she? In addition, the teachings of these chapters announce themes that are important for the rest of the Gospel.

While John 2 relies on signs to introduce Jesus' public mission, each of its three parts (2:1-12; 2:13-22; 2:23-25) treats the signs somewhat differently. In the first part, the sign discloses Jesus' glory (2:11); in the second, the sign is his word (2:19); in the third, the signs produce inadequate faith (2:24-25).

The story of what occurred at the Cana wedding is remarkable for what it does not say: Why were Jesus and his disciples, as well as his mother, invited? Who was the groom? How is it that Jesus' mother sensed that he would solve the problem? Why did Jesus respond so rudely to her? Because these matters are ignored, each detail the story does include is all the more important for conveying the meaning of a "miracle" ("the water that had become wine," 2:9). The narrator says what Jesus' deed means—it "revealed his glory"—but leaves it for us to figure out what this explanation means.

So we look closely at the significance of the details for the story as a whole: The empty jars were available for "the Jewish rites of purification"; after Jesus ordered the jars filled with water, he had some of the liquid sent to the manager of the wedding feast, who then complained to the bridegroom that contrary to custom "the good wine" is now being served last. The whole situation is unexpected: The original supply of wine was inadequate, but now the good wine will be served in abundance to those who cannot appreciate its superior quality because they have "become drunk." What begins as a dilemma of insufficiency of the ordinary ends as a surprising abundance of the extraordinarily good. Why? Because Jesus transformed the anti-defilement water into the positive wine of celebration. Other details add to the implied meaning: A wedding is a well-known metaphor for celebrating the arrival of the time of salvation (recall Mark 2:18-19); that the good comes last suggests the "last times," the end of the old age and the beginning of the new; that Jesus provides wine agrees with the widespread view of the time that wine is the drink of the gods.

> **What begins as a dilemma of insufficiency of the ordinary ends as a surprising abundance of the extraordinarily good.**

Here then, Jesus "revealed his glory" not by showing he could make better wine out of plain water but by transforming what was to be used merely to purify into what is life-celebrating wine.

John suggests that this transformation manifests Jesus' glory, "the glory as of the Father's only Son" (1:14). Why then did Jesus not reply to his mother's report, "They have no wine," by saying, "I'll take care of that"? Why did he say instead, "My hour has not yet come" (2:4)? Because, in John, Jesus' "hour" is the time of his death, not the opportunity to do good. By transforming water into wine now, at the beginning of the story, Jesus foreshadows at Cana the significance of his death at the end—as the event by which he supplies the wine of life to those who have exhausted their resources. By not allegorizing the story, so that every item in it stands for something else, we can understand that this first sign points ahead to the other signs.

With the Cana sign belongs the story of Jesus' action in the Temple (2:13-22) because both have to do with Jewish religious practices. After Jesus had expelled cattle, sheep, doves, and money changers, he is asked for a sign that authorizes this disruption. This request for a sign reminds us of the similar request in Mark 11:28-33 where Jesus refused the request and especially of the request in Matthew 16:1-4 where he said that the only sign is the sign of Jonah. In Matthew 12:38-42 the sign of Jonah points to Jesus' resurrection. Also in John 2:19 Jesus responds by pointing to his resurrection, but here he veils the reference: "Destroy this temple, and in three days I will raise it up." Since Jesus is in the Temple when he says this, "the Jews" naturally assume he is referring to the building. How are they to know "he was speaking of the temple of his body" (2:21)? Not even the disciples understood what he meant until after his resurrection. Here is another instance in which Jesus spoke in a way that the usual meaning is the wrong one for those who do not understand that Jesus has the other meaning in mind.

By reporting that Jesus used words that are misunderstood whenever they are taken literally, John clearly implies that the words central to Jesus' message are like signs—deeds that a person can see without perceiving the sign in the deed. Just as we can observe the action without "seeing" its sign-meaning, so we can hear what Jesus says plainly and still not "hear" what he conveys. Indeed, whenever Jesus' words have a double meaning, the literal meaning is factually correct but actually wrong. So, as we saw earlier, when Jesus says, "I am the bread that came down from heaven," people object because they know his parents (6:41-42); people with known parents have not arrived on the scene by descending from heaven. Correct but beside the point Jesus is making:

As the *Logos* enfleshed, he came from God's presence.

According to the concluding paragraph of John 2, faith based on seeing signs is not adequate. The passage does not explain this negative assessment, but Jesus' conversation with Nicodemus in John 3 provides a clue. Before examining that episode, one detail in 2:24 merits notice: Jesus "would not entrust himself" to those who believed on the basis of seeing his signs because he knew "what was in everyone"—their inner life, the disposition of their hearts. But to whom does Jesus entrust himself? To his disciples, as John 13–17 shows. Just now, however, it is enough to ponder what is implied: Not only does the disciple entrust himself or herself to Jesus (as the word *disciple* implies), but Jesus entrusts himself to the disciple as well. That is how any one of us becomes a child of God (1:12-13)—by this mutual entrustment.

John 3 reports two conversations, one between Jesus and Nicodemus (3:1-21), the other between John the Baptist and his followers (3:22-30). Nicodemus appears only in John—here, in 7:45-52 where he speaks up on behalf of Jesus, and in 19:39-42 where he helps to bury Jesus.

Nicodemus began his nocturnal visit by making what is nearly a confession of faith: "Rabbi, we know that you

> By transforming water into wine now, at the beginning of the story, Jesus foreshadows at Cana the significance of his death at the end—as the event by which he supplies the wine of life to those who have exhausted their resources.

are a teacher come [the Greek perfect tense, used here, means 'has come and now is here'] from God; for no one can do these signs that you do unless God is with him" (3:2; RSV). But Jesus does not congratulate Nicodemus for drawing the right conclusion from the signs. Nor does Jesus explain the response he does make: "No one can see the kingdom of God without being born *anōthen*" (which means either "from above" or "from the beginning," that is, all over again). The narrator's comment at 2:25 gives the clue for our understanding Jesus' response: Because Jesus knew "what was in everyone," he knew that what Nicodemus needed was not affirmation but being born "of God" (1:13). (While the kingdom of God is the energizing center of Jesus' message and mission in the Synoptics, he mentions it only twice in this Gospel—here it probably means eternal life.) Nicodemus, of course, takes *anōthen* to mean "all over again" (3:4). So in 3:5-7 Jesus paraphrases being born *anōthen* as a matter of being born "of water and Spirit" (an allusion to baptism), and then goes on to comment on the mysterious working of the Spirit (*pneuma* means either "spirit" or "wind"). We may sympathize with Nicodemus's confusion, but Jesus seems to have sensed that Nicodemus did not understand what his own words about Jesus implied ("you are a teacher come *from* God"), for one who comes *from* God (that is, is not simply sent *by* God) can be expected to speak of "heavenly things," that is, things that do not fit ordinary reality as commonly understood. "A teacher of Israel" should have known this.

Although Jesus appears to keep on speaking, it is not clear that he continues to speak to Nicodemus, for in 3:11 Jesus begins by addressing him ("I tell you" [singular *you*]) but then switches to address a group ("yet you [plural] do not receive our testimony"). This change suggests that here Jesus speaks on behalf of the Christian community ("we speak") as it addresses the Jewish community. Then in 3:13, Jesus speaks to no one in particular. This is why many interpreters regard 3:13-21 (or even 3:16-21) as the Evangelist's commentary, given as the teaching of Jesus (so also in 3:11). In other words, this is John's way of claiming that the church's message is the message of Jesus himself. Accordingly, in 3:13-21 Jesus speaks about himself without using "I" (he does not say, "God so loved the world that he gave me").

At 3:14-15 Jesus for the first time alludes to the meaning of his death on the cross. He refers to the story in Numbers 21:4-9, where those bitten by the serpents did not die when they looked to the bronze serpent that Moses made and mounted on a pole. Jesus does not compare himself with the serpent. Rather, he compares the "lifting up" of Moses' serpent with the "lifting up" of the Son of Man—that is, with Jesus lifted on the cross—because just as the Israelites lived when they looked to the serpent on the pole, so now "whoever believes in him" (the crucified Son of Man, Jesus) will have eternal life. This comparison prepares us for 3:16, according to which eternal life for everyone who believes in Jesus is God's purpose in giving his only Son, that is, giving him to death.

From the Gospel's angle, 3:17-21 is just as important as 3:16, if not more so, because these verses express a distinctive emphasis in John—that both eternal life and the judgment occur now, depending on how we respond to Jesus. John 3:36 makes the same point: "Whoever believes in the Son *has* [not *will have*] eternal life; whoever disobeys the Son [that is, does not respond positively by believing] will not see life, but must endure God's wrath." The same point is made again and again (see, for example, 5:24).

We will see that while Jesus also speaks of life after death, his emphasis is on the opportunity to receive eternal life now, before a person actually dies, because eternal life is what Jesus *gives* to those who believe in him by believing his claims. He can give eternal life because he is the *Logos* ("in him was life," 1:4), now enfleshed. As the Prologue implies, to meet Jesus is to meet the Creator (1:3), the source of life; to believe in his name is to entrust one's life to him and to receive what he gives. But to refuse the Creator/*Logos* enfleshed is to be "condemned already," for no future judgment can have more fatal consequences than saying no to one's Creator. While "God did not send the Son . . . to condemn the world" (the world of humanity, not the earth), condemnation is the inevitable result of refusing the sent Son. John 3:19-20 expresses this understanding in terms of light and darkness (reminding us of the Prologue): "And this is the judgment, that the light has come into the world [the Incarnation has occurred], and people loved darkness rather than light because their deeds were evil. For all who do evil hate the light and do not come to the light," for the light exposes them and their deeds.

When Signs Give Way to Disclosure

Jesus' midday conversation in Samaria (John 4:4-26) differs markedly from his nighttime exchange in Jerusalem, not simply because the latter was with a Jewish male teacher while the former was with a Samaritan female, but also because the woman becomes Jesus' herald to the Samaritans, as John the Baptist was Jesus' herald to Israel (1:19-28). Besides, Nicodemus is deferential; this woman is feisty. Also, with Nicodemus Jesus speaks in general terms about birth *anōthen*, but with the woman Jesus speaks explicitly of himself. Finally, whereas Jesus' exchange with Nicodemus goes nowhere because they talk past each other, the conversation with the woman results in the Samaritans' acknowledging that Jesus is "the Savior of the world" (4:42)—a confession without parallel in the entire Gospel. Thus John underscores (by contrast) the Prologue's line, "his own people did not accept him"—but the Samaritans did. In John this is Jesus' only encounter with Samaritans, and its character is completely different from that reported in Luke 9:52-56 where a Samaritan village refused hospitality to Jesus and his disciples.

Since Jesus discloses his identity (John 4:25-26) as well as his significance as the one who gives the water of eternal life (4:14), John implies that here, as in Cana, Jesus ultimately "revealed his glory" (2:11), though it all began when, "tired out by his journey" (4:6), he asked for a drink. That is, "his glory" was not visible; only he could disclose it by what he said.

Jesus hints that the water he can give is not ordinary well water ("living water" can mean running water, but here the expression has another meaning); but the woman, like Nicodemus, takes his words literally, and so she taunts him for offering well water when he has neither bucket nor rope ("the well is deep"). She also mocks him for implying that he is greater than the patriarch Jacob (a truth she does not recognize). Jesus now points out that those who drink this well water will be thirsty again, but those who drink his water "will never be thirsty." Why not? Because the water he gives "will become *in them* a *spring* of water gushing up to eternal life." She still takes him literally, and so asks for this water "so that I may never be thirsty or have to keep coming here to draw water" (4:15).

Jesus, having exposed her misunderstanding, which he does not correct, now changes the subject in order to expose her moral life: He asks her to bring her husband. When she admits she doesn't have one, Jesus tells her that she already has had five, and that the man she is living with now is not her husband. She concludes that a stranger who can know this about her past must be "a prophet." Like Nicodemus, who came close to drawing the right conclusion from the "signs" that Jesus did, she comes close to identifying Jesus rightly on the basis of his remarkable knowledge of her past and present.

Having raised a religious motif (calling Jesus a prophet), the woman shifts the conversation away from her own life in order to talk about the difference between Samaritan and Jewish religions, symbolized by the conflict over the right place to worship (4:20). Jesus does not argue the Jewish case for Jerusalem. Instead, he predicts that a time will come "when you [Samaritans, the *you* is plural] will worship the Father neither on this mountain nor in Jerusalem." Then he criticizes Samaritan religion: "You [plural] worship what you do not know; we [Jews] worship what we know, for salvation is from the Jews," not from the Samaritans.

But salvation's being "*from* the Jews" does not mean it is only *for* the Jews, for Jesus continues: "But the hour is coming, and is now here, when the true worshipers will worship the Father in spirit and truth," for that is the kind of worshipers God wants (4:23). "God is spirit, and those who worship him must worship in spirit and truth." The woman neither questions nor disputes this statement, but

> John's Gospel never allows us to take for granted the faith we already have or to assume too readily that we really do believe.

instead picks up on Jesus' prediction ("the hour is coming") and ignoring the "and is now here," says, "I know that Messiah is coming . . . . he will proclaim all things to us" (4:25). Thereby she implies, "You may be a prophet all right, but when it comes to redefining the worship of God, I will depend on what the Messiah will say." Who can object to such a tactful and devout comment? But this is the opening Jesus needs: "I am he, the one who is speaking to you."

Just when we want to know how the woman responded to this self-disclosure, the disciples arrive with lunch and the conversation ends. The woman, returning to the city without the water jar, invites her fellow Samaritans, "Come and see a man who told me everything I have ever done! He cannot be the Messiah, can he?" (The question implies she is not quite ready to believe Jesus but is considering it.) And they do come, and they believe in Jesus—but as the Savior of the world, not merely the Messiah. Moreover, they invite him "to stay with them; and he stayed there two days" (4:40)—bringing to an end what the narrator pointed out in 4:9: "Jews do not share things in common with Samaritans."

The unit (John 2–4) ends where it began, in Cana (4:46-54). Here Jesus is met by a "royal official" who begs him to come to Capernaum to heal his son who is about to die. Just as Jesus replied curtly to his mother's report, "They have no wine" (2:3-4), so now he responds brusquely,

"Unless you [plural] see signs and wonders you will not believe" (4:48). The man had not asked for a sign so that he might believe. But the father is undeterred: "Sir, come down before my little boy dies." Jesus does not go. Instead, he tells the father to go: "Go; your son will live." And the father "believed the word that Jesus spoke to him and started on his way" (4:50). He believed without seeing signs and wonders. It turned out that the "sign and wonder" occurred exactly when Jesus said, "Your son will live" and when the man believed Jesus. When he arrived home, "his whole household" also believed.

And so the curtain comes down on Act I. The audience (readers) has been introduced to the important themes of this drama—transformation (water into wine), birth *anōthen*, eternal life or judgment now, the rejection of Jesus, Jesus as the world's Savior. When the curtain rises on Act II, the tensions set up in Act I will develop; for the words and deeds of Jesus will produce ever-increasing conflicts. Given what is in the human heart, revealed glory will have that kind of results.

So Then

The writer has constructed this Gospel in such a way that we first learn who Jesus really is so we can also understand why he is so decisive: The Prologue asserts that, as the *Logos*, he is the self-expression of God who became a particular person, Jesus.

This week's study of John 2–4 took us a step further, showing us Jesus' doing what he came to do and how he went about doing it. In John Jesus acts and speaks differently from the way he acts and speaks in the first three Gospels: His marvelous deeds are "signs," and he often uses words with two meanings that his hearers regularly misunderstand. Those who are in on the truth of Jesus' identity hear his meaning in the ambiguous words, just as they understand what the signs signify. Jesus never helps the hearer, whether Nicodemus or the woman at the well, understand what he means. He simply confronts them with his ambiguous language (except for his "I am he" to the woman). How they respond shows whether they get it or not (this is true also of the woman to whom he disclosed his identity).

How then do we read this Gospel? As believers we readily and naturally identify with Jesus, for we already know—more or less—what he is talking about. And so we may find ourselves marveling at Nicodemus's and the woman's obtuseness—"Why don't they get it?"—forgetting that they have not read the Prologue.

Another way of reading this Gospel is to identify with the people Jesus meets so that what he says to those who ask for an authorizing sign or to Nicodemus or to the woman or to the royal official, he says also to us. If we first identify with them, then we find that we too are confronted by the strange words and deeds of Jesus that require us to decide whether he is right—so right that we allow ourselves to be changed by them. John's Gospel never allows us to take for granted the faith we already have or to assume too readily that we really do believe. We hear the call to believe on every page.

Do You Want to Become His Disciples, Too?

John 1–4 implies that the disciple joins those who confess (1) that the enfleshed *Logos* "lived among us, and we have seen his glory"; (2) that "from his fullness we have all received, grace upon grace"; (3) that "we have found the Messiah" and need look no farther. In short, to be disciples is to allow ourselves to be transformed by accepting what Jesus gives because of who he is. This "allowing by accepting" reaches so deeply into us that it turns into being born *anōthen*. The impossible happens because the breeze of the Spirit "blows where it chooses." By telling us this, John's Gospel offers the gospel—that by believing in Jesus, we begin all over again, repeatedly. Where is it written that a disciple needs to be born *anōthen* only once, especially if the Spirit blows "where [and when] it chooses"?

Describe the Jesus you encountered through his signs.

_____

_____

_____

_____

_____

Prayer

I have seen your power and your glory
    in the place of worship.
Your love means more than life to me,
    and I praise you.
As long as I live, I will pray to you.
I will sing joyful praises and be filled with excitement
    like a guest at a banquet.

I think about you before I go to sleep,
    and my thoughts turn to you during the night.
You have helped me,
    and I sing happy songs in the shadow of your wings.
I stay close to you,
    and your powerful arm supports me.

(Psalm 63:2-8, CEV)

25 In Him Was Life

Very truly, I tell you, anyone who hears my word and
believes him who sent me has eternal life, and does not
come under judgment, but has passed from death to life.

(John 5:24)

They Have No Wine

For some of us, life has been so good, so fulfilling, we cannot think of what
we would change without being frivolous. Others of us find that for some reason
a good life has gone flat, has lost its sense of purpose and meaning, but we still
go through the routines. But many of us, whether hustling from one part-time
job to another or working ever longer in the full-time position we finally have
gotten, find ourselves saying, "This is no life." All of us know that sheer
existence—even a comfortable one—is not real life. There must be more to it.

Beginning With Moses and All the Prophets

The story of Jesus takes a turn at John 5; here begin opposition to Jesus and
the portrayal of his responses to it. Reading John 5–7 without interruption lets us
see how Jesus' mission takes shape through the issues it raises.

Day 1 John 5–7; Romans 6:20-23; Daniel 12:1-4

(1) Note that in John 5 the story leads up to an important pronouncement by Jesus (5:17), a
twofold explanation of Jesus' persecution (5:16, 18), and culminates in Jesus' discourse
(5:19-47). Observe that its various topics suggest that it assembles teachings given on several
occasions, as does the Sermon on the Mount.

(2) Note that many manuscripts omit 5:4, which explains the man's comment in 5:7.

(3) Observe that although Genesis 2:2-3 says that God rested on the sabbath, in John 5:17 Jesus claims that he and his Father are "still working" (on the sabbath): How is God still working? Note that some people infer that Jesus is making himself equal with God (5:18) and that this charge becomes the starting point of Jesus' discourse in 5:19. Note that what 3:32-35 says about Jesus' words 5:19-20 says about his deeds.

(4) Observe carefully that 5:24 and 5:28-29 express two views of "life"—eternal life now (5:24) and life after death (5:28-29).

(5) Note that John 5:30-47 returns to the theme of witness/testimony (3:31-33) and that in 5:32-33 Jesus bears witness to John, who had borne witness to him. Note also that Jesus claims to have a greater witness than John—his God-given "works" and Scripture (5:36-39). Observe how 5:37 echoes 1:18 and how 5:40 echoes 1:11.

Day 2 John 6:1-24; Mark 6:30-56

(1) Note that also in Mark 6 the story of the feeding is followed by the story of Jesus' walking on the sea.

(2) Observe what the crowd inferred when they saw the "sign" Jesus did (John 6:14). Note that the expected "prophet" probably alludes to Deuteronomy 18:15.

Day 3 John 6:25-59; 1 Corinthians 10:1-13; Exodus 16; Isaiah 55:1-5; Psalm 78:17-32

(1) Note that John 6:25-59 repeatedly refers to certain details of Exodus 16 (and Psalm 78:17-32), that John 6:27 alludes to Isaiah 55:1-5, and that John 6:45 alludes to Isaiah 54:13.

(2) Note the similarity and difference between John 6:30 and Mark 8:11. Note that in John 6:32-34 the people's request for bread echoes the woman's request for water in 4:13-15.

(3) Note that 6:40 and 6:54, like 5:24, 28-29, also combine eternal life now with the promise of future resurrection life.

(4) Observe that Jesus' descent from heaven (6:38) is a way of referring to the Incarnation.

(5) Note that 6:51 identifies Jesus' life-giving bread with his "flesh"—an allusion to his death. Observe the allusions to the Eucharist in 6:53-56.

Day 4 John 6:60–7:13; 3:1-15; Leviticus 23:33-36; Deuteronomy 16:13-17

(1) In 6:60-71, notice the progression: Many disciples are offended by what Jesus had said in 6:53-58 (as were the people in 6:41-42); then Jesus challenges them even more in 6:62 (as in 6:43-44); then many cease being disciples (6:66); then Jesus challenges the Twelve (6:67); then Simon Peter makes his confession (6:68-69, John's equivalent of Matthew 16:16); then Jesus alludes to the betrayer. Observe that what John 1:11-13 says of "his own people" 6:60-71 says of his disciples.

(2) Note that in 3:13 Jesus speaks of himself as the Son of Man who has descended from heaven and that in 6:62 he alludes to his return by ascent.

(3) Observe that 7:1 recalls 5:18 and that 7:6 and 7:8 recall 2:4.

Day 5 John 7:14-52; Deuteronomy 17:2-7; Micah 5:2-5; Zechariah 7:8-14

(1) Note that 7:14 does not say what Jesus taught and that 7:15 sets the stage for 7:16-18. Compare the same question about the source of Jesus' teaching in 7:15 with Mark 6:2-4 and Luke 4:22. Observe also that in John Jesus answers the question, whereas in Mark and Luke he does not. Note also that his answer (John 7:16-18) recalls 3:31-35.

(2) Notice how in 7:19 Jesus deliberately provokes his hearers who had been impressed by his teaching (7:15). Note that 7:21-23 (and Jesus' question in 7:19) refer the readers to 5:1-18.

(3) Notice how common knowledge of where Jesus came from (7:27, an allusion to 6:42) prevents understanding that Jesus really comes from God (7:28-29). Note how the same issue is debated in 7:40-43, 52. Recall that the birth stories in Matthew and Luke account for the fact that Jesus came from both Galilee and Bethlehem.

(4) Note that John 7:37 implies that Isaiah 55:1-5 comes true in what Jesus offers. Note also that the quotation from "scripture" in John 7:38 is not in the Bible. Note that the glorification of Jesus refers to his death on the cross.

Day 6 Read and respond to "In Him Was Life" and "Do You Want to Become His Disciples, Too?"

Prayer Concerns

234

In Him Was Life

John's Prologue announces what the event of Jesus was all about—the arrival of the enfleshed *Logos* in whom was life, but whose identity was acknowledged only by the few who accepted him. Those who did were given a new life because they were "born . . . of God." Greek has two words for "life": One (*bios*, from which *biology* is derived) is ordinary life; the other (*zōē*) is used in John for a *kind* of life so different from ordinary day-to-day existence that it is called "eternal life." Whatever is "eternal" is not transient. Since the offer of eternal life is *what* was really going on in the event called Jesus, the story of the event shows *how* this offer was made. Because the Prologue says that Jesus was refused, we also expect to find accounts of that refusal. John 5–7 reports both the offer and the refusal and so takes us deeper into the meaning of Jesus' mission.

During Jesus' conversation with the Samaritan woman, he disclosed that he was the giver of "a spring of water gushing up to eternal life." John 5–7, using different language, shows us how Jesus disclosed himself as the life-giver to "his own people" and what happened as a result. In other words, these chapters show us what happens when the message of Jesus is the messenger himself.

The Words of the Word

By reporting only a few of Jesus' wondrous deeds (there are only seven "signs"), John's accent falls heavily on Jesus' teachings. Frequently, the wondrous deeds themselves provide the occasion for Jesus' teaching. Also, in John 6:63, Jesus says why his words are so important: "It is the spirit that gives life; the flesh is useless. The words that I have spoken to you *are* spirit and life." A few verses later, Simon Peter acknowledges that Jesus has said the truth: "You have the words of eternal life. We . . . know that you are the Holy One of God" (6:68-69). Responding rightly to Jesus in

> **Responding rightly to Jesus in this Gospel requires us to understand the connection between the life that Jesus gives and his utterances.**

this Gospel, then, requires us to understand the connection between the life that Jesus gives and his utterances. In John Jesus speaks differently from the way he speaks in the Synoptics. For instance, John has no parables; Jesus mentions the kingdom of God only twice (3:3, 5); he talks repeatedly about himself and his relation to the Father yet never says "our Father" or "your Father" (except in 20:17, after his resurrection). These differences invite comment.

What the narrator says about Jesus' signs surely applies to his words too: "Those [signs] written here have been recorded in order that you may believe that Jesus is the Christ, the Son of God, and that through this faith you may have life by his name" (20:31, REB). Whether the translation reads "that you may come to believe" or "that you may continue to believe," John claims that true life comes to those who respond positively to Jesus' deeds and words by entrusting themselves to him.

When Jesus says his words are spirit and life, he means they are life-giving to those who accept them. Simon Peter acknowledges this when he says Jesus has "the words of eternal life," for the phrase does not mean "the words *about* eternal life." Jesus' words have this power because they are utterances of the enfleshed Word. In John Jesus does not speak as a divinely inspired prophet or as an unusually wise sage; he speaks rather as God's self-expression who has become a human being. As the enfleshed *Logos*, in whom was life because God is the source of life, he can give life. But he does not do so by touching people (as if life flowed from his fingertips into those he touched); were that the case, he could impart life only to those with whom he made physical contact. So, in contrast to the Synoptics, none of Jesus' healings in John involves touching the person. Rather, the enfleshed Word relies on his words, which bring life when they are believed. And to offer this life, he speaks about himself because the message is the messenger. He does not talk *about* God; he speaks *as* God's self-expression. We should not be surprised that those who hear him are offended by what he says, nor that we too are startled, and perhaps offended as well, by what he says. We should be surprised if we discover that we have been taking the truth of what he says for granted.

In the Synoptics Jesus' mission is energized by the coming of God's kingdom, which he interprets and makes real by his exorcisms, healings, and way of life so that his hearers can respond by repenting, by making a U-turn with their lives. In John, Jesus offers eternal life because in this Gospel eternal life is what life in God's kingdom really means. (However, the meaning in John should not be read back into the Synoptics; each Gospel has its own truth that should be retained.)

Because the eternal life that Jesus gives and the believer receives is not enhanced physical existence (a better *bios*), Jesus calls for faith, for believing what he says, because only by believing can anyone receive the kind of life (*zōē*) he came to give. But the believing itself does not confer eternal life; that would be saving oneself. In John believing Jesus' words is accepting them deeply enough that a person allows himself or herself to be changed. So, in John Jesus never calls for repentance (neither *repent* nor *repentance* occurs in this Gospel or in the letters of John), for repentance is a moral change that turns life Godward. Nor does Jesus describe or define eternal life, and except for 13:17 and 20:29, he pronounces no believer blessed. In John he does not identify with or consort with the outcasts, sinners, tax collectors, the poor, or any other group; for in his eyes everyone needs eternal life. On the other hand, lack of eternal life is not the result of being in a particular group. Given the power of "the world," the only way he can offer eternal life to all is by speaking bluntly, explicitly, and often confrontationally about himself. And given who he really is, he cannot speak about himself without speaking of his relation to God. In making himself known, he makes God known at the same time.

> In John, Jesus offers eternal life because in this Gospel eternal life is what life in God's kingdom really means.

Making God Known

The Prologue ends with the declaration that while "No one has ever seen God," the only Son "has made him known," literally, "has exegeted him" (John 1:18). Yet, apart from the statement that "God is spirit" (4:24), everything Jesus says about God pertains to the relation between himself and God. Moreover, in some of this week's passages, Jesus says that his role as life-giver expresses this relationship. Indeed, in John, Jesus'

relation to God (Son to Father) and Jesus' relation to people (as life-giver) are two sides of the same message because the latter depends on the former.

John 5:19-47 is the first extended exposition of these themes and carries forward the succinct summary in 3:31-36. The sabbath healing of the lame man by the pool (5:2-18) sets the stage by alerting the readers to several themes: (1) The man was healed instantly as the result of Jesus' word alone (5:8-9); (2) although both the healed and the healer broke the sabbath (the former by carrying his mat, the latter by healing), the storyteller uses the incident to explain why Jesus was persecuted (5:16); (3) Jesus' justification for healing on the sabbath ("My Father is still working, and I also am working," 5:17) claims the right to do as God does; (4) the real issue is that in calling God his Father Jesus was "making himself equal to God" (5:18)—though no one actually accuses Jesus of this. This comment is the narrator's interpretation of what lies at the heart of Jesus' controversies. The interpretation also reminds the readers that Jesus is the incarnate *Logos* who not only was "with God" but also "was God" (1:1). Also, Jesus' equality with God was at the heart of the church's debate with Judaism in John's own day. In other words, the narrator's comment anchors what the church believes about Jesus in what Jesus believed about himself. The theme of Jesus' equality with God appears precisely here because this issue points to what Jesus is about to say in the verses that follow.

In 5:19-29, Jesus does say remarkable things about his relation to the Father. The cumulative force of these claims may be easier for us to grasp if we paraphrase and itemize them before commenting on them.

- The Son is not autonomous; he can do only what he sees the Father doing; in fact, the Son does what the Father does (5:19).
- The Son is more than an observer who copies the Father; for the Father, who loves the Son, shows him everything that he does (5:20; also 3:35).
- Just as the Father resurrects the dead, so "the Son gives life to whomever he wishes" (5:21).
- The Father has even turned over to the Son the role of judge, so that all may know the Son when they know God; consequently, whoever does not honor the Son does not honor the Father either, for the Father "sent him" (5:22-23).
- So closely does Jesus repeat what God does that whoever hears Jesus' word (that is, heeds and obeys) believes God, and that person *has* eternal life; in fact, because the Son is the

judge, that person "does not come under [the last] judgment but has [already] passed from death to life" (5:24).

- Additionally, the future resurrection (5:28-29) is also the work of the Son (5:25). The effect of placing these two views side by side is clear: Jesus is *the* life-giver. To the living he gives eternal life now; in the future, he will give resurrection life to those who have done good before they died. The living who believe will not "come under judgment" (5:24), but those who have done evil cannot avoid it.

Again we see how utterly important the Prologue is for the way we are to read this Gospel. If we keep the Prologue in mind, everything makes sense, though it is not easy to understand. Without the Prologue, what Jesus says does not make sense but reads like baseless boasting and sheer arrogance. In 5:18 Jesus does claim to be "equal to God" because he knows who he is. God is "the Father" and he is "the Son" because in this Gospel "the Son" replicates the Father. This Father-Son language has nothing to do with gender and everything to do with making the God-reality effective on earth. The rationale that permeates the use of this imagery would be exactly the same if Jesus had spoken of Mother-Son: for in John "Son" is the expression of the divine origin.

In John only Jesus is Son of God. Although believers are called "children of God" (1:12), Jesus never says his disciples, or those who believe in him, become "sons of God." Likewise, in John Jesus never refers to God as "your Father" until after the Resurrection (20:17). Here John differs from the Synoptics (as in Matthew 5:16, 48; 6:4; Mark 11:25; Luke 6:36; 12:30, for example).

In John 5:31-47 Jesus' assertiveness turns aggressive as he defends his mission by speaking of witness or testimony. The argument assumes the biblical view that two witnesses are needed to establish guilt in court. The argument moves in several steps: (1) Jesus says, "If I testify about myself, my testimony is not true" (5:31)—not because what he says is false but because self-witness is not valid in court. (2) But "there is another who testifies on my behalf, and I know that his testimony to me is true"—specifically, John the Baptist (5:32-35). (3) Jesus has a more important witness than John's witness—"the works that the Father has given me to complete . . . testify on my behalf that the Father has sent me" (5:36). (The "works" include everything significant that Jesus does.) John and these works are two visible witnesses, and they are present for all to see. (4) But two additional witnesses are even

greater than those: One is the Father, whose witness is rejected because people do not believe Jesus "whom he has sent" (5:37-38); the other is Scripture—the very Scriptures that his opponents "search" because they think that in them they will have eternal life. Yet it is precisely these that "testify" on behalf of Jesus (5:39). So Scripture (Moses) turns into the accuser of those who rely on Scripture to discredit Jesus. "If you believed Moses, you would believe me, for he wrote about me" (5:46); that is, what "Moses" is all about (a life-giving relation to God) is what Jesus is all about. Jesus does not deny that a person can find eternal life by searching the Scriptures. What he does deny is that eternal life can be found by a search that misses the meaning of Jesus.

> In John, Jesus' relation to God (Son to Father) and Jesus' relation to people (as life-giver) are two sides of the same message because the latter depends on the former.

While Jesus has declared as forthrightly as possible the ground of his mission as the life-giver—namely his relation to the Father—he has said little up to this point about *how* he imparts eternal life or how it is to be received. John 6 takes up these themes.

The Living Bread That Dies

John 6 begins with a sign, the feeding of the large crowd; here as in the previous chapter, Jesus' deed is the springboard for an extended discourse. However, whereas in John 5 the discourse is Jesus' response to criticism, in John 6 the discourse is separated from the feeding story by 6:15-25, which reports Jesus' rejection of the crowd's intent to "take him by force to make him king." By isolating himself, Jesus avoids a confrontation with the crowd; it is not deterred, however, despite nightfall. The next day they found him in Capernaum, where Jesus rebuked them for seeking him for the wrong reason—"because you ate your fill of the loaves" (6:26). This saying leads into the discourse.

Alluding to Isaiah 55:2, Jesus begins by urging people to work, not for perishable food but for the "food that endures for eternal life" (6:27). The crowd accepts this admonition and asks what they are to do "to perform the works of God" (6:28). For Jesus, however, only one "work" is required: believing in him as God's sent one (6:29)—and that is not a work, an achievement. The crowd does not dispute his words but asks for a sign that will justify putting their faith in him. So, referring to Moses and the manna ("He gave them bread . . . to eat," 6:31), they ask directly, "What work are *you* performing?" What they cite as Scripture is a summary statement that draws on various texts (especially Psalms 78:24; 105:40, as well as the story in Exodus 16).

Jesus first corrects this statement at three points: (1) "*He*" does not refer to Moses, as they think, but (2) to God, the Father who *gives* (present tense) (3) "the *true* bread from heaven" (John 6:32-33). Since God also gave the manna, Jesus implies that the bread the Father gives now is superior to the manna the Father gave then. Jesus continues, "For the bread of God is that which [or "he who"; the Greek can mean either] comes down from heaven [present tense] and gives [present tense] life to the world" (6:33). As the woman at the well asked for the water Jesus gives (4:15), so the crowd asks, "Sir, give us this bread always" (6:34). But as soon as they realize that this bread is Jesus himself, they no longer ask for it.

In the first part of Jesus' discourse that follows (6:35-47), Jesus speaks of himself as the bread that gives life to those who come to him and so show that they believe in him. As in John 5, they have eternal life now and will be resurrected "on the last day." In the second part of the discourse (6:48-58), Jesus indicates why the bread that he is surpasses the manna from heaven: The Israelites who ate the manna died, but "this is the bread that comes down from heaven, so that one may eat of it and not die" (6:50). Jesus' teaching moves now in a somewhat different direction; now the benefit that the bread from heaven confers depends on *eating* it—a metaphor for internalizing the meaning of Jesus as the bread. (In other words, one must "take in" the meaning of Jesus.) That the eater will "not die" implies that one becomes immortal, as 6:51 indicates: "Whoever eats of this

This Father-Son language has nothing to do with gender and everything to do with making the God-reality effective on earth.

bread will live forever." The rest of 6:51 shows that ingesting the meaning of Jesus entails more than assimilating an idea into one's thinking: It entails "taking in" the meaning of an event, Jesus' self-giving; for the bread that Jesus gives for the life of the world is his "flesh"—his actual existence as a human being that resulted from the enfleshment of the *Logos*. Paradoxically, ingesting the *death* of the Word enfleshed brings immortal *life*. To paraphrase, this life comes to those who live by Jesus' self-giving death. No wonder people objected: "How can this man give us his flesh to eat?" (6:52).

Jesus does not answer the question; instead, he becomes even more adamant: "Unless you eat the flesh of the Son of Man and drink his blood, you have no life in you" (6:53), for only by "eating and drinking" (internalizing) the life-bearing, life-giving enfleshed *Logos* can one benefit from the identity of Jesus. (Jesus' declaration is all the more shocking because drinking blood of any kind is expressly forbidden in Leviticus 7:26-27.) But Jesus still has not finished: "Those who eat my flesh and drink my blood have eternal life, and I will raise them up on the last day" (John 6:54). Jesus does not explain how this works, but he does state the basis on which he imparts eternal life: "Those who eat my flesh and drink my blood abide in me and I in them." That is, when his meaning is internalized, he becomes an enduring presence who continues to nourish the true, eternal life of the believer.

We may be offended by this discourse, but we are not the first, for according to 6:60 many of Jesus' disciples had the same reaction; in fact, many "turned back and no longer went about with him" (6:66). But those who remained shared Simon Peter's confession, "Lord, to whom can we go? You have the words of eternal life. We have come to believe and know that you are the Holy One of God." But even now Jesus maintains his confrontational manner, and so instead of blessing Simon Peter (as in Matthew 16:17), he points out that he chose the Twelve in the first place (see also John 15:16).

At the same time, since Jesus is the enfleshed *Logos* on earth, his work is God's work, so those whom Jesus chooses are those whom God gives him, the result of God's work (6:37-39). Jesus' choosing and God's giving make the same point: A person becomes a disciple by responding, not by volunteering. In other words, God is at work in the positive response to Jesus' mission: "No one can come to me unless drawn by the Father who sent me" (6:44). An essential part of Jesus' work of making God known is disclosing that everything pertaining to a person's life-giving relation to Jesus depends on God's act in sending the Son. Were that not the case, then Jesus would not really be the bread from heaven; he would be only the bread from Nazareth.

Jesus' whole discourse about bread is thoroughly metaphorical or figurative; to read it in any other way is to repeat the error of his hearers who took his words literally. Metaphors work, however, because their literal meaning is known and so make it possible to understand what is meant when the words are used "improperly." For instance, we understand "Mary is the family's anchor" because we know that an anchor keeps the boat from drifting. If we do not know the literal meaning of "anchor," we miss the metaphorical meaning in "Mary is the family's anchor." This simple illustration may be useful in understanding Jesus' metaphors in this Gospel.

(1) Jesus' use of "bread" assumes what was universally true in his culture—bread was basic, the essential part of the diet. Jesus did not say, "I am the artichoke." (Those who translate the Bible into languages of people who do not eat bread regularly search for some equivalent in their diet.)
(2) When Jesus spoke of eating his flesh and drinking his blood, he was alluding to the expression "flesh and blood," to what is truly and characteristically creaturely, as when Paul said, "Flesh and blood cannot inherit the kingdom of God" (1 Corinthians 15:50), or when Jesus told Peter that "flesh and blood" did not reveal Jesus' true identity but God (Matthew 16:17). In Jesus' talk of eating his flesh and drinking his blood, *eating* and *drinking* too are metaphors—words for ordinary acts that convey meaning effectively *because* we know that literally they are the wrong words (Mary is a person, not an anchor). When metaphors are effective, they make us think about the subject matter in fresh ways. More than that, a good metaphor says what cannot be said as effectively in any other way. To speak metaphorically about Jesus' bread metaphor, we can say that it gives us something solid to chew on. (See "The 'I Am' Sayings of Jesus," page 241.)

John 7 carries forward the motif of Jesus' conflict with his opponents who do not understand him because they take his words literally while he uses them metaphorically. Thus, the people are not willing to acknowledge that he is the Messiah because they know where "this man is from [Nazareth]; but when the Messiah comes, no one will know where he is from." This remarkable

statement shows that by relying on what is right (Jesus is from Nazareth, and no one knows where the Messiah will come from) they cannot see that Jesus really comes from God (7:25-31). Likewise, when Jesus says he will soon go to the One who sent him, and that the people will look for him but not find him, they wonder whether he is going abroad (7:32-36). The controversies Jesus generates by his way of speaking are continued in John 8–9.

So Then

We find it easy to read John 1–4 as a report of what happened "back then"; we tend to read such reports as observers of "what was going on," even when Jesus is speaking. But when we come to John 5–7 we find it harder to be observers, for here Jesus makes claims that somehow confront us no less than they confronted those to whom he spoke "back then." This sense of being confronted is reinforced by the fact that Jesus often uses the present tense:

"My Father is still working, and I also *am working*" (5:17).
"Whatever the Father does, the Son *does* likewise" (5:19).
"The Son *gives* life to whomever he wishes" (5:21).
"Anyone who hears my word . . . *has* eternal life" (5:24).
"My Father . . . *gives* you the true bread from heaven" (6:32).
"The bread of God . . . *gives* life to the world" (6:33).
"I *am* the bread of life" (6:35, 48).
"Whoever believes *has* eternal life" (6:47).
"Those who eat my flesh . . . *have* eternal life" (6:54).

We find ourselves agreeing with the officers who explained why they did not arrest Jesus: "No man ever spoke like this man" (7:46, RSV)—at least not to us.

And that is precisely the point. This man spoke differently because he was different—the *Logos* enfleshed, the Creator in the form of this particular creature, God's self-expression among us, presenting himself as the one through whom we receive eternal life by our feeding on who he is.

And by what he did for us—give his flesh. In Jesus' assertion, "The bread that I will give for the life of the world is my flesh" (6:51), all the words are simple and the structure of the sentence is not complicated; but the thought is both complex and profound, perhaps distressingly so. To begin with,

Jesus the bread gives the bread—that is, he gives himself. Moreover, in saying that the bread he gives is his flesh, Jesus asserts that what he gives is his actual, physical, tangible body-self—the very flesh that the *Logos* became. Given the importance of bread in Jesus' social world, this implies that we are sustained daily by that present-tense self-giving.

Finally, the life of which he speaks is eternal. Such life is not merely endless; it is of a different order altogether. Life is eternal not simply when there is more of it; rather it is eternal when it has a different quality, a quality derived from the *Logos*, and so is indestructible even if the person actually dies. And to our amazement, this indestructible life is made possible by the self-giving of Jesus' destructible flesh. To receive a quality of life that is eternal, we live by what Jesus did (we eat the bread he *is* and *gave*). And if we live by what he did, then we can accept our own dying as well; for the one who imparts eternal life now also promises to raise us up from death "on the last day."

Do You Want to Become His Disciples, Too?

If we follow the clue in John 6:66-69, we will discover there are times when being a disciple means staying with Jesus even though we may be as offended by what he says as were those who abandoned him. In fact many, in their own experience, have found it to be true, that being offended is an important part of being a disciple, perhaps even an essential part. Why? Because being offended reminds us we follow by believing, not by figuring the odds or by calculating the cost-benefit ratio favorably. In believing, we know that Jesus draws us to him, not the other way around. He said so: "Did I not choose you?" The disciple is glad that is how it is.

What do Jesus' claims about himself reveal to you about his relationship to God? What response do his claims require of you?

Prayer

I depend on you,

    and I have trusted you since I was young.

I have relied on you from the day I was born . . . .

Don't throw me aside when I am old;

    don't desert me when my strength is gone . . . .

All day long I will tell the wonderful things you do

    to save your people.

But you have done much more

    than I could possibly know.

I will praise you, LORD God,

    for your mighty deeds and your power to save.

(Psalm 71:5-6, 9, 15-16, CEV)

The "I Am" Sayings of Jesus

Jesus' claim "I am the bread of life" (John 6:35, 48) is one of a number of such self-proclamations: "I am the light of the world" (8:12; 9:5); "the gate for the sheep" (10:7); "the good shepherd" (10:11); "the resurrection and the life" (11:25); "the way, and the truth, and the life" (14:6); "the true vine" (15:1). Despite their variations, they have several common features: (1) Each is a metaphor, not a simile (a simile compares; Jesus did not say, "I am like bread"). In a metaphor, a word that is literally inappropriate is used to make a point on another level, as in "he's a bear" or "the lecture was thin soup." Often a good metaphor shocks because it intends to jar the reader or hearer into viewing the subject matter quite differently. Shock is precisely the effect of Jesus' saying, "I am the bread." (2) Each of the "I am" sayings is followed by an invitation expressed in language appropriate to the metaphor—bread: never be hungry; light: never walk in darkness; gate for the sheep: enter, and so forth. These invitations too are metaphors for the human condition that is being met by Jesus—hunger, darkness, being outside the fold. Consequently, Jesus' "I am" statements confront us with an understanding of ourselves as needing what Jesus offers and so invite us to confess that Jesus is indeed the bread by which we live, the light that dispels our darkness, the gate through which we enter as the flock of God, the way that defines how we live. (3) Yet nowhere in this Gospel does anyone say such things *about* Jesus; that is, no one says, "He is the bread," and so forth, even though this response is the desired one. By restricting the use of these metaphors to Jesus' own words, this Gospel makes it clear that we do not decide who Jesus is for us; instead, Jesus accosts us with his claim, his offer, and we are to respond to it. The initiative is always with Jesus. Christian theology has language for this persistent initiative on Jesus' part— prevenient grace.

Occasionally we find another kind of "I am" on Jesus' lips—one that is not followed by a metaphor at all but simply says, "I am." Translations, however, usually read "I am he" (as in 8:24). This remarkable self-proclamation appropriates God's own self-disclosure as expressed in Isaiah 43:10, 25 (also rendered "I am he"), also Exodus 3:13-14 ("I AM"). In other words, when Jesus simply says, "I am," he implies that what God is, he is. The Prologue told us so.

26 Yet the World Did Not Know Him

Jesus said, "I came into this world for judgment
so that those who do not see may see, and those
who do see may become blind."

(John 9:39)

They Have No Wine

When I know I'm right and you're wrong, the stage is set for an argument. Once the argument begins, we dig in our heels because each of us wants to prevail. So instead of hearing the other out, we start planning our rebuttal while the other is still speaking. The less we take in what the other person is saying, the more closed our mind becomes. We cannot see that it is possible to lose the argument and gain the truth.

Beginning With Moses and All the Prophets

This week's readings (John 8–10) continue the account of Jesus' controversies in Jerusalem, begun at 7:1-2. Note that according to 7:14 Jesus was teaching in the Temple; not until 8:59 did he leave it. Observe that according to 7:37, what follows was said "on the last day of the festival," including all of John 8; thus John 7–8 presents Jesus' teachings in the Temple during Sukkoth. (Note that this detail allows the readers to understand the force of what Jesus says to the high priest after his arrest, 18:19-21.) Not until 10:40 does Jesus leave the city—to avoid arrest (10:39).

Day 1 **John 8:1-30;** 3:19-21; 12:35-36, 46; Deuteronomy 19:15-21; Isaiah 43:10-13

  (1) Note that 8:12 is a typical "I am" saying. Note that the Pharisees do not deny what Jesus claims about himself but instead invalidate it on procedural grounds: Testimony about oneself is not valid (8:13). Note that Jesus' exchange with the Pharisees (8:16-19) is based on two meanings of the word *father*.

  (2) Observe that the narrator's comment at the end of John 8:20 concerns the determined time of Jesus' death. Note that Jesus' words about his departure (8:21) more or less repeat 7:34 and that neither was understood (compare 7:35-36 with 8:22).

(3) Note that while in John 7 Jesus does not respond to the Jews' puzzlement, in 8:23-24 he offers an explanation of his words. Note that in 8:24 Jesus makes freedom from sin depend on believing who he is ("I am"). Observe that at 8:25 the alternate translation in the footnote (NRSV) makes more sense here. Note that in 8:27-28 the narrator explains why Jesus said what he did in 8:18-19. Note that Jesus promises that *after* his death ("when you have lifted up the Son of Man") they will realize that he is "I am."

Day 2 **John 8:31-59;** Romans 6:12-23; Sirach 44:19-21

(1) Observe that in today's reading (John 8:31-59) "the Jews who had believed in him" (8:31) do not comprehend Jesus and that this leads to the Gospel's bitterest exchange between Jesus and "the Jews." Note that Jesus' claim to be "I am" almost got him killed (8:59).

(2) Note that the exchange degenerates into name-calling (8:48, 52) and ridicule (8:57) because Jesus repeatedly challenges the bases on which people rely for their security apart from Jesus (8:33, 39-41, 52-53, 57). Note also that each of Jesus' responses exposes ever more clearly the gulf between him and his opponents, thereby making concrete what he said in 8:23-24.

(3) Observe carefully how much of the dispute hinges on the idea that parentage determines who and what a person is. Note that this idea accounts for the attempt to kill Jesus (8:40; see 7:1, 25) and for the charge that the real "father" of "the Jews" is not Abraham as they claim (8:33, 39-40) or God (8:41), but the devil (8:44).

Day 3 **John 9;** Exodus 20:1-6; Proverbs 15:29

(1) Note that the important story in John 9 is not connected to either John 8 or John 10. Note also that although Jesus' healing caused controversy (as in John 5), this time the controversy is not *with* Jesus but *about* him. (Note that as in 5:13, here too Jesus disappears from the scene; he reappears at 9:35-41.)

(2) Note that the story emphasizes that the man was *born* blind (9:1-3, 19-20, 32)—that is, he is not responsible for his condition (though Exodus 20:1-6 might suggest that he is). Observe how Jesus' statements in John 9:3-5 move from one theme to another by word association: God's *works*; Jesus *works* while it is day*light*; he is the *light* of the world. Note that Jesus used spittle (as in Mark 7:33; 8:23), though differently. Note also that the healing (John 9:7) did not occur in Jesus' presence but in obedience to his command (as in 4:50-53), and that this explains why the first dispute is over whether a healing did in fact occur.

(3) Observe how controversies (9:13-24) begin with an argument over whether Jesus' violation of the sabbath disqualifies him as a man from God (recall Nicodemus's words in 3:2); note also how the question in 9:16 becomes an unequivocal assertion in 9:24.

(4) Note how 9:39-41 serves as a commentary not only on the story in John 9 but also on the entire Jesus story in John, and note that understanding the commentary requires one to grasp the double meaning of *seeing* and *blindness*.

Day 4 John 10:1-21; Ephesians 2:11-22; Psalm 23; Ezekiel 34:11-16, 23-31; Zechariah 11:4-9

(1) Note that in John 10:6 the narrator rightly calls Jesus' words in 10:1-5 a "figure of speech," not a parable (parables have plots) or an allegory (which assigns a separate meaning to each item). Were it an allegory, we would ask whether the sheepfold is the church, who the thief and bandit are, whether the gatekeeper is the clergy, and so forth. Observe that in 10:7-10 Jesus himself identifies the point: He is the gate.

(2) Observe that in 10:11-18 Jesus uses the image of the shepherd to speak of his death. The Old Testament readings remind us that sheep and shepherd imagery was well-established in Scripture.

(3) **GC 26-1** Compare the double accusation against Jesus in 10:19-21 with that in 8:48 and with similar accusations in the Synoptics (Matthew 9:32-34; 12:22-24; Mark 3:20-22).

Day 5 John 10:22-42; Leviticus 24:10-23; Psalm 82

(1) Note that in John 10:25-26 Jesus gives two reasons why he does not answer the question in 10:24: He has already answered it (but on his terms, not theirs), and they did not believe it. Note also the reason they do not believe. Observe that the manuscripts differ widely in the wording of 10:29; for example, according to one version the subject matter is the giver (NIV), while in another, it is the gift (NRSV).

(2) Observe that Jesus' claim in 10:30 provokes the charge of blasphemy, an accusation that recalls 5:18. Note that Jesus' response (10:34-35) is taken from Psalm 82, which envisions God addressing the heavenly council of divine beings, an old image. Note also that Jesus does not refer to "our law" but to "your law" (John 10:34).

(3) Note that after another attempt to stone Jesus (10:31; see 8:59) and then to arrest him (10:39; see 7:30), Jesus returned to the locale where John had baptized (10:40); with this detail and the reference to the witness of John the Baptist the narrative comes full circle.

Day 6 Read and respond to "Yet the World Did Not Know Him" and "Do You Want to Become His Disciples, Too?"

Prayer Concerns

Yet the World Did Not Know Him

Jesus has been confronting the world and evoking its hostility as a result since John 5. John 8–10 brings the world's hostility to a head. In fact, had Jesus not left the scene, he would have been arrested (10:39-40). No doubt John assumes that readers do not need to be told again that Jesus eluded arrest because "his hour had not yet come" (7:30). When it arrives, he will know it (12:23, 27; 13:1; 17:1). Until then Jesus attacks "the Jews" with growing vehemence, but he does not allow himself to be arrested. Since Jesus himself is a Jew, indeed hailed as "King of the Jews" at the beginning and killed as such at the end of the story, why are his opponents called "the Jews"?

"The Jews" in John

We first see how this Gospel portrays "the Jews," and this means distinguishing what Jesus says *to* them from what the narrator says *about* them; they are closely related because the narrator presents himself as knowing what Jesus thinks (for example, 2:23-25; 6:61, 64; 13:1-3; 19:28).

Since the phrase "the Jews" appears on Jesus' lips only four times (4:22; 13:33; 18:20, 36), the difficulties arise mostly from the narrator's use. What he means to convey by this phrase is not obvious because the Greek word *Ioudaioi* can be translated either "Jews" or "Judeans." In some passages the word clearly refers to Jewish people (as in 2:13, "the Passover of the Jews," and 3:1, "Nicodemus, a leader of the Jews"). The troublesome passages are those in which the *Ioudaioi* are openly hostile to Jesus. So scholars continue to debate whether the narrator is referring to hostile Judeans (who are Jews, of course) or to "the Jews," in which case he would appear to be implicating the Jewish people in the hostile responses to Jesus (5:16-18; 8:48, 52, 57; 9:22; 10:24, 31, 33—all of which should be read carefully). Most scholars acknowledge that while *Ioudaioi* can be translated as "the Judeans" in some passages, in most cases it should be translated as "the Jews." (Occasionally John identifies Jesus' opponents as Pharisees, as in 7:32; 8:13; 9:16, 40; 11:57, for example; Sadducees are never mentioned, and scribes only in 8:3.)

As a general rule, we can say that when the hostility against Jesus is centered in theological issues, this Gospel often refers to Jesus' opponents as "the Jews," even though in John Jesus never argues with anyone who is not a Jew. From beginning to end Jesus is a Jew among Jews. Why, then, does this Gospel make a point of saying that those who failed to understand Jesus or those who became hostile because they did understand were "the Jews"?

To answer the question, we first note what Jesus said *to* them, and that means attending to the theological issues in his exchanges with them. Consistently, these issues are christological—that is, they concern the identity of Jesus and his significance for the human situation. And that means they concern the gospel in John's Gospel. Christological issues have appeared already in 5:18-42; 6:41-51; 7:15-24.

The issues that "the Jews" and Jesus were arguing about (his relation to God and God's deeds, whether he does impart eternal life, and so forth) were the same issues the church in John's time was debating with the Jewish community. Consequently, the narrator in John calls Jesus' theological opponents "the Jews" because most non-Christian Jews had regularly objected to the Christian understanding of Jesus' identity and significance. If John had written an extended essay, he might have explained how the issues that divided Christians (many of whom were Jewish) and non-Christian Jews in his day were rooted in the divisions caused by Jesus himself. Instead, he wrote a narrative that shows this to be the case.

> **From beginning to end Jesus is a Jew among Jews.**

Because Jesus himself is a Jew and tells the Samaritan woman that "salvation is from the Jews" (4:22), Jesus' harsh words to "the Jews" are not anti-Semitic or anti-Jewish. However, when combined with the narrator's words about "the Jews," they certainly sound that way in the mouth of a Gentile.

The Prologue gives us a clue to the way we should understand the portrayal of "the Jews" as well as Jesus' words to them. John 1:10-11 says, "He was in the world, and . . . the world did not know him. He came to what was his own, and his own people did not accept him." This wording clearly suggests that his own people's refusal was the concrete, historical form of the world's not knowing him. According to the logic of the

Prologue, then, we might say that if Jesus had been a Greek among Greeks or a Roman among Romans (or an American among Americans), he would have said comparable things about his fellow Greeks, Romans, or Americans, because what Jesus' words address is not the hearers' Jewishness but the character of "the world" in the hearers Even so, we can appreciate the fact that Jews are not pleased to be regarded as representatives of "the world."

"The World" in John

"The world" is mentioned in almost every chapter of John's Gospel. The word *kosmos* can refer to the physical universe or world, as in "before the world existed" (John 17:5) or "the world itself could not contain the books" that could be written about Jesus (21:25). But in John the word has a loaded content, for it usually refers to the nonphysical reality that shapes (that is, misshapes) human life. In the Prologue both meanings are found side by side: "The world came into being through him [that is, the universe]; yet the world did not know him." In the second part of the statement, the meaning has shifted, for the physical universe is not something that "knows"; now the term refers to the human "world," the human mindset that does not acknowledge the one to whom all things and all persons owe their existence. In other words, "the world" is not the earth *on* which we live; it is the mindset *in which* we live; it also lives *in us*, as a set of assumptions about what is real and true, as habits and patterns of living. An analogy may help: We live in secularity, and secularity lives in us. To oversimplify the Prologue, creation has become "world," turned away from its Creator, even when (and perhaps especially when) it is being "religious." Neither the author nor Jesus explains all this; but both assume it—the author in what the Prologue asserts, Jesus in the way he talks about "the world."

> "The world" is not the earth *on* which we live; it is the mindset *in which* we live; it also lives *in us,* as a set of assumptions about what is real and true, as habits and patterns of living.

The mindset called "the world" is more than an attitude; it is a power. In fact, it has a ruler (that is, Satan, 14:30; 16:11) into whose domain the Father sent Jesus and from which he will depart. Because Jesus sees "the world" as an active power and domain, he speaks of it as if it were a person: It sees (14:19), hates (15:18), does not know (1:10; 17:25) or receive (14:17); yet it can believe (17:21) and know (17:23), which is why Jesus spoke to it (18:20). "The world" is so determining of human life that Jesus can say that a person is derived "from" it (literally, "of the world"), though Jesus himself is not: "You are of this world, I am not of this world," 8:23); he is in the world but not of it. Although he entered "the world," he never became "of" it.

The more clearly we understand John's negative view of "the world," the more striking and startling is the gospel in John's Gospel: "God so loved the world that he gave his only Son, so that everyone who believes in him may not perish but may have eternal life" (3:16). Given John's portrayal of "the world," this declaration is the great *nevertheless* that becomes the story of Jesus in John.

Jesus in John

The great *nevertheless* appears as the discontinuity between Jesus and "the world," and is particularly evident in the ways in which Jesus talks about himself and his task. In the Synoptics Jesus occasionally says why he "came" (Matthew 5:17; 9:13; 10:34; 20:28); but in John, when Jesus speaks of his "coming," he links it rarely with service but regularly with his authority: He came in the Father's name (5:43), not on his own (7:28; 8:14). He even says he came "down from heaven" (6:38, 41). Most of all, he refers to himself as the one who has been "sent" and speaks of the Father as the sender (for example, 5:23-24, 37-38; 6:29, 38-39; 7:16, 28; 8:16, 18; 9:4; 10:36; 11:42; 17:3, 18, 21). Never is Jesus one who has been "called" or "chosen" by God. Though he is from Nazareth and his parents are known (6:42), he is really an outsider who has come from the presence of God (1:18) into "the world" where he remains a stranger.

So "the world" did not welcome the *Logos* enfleshed, the stranger in its midst. It did not "master" the light that entered its darkness ("mastered," both in the sense of "overcome" and "understood"). What occurred instead was failure to understand, conflict, and the demonization of the messenger (8:48, 52) in response to Jesus' harsh denunciation of them ("you are from [of] your father the devil," 8:44).

In John, Jesus' public mission is consistently confrontational, because this approach is required if he is to break open the deceptive self-confidence of "the world" in order to save it. To put "the world" straight about what it "knows," Jesus deliberately uses words with double meanings; and he exposes the gulf between his truth and the facts on which "the world" relies to discredit him. He broke the sabbath (5:18; 9:14, 16); he cannot be the Messiah because they know his mother and father (but not his Father). He is confrontational even with his followers (6:60-71); never does he assume the role of a tutor who helps people understand what he means. When he does explain something, he deepens the hearers' dilemma, as in 8:47: "Whoever is from [of] God hears the words of God. The reason you do not hear them is that you are not from [of] God."

> **In John, Jesus' public mission is consistently confrontational, because this approach is required if he is to break open the deceptive self-confidence of "the world" in order to save it.**

John 8, in fact, shows how much "the world" remains in those who believed in him. To them he promised, "If you continue in my word, you are truly my disciples; and you will know the truth, and the truth will make you free" (8:31-32). But instead of accepting this promise, they contested their need to be freed: As Abraham's descendants, we "have never been slaves to anyone. What do you mean . . . , 'You will be made free'?" When Jesus goes on to explain that he is talking about liberation from the enslaving power of sin (8:34-36), their insistence that Abraham is their father degenerates into a bitter dispute in which Jesus says their real father is the devil, a murderer and "a liar and the father of lies." When the dispute ends, those who had "believed in him" at the outset now "picked up stones to throw at him." Alas, this was not the last time that believers failed to become true disciples because they did not "continue" in his word and so come to know the truth that frees them from the enslaving power of "the world."

The disputes that followed Jesus' announcement, "I am the light of the world" (8:12), began with a procedural point: Testimony to oneself is not valid. The Pharisees did not challenge what Jesus had claimed. Nor did he explain beyond what he added: "Whoever follows me will never walk in darkness but will have the light of life." The unusually detailed story of the healing of the man's blindness in John 9, however, shows how this promise is fulfilled while Jesus is in Jerusalem. This story is one of the three long stories in John, the others being Jesus' exchange with the Samaritan woman in Chapter 4 and the raising of Lazarus in Chapter 11. One reason the story is so prominent is that what it reports is not the restoration of sight lost but the gift of sight to a man who was *born* blind (stated six times). This "sign" is greater than healing a thirty-eight-year illness (John 5), but not as great as bringing Lazarus back to life. The story focuses on the healed man because this healing sign signifies what can happen when one receives "the light of life"—disputes, fear (of what might happen if one is linked to Jesus), and faith.

The storyteller's art here is evident in the repetition of what Jesus actually did (9:6, 11, 15, 26-27) and in the way this repetition increases the dramatic quality of the story. The same art appears in the way the beginning of the story (9:1-5) coheres with its ending (9:35-41), tying the whole account together, thereby helping the readers understand what was going on in the healing and its consequences. Consequently, the beginning and ending of John 9 merit our close attention.

The very first line tells us that the man was "blind from birth"; but the disciples ask whether the man's blindness was God's punishment for his sin or for that of his parents (the disciples assume it must be somebody's fault perhaps because according to Exodus 20:1-6, punishment for sin can go on for several generations). Jesus, however, rejects this assumption and instead asserts something that fits his mission: "He was born blind so that God's works [the plural is important] might be revealed in him." In adding, "As long as I am in the world, I am the light of the world," Jesus points ahead to the meaning of what he is about to do—give light to the man who has never seen daylight. In doing so, "God's works" are revealed in the man, visible for all to observe.

As the story ends (John 9:35-41), Jesus responds to the man's confession of faith by declaring, "I came into this world for judgment so that those who do not see may see, and those who do see may become blind" (9:39), a remarkable reversal.

Both parts of this declaration have occurred in the story: The man now sees, and the Pharisees who have both raised objections and declared Jesus to be "a sinner" (9:24) have become blind to the truth about Jesus. Still they understand what Jesus' word implies about them and so object: "Surely we are not blind, are we?" But Jesus has the last word: "If you were blind, you would not have sin. But now that you say, 'We see,' your sin remains." Here inability to "see" the truth is not a sin, just as the man's blindness from birth was not the result of sin, something for which he or his parents were responsible. Sin is claiming to "see" the truth while actually not "seeing" it at all. So long as they claim to "see," their "sin remains." In healing the man and in causing the Pharisees to expose their own blindness, Jesus accomplishes both of God's "works"—healing and judgment. Moreover, the man is healed by obeying Jesus' word, and then he confesses his faith in response to Jesus' words about himself. His responses too are "the works of God."

Again, Jesus' deed generates controversy (as in 6:52; 7:12, 40-43), a division within the people of God. Here, however, the dispute is not with Jesus himself but about him, and it has several aspects, each of which reflects issues that divide John's church from the Jewish community. The first dispute is over whether Jesus was in fact a healer (9:8-12); the second concerns the possibility of being "put out of the synagogue" for confessing Jesus to be the Messiah (9:18-23); the third concerns the truth about Jesus. The importance of this third aspect is underscored by the fact that it is pursued twice, first in 9:13-17, then in 9:24-34 as well.

John 9:13-17 is especially interesting in light of Nicodemus's opening remark, "We know that you are a teacher come from God; for no one can do these signs that you do, unless God is with him" (3:2, RSV). In the dispute in John 9, however, the sign (the healing) is used as evidence that Jesus is "not from God, for he does not observe the sabbath" (9:16). In 9:24-34, the man turns this same argument on its head: Jesus opened the man's eyes; God "does not listen to sinners, but he does listen to one who worships him and obeys his will" (the man assumes that this allusion to Proverbs 15:29 describes Jesus); therefore, Jesus is "from God," for if that were not the case, "he could do nothing," and he would not have done what had never been done before. What the man's

parents feared might happen to them (9:22-23) now happens to him: He is thrown out. His last words are those of a person whom Jesus has enabled to see and to "see" the meaning of what he has done: "Lord, I believe."

In John 10 God's *nevertheless* to "the world" is carried out by Jesus' own *nevertheless* while "in the world"—namely, by being "the good shepherd [who] lays down his life for the sheep" (10:11). He is the opposite of the wicked shepherds portrayed in Ezekiel 34, who for their own benefit fleece the sheep instead of feeding them. When Jesus says that he must bring "other sheep" also into his fold so there will be one flock and one shepherd, he takes on God's role: "I myself will search for my sheep, and will seek them out .... I will rescue them from all the places to which they have been scattered .... I will bring them out from the peoples and gather them from the countries .... I will feed them with good pasture .... I myself will be the shepherd of my sheep" (Ezekiel 34:11-15). In John 10:1-18 Jesus draws on Ezekiel to express his dual role—first as the one through whom people find life (the gate to good pasture), then as the Good Shepherd who does not flee death but voluntarily gives his life so that his sheep will have life that is eternal.

Like the shepherd, the sheep live in "the world" where they are in danger of being led astray by strangers, exploited by thieves and bandits, abandoned by hired hands who do not really care for the flock and so allow the wolves to ravage them. "The world" is that kind of place.

So Then

We should not be surprised if we find ourselves responding to John's Gospel as Jesus' disciples responded to his gospel, "This teaching is difficult; who can accept it?" (John 6:60). Often we too find that understanding eludes us and what we do understand exposes the extent to which we are still "of" the world and yet promises us life so different that it is called eternal. We can never master this Jesus; instead, he somehow masters us—in both senses of the word *master*. We struggle along in his company because we know there is no one else to whom we can go because he has "the words of eternal life" (6:68). He makes known to us that reality we call "God," the invisible source of the great *nevertheless* that is for us because it is against "the world" in us.

Do You Want to Become His Disciples, Too?

Before answering this question, notice what is implied for discipleship in what Jesus says about the relation between himself—the Good Shepherd—and the sheep. They "hear his voice," they are known individually (by name), and they know the shepherd; they belong to the shepherd and are led by him. In a dangerous and hostile environment, they are safe because the shepherd dies for them voluntarily. The passage is not designed to evoke the question, "Do you want to be a sheep?" for it assumes the disciples are Jesus' flock already. But the passage does invite us to ask ourselves whether we do hear his voice speaking to us personally and whether we do indeed follow his lead. The passage suggests being a disciple is not a matter of following Jesus "sheepishly" but a matter of letting him take us to the good pasture.

Who is this Jesus that the world you know does not recognize or accept?

_____

_____

_____

_____

_____

Prayer

I will listen to you, LORD God,
because you promise peace to those
    who are faithful and no longer foolish.
You are ready to rescue everyone who worships you,
    so that you will live with us in all of your glory.

Love and loyalty will come together;
    goodness and peace will unite.
Loyalty will sprout from the ground;
    justice will look down from the sky above.

(Psalm 85:8-11, CEV)

27 That They May Believe

Jesus said to her, "I am the resurrection and the life.
Those who believe in me, even though they die, will live."
(John 11:25)

They Have No Wine

Who of us has not looked back with regret because we missed an opportunity?
"I should have applied for that job after all." "If I had rearranged my schedule so
I could see Julie's soccer games . . . ." It's hard to decide which we regret more,
an opportunity offered and declined or one we didn't recognize in the first place.
The one shows we were too reluctant to venture; the other, that we did not see
the possibilities.

Beginning With Moses and All the Prophets

In John 11–12 we reach the climax of Jesus' public mission, capped by his
greatest sign, the raising of Lazarus. The story has several levels of meaning.
In addition, it summarizes Jesus' role as life-giver in the previous chapter, and it
looks ahead to his death. These chapters repay careful study. That's why there
are so many things to look for in your daily reading of Scripture.

Day 1 John 11:1-44; 5:19-29; 1 John 1

(1) Note that the story of Lazarus has three phases: John 11:1-16, 17-37, and 38-44.
(2) Note that the reference to Mary in 11:2 assumes the readers know the story that has not yet
been told but appears in 12:1-8. Note also that 11:3 assumes what is reported at 10:40.
(3) Observe that according to 11:4-6 Jesus foresees the result of Lazarus's illness and delays his
return in order to underscore the result. Note that he makes a similar point after he learns that
Lazarus has died (11:14-15); this repetition alerts the readers to expect something unusual.
Recall that 9:3 makes a similar point.

(4) Note that both sisters blame Jesus for Lazarus's death (11:21, 32), though only Martha also tactfully suggests that Jesus can still get God to do something. Note that Martha expresses the widespread view of future resurrection; note especially her response to Jesus' self-proclamation (11:25-27).

(5) Observe that Jesus' prayer (11:41-42) and what follows confirm what Martha had said in 11:22 and also alludes to Jesus' word in 11:15.

(6) Observe how the story fulfills Jesus' promise in 5:19-29.

Day 2 John 11:45-57; 1 John 3:1-10; Wisdom of Solomon 2:12-24

(1) Note that in John 11:45 the raising of Lazarus is a sign that prompts belief in Jesus; see also 7:31; 10:40-42.

(2) Observe that what Caiaphas regards as a political expedient, the narrator sees as the unwitting statement of the truth (11:49-52). Observe that 11:52 recalls 10:16.

(3) Note that 11:55-57 serves to heighten the readers' sense of anticipation—a mark of good storytelling.

(4) Note how the passage from the Wisdom of Solomon fits today's reading from John.

Day 3 John 12:1-19; Mark 14:3-9; 11:1-11; Matthew 21:1-17; Luke 10:38-42; 19:28-44; Psalm 118:19-29; Zechariah 9:9-10

(1) GC 27-1 Note that the story in Mark 14:3-9 has a different setting in John 12:1-8. Note also that "Martha served" in 12:2 seems to reflect John's knowledge of Luke 10:38-42. Note that whereas in Mark 14:4 "some" complained; in John it is Judas, also characterized as a thief. Note also that the presence of Lazarus tells the readers that he really has been restored to life.

(2) Observe that in John 12:9-11 Lazarus has become both an object of curiosity and the reason many "were believing in Jesus" and that this response prompts the plot against Jesus.

251

(3) **[GC 27-2]** In John 12:12-15 note that Jesus responds to the crowds (whose reasons for meeting him are given in 12:17-18), whereas in the Synoptics Jesus takes the initiative and the crowds respond to him (Mark 11:1-11; Matthew 21:1-17; Luke 19:28-48). Observe also that John's story of Jesus' arrival emphasizes the acclamation (12:13, taken from Psalm 118) and the fulfillment of Zechariah 9:9. Note the similarity between John 2:22 and 12:16 and that these observations anticipate what Jesus will promise in 14:26.

Day 4 John 12:20-43; Mark 14:32-42; Matthew 16:24-28; Psalm 89:19-37; Isaiah 6:1-10; 53

(1) Note that Jesus responds to the Greeks' request by speaking of his death, implying that the Gentiles will see Jesus only after his death (12:24).

(2) Notice how John 12:25 adapts Matthew 16:25 into John's vocabulary.

(3) Observe carefully what Jesus says about his impending death in John 12:27-33. Note that he speaks of it as his "hour" (see also 2:4; 7:30; 8:20). Though John does not report Jesus' prayer in Gethsemane (Mark 14:32-42), note that he does have Jesus speak of his death as a cup he must drain (John 18:11). Note especially that Jesus regards his death as glorification (12:23, 28).

(4) Note that the heavenly voice (12:28) looks back to Jesus' mission and ahead to his death. Note how Jesus understands the purpose of the voice (12:30).

(5) Observe that Jesus regards his death as "the judgment [condemnation] of this world" ("the ruler of this world" is not Caesar but the devil).

(6) Note that in 12:33 the narrator explains what Jesus means in 12:32. Note that the ceaseless presence of the Messiah is probably inferred from Psalm 89. Note that John 12:32 expects the readers to recall 3:14.

(7) Observe that from the latter half of 12:36 through 12:43 the narrator comments on Jesus' whole public mission and that Jesus has the last word in 12:44-50. Note that despite 11:47-48 and 12:17-19, the narrator sees the overall result of Jesus' signs as failure (but then modifies this verdict in 12:42-43 just as the Prologue did in 1:11-12). Observe that the narrator sees this failure as the fulfillment of Isaiah 53:1. Note that John 12:41 sees *God's* command to Isaiah (Isaiah 6:1-10) fulfilled in *Jesus'* mission: "so they could not believe." Observe that John 12:42-43 recalls 9:22.

Day 5 John 12:44-50; 1 John 2:7-11; 5:1-5

   (1) In 12:44-50 note that Jesus restates the major themes of his message and that the narrator signals the importance of these words by saying, "Jesus cried aloud" (as in 7:28).

   (2) Observe that the passage begins with Jesus' relation to God (12:44-45), moves to the purpose of his coming (12:46-47), then to the consequences of persons' rejecting his word (12:48), and ends with his return to the Father (12:49-50); note this same sequence of themes in the Prologue.

   (3) Note that Jesus summarizes his mission by paraphrasing what he had said before and will say again:
- the sent and the Sender (12:44-45; 5:24, 30; 6:29, 39; 11:42; 13:20; 17:8, 21)
- Jesus as the light (12:46; 8:12; 9:5; 12:35-36; also 1:4-5, 7-8; 3:18-20)
- Jesus came to save, not to judge (12:47; 3:17)
- those who reject him have a judge (12:48; 3:17-19)
- the Father gave Jesus tasks (12:49; 4:34; 5:36; 9:3-4; 10:25, 37; 15:24; 17:4)
- Jesus is not "on his own" (12:49; 7:28-29; 8:42)
- the Father's will is eternal life (12:50; 6:40)
- Jesus speaks God's words (12:50; 3:34; 14:24; 17:8, 14)

Day 6 Read and respond to "That They May Believe" and "Do You Want to Become His Disciples, Too?"

Prayer Concerns

That They May Believe

Some form of the verb *believe* appears in almost every chapter of John (over ninety times, beginning with 1:7 and ending with 20:31), yet the nouns *faith* and *belief* are never used, either by Jesus or the narrator. This feature of John can be neither overlooked nor taken for granted, for it is hardly accidental. Since Jesus' last public utterance (12:44-50) repeats many themes of his message to the world, this is an appropriate point to call attention to the unusual emphasis on the verb *believe*.

Generally speaking, verbs express some kind of action or state of being, whether observable or unobservable. Jesus' message in John intends to evoke an action that he calls "believe." He does *not* ask people to "believe in faith"; he does ask them to believe that certain things are so true that persons ought to act on them. To "believe" is to commit oneself. What Jesus says about believing, the narrator underscores by using the same expressions himself.

First, although Jesus sometimes speaks simply of believing, more often he mentions what is to be believed, usually something about himself. Thus at Lazarus's tomb Jesus tells God that he prays so that the crowd "may believe that you sent me" (11:42). In 16:27 he tells the disciples they "have believed that I came from God." *Second*, Jesus asks the disciples to believe what he says about his relation to the Father: "Believe me that I am in the Father and the Father is in me" (14:11). *Third*, in 8:24 he tells his opponents that they will die in their sins unless they "believe that I am he" (literally, "that I am"). *Fourth*, just as the narrator reports that people believed "in him" (2:11; 7:31; 10:42), so Jesus speaks of believing "in me" (6:35; 11:26; see also 9:35 and 12:36). In John's Gospel, whoever believes *in* Jesus also believes *what* he says about himself and his mission.

> **In John's Gospel, whoever believes *in* Jesus also believes *what* he says about himself and his mission.**

Jesus Confronts the Living and Summons the Dead

Of all the signs Jesus did to signify the purpose of his mission, summoning Lazarus from the tomb four days after his death is surely the most important. While an earlier sign generated efforts to do away with Jesus (John 5:16-18), this sign triggered the plot to kill him (11:45-53) and Lazarus as well (12:9-11). Yet, important as Lazarus is in this Gospel, he never says a word; the Evangelist keeps the focus on Jesus. Lazarus's sisters speak because what they say keeps the readers' eyes on Jesus. Similarly, in the story of Mary's anointing Jesus' feet (12:1-8), we are left to surmise her motivation and her opinion, for what matters are her deed and Jesus' words.

In John's story line Jesus' response to Lazarus's illness and death, together with its aftermath (11:1-53), interrupts his withdrawal from Jerusalem because of hostile action against him (10:31, 39-42; 11:8). Indeed, Jesus' absence from the area around Jerusalem is an essential part of the story: (1) It underscores Jesus' deliberate delay before returning, "so that the Son of God may be glorified" when he arrives in Bethany (11:4-6); (2) Jesus' absence sets the stage for the sisters' complaint that their brother would not have died if Jesus had been there, just as it accounts for the "stench" at Lazarus's tomb (11:39); (3) Jesus' absence allows the disciples to say that he will risk death by returning to Judea (11:7-8, 16). Jesus' response about "those who walk during the day" and "those who walk at night" (11:9-10) seems quite beside the point—until we see that he regards the disciples' warning as evidence that "the light is not in them." They have not internalized Jesus' conviction that he will die when his "hour" comes—not before—and that therefore his decision about returning is not a matter of calculating the odds about his safety.

Jesus' next exchange with the disciples (11:11-16) shows two things about them. On one hand, they misunderstand Jesus when he uses words with two meanings (here, *asleep* and *awaken*) as did Nicodemus and "the Jews" earlier. As John sees it, truly understanding Jesus will occur after his departure. On the other hand, as with Caiaphas (11:49-52), what the disciples say is more true than they realize. They say that if Lazarus has "fallen asleep, he will be all right" (NRSV); "he will recover" (RSV and REB); "will get better" (NIV), but none of these translations captures the dual meaning of the Greek, which also means "he will be saved." John does not idealize the disciples or present them as models to be imitated; in fact, his portrayal of them is remarkably like his portrayal of "the world"—until after Jesus' death and the coming of the Spirit.

Many readers, accustomed to visualizing Jesus as always responding to human need, are puzzled and perhaps put off by his delay in responding to the sisters' message—especially since Lazarus was "our friend" (11:11, 35-36). But in John everything Jesus says and does is for the sake of expressing who he is and why he has come. The delay makes this intention evident.

When Jesus arrives in Bethany, he first must respond to the sisters. Even though it was Mary who "knelt" at Jesus' feet to show reverence and who later anointed his feet with expensive perfume (12:1-8), her role is not as important as Martha's. After complaining about Jesus' absence, Martha points out that it's not too late for Jesus to do something because God answers his prayer (11:21-22). Jesus does not dispute her comment; indeed, at the tomb he confirms her point (11:41-42). But just now he responds by saying, "Your brother will rise again" (11:23), which is probably not what Martha wanted to hear. She thinks Jesus is simply referring to the future resurrection, which she affirms, "I know that he will rise again in the resurrection on the last day."

Now Jesus confronts her in three ways: He (1) gives an "I am" saying, "I am the resurrection and the life"; (2) offers a twofold explanation of resurrection, "Those who believe in me, even though they die, will live, and everyone who lives and believes in me will never die"; and (3) finally asks her directly, "Do you believe this?" (11:25-26). Like other "I am" sayings, this one too states the meaning of Jesus: He is the one through whom life is transformed radically when it is rightly related to its Creator.

In the first part of the explanation, Jesus restates what Martha said but then qualifies it by promising life after death to "those who believe in me" instead of simply relying on the hope of the general resurrection, as she had implied. Earlier Jesus himself had referred to this general resurrection when he said that all who hear the voice of the Son of Man will come out of their graves, whether they have done good or evil (5:28-29). But now, in speaking to Martha, he speaks of "those who believe in me" because he wants to elicit her believing.

The second part of the explanation ("everyone who lives and believes in me will never die") strikes us as strange, partly because "lives" seems unnecessary (who else would do the believing?), and mostly because "will never die" appears to contradict the first part of the explanation, which admits that believers do die. Understandably, commentators have offered various interpretations. One possibility takes account of the fact that "will never die" actually translates the unusual Greek that literally says "will not die into the age" and can be rendered as "will not die forever" (which is not the same as not dying at all). A more likely interpretation holds that the unusual Greek refers to the believers' life that is eternal, not destroyed by death. On this basis, the two conceptions stand side by side (future resurrection life and present eternal life) as they do also in 5:24-25. Here 5:24 promises,"Anyone who hears my word and believes him who sent me *has* eternal life, and . . . has passed from death [here, ordinary life apart from Christ] to life [real existence, eternal life]"; and 5:25 promises, "The dead will hear the voice of the Son of God, and . . . will live [again]" (see 6:40).

Why are these two conceptions placed next to each other? If believers receive a life that is eternal (qualitatively different and so not vulnerable to death), why is also a resurrection promised? Both are essential because alone each is incomplete: By itself, the traditional Jewish hope of future life after resurrection does not take enough account of the new kind of life that comes to those who believe in Jesus; and by itself, presently enjoyed eternal life does not reckon seriously enough with either the fact of death or Jesus' own resurrection as a pledge of what can be expected. The two conceptions do not contradict each other; they complement each other.

Jesus' question to Martha, "Do you believe this?" calls for a decision that cannot be avoided. What Jesus now asks explicitly has been implicit throughout the Gospel, beginning with 3:16 at least. In other words, Jesus gives Martha the opportunity to believe and so to receive eternal life. If she seizes the opportunity, she will experience what Nicodemus forfeited—being "born" *anōthen* (anew or from above). Her reply shows she did not repeat Nicodemus's forfeiture: "Yes, Lord, I believe that you are the Messiah, the Son of God, the one coming into the world" (11:27). Additionally, she has reached the goal of the Gospel of John itself, "written so that you may come to believe [or 'may continue to believe,' as many manuscripts read] that Jesus is the Messiah, the Son of God, and that through believing you may have life [that is, eternal life] in his name" (20:31). Lazarus will receive more life that is temporal; she has received life that is eternal.

Although Jesus apparently met Martha privately, his meeting with Mary was a public event, for she was accompanied by "the Jews" who had been consoling her at home (11:31). Here "the Jews" are not Jesus' opponents. Indeed, when they see him weep, they say, "See how he loved him [Lazarus]" (11:36), though some shared the sisters' complaint that Jesus might have prevented Lazarus from dying had he been there.

> **In his weeping, Jesus' humanness becomes evident as nowhere else in John. The *Logos* really did become flesh.**

John's description of the scene with Mary and the consoling Jews emphasizes weeping (not merely shedding tears but bewailing). Intriguing is the narrator's comment that when Jesus saw all this wailing, "He was greatly disturbed in spirit and deeply moved" (11:33). Here the translation, "He was moved with indignation and deeply distressed" (REB) catches better the intense anger implied by the Greek word. Mark 14:5 uses the same word of the disciples' response to the woman who used expensive ointment to anoint Jesus: "They rebuked her harshly" (NIV). The point is not that Jesus too is grieved over the death of his friend and cannot conceal his emotions but rather that all the wailing makes him deeply angry. John uses the same word to describe Jesus at the tomb (John 11:38), perhaps implying that Jesus is deeply angered by the fact of death that he now confronts. When 11:35 says, "Jesus began to weep," the Greek text uses a different word from that in 11:33, a detail hidden when translators use "weep" for both. Whereas 11:33 refers to wailing (which can include weeping), 11:35 explicitly refers to shedding tears—which is why the Jews concluded that Jesus had really loved Lazarus. In his weeping (11:35), Jesus' humanness becomes evident as nowhere else in John. The *Logos* really did become flesh.

The point of the whole story—the raising of Lazarus—is made with utmost brevity: The tomb having been opened, Jesus shouts, "Lazarus, come out!" And out he comes, as he was put in—"his hands and feet bound with strips of cloth, and his face wrapped in a cloth." Jesus says nothing more to him, but simply tells an unspecified "them" to "unbind him, and let him go." And Lazarus says nothing at all. Thus John reports that Jesus fulfilled his promise made earlier: "The hour is coming, and is now here, when the dead will hear the voice of the Son of God, and . . . will live" (5:25).

When John goes on to report the frustration of "the chief priests and the Pharisees," he has *them* use his own theological language: "This man is performing many signs" (11:47). What occurred at the tomb is indeed Jesus' last, greatest, and most significant sign; and it prompted many of the wailers and weepers to believe in him. Others, however, reported to the Pharisees what Jesus had done—that is, they could not deny that Lazarus had come out of the tomb when Jesus summoned him to life, for they had been there; yet they did not believe in Jesus as a result. So John shows that even this greatest sign does not make believing inevitable; a person can see what happened and still not believe. John offers an explanation for this in 12:37-41.

The way the Lazarus sign is told differs from the way other signs are reported. Elsewhere, Jesus' deed comes first and then provokes a response that provides him the occasion to present and usually to defend his teaching. But here the teaching comes first (in Jesus' words to Martha), and the sign follows. This unusual sequence is neither accidental nor irrelevant; rather, it expresses an important theme of this Gospel's theology, one aspect of which we have already noted: Martha's confession *in* the Gospel story anticipates what the text *of* the Gospel hopes to achieve in the readers. To this we can now add another aspect: Martha believes what Jesus says *before* (that is, without) seeing the Lazarus sign and so actualizes Jesus' later words to Thomas (who insisted that he would not believe Jesus was resurrected until he touched the wounds), "Blessed are those who have not seen and yet have come to believe"

> **Martha's confession *in* the Gospel story anticipates what the text *of* the Gospel hopes to achieve in the readers.**

(20:29), namely, the readers! Apart from Jesus, the real hero of the story is Martha, who believes, not Lazarus. He is a walking sign of what Martha believes. She receives eternal life; but he receives only a reprieve from death, a "sign" that Jesus is the life-giver. While Lazarus is restored to the life he had before (12:1-2), he was not resurrected, only resuscitated.

The difference is not merely a matter of words, for while every resuscitation (including those that occur in today's hospitals) is a marvelous event, no resuscitation is a resurrection as the New Testament understands it—transformation into another mode of existence, one no longer subject to death. On this point Paul speaks for the whole New Testament when he writes, "Christ, being raised from the dead, will never die again; death no longer has dominion over him" (Romans 6:9), and in 1 Corinthians 15:50-53, where he explains that our resurrection (like Christ's) means that "the dead will be raised imperishable, and we [who happen to be alive at the time] will be changed. For this perishable body must put on imperishability, and this mortal body must put on immortality."

A Reader's Guide to the Passion Story

In the Synoptics, the Passion predictions—especially important in Mark (Mark 8:31-33; 9:30-32; 10:32-34)—prepare the reader for the Passion story. These predictions are completely absent from John. Yet this Gospel too prepares the reader for Jesus' death; however, it does so in its own way. In fact, almost from the beginning of his mission, Jesus alludes to his death as in "My hour has not yet come" (John 2:4) and in his response when questioned about his authority to "cleanse" the Temple (2:18-21). Subsequently, when he refers repeatedly to his death, he does not predict details of the Passion story as in the Passion predictions but speaks of its significance for the human condition. In this way John shapes the readers' understanding of Jesus' death before it happens, particularly in 11:55–12:50.

Jesus' first clear reference to his death appears in John 6, where he speaks of himself as "the living [life-giving] bread that came down from heaven." After promising that "whoever eats of this bread will live forever," he adds, "and the bread that I will give for the life of the world is my flesh," his physical existence (6:51). Later he expressed this self-giving as "the good shepherd [who] lays down his life for the sheep" (10:11), said even more plainly in 10:15, "I lay down my life for the sheep." A few verses later, he is even more explicit: "For this reason the Father loves me, because I lay down my life in order to take it up again. No one takes it from me, but I lay it down of my own accord. I have power [authority] to lay it down, and I have power to take it up again. I have received

this command from my Father" (10:17-18). Here Jesus' free self-giving to death carries out his obedience to God, because this is how God "gave his only Son." In John neither the plot against Jesus nor the understandable reasons for it make Jesus the helpless victim of human schemes, for these are but the means that facilitate his free self-giving. "The world" may think it takes Jesus' life from him, but Jesus says he gives it.

Jesus also speaks of his death as his departure and return to the Father who sent him: "I will be with you a little while longer, and then I am going to him who sent me" (7:33). Likewise, in 8:14 he says, "I know where I have come from and where I am going, but you do not know where I come from or where I am going," and in 8:21: "I am going away . . . . Where I am going, you cannot come." In the first instance the hearers do not understand that Jesus is referring to his death because they take his words at face value and wonder whether he intends to travel to "the Dispersion among the Greeks" (7:35). In the second instance they do understand that he is speaking of his voluntary death but misunderstand it as suicide: "Is he going to kill himself?" (8:22). The readers know, of course, that Jesus' voluntary death is an act of self-giving for the sake of the world.

> ## "The world" may think it takes Jesus' life from him, but Jesus says he gives it.

What Jesus says in 12:23-25 as well as its setting are important for this Gospel's understanding of Jesus' death. The passage contains three elements of that understanding: (1) "The hour has come." Both the narrator and Jesus have spoken of this hour before (2:4; 7:30; 8:20) or of his "time" (7:6, 8), and both will do so again (13:1; 17:1). His "hour" expresses the idea that the time of Jesus' death has been set by God. In John Jesus knows when that "moment" has arrived (though neither he nor the narrator says how or when he knows it). In fact, John never explains how Jesus knew anything that he knew. What matters is our knowing that he knew it. At the right time, he will lay down his life; it will not be taken from him (10:18). And when that time arrives, he will not evade it because his mission has this purpose in view from the start (12:27). **GC 273** The "hour" has the same theological function in John as the emphasis on the *necessity* of the Passion in the Synoptics (Matthew 16:21; Mark 8:31;

Luke 9:22; 17:25; 24:7, 44); both deny that Jesus' death was a fluke; both assert that it fit God's purpose.

John does not imply that Jesus had a dark sense of foreboding, for Jesus acts out of his knowledge of the Father's will rather than out of his sense of the way "things are moving." This Gospel does not make it easy for us to understand Jesus' view of his death. In fact, the more it guides our thinking about Jesus' death, the greater the challenge to believe that Jesus was right.

(2) Jesus' shameful death on the cross is his glorification: "The hour has come for the Son of Man to be glorified" (John 12:23). So Jesus can say, "Father, glorify your name" (12:28); that is, when Jesus is glorified by the shameful cross, God is glorified because Jesus does God's will. John goes on to say, "A voice came from heaven, 'I have glorified it [Jesus' mission], and I will glorify it again'" (in the death and Resurrection). Jesus did not need to hear this voice, but the crowd (like the readers) did (12:30), perhaps lest they think that Jesus' death was a tragedy. Earlier Jesus had declared, "If I glorify myself, my glory is nothing. It is my Father who glorifies me" (8:54). In his prayer later, Jesus says, "Father, the hour has come; glorify your Son so that the Son may glorify you .... I glorified you on earth by finishing the work that you gave me to do. So now, Father, glorify me in your own presence with the glory that I had in your presence before the world existed" (17:1, 4-5). Here the glorification of Jesus that marked his mission is completed by the return of the *Logos*, the Son, to the Father. John refuses to let the readers separate Jesus' glory in his wonderworking signs from his glory on the cross and rather insists that the event of Jesus as a whole glorifies God, who glorifies him. The Prologue invites us to see the glory throughout the whole event and supremely in the cross. For John the glorification of Jesus occurs not only after the cross but in it. (See " 'Glorification' in John," page 261.)

(3) The setting of Jesus' words in 12:25 also invites comment. When Jesus learns that "some

> The glorification of Jesus that marked his mission is completed by the return of the *Logos*, the Son, to the Father.

Greeks" want to see him (12:20-22), he does not respond by saying, "Well, if my own people will not accept what I have to say, maybe these Gentiles will." Instead, by speaking of his death, he clearly implies that Gentiles will "see" him after the glorification is completed. That is, his mission, like a grain of wheat, will bear much fruit only after it dies (and sprouts), as he observes in 12:24. In other words, without his death and resurrection he would be just "a single grain," a remarkable event in Jewish history but without the capacity to redeem "the world."

Another interpretation of Jesus' death in John 12 is stated in 12:32: "And I, when I am lifted up from the earth, will draw all people to myself." Being "lifted up" has a double meaning: It refers to Jesus' return to the Father by going "up" to heaven (alluded to in 6:62) *and* to his being "lifted up" on the cross, as the narrator points out. Jesus has spoken before of his death as the lifting up of the Son of Man (8:28), and before that compared this lifting up to Moses' lifting up the serpent in the wilderness (3:14). In 12:32 he points to the universal impact of his death (he will "draw all people" to himself) because the whole passage is part of his response to the Greeks' desire to see him. That is, Gentiles will see him when he draws also them to himself. And we are the Gentiles.

Failure or Fulfillment?

In bringing the story of Jesus' public mission to a close, the narrator first explains why Jesus' signs failed to elicit believing (John 12:37-43), then gives Jesus the last word (12:44-50), in which he summarizes the role of his words for those who do not believe and for those who do. The narrator's interpretation (12:37-43) is complex because it consists of his inferences from a particular interpretation of Isaiah. So we have to interpret John's interpretation of passages from Isaiah, which he used to interpret Jesus.

John is not alone in using these passages, for Paul uses Isaiah 53:1 to refer to those who have not believed the gospel (Romans 10:16). Mark uses Isaiah 6:9-10 to account for people's inability to understand Jesus' parables (Mark 4:11-12), and Acts 28:26-27 uses the same passage to account for Jewish unbelief. John 12:37-43 is complicated further by the fact that while 12:38 quotes the Septuagint exactly, 12:40 does not agree completely with either the Hebrew or the Greek Bible. John, like other writers of the day, adapted the wording to fit his point better.

In Isaiah 53 (cited in John 12:38) the nations marvel that they did not recognize God's servant but instead disdained him. Perhaps John assumed that the readers would recall the whole chapter when he quoted only the first verse:

"Lord, who has believed our message,
and to whom has the arm of the Lord been revealed?"

In any case John apparently regards the first verse as a rhetorical question, whose implied answer is "no one" (or almost no one). Also, in John "our message" refers to the words Jesus speaks (12:44-50) just as John understands "the arm of the Lord" as Jesus' mighty deeds, the signs that did not get the desired response. To our amazement, the narrator goes on to use Isaiah 6:9-10 to explain why the people *could* not believe. In Isaiah 6, the prophet is told,

"Make the mind of this people dull,
and stop their ears,
and shut their eyes,
so that they may not look with their eyes,
and listen with their ears,
and comprehend with their minds,
and turn and be healed" (6:10).

But what is commanded in Isaiah is now quoted in John as a report of what has happened: "He *has* blinded their eyes," and so forth. Evidently John saw in Jesus' mission (particularly in the signs) the fulfillment of the command to Isaiah; that is, what Isaiah was told to do, Jesus did. Therefore the people "could not believe."

The narrator recognizes, however, that "many, even of the authorities" (the word used to describe Nicodemus) did believe in Jesus but did not confess this belief openly, lest they "be put out of the synagogue"—the same fear that John attributed to the parents of the formerly blind man (9:22). This danger fits John's time rather than the time of Jesus, even though those who responded positively to Jesus probably were under pressure from the start. We only wish the narrator had said more about those who did believe and did not fear expulsion.

Failure or fulfillment? In the last analysis, that alternative is too stark, for Jesus' mission was both. More troubling to most readers is the claim that people "could not believe" because Jesus had "blinded their eyes and hardened their heart" *so that* they were unable to believe. However, remember that in English, as in Greek, "so that" can express either purpose (in order to) or consequence (so that as a result). Jesus made the same point in 9:39: "I came into this world for judgment so that those who do not see may see, and those who do see may become blind."

> The sort of believing Jesus calls for in this Gospel is not an easy assent to nice ideas.

So Then

The sort of believing Jesus calls for in this Gospel is not an easy assent to nice ideas. For one thing, this Jesus does not allow us to separate the message from the messenger, for he calls on people to believe "in him" and then also insists that one believes "*in him*" when one believes *him*. And this Jesus is neither a simple, one-dimensional figure nor one who meets our expectations. If we are baffled, we are also intrigued and find ourselves suspecting that he is right, even if we do not fully understand why he is right. In fact it is just his strangeness that is the secret of his power to attract and change us. Who needs a Savior just like us?

Do You Want to Become His Disciples, Too?

Because John 1–12 concerns Jesus' public mission to the world, these chapters do not say much about what it means to follow such a Jesus. That is reserved for John 13–17. But already we can sense what is coming: The heart of the call to discipleship is the call to believe in Jesus so deeply that we are not afraid to find ourselves on the outside of whatever "synagogue"—perhaps even a church, as some believers have found out from time to time. Yet we do not decide to become outsiders in order to be believers or to prove we are believers. It's the other way around, for self-alienation no more leads to believing than being a fool makes one "a fool for Christ." The point is that discipleship entails being willing to become an outsider to "the world" for the sake of "the world" as was true in Jesus' case. And that's not easy. It wasn't meant to be.

Who is this Jesus you believe in? How does what you believe conform to what Jesus says about himself?

_____

_____

_____

_____

_____

Prayer

Our Lord, in all generations you have been our home.
You have always been God—

> long before the birth of the mountains,
> even before you created the earth and the world.

At your command we die and turn back to dust,

> but a thousand years mean nothing to you!

They are merely a day gone by

> or a few hours in the night. . . .

Teach us to use wisely all the time we have.

(Psalm 90:1-4, 12, CEV)

"Glorification" in John

Even though such words as *beautify* and *magnify* mean "make beautiful" or "make great," when used of God, *glorify* does not mean that we *make* God glorious but rather that we acknowledge the gloriousness that already characterizes God. So Jesus' glorification of God is really another way of saying what the Prologue asserts: Jesus, the enfleshed *Logos*, made God known not by teaching doctrines about God but by making God's "Godhood" effective in human life. To know God in this sense is more than being informed *about* God; it is to have a sustaining, life-giving relation *to* God. That, according to John, is what Jesus' entire mission aims to achieve. When that occurs, Jesus "glorifies" God, for then God's Godhood becomes real in human life. Likewise, when God "glorifies" Jesus, the Son, God makes Jesus' word and work effective for those who believe. Because Jesus' mission reaches its climax on the cross, that is where the reciprocal glorification of God and Jesus takes place. When glorification occurs, glory is disclosed; for glory can be understood as true excellence made manifest. But only in our believing is God's glory manifest in Jesus.

28 Jesus' Legacy

**By this everyone will know that you are my disciples,
if you have love for one another.**

(John 13:35)

They Have No Wine

When death takes the family matriarch or patriarch, the hub that centered the spokes of the wheel, those still living sense the loss of someone whose place no one can take. But how to honor the departed? With a gravestone? or a sapling? In some cultures the family assembles on the anniversary of the death to remember the deceased. Remembering is especially important when we appropriate for ourselves the good that the departed stood for so that it can flower in us. If we falter here, we will be out of wine sooner than we think.

Beginning With Moses and All the Prophets

John 13–17 has no equivalent in the other Gospels (though in a very limited way Luke comes closest). The entire section has the same setting, the Last Supper (*not* Passover; 13:1). The section falls naturally into three parts: (1) Chapter 13, the footwashing, Judas's betrayal and Peter's denial signaled; (2) Chapters 14–16, Jesus' farewell discourse to the disciples; (3) Chapter 17, Jesus' prayer.

Day 1 John 13; Luke 22:1-34; 1 John 3:18-24; Psalm 41:5-12

(1) Note how carefully the narrator sets the stage (in John 13:1-3) for Jesus' surprising act, described in unusual detail (13:4-5). Note that the theme of future understanding (13:7) has appeared before (12:16; implied at 2:22). Note that in 13:8 Jesus gives one interpretation of the footwashing and in 13:14-17 he offers another.

Day 5 John 17; Romans 8:28-39; Ephesians 4:1-16; Philippians 2:1-13

(1) Note that because no change of location is reported in John 17:1, the disciples overhear Jesus speak to God about the significance of his mission for them.

(2) Note that the disciples are Jesus' own because the Father "gave them" to him (17:6, 9); note also that this theme restates what Jesus says in 6:44, 65 and what is implied at 10:3-5, 14, 26, 27. Observe the similarity between what Jesus says in 10:28-29 and 17:12.

(3) In 17:15 (NRSV), note the difference between the preferred and alternative translations.

(4) Observe that 17:18-19 is the springboard for Jesus' prayer for those who believe as a result of the disciples' mission (17:20-23). In light of "that they may all be one," recall what Jesus said about the one flock in 10:16. Observe that a comparable concern for the unity of the church is found in Ephesians 4:1-16.

Day 6 Read and respond to "Jesus' Legacy" and "Do You Want to Become His Disciples, Too?"

Prayer Concerns

Jesus' Legacy

In ancient times the farewell speech by a significant figure was regarded highly, for it afforded the speaker opportunity to sum up the meaning of a life's work, and to do so in a way that provided guidance for the future. In Greek literature, the most famous farewell speech is that of Socrates. In the Old Testament, we have Jacob's last words in Genesis 49 and Moses' final blessing in Deuteronomy 33. In the New Testament, we have Paul's farewell to the elders of the Ephesian church (Acts 20:17-38) and Jesus' farewell in John. John's readers would not have been surprised to find Jesus speaking as he does—looking backward and forward—at this point in the story.

Since farewell discourses were written after the speaker was off the scene, what the writer has the speaker foretell corresponds to the issues that face the writer and his readers. So John's readers would have understood themselves to be addressed in what Jesus said to the disciples at the supper "back then." The same holds true of us when we read John 13–17 "with the grain," and not as eavesdroppers.

The Last Supper

We already noted that in the Synoptics Jesus institutes the Lord's Supper but does not do so in John, where Jesus' final meal with his disciples is the Last Supper. Consequently, in John there are no words of institution ("This is my body," and so forth). Instead, Jesus speaks extensively with his disciples before praying. What transpired during the meal (John 13) prepares the readers for the discourses (14–16) and the prayer (17) that follow.

The deliberate, solemn, and unprecedented beginning of John 13 signals the importance of what follows. We even learn what was in Jesus' mind and what had occurred in Judas's heart (13:1-3). Then Jesus, to whom the Father has given all things, takes the role of a slave who has nothing and washes and dries the disciples' feet. To Peter's objection Jesus replies, "Unless I wash you, you have no share with me" (13:8)—that is, this washing somehow makes Peter a partner with Jesus. In this action Jesus establishes the disciples' solidarity with him, their participation in him, in what his lifework represents.

In the discourses in John 14–16, Jesus uses various words to express this solidarity, this participation. Here he speaks of it as being made "clean" because that fits the footwashing setting.

Did Jesus wash Judas's feet? The narrator does not say but seems to imply that he did, for Jesus recognized that "You [plural] are clean, though not all of you" (13:10); this observation hardly means that Jesus had not yet gotten around to all the disciples. In other words, in Judas's case the footwashing was in vain. But Jesus, knowing what Judas would do, did not make his own action depend on that of Judas, just as he did not omit washing Peter's feet because of Peter's impending denial. Thus John suggests that Jesus' love is not conditional; rather, it should change conditions. The entire scene dramatizes the significance of Jesus' mission as a whole. In fact, the detail that Jesus took off his robe and then, when he had finished, put it on again (13:4, 12) and returned to the table, symbolizes his leaving his glory to enter the world and his return from the world to glory.

In 13:12-17 Jesus offers another interpretation of his deed, this time emphasizing the self-humbling that his coming into the world expressed: The teacher acts as slave of the students so that they will do for one another as he has done for them. Many readers recall that Paul made a similar point of Jesus' self-humbling in Philippians 2:1-13, especially in 2:6-8: He "emptied himself, taking the form of a slave."

Even though Jesus believed that Judas's betrayal fulfilled Scripture (John 13:18, referring to Psalm 41:9), he did not take Judas's action lightly. According to John 13:21, Jesus was "troubled in spirit" ("troubled" translates the same word used in 11:33 rendered as "deeply moved," NRSV). When the beloved disciple wants to know who the betrayer is, Jesus says, "It is the one to whom I give this piece of bread," and then gives it to Judas, who accepts it. *Then*, says the narrator, "Satan entered into him," taking complete control in order to bring about what Satan had already put into Judas's heart (13:2). John implies that Jesus gave a piece of bread to all the disciples, for had he given it only to Judas, the others would have known he was the betrayer. But when Jesus tells him to "Do quickly what you are going to do," the other disciples do not realize Jesus is telling him to proceed promptly with the betrayal; instead, they draw other conclusions. The concluding comment "And it was night" does more than report the time of day. Jesus' hour was "the world's" darkest night.

Once Judas has gone, Jesus speaks of his death as his glorification that results from God's action.

But he also interprets his earlier command to the disciples to wash one another's feet as he had washed theirs; for now he says, "I give you a new commandment, that you love one another. Just as I have loved you, you also should love one another." In fact, by this reciprocal love "everyone will know that you are my disciples" (13:31-35). In the discourse that follows, Jesus again commands them to love one another (15:12, 17). In John Jesus never asks the disciples to love the neighbor (as in Mark 12:28-31) or to be a neighbor (as was the good Samaritan in Luke 10:29-37), let alone love the enemy (as in Matthew 5:43-48). Instead he asks them to love one another and speaks even more often of their loving him (14:15, 21, 23, 24, 28) and of his exemplary love for them (13:34; 15:9, 12). Many of John's readers today are perplexed by this emphasis on reciprocal, intragroup love, for it seems so out of character with the outward-oriented love commanded by Jesus in the Synoptics.

Remembering that farewell speeches let the speaker emphasize what is important for the writer's own time, the proper question is, Why did John have Jesus speak only of the believers' love for Jesus and of their reciprocating love for one another? Did his first readers need just this emphasis, for reasons we can only surmise? The First Letter of John (probably written by a different author at a slightly later time) may well offer a clue. First John 3:11-17 implies that some Christians have become callous toward the needs of fellow Christians, as does 1 John 4:7-21. (The readers of First John also face theological problems, as in 1 John 2:18-29 for instance.) In other words, the author of John's Gospel may have Jesus emphasize reciprocal love (and love for Jesus) because when he wrote, the problems addressed in First John were already becoming apparent. Besides, the writer of the Gospel, like the writer of the letter, sees the church in a hostile world (John 15:18-25; 16:2; 17:14-16; 1 John 2:15-17; 3:1; 5:4-5). In such circumstances, mutual love is essential lest the community fragment under pressure.

> Mutual, reciprocal love within the Christian community remains an essential obligation today, for without it the church blurs its witness to Jesus' love.

Picture the situation of John's readers: Threatened by ostracism from the Jewish community, facing the possibility of martyrdom (John 16:2-4), and perhaps splitting up over the very theology the Gospel of John emphasizes (see 1 John 2:18-23) so that the faithful must assess those who claim to be prophets (1 John 4:1-6), they need to remember that callousness toward the needy brother or sister is inconsistent with God's love. Mutual, reciprocal love within the Christian community remains an essential obligation today, for without it the church blurs its witness to Jesus' love.

Important as it is to get a sense of how Jesus' words about love might have been especially significant in John's church, we remember that Matthew's church faced similar problems (Matthew 24:9-13 for example); however, Matthew did not hesitate to include both Jesus' command to love the enemy and pray for the persecutor and his criticism of mutual love: "For if you love those who love you, what reward do you have? Do not even the tax collectors do the same?" (Matthew 5:44-46). Those who put the New Testament together did not intend to offer us a choice between John and Matthew; rather by including both they require us to be wise enough to know when and where one needs to be heeded more than the other.

The Final Discourses

Some of Jesus' teachings in John 14–16 are among the best-known and most loved in the whole Gospel and are used regularly at memorial and funeral services. At the same time, these chapters also contain passages that, when placed side by side, leave the careful reader wondering what to conclude.

But first, another matter invites attention— Jesus' response to Thomas's objection, "Lord, we do not know where you are going. How can we know the way?" Jesus replies, "I am the way, and the truth, and the life. No one comes to the Father except through me" (14:5-6). When Jesus' reply is cited in debates over the relation of the Christian religion to other religions, there is often some slippage away from John's perspective. For one thing, Jesus is not talking about Christianity's relation to other religions at all. In John's Gospel, the saying clearly answers Thomas's question, which concerns Jesus' departure to the Father's house (God's heavenly abode). Jesus claims to be the way to the presence of God, and in 14:3 this involves his departure and return to bring believers to God's house (presumably at their death).

267

Most important, remember that the Jesus who says this is not a rabbi from Nazareth but the enfleshed *Logos* through whom God created everything, including people. So if no one was created apart from the *Logos*, if no one's life is derived directly from the Father, then it follows that no one going to God can bypass the *Logos* enfleshed either. So what Jesus' assertion calls for is pondering the fact that his claim to be the sole access to God is the inevitable consequence of being the sole one through whom God created everyone. In John, Jesus' exclusiveness and his universality as *Logos* are as inseparable as two sides of the same sheet of paper. Again we see why the Prologue is so important: It tells us who became Jesus. In short, according to John, Jesus is the sole way to God not because he is superior to Buddha or Muhammed or Moses but because he is the *Logos* enfleshed. Without that, the assertion collapses. With it Jesus' claim may still be offensive but at the same time also a promise.

> In John, Jesus' exclusiveness and his universality as *Logos* are as inseparable as two sides of the same sheet of paper.

Of these chapters' side-by-side statements that perplex us, the most important are those that refer to *who* will come after Jesus has departed. On one hand, Jesus promises that he will come (14:3, 18, 28; 16:22) or that he and the Father will come (14:23). On the other hand, he promises a *replacement*, the "Advocate" (NRSV, which translates *paraklētos*), the Spirit (14:16, 26; 15:26; 16:7). Furthermore, not only does Jesus refer to the Spirit as "another Advocate" (implying he is the first one, 14:16), but he says clearly that the Advocate will come only if he has gone away; Jesus and the Advocate cannot be present at the same time (16:7). So we wonder how these promises are related. How are they to be combined into one teaching?

Probably we should not combine them at all but keep them separate. That is, apart from 14:3 (which might refer to Jesus' coming to the dying believer) and 14:23 (which speaks of Jesus and the Father coming to reside with the disciples), all the other passages about Jesus' coming refer to his coming to the disciples at Easter (14:18, 28; 16:22) and so should be read in light of the Easter story in 20:1-29. In fact, what 16:23 foresees ("on that day

[when the disciples' pain will turn into joy, 16:20-22] you will ask nothing of me") is exactly what the Resurrection appearances show: The disciples do not ask; Jesus speaks. Keeping the promises separate avoids regarding the coming of the Spirit as John's reinterpretation of the Second Coming of Christ, a view sometimes advanced. In short, Jesus' coming to the disciples refers to the Resurrection; the coming of the Spirit, to something else.

If the foregoing way of reading John is on target, the way is open to consider what Jesus says about the coming of the Spirit, whom he consistently calls "the Paraclete." No translation does justice to the Greek word, which literally means "one called to be alongside" to help; "Advocate," "Helper" as an alternative, NRSV; "advocate," REB; "Counselor," NIV. The New Jerusalem Bible consistently keeps the word *Paraclete*, the English form of *paraklētos*. Actually, what Jesus is talking about cannot be found in the meaning of the word itself but only in what he says about the Paraclete's function.

First, the Paraclete will be *with* and *in* the disciples permanently (14:16-17). Whereas Jesus came and departed, the Spirit will come and remain. Since Jesus says that his departure is necessary for the Paraclete to come, we may infer that the transient event of Jesus makes the continuing presence of the Spirit possible. To restate it, without the temporary event of Jesus in the time of Pontius Pilate, there would be no permanent experience of the Spirit in the Christian community.

Second, the gulf between Jesus and "the world" will continue; therefore "the world cannot receive" the Spirit, for "it neither sees him [at work?] nor knows him" (14:17). In short, "the world" is on one side of the gulf; Jesus, the Spirit, and the disciples are on the other side. In 15:18-25 Jesus says the world hates the disciples as it first hated Jesus, and for the same reason: Neither Jesus nor the disciples "belong to the world" (literally, are *of* the world). True, Jesus was never *of* the world but the disciples had to be chosen "out of the world" (15:19). In fact, Jesus could choose them out of the world because he was not *of* the world.

In 16:8-11 Jesus explains further the Paraclete's relation to the world: When he arrives (and dwells *with* and *in* the disciples), he will function as the prosecuting attorney in a cosmic court, where he will "prove the world wrong." As a result, the world will be convicted and proved wrong on three counts—sin, righteousness, and judgment. Jesus' brief explanation of this invites additional explanation.

First, because the world does not believe in Jesus, it does not know what sin really is, though it thinks it does when it seeks Jesus' death because he healed on the sabbath (5:16; 9:16) and implied his equality with God (5:17-18). The world also thought he was a sinner, for it accused him of blasphemy (10:31-36), being demon-possessed (7:20; 8:48; 10:19-20), and of leading the people astray (7:47). The presence of the God-sent Spirit in the ongoing community is here regarded as convicting evidence that the world was wrong, and that Jesus was right in regarding the world's refusal to believe in the Son as the decisive sin—"You will die in your sins unless you believe that I am he [that I am]" (8:24; see also 9:41 and 15:22-25). John 16:8-11 does not mean to say that the world has no sense whatever of sin; the sin in view here is centered in declaring Jesus to be "a criminal" (18:30).

Next, because Jesus goes to the Father, the world is wrong about righteousness (rightness, what conforms to God's will). Why? Because Jesus' return to the Father shows that the Father deems Jesus to be right in what he said and did. Jesus' return to the Father who sent him vindicates Jesus' claims to do as the Father told him to do—a point Jesus made repeatedly (5:30; 6:38-40; 8:55; 12:49). The Spirit proves that the world is wrong and Jesus is right in obeying God by giving his life voluntarily: "No one takes it from me, but I lay it down of my own accord . . . . I have received this command from my Father" (10:18). In short, the world is wrong about righteousness because it does not understand that Jesus' voluntary self-giving is his righteousness, his obedience to God's will.

Finally, "the ruler of this world has been condemned" precisely when the world condemned Jesus to death; therefore the Spirit who comes afterward proves that the world was wrong about judgment, for it does not know what true judgment (God's judgment) really is. Had the Spirit not come, had there been no ongoing community in which he resides, the world's judgment would have been validated.

The image of the Spirit or Paraclete as a prosecuting attorney in a cosmic court (an ancient image) implies that the work of the Spirit is done in the community of believers who are "on trial" because they are harassed and live under the threat of death (16:1-2). But the Spirit does not inspire believers to be prosecuting attorneys, always accusing the world. Rather, the presence of the Spirit with the community itself is the evidence that proves the world is wrong about sin, righteousness, and judgment because the Spirit enables the Christian community to be *in* the world but not *of* it.

Another saying about the Spirit appears in 16:13-15, where Jesus says, "When the Spirit of truth comes, he will guide you into all the truth; for he will speak not on his own [just as Jesus did not speak on his own], but will speak whatever he hears, and he will declare to you the things that are to come. He will glorify me, because he will take what is mine and declare it to you. All that the

> **The Spirit is in no way autonomous; rather, the truth into which he will guide the community is nothing other than the truth of Jesus, whose truth is that of the Father.**

Father has is mine. For this reason I said that he will take what is mine and declare it to you." In other words, the Spirit is in no way autonomous; rather, the truth into which he will guide the community is nothing other than the truth of Jesus, whose truth is that of the Father. Later, Christian theology wrestled with the right way to express what is implied here about the relation of the Father, Son, and Spirit, and formulated the doctrine of the Trinity as a result. But the concern of this passage is the role of the Spirit in the believers—to interpret the meaning of Jesus, who interprets the meaning of God. The most dangerous thing a person can do with this passage is to quote only the first part—which promises that the Spirit will guide into all truth—and ignore the rest. Whenever that occurs, Christians' "spiritual experiences" displace Jesus himself. And then, the Spirit indeed "speaks on his own." But the passage (16:13-15) insists that going deeper into the truth by the aid of the Spirit does not take one farther from Jesus but ever more deeply into the meaning of Jesus.

What Jesus says in 14:26 makes the same point: The Holy Spirit "will teach you everything, and remind you of all that I have said to you." This reminding is more than sheer recollection of Jesus' words; otherwise, we would have no need for the Spirit to "teach," for memorizing would be sufficient. Here too the experience of the Spirit is not a substitute for Jesus; rather, the Spirit facilitates continual learning of what Jesus' teachings mean. This saying, like 16:13-15, also implies that simply learning the facts about what Jesus actually said and did is not enough. We must continually learn through the Spirit what Jesus' words and actions mean because their meaning was not evident when Jesus said and did them. Recall that in 16:12-13 Jesus says, "I have many things to say to you, but you cannot bear them now. When the Spirit of truth comes ...." Indeed, the Gospel itself is written from this standpoint—the post-Easter, Spirit-taught meaning of Jesus. While the writer never claims to be inspired, he does report that Jesus said that the Spirit "will testify on my behalf. You also are to testify because you have been with me from the beginning" (15:26-27). Thus the Spirit-taught church is to absorb and repeat the Spirit's testimony about Jesus. In doing so, the church will "keep" Jesus' word (14:23)—not simply be preserving it, but by living it.

The Spirit's coming to be *with* and *in* the disciples in no way overshadows their relation to Jesus. Jesus speaks not only of his words but also of himself *abiding in them* and of their abiding *in him* (15:4-9), and *in his love* (15:10). To express this reciprocal indwelling, Jesus uses another *I am* saying: "I am the true vine" (15:1). This image allows him to emphasize the necessary participation of the disciples in him: "Just as the branch cannot bear fruit by itself unless it abides in the vine, neither can you unless you abide in me. I am the vine, you are the branches. Those who abide in me and I in them bear much fruit, because apart from me you can do nothing" (15:4-5). And failure to bear fruit has serious consequences: The fruitless vine is pruned away by God the vinegrower and burned (15:1-2, 6).

While this language recalls what John the Baptist said (Matthew 3:10) and what Jesus said in the Sermon on the Mount as well (Matthew 7:15-20), they spoke of fruit trees, not vines. More important are the uses made of the image of burning fruitless branches. The Baptizer uses the image to urge repentance, a moral and spiritual U-turn in order to be prepared for the judgment. In the Sermon on the Mount, Jesus uses the image to express judgment on the false prophets who are bad trees bearing bad fruit—a harmful influence on the community. In John, however, Jesus talks neither of repentance (as noted, the word never appears in this Gospel or in the letters of John) nor of good and bad fruit but rather of "fruit" (John 15:4), "much fruit," (15:8) and "fruit that will last" (15:16, the same word that is translated "abide" in the previous paragraph). In other words, in John fruit-bearing itself is the point, and here that means

being (or becoming, depending on which manuscripts are translated) Jesus' disciples.

The reader who senses that the thought is moving in a circle is right: The disciples are to bear fruit; those who bear fruit are (or become) disciples. In other words, the point of being a disciple is to be a disciple, not to achieve something else, something better or more

> **The point of being a disciple is to be a disciple, not to achieve something else, something better or more important.**

important. Nor is being a disciple a stage through which one passes on the way to a preferred, advanced status; for all the "abiding" language means "remaining," not sojourning. Those whose abiding is expressed as obedience to Jesus' commands are called his "friends" (15:15)—friends he loved so much that, according to 15:13, he voluntarily died for them. We have no reason to think that John, in reporting that Jesus says the disciples are not his slaves but his friends, is criticizing Paul, who calls himself Christ's slave; further, Paul writes often of being "in Christ."

John's way of portraying the work of the Spirit differs from Paul's view of the Spirit. For Paul the Spirit is enabling power, power that enables some to speak, others to work miracles, still others to speak in tongues, and so forth—new capacities understood as gifts of the Spirit (1 Corinthians 12). Not in John. Here the Spirit is interpreting presence, reminding and teaching. By including both Paul and John the New Testament is not offering us a choice but an enrichment; for without John we might easily assume that the Spirit does mostly the unusual, and without Paul we might think that the Spirit works mostly on the brain.

Jesus' Concluding Prayer

Luke often reports that Jesus prayed (Luke 3:21; 5:16; 6:12; 9:18, 28; 11:1) but only twice says what he prayed (once in Gethsemane, 22:42; once on the cross, 23:34). But John never says that Jesus prayed without reporting also *what* he prayed (John 11:41-42; 12:27-28; 17). In John 17 Jesus first asks the Father to glorify him in the appointed hour of his death (17:1-5), next recounts his mission's import for the disciples (17:6-19), then prays for future believers (17:20-24) before concluding in 17:25-26 that he has made the

Father's name known. The themes of the prayer, however, overlap the various parts. For the readers the prayer serves as a focused reminder of what Jesus said before and so prepares them for the Passion story that follows.

Because Jesus has in view his mission as a whole, he speaks of it as already finished, though the climax is yet to come; so "finishing" in 17:4 translates a form of the same verb that he uses at the very end of his life, "It is finished" (19:30). So too, in 17:11 he speaks as if he were already returning to the Father: "I am no longer in the world . . . and I am coming to you" (also 17:13); and in 17:12 he says, "While I was with them," although he is still with the disciples at the supper. Jesus can speak of his mission as completed because the Passion story will change neither his mission's character nor its purpose. In John, theologically what will happen then dramatically and definitively enacts what has already occurred, and brings it to completion.

Since Jesus prays from the standpoint of his whole mission completed, we can understand why his words about the disciples are more positive than before. The disciples have received the words that Jesus received from the Father, know that he came from the Father, and have believed that God sent him (17:8, 25)—everything Jesus asked for in his mission. Moreover, he has "been glorified in them." Further, he has "sent them into the world" as he has been sent (17:18). Jesus alludes to the betrayer (17:12) but not to the denier, nor is there any hint now that the disciples did not understand him. So too, the standpoint of the finished mission accounts for the fact that in 17:14 Jesus says "the world has hated" the disciples, something 16:1-2 foresees and 15:18-21 explains in advance.

Jesus also prays for John's readers, "those who will believe in me through their word," and specifically "that they may all be one" (17:20-21). The context suggests that what Jesus asks for is not only the unity of the later believers among themselves but also their oneness with the disciples—the unity of the church across the years. Moreover, the unity of the church for which Jesus prays is to reflect his unity with God, "so that they may be one, as we are one, I in them and you in me, that they may be completely one" (17:22-23). The purpose of this remarkable unity (impossible without mutual love) is "so that the world may know that you have sent me and have loved them even as you have loved me" (17:22-23). The similarity between this statement and 17:21 shows that believing and knowing are inseparable, for a person cannot believe that God sent Jesus without

knowing that he did, nor can a person know that God sent Jesus without believing. In 14:31 the world's knowing depends on Jesus' love of God, expressed in his death. What is new here, then, is that the world's knowing and believing are to be the result of the church's unity. Thus the church's life is to bear witness to the identity and significance of Jesus, a witness to the very world that hates the believers so that perhaps the world will cease to refuse the light. Whether or not John foresaw the problems that surface in First John (including denial of the Incarnation in 1 John 4:2-3 and schism in 1 John 2:18-19), his Gospel would have been read by those whom the letter addresses; and they may well have prayed that Jesus' prayer would be answered. Fortunately, many of today's divided Christians still do; unfortunately, not all of them do.

So Then

John 13–17 gives us much to think about, unusually so— the example of Jesus, the necessity of remaining with Jesus, the role of the Spirit, the church's relation to the world—to name the most obvious. Two of Jesus' assertions are not to be overlooked—the one that "it is to your advantage that I go away," for otherwise the Paraclete will not come (16:7); the other that believers will "do the works that I do and, in fact, will do greater works than these, because I am going to the Father" (14:12). The one is as challenging as the other. The first closes the door to that wistfulness that says, "If only I had been there!" The other opens the door to discovering what can happen when believers remember Jesus and are led deeper into his meaning because the Paraclete has come to stay.

Don't overlook the fact that in these chapters Jesus speaks of the believers' joy, not their happiness. In 15:11 he says, "I have said these things to you [he has just spoken of the vine and the branches] so that my joy may be in you, and that your joy may be complete [literally, 'fulfilled']." And in 16:22, having promised that the disciples' pain at his death will "turn into joy," Jesus goes on to say, "So you have pain now; but I will see you again [after the Resurrection], and your hearts will rejoice, and no one will take your joy from you." Were he to wander into some joyless churches today, he might shake his head and say, "I must have been talking about someone else," for a joyless believer is a contradiction in terms. Jesus' legacy embraces joy as well as the obligation to love; both are generated by what he has bequeathed to us by his remembered word.

Do You Want to Become His Disciples, Too?

Before answering yes, perhaps we should ponder the likelihood that the most challenging obligation Jesus lays on the disciples is that they should love *one another*! Often it seems easier to love the poor, the marginalized, the victimized, especially when we ourselves are secure; for then we have the satisfaction of doing something for "them." But the fellow believer, whose prejudices we abhor, whose pride we disdain, whose lackadaisical attitudes and unreliability make our own church work more difficult? To love such people is asking a lot. Yet if "charity begins at home," so does love. Fortunately, Jesus did not ask us to like one another or even to agree with one another, not even to put up with one another, but to exercise the love that he exemplified when he washed feet. That kind of love seeks the well-being of the other. Even if Christians' reciprocal love is neither the whole story nor one of the "greater works," it is at least a sign that we do care, a sign signifying that our feet too have been washed. The call to discipleship includes the invitation to fill our basins and get our towels. Feet are waiting to be washed.

What have you learned about Jesus that you want to pass on to others? (Before answering this question, reflect on and respond to what is called for on page 273.)

_____

_____

_____

_____

_____

Prayer

You created me and put me together.
Make me wise enough to learn
    what you have commanded . . . .
I serve you, LORD. Comfort me with your love,
    just as you have promised.
I love to obey your Law! Have mercy and let me live . . . .
Show that you love me and let me live,
    so that I may obey all of your commands.

(Psalm 119:73, 76-77, 88, CEV)

Jesus' Farewell
John 14–17

Describe how Jesus' farewell words to his disciples also address you as a disciple.

What comfort and guidance do you draw from Jesus' farewell words?

273

29 Mission Completed

Pilate asked him, "So are you a king?" Jesus answered, "You say that I am a king. For this I was born, and for this I came into the world, to testify to the truth. Everyone who belongs to the truth listens to my voice."

(John 18:37)

They Have No Wine

Innocent suffering gives us moral agony, for we can't make sense of it, though we are convinced it must make sense somehow to someone. So too, we are perplexed when we see someone willing to suffer for another's benefit. With so much moral darkness about, how is it there are also these flickers of goodness? Where did they come from? What sustains them? If we think long enough and deeply enough, we may ask ourselves, Why am I suspicious of those who suffer willingly for others? Do I hope, or do I fear, that someday I might depend on such a person?

Beginning With Moses and All the Prophets

This week's readings return us to familiar territory—the Passion story and the Easter discoveries. Because we already noted how John's Passion and appearance stories differ from Mark, here we will compare John and Luke while focusing on John. We will also observe this Gospel's literary artistry. The Resurrection appearances are included in the study of the Passion story because John, more than any other Gospel, regards them as part of the completion of Jesus' mission.

Day 1 John 18:1-27; Luke 22:39-71

(1) Note that John 18:1-2 explains why Judas knew where Jesus would be found, whereas Luke 22:39, 47 does not. Note that only John mentions the garden, and only Mark and Matthew give the name of the place (Mark 14:32; Matthew 26:36).

274

(2) Observe that Judas need not identify Jesus in the dark with a kiss (as in Mark 14:43-45; Luke 22:47-48) because here Jesus identifies himself (John 18:4-5). Observe that Jesus' self-identification ("I am he," literally, "I am") causes the crowd to fall to the ground—because they recognize that "I am" is the self-proclamation of the divine (see "The 'I Am' Sayings of Jesus," page 241).

(3) Note that only John says who cut off the ear of the slave and that only in Luke does Jesus heal the wound (John 18:10; Luke 22:49-51). Observe that although John has no Gethsemane story, Jesus' rebuke of Peter (18:11) echoes Jesus' prayer in Luke 22:42.

(4) **GC 29-1** Note that John divides the story of Peter's denial into two parts (John 18:15-18 and 18:25-27) and places Jesus' exchange with the high priest between them; as a result, the story moves smoothly from the cock's crow at dawn to the transfer of Jesus to Pilate "early in the morning" (18:28). Note that John does not report Peter's response to the cock's crow, as does Luke 22:61-62, and that John explains how Peter got into the courtyard (John 18:15-16) but Luke does not (Luke 22:54-55).

(5) **GC 29-1** Observe that in John Jesus is not taken to the Sanhedrin (the council) as in Luke 22:66, but only to Annas (John 18:12-14, note the cross-reference to 11:45-53), and that what transpires there (18:19-24) differs from what is reported in Luke 22:54, 66 (nothing in John corresponds to Luke's report of Jesus before the Sanhedrin in 22:67-71).

Day 2 John 18:28–19:16; Luke 23:1-25

(1) Observe the literary skill with which the narrator tells the story of Jesus before Pilate. The action moves in and out of Pilate's headquarters.

(2) Note that in John 18:31 Pilate recognizes that the priests have already judged Jesus to be "a criminal" on the basis of Jewish law (18:30) and so refuses to get involved. Note also that the Jews' response shows that Jesus' punishment too has already been decided but needs to be legalized by Rome. Note that in 18:32 the narrator reminds the readers of 12:32-33, where Jesus speaks of his death as being "lifted up"—that is, on the cross. Note also that the narrator's comment assumes that the Jewish authorities had authority to stone to death certain offenders but wanted Rome to crucify Jesus, yet did not say so until later (19:6).

(3) **GC 29-2** Observe that in questioning Jesus privately (18:33-38), Pilate attempts to learn whether Jesus claims to be "the King of the Jews"—a claim that would justify crucifixion. Note that Jesus' counter-question aims to disclose whether Pilate's question is sincere. Note that Jesus redefines his kingship (not "of" this world), and that 18:38 implies that Pilate understood Jesus and so found "no case against him" but offers to release "the King of the Jews" in order to taunt the Jews (18:39). Note also that whereas in Matthew 27:16-21 Pilate twice offers a choice (Barabbas or Jesus), in John he mentions only Jesus (18:39) but the crowd calls for Barabbas instead. Did Pilate release Barabbas?

(4) Note that Pilate is frightened by the real charge against Jesus (John 19:7-8). Note that Jesus does not tell Pilate where he (Jesus) is from but does tell him where Pilate's power is from (19:9-11).

(5) Observe how Pilate was outmaneuvered (19:12). Note that the narrator reminds the readers of the irony of the situation: On "the day of Preparation for the Passover," celebrating Israel's liberation from Egypt, the chief priests tell Pilate, "We have no king but the emperor" (19:15).

Day 3 John 19:17-30; Mark 15:21-39; Luke 23:26-49; Psalms 22:1-21; 69:9-21

(1) Note that John 19:17 points out that Jesus carried his cross "by himself," whereas the Synoptics say that Simon was coerced into doing it for him (Luke 23:26).

(2) **GC 29-3** Note that John does not identify the two crucified with Jesus as "criminals" as does Luke 23:32. Observe that John does not say Jesus asked God to forgive his crucifiers (as in Luke 23:34) or that he was mocked (23:35-40) or that he responded positively to the penitent criminal (23:40-43).

(3) Observe that while all the Gospels report the casting of lots for Jesus' clothes, only John tells us that the exact details fulfilled Scripture (Psalm 22:18).

(4) Note that in John, among the women standing near the cross (not "at a distance" with "all his acquaintances," as in Luke 23:49) were his mother and the beloved disciple, and that only in John does Jesus make provision for her (John 19:25-27).

(5) Note that the narrator regards Jesus' admission that he is thirsty as a fulfillment of Psalm 22:15 (the narrator might imply that what was given Jesus fulfilled Psalm 69:21).

Day 4 John 19:31-42; Luke 23:50-56; Exodus 12:43-49; Deuteronomy 21:22-23; Psalm 34:15-22; Zechariah 12:10-11

(1) Note that only John reports that the soldiers pierced Jesus' side but did not break his legs as Pilate had ordered (John 19:31-34); note also that the narrator regards the latter as the fulfillment of Exodus 12:46 (which pertains to the lamb eaten at Passover) and the piercing as the fulfillment of Zechariah 12:10-11 (which, in turn, might allude to the suffering servant in Isaiah 52:13–53:12). Note also the narrator's keen interest in the truth of the story (19:35).

(2) Note that the narrator assumes he does not need to explain what the flow of blood and water means or why it is important.

(3) GC 29-4 Note that only John says Nicodemus helped Joseph of Arimathea to bury Jesus (John 19:39-40), though he does not explain how they got together on the project. Note that whereas Nicodemus brought a huge amount of spices with which to bury Jesus, in Luke women brought them *after* Jesus was buried and the sabbath had passed (Luke 23:56; 24:1).

Day 5 John 20; Matthew 28:16-20; Mark 16:1-8; Luke 24:1-53

   (1) Note that from the emptiness of the tomb Mary Magdalene infers that someone has removed Jesus' body to an unknown place, not that Jesus has been raised from the dead.
   (2) When the beloved disciple saw the empty tomb, he "believed" (20:8). Note that we are not told what he believed—that Jesus had been resurrected? that the tomb was really empty?
   (3) [GC-29-5] Note that whereas the Synoptics say that angelic figures first announced Jesus' resurrection (Matthew 28:2-7; Mark 16:5-7; Luke 24:4-5), in John Mary learns of Jesus' resurrection from Jesus himself (20:18).
   (4) Note that only after the Resurrection does Jesus say that his Father/God is also the disciples' Father/God (20:17). What does this imply about becoming "children of God" in John 1:12-13?
   (5) Observe that on Easter night Jesus appears "among" the disciples (not confrontationally in front of them), despite locked doors (implying that this is indeed Jesus but that he is now different). Note also that their rejoicing (20:20) fulfills Jesus' word in 16:20-22. Note as well that Jesus' words about "sending" the disciples carries out 17:18.
   (6) Note that here for the first time Jesus speaks of forgiveness (20:23), and he authorizes the disciples to give or withhold forgiveness in a way that recalls Matthew 16:19.

Day 6 Read and respond to "Mission Completed" and "Do You Want to Become His Disciples, Too?"

Prayer Concerns

Mission Completed

John 18–20 is the most integrated, smoothly flowing, extended narrative in the whole Gospel. Here John's narrative is closer to that of the Synoptics while still remaining distinct in content. Suggestions of things to look for in assigned Scripture repeatedly point to certain similarities and differences between John and Luke in order to assist a more careful reading of John, one that does not unwittingly read the Synoptics into John. Because John 18–20 is a coherent account of the way Jesus completed his mission, it deserves careful attention.

As the climax of the Gospel, John 18–20 repeatedly draws our attention to what Jesus said and did before his arrest. John 13–17 also does this. As a result, Chapters 18–20 reinforce in story form what John 13–17 gives as largely discourse. So, we'll look back at the whole Gospel through the lens of John 18–20.

Do Not Judge by Appearances

Jesus' counsel in John 7:24, though addressed to his opponents, also tells us how to read John's Passion story as the Gospel's climax. That is, if we were to judge what went on by appearances, we would read the Passion story as Jesus' defeat: He was betrayed by Judas (18:2); "arrested . . . and bound" (18:12); denied three times by Peter (18:15-18, 25-27); flogged, mocked, and humiliated (19:1-5); used by Pilate to taunt the Jews, "Here is your King!" (19:14); crucified with two others similarly subjected to Rome's most horrible mode of execution (19:18); his clothes divided among his crucifiers and his seamless tunic the prize given by the throw of the dice (19:23-24); his thirst assuaged with wine gone sour (19:28-29). No wonder his last words, "It is finished," can also mean, "It's over!" And while his legs were not broken, his side was pierced to make sure he really was dead (19:31-34). At the supper his last words to his disciples were, "Take courage; I have conquered the world" (16:33). Judged by appearances, he surely was wrong, for he turned out to be helpless and unhelped, a victim not a victor.

But surely John did not report that Jesus claimed to have defeated the world in order to show how mistaken he proved to be; rather, John included that remarkable declaration because he was convinced Jesus was right. We may surmise that this conviction was rooted ultimately in another conviction, namely, Jesus' resurrection. And that conviction was confirmed by the experience of the Spirit that keeps unfolding the truth of what Jesus said.

But if Jesus had been right all along, despite appearances, then John's task was clear: to write the Jesus story in such a way that the real truth about him was not apparent because it did not fit appearances. Consequently, in this Gospel few things are what they appear to be; rather, most events, and most of what Jesus says, mean something more, and often other than what they appear to mean. Students of language identify such speech and writing as irony. The storyteller who uses irony counts on the hearer

> **John's task was clear: to write the Jesus story in such a way that the real truth about him was not apparent because it did not fit appearances.**

or reader to recognize irony, even though persons in the story do not. In fact, the more the reader sees the irony, whether in what was said or in the situation in which it was said, the more the reader understands what is really going on in the story. The reader who is aware of the writer's use of irony is in a privileged position because the reader does not need to wait until the end of the story to grasp the deeper meaning in the story but is aware of the meaning all along. By using irony, the Gospel writer lures the attentive reader into sharing his understanding of the real meaning of what is being reported. With these observations in mind we look at how John writes about Jesus and Pilate (18:28–19:16).

Two aspects of the setting are ironic. First, the priests, who want the pagan Roman to carry out what they have decided, do not enter Pilate's "headquarters" because they do not want to become defiled. (From John's angle, they are already "defiled" by their decision regarding Jesus.) So they remain outside, in effect making Pilate, the embodiment of Roman power, come to them (irony applied to Rome). This leads to the second ironic aspect: Pilate goes back and forth (seven times) between Jesus and the priests. Pilate is caught between his subjects and his prisoner. The more he appears to exercise his power (and moral judgment in finding no case against Jesus), the less power he actually has; for he is manipulated and finally cornered by the shout, "If you release this man, you are no friend of the emperor. Everyone who claims to be a king sets himself against the emperor" (19:12). Thus Pilate, who according to appearances has ample power, is in a position where he must decide whether to be a friend of Caesar or befriend his prisoner. The irony of the situation expresses the narrator's disdain for priests and Pilate alike and invites the readers to share it.

Sometimes a writer uses irony to show that the real truth is the opposite of what appears to be the truth. Such is clearly the case in 19:2-5, which reports that Jesus was crowned with thorns and dressed in royalty's purple robe. The soldiers even "kept coming up to him, saying, 'Hail, King of the Jews!' and striking him on the face." To all appearances, this prisoner is not king but victim. Yet the readers who see the irony of it know that Jesus really is the King of the Jews. And Jesus too, knowing that his kingship is not "of" this world (18:36), accepts the irony of this mockery and then comes out of the building (note that he was not brought out) and "wearing the crown of thorns and the purple robe" presents himself to the crowd (19:5). Pilate, seeing the irony of the situation, sneers at the crowd, "Here is the man!" The crowd calls for his crucifixion. Again Pilate taunts them, "Take him yourselves and crucify him," knowing full well that only he could give the order. When he has "the King of the Jews" posted on the cross—in three languages so no one would miss it—he expresses the truth while mocking it.

Words that have more than one meaning are especially useful for irony because the writer and the readers who are in on the secret know what is really being said while the persons to whom it is said understand something else. A clear instance of this is Jesus' response to Pilate's claim to have "power to release you, and power to crucify you." When Jesus replies, "You would have no power over me unless it had been given you from above (*anōthen* again), Pilate might well have taken this to refer to his appointment by Caesar; but Jesus means that Pilate's power over him is God-given (19:10-11)—and Pilate doesn't know it.

The whole depiction of Jesus before Pilate is ironic in detail after detail, for when judged by appearances, Jesus is on trial; yet the story is told in such a way that perceptive readers know the opposite is true: Pilate is on trial before Jesus, and he does not realize that in condemning Jesus he is condemning himself. John writes this way because he believes Jesus was right in saying that the Paraclete would prove the world wrong about judgment because the ruler of this world (including Satan's Roman agent) is judged (16:8-11).

John's readers have been alerted repeatedly to the irony of what we call "the Passion story"—itself an unwitting irony as far as John is concerned, since this Gospel does not emphasize Jesus' suffering but his glorification. Perhaps we should call John 18–20 "The Glorification Story." We recall that when Jesus learned of some Greeks' interest in seeing him, he responded, "The hour has come for the Son of Man to be glorified" (12:23; also 17:1). At the supper, after Judas's departure, Jesus said, "Now the Son of Man has been glorified, and God has been glorified in him . . . . God will also glorify him in himself and will glorify him at once" (13:31-32). Jesus can also speak of his impending glorification: "So now, Father, glorify me in your own presence with the glory that I had in your presence before the world existed" (17:5). In other words, Jesus' final glorification begins in his humiliating death on earth and ends in the Father's presence. For John Jesus' death and resurrection are two "moments" in one event, his return to the Father. The world thinks it got rid of him; the readers know otherwise.

> For John Jesus' death and resurrection are two "moments" in one event, his return to the Father. The world thinks it got rid of him; the readers know otherwise.

It Is Finished

Although Jesus' last words do not say what is finished, the reader knows Jesus is not referring just to the Crucifixion but to the entire "work" that the Father gave him to do. Accordingly, "is finished" correctly translates the perfect tense, which ancient Greeks used to express completed action with continuing results. For example, "the bucket is filled" means that it was filled and remains filled; "the bucket was filled" does not indicate whether it is still filled or was tipped over afterward and is now empty. Jesus' last words not only say that his task was finished but that it remains completed.

These words also point us back across the Gospel's whole account. To begin with, as mentioned repeatedly, Jesus' death occurs at the right time, when his "hour" has come, not before, as both the narrator (John 7:30; 8:20; 13:1) and Jesus (2:4; 12:23, 27; 17:1) point out. John does not confuse the readers by mentioning the literal hour of the day when Jesus was crucified and when he died (as does Mark 15:25, 34), for in John this "hour" refers to the whole series of events from the arrest to the death. At the same time, in keeping with John's penchant for double meaning, the "hour" occurs on the day of preparation for the Passover, which begins at sundown (that year Passover coincided with the sabbath; John 19:31); and the narrator reminds the readers that "it was about noon" when Pilate handed Jesus over to be crucified (19:14-16). Jesus died at the same "hour" Passover lambs were being slaughtered for the meal that night. John does not point this out, for he assumes his readers will understand the implication of this detail. John may also have assumed his readers would recall the way Isaiah depicted God's servant:

"He was oppressed, and he was afflicted,
    yet he did not open his mouth;
like a lamb that is led to the slaughter,
    and like a sheep that before its shearers is silent,
        so he did not open his mouth" (Isaiah 53:7);

nor did Jesus during one encounter with Pilate in John 19:8-9.

Next, when Jesus' "hour" arrived, he laid down his life voluntarily (John 10:17-18; 12:27). Accordingly, this voluntariness is carried out in the story of his arrest. Judas brought a detachment of soldiers (*speira* is the Greek for the Latin *cohors*, 600 troops, though the unit may not always have had its full number), together with the police from the chief priests and Pharisees—as if to capture an insurrectionist and his followers (another bit of irony). In response Jesus identified himself and asked that his followers not be arrested with him (18:3-8). In John the disciples did not flee; they were spared arrest by Jesus' intervention on their behalf, implying fulfillment of 10:15. In other words, Jesus was not captured; he gave himself up. Judged by appearances, of course, he had little choice; but what John wants us to see is that Jesus was true to his word: No one takes the life of one who lays it down (see 10:18). Consistently then, when Jesus stands before Pilate and says that his kingship is not "of" this world, he explains that if it were of this world, his "followers would be fighting" to prevent his arrest (18:36). This comment reminds us of Jesus' rebuke of Peter, who

had used a sword to cut off Malchus's ear (18:10-11), as well as of the earlier time when Jesus eluded the crowd he had fed because he "realized that they were about to come and take him by force to make him king" (6:15). Had he not evaded the crowd, he would have agreed that his kingship is of this world.

Another instance when details in the Passion story take us back to earlier parts of the Gospel appears when the Jews point out that Jesus "claimed to be the Son of God" (19:7). We recall that his relation to God—his referring to God as Father— had already prompted efforts to kill Jesus (5:17-18; 10:33-39). Now this issue is made the key factor in the strategy—and it works.

Finally, John's account of Jesus' burial also reminds us of what had been said earlier. In the first place Joseph of Arimathea was a disciple, "though a secret one because of his fear of the Jews" (19:38)—a fear mentioned several times before (7:12-13; 9:22-23; 12:42-43) and perhaps implied in the detail that Nicodemus came to Jesus at night. Ironically, Joseph feared the Jews but not Pilate. Perhaps John hints that Nicodemus too was a secret disciple, for not only does he join Joseph, but when he spoke up for Jesus (7:45-52), the Pharisees came close to calling him a follower of Jesus: "Surely you are not also from Galilee, are you?"

> **Jesus' public mission was not terminated; it was completed and remains finished.**

Taken together, these various threads leading back to earlier parts of the Gospel imply that Jesus' public mission was not terminated; it was completed and remains finished. Nor was it broken off prematurely, as if it were a tragedy. That's why, John suggests, Jesus, having been "lifted up," now draws all people to himself. Jesus' "work" does not need to be finished; it needs only to be understood and appropriated.

So That the Scriptures Might Be Fulfilled

However much John differs from the Synoptics, all four Gospels point out that certain aspects of the Passion story "fulfilled" Scripture. The fact that they often quote different passages shows that each Gospel writer had his eye on what mattered to him. Moreover, sometimes a passage in the Old Testament influenced the way an Evangelist told the story even though he does not actually quote it; Isaiah 53 might have had just such an influence, as seen already.

Within John 18–19, the narrator calls attention to the fulfillment of Scripture only in connection with the Crucifixion scene itself, beginning with the division of Jesus' clothes (19:23-25). He quotes both lines of Psalm 22:18:

"They divided my clothes among themselves,
    and for my clothing they cast lots."

He sees the first line fulfilled when the soldiers "took his clothes and divided them into four parts," and the second line fulfilled when they "cast lots" to see who would get the seamless robe. Even in these details, Scripture came to pass in Jesus.

Also Jesus' thirst fulfills Scripture, evidently alluding to Psalm 22:15:

"my mouth [literally 'my strength'] is dried up
    like a potsherd,
and my tongue sticks to my jaws."

The other Gospels too report that Jesus was given sour wine, but in different circumstances: In Matthew and Mark he was given sour wine when he cried out, "My God, my God, why have you forsaken me?" (Psalm 22:1; Matthew 27:46-48; Mark 15:34-36), whereas in Luke the soldiers give it while saying, "If you are the King of the Jews, save yourself!" (Luke 23:36-37). In John Jesus' thirst underscores what the Prologue says: The *Logos* became *flesh*.

The third time the narrator calls attention to the fulfillment of Scripture appears at John 19:36, after he has reported that the soldiers did not need to break Jesus' legs to hasten his death because he was already dead, and that instead, for no stated reason, one of them stuck his spear into Jesus' side, from which blood and water flowed. The narrator sees Scripture fulfilled both in what did not happen to Jesus (his legs were not broken) and in what did happen (his side was pierced), and so he first quotes the prohibition against breaking the bones of the lamb eaten at Passover (Exodus 12:46; Numbers 9:12) and then Zechariah 12:10, which refers to the "pierced" one. By quoting the prohibition, the narrator suggests that Jesus is killed like a Passover lamb and also that the compliance with God's will that marked Jesus' mission is completed even after he died. Interestingly, the reference to the unbroken bones might also allude to Psalm 34, which celebrates God's care for the righteous sufferer, saying at 34:20,

"He keeps all their bones;
    not one of them will be broken."

If this Psalm is also to be recalled, then the narrator would be suggesting that despite appearances, God cares for this righteous sufferer Jesus. John is quite capable of suggesting both meanings.

The narrator insists that blood and water really did come out of Jesus' pierced side, but he does not say what this signifies (John 19:34). So we are not surprised that all sorts of interpretations have been advanced or that the debate continues over the physiological correctness of the report. Some interpreters see here an allusion to the two sacraments (blood referring to the Eucharist, water to baptism); for others, the point is simpler: It emphasizes that Jesus really was human.

Instructive as it may be to see where and how John calls attention to the fulfillment of Scripture, many readers today may wonder why this emphasis is important in the first place. They are not the first to wonder. Indeed, the relation between the Old Testament and what Jesus said and did has engaged Christian theology since the first century. As we saw in connection with Matthew, "in order that Scripture might be fulfilled" can also mean "with the result that Scripture was fulfilled." That is, the formula "in order that" usually does not refer to the motivation of the doer but to the deed's correlation with the sacred text. Thus John did not mean that the recalling of Psalm 22:15 motivated Jesus to say he was thirsty in order to make a point; rather, as a result of Jesus' saying he was thirsty, Scripture was fulfilled.

The correlation between the text and the event in Jesus' life is more important for what it implies about God than for what it says about the event itself. Why? Because what was written long ago has happened, has been actualized. The truth of an actualized word is no longer a promissory note, for it has been "paid off" by what happened. And since John, like the rest of the New Testament writers, was convinced that the words of Scripture are God's word, the fulfillment of Scripture means that God's word has been kept in Jesus and his mission. And this word-keeping God can be trusted, and the Jesus in whom the word was kept can be believed.

So Then

John's story of Jesus' "passion" is a standing dare to see the triumph in the defeat, the victory in the victim, the glorification in the humiliation— not because we are so smart but because that is how God is made known in this kind of world.

Except for the beloved disciple, the disciples play no role in what occurred after Jesus was arrested. Not even Peter's denial affects the story itself. In John this story is not about Jesus *and* the disciples but the story of Jesus *for* the disciples. As his words to the soldiers in the garden make clear, he allows himself to be arrested so the disciples can go free. The disciples are the beneficiaries of what Jesus did and of what was done to him. So being a disciple means living by the knowledge that one is a beneficiary, not a contributor. The beneficiary does not try to defend Jesus, as Peter found out at Malchus's expense. The disciple who is unwilling to be a beneficiary somehow ends up with Peter, saying, I am not one of *this* man's disciples.

Do You Want to Become His Disciples, Too?

To live as beneficiaries is to live in awe of what Jesus has done for our sake and in gratitude to God. To live as beneficiaries is also to become like the benefactor who was not awed by Roman power and so unmasked its pretensions. It is to care for the vulnerable even in the midst of our own suffering, as Jesus cared for his mother. It is to receive his peace when fear makes us lock doors and to rejoice when the Lord makes his presence known. It is to be sent as he was sent.

In other words, the real question is not, What are we to make of John's Passion story? but rather, What will this story make of us?

In what sense are you a beneficiary of who Jesus is and what he did, and what difference does that make in your living?

_____

_____

_____

_____

_____

Prayer

You have looked deep into my heart, LORD,
    and you know all about me.
You know when I am resting or when I am working,
    and from heaven you discover my thoughts.

You notice everything I do and everywhere I go.
Before I even speak a word,
    you know what I will say,
and with your powerful arm
    you protect me from every side.
I can't understand all of this!
    Such wonderful knowledge is far above me.

(Psalm 139:1-6, CEV)

283

30 Looking Back at Jesus' Future

> Jesus said to him, "If it is my will that he remain until I come, what is that to you? Follow me!"
>
> (John 21:22)

They Have No Wine

The future fascinates us, but we are of two minds about it. We want to know what will happen as well as how and when it will happen. To satisfy our curiosity, a huge industry has developed, from fortunetellers to futurologists. On the other hand, we're not sure we want to know what lies ahead, whether vast climate changes or a dread disease. In any case, how can we be ready for whatever comes our way?

This Time: Beginning With John 21

This concluding lesson provides opportunity to look back at the Gospels, all of which end by looking forward. But we would shortchange this opportunity if we examined only the various ways the Gospels end, because the impact of each ending depends on what leads up to it. Therefore, after first reading John 21, we will reread each of the four Gospels from beginning to end.

The suggestions of things to look for are changed to make this rereading fruitful. Day 1 suggestions as usual call attention to details of the text. But for Days 2–5, the initiative is yours, for you are asked to look for up to six passages that strike you as expressing the characteristic or distinctive emphasis of each Gospel as a whole and to list these passages in the space provided. Keep in mind that a list of your *favorite* passages might not be the same as a list of passages you see as characteristic of each Gospel. Your reading might be more stimulating if you now use a translation you have not used before.

Day 1   John 21

(1) Note that John 20:30-31 looks like the end of the Gospel and that some scholars regard John 21 as a later addition.

(2) Note that 21:1 alerts the reader to the narrator's purpose—to tell a story showing *how* Jesus "showed himself."

(3) Observe that the story has four episodes—21:2-8; 21:9-14; 21:15-19; 21:20-23—followed by a conclusion in 21:24-25. Note also that in addition to Jesus, Simon Peter links all four episodes.

(4) Observe that not even here do we learn the name of the disciple "whom Jesus loved." Note also that although 21:24 says he wrote "these things," we are not told exactly what "these things" are—Chapter 21? the whole Gospel? Note also that 21:24 is the word of someone *about* the beloved disciple and so functions as the seal of a notary public would.

(5) Recall that the beloved disciple—"the one whom Jesus loved"—appears first at 13:23-25 and 19:26-27; *probably* at 19:35, and *perhaps* as "the other disciple" at 18:15-16 and 20:3-4, 8.

(6) Observe that *if* he was John, one of Zebedee's sons (as tradition has held), 21:2 ignores the opportunity to say so.

Day 2 Read John 1–21, with an eye to finding up to six passages that most clearly express what this Gospel wants the reader to understand about Jesus. Record these passages in the space provided.

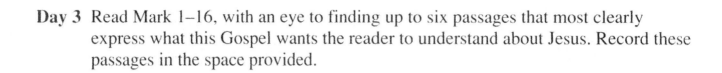

Day 3 Read Mark 1–16, with an eye to finding up to six passages that most clearly express what this Gospel wants the reader to understand about Jesus. Record these passages in the space provided.

Day 4 Read Matthew 1–28, with an eye to finding up to six passages that most clearly express what this Gospel wants the reader to understand about Jesus. Record these passages in the space provided.

Day 5 Read Luke 1–24, with an eye to finding up to six passages that most clearly express what this Gospel wants the reader to understand about Jesus. Record these passages in the space provided.

Day 6 Read and respond to "The Lord's Breakfast" and "Do You Want to Become His Disciples, Too?"

Prayer Concerns

The Lord's Breakfast

Is it a coincidence that the Gospel that gives us the story of the Lord's Supper also has the story of the Lord's breakfast?

This story, like all the stories of the resurrected Jesus' appearances, appeals to the imagination by leaving so much unsaid. This feature is true of the stories of the pre-Easter Jesus as well. The intent of this feature, we may surmise, is not to invite the readers to fill in the gaps but rather to attend imaginatively to what is actually said—particularly in the case of the appearance stories. Why? Because we can only imagine what it was like to meet the same Jesus who is no longer the same because God has done for him what God has not yet done for anyone else (recall the distinction between resurrection and resuscitation).

This observation makes John 21:1 all the more suggestive: What follows shows *how* Jesus "showed himself." The identity of Jesus is self-disclosed in this way—by what happened at this breakfast at the beach. (Notice that Jesus does not demonstrate that he has been raised from the dead; John 20 already made that point.) What then does this story convey about Jesus now that he has been resurrected? That from the shore, facing the rising sun, he could see the school of fish better than those in the boat above the fish? That he wanted to humiliate Peter, who already was embarrassed by his nakedness? Hardly. We do better by asking how each episode discloses something about the post-Resurrection Jesus, something important for the disciples in the future.

Episode 1: The Memorable Catch of the Day (John 21:2-8). The narrator sets the scene by simple, matter-of-fact realism, though we are not told why the disciples had already gathered at the lakeside. (In John Jesus does not promise to meet the disciples in Galilee as in Mark 14:28; 16:7; see also Matthew 28:5-7.) Nor are we told why only these seven were there or why Peter decided to go fishing (in this Gospel neither he nor Zebedee's sons are identified as fishermen). Equally matter-of-fact is the result of their effort: "But that night they caught nothing" (John 21:3). At just this reported failure, the story introduces Jesus, unrecognized, who knows the men had fished in vain. He also knows where they will succeed if they do as he

"Come and have breakfast"

says. And he is right. Suddenly, they have too many fish to manage easily. That's when the beloved disciple tells Simon Peter, "It is the Lord!" (not simply "Jesus"). The news startled Simon Peter into such confusion that he not only put on some clothes but also foolishly jumped clothed into the water, leaving the others to cope with the full net as best they could. Were this a scene in a movie, the audience would roar with laughter at this comic figure. So in this opening episode the Lord discloses himself as one who does not need to be informed because he knows the whole situation without being among the men, and as the one whose concern for the disciples exposes Simon Peter's foolish concern for his self-image when in fact he is naked before the Lord who sees reality.

Episode 2: The Embarrassed Silence (John 21:9-14). Jesus is now the host at the breakfast, as he had been at the supper. When Jesus asks the disciples to bring some of the newly-caught fish, Simon Peter alone hauls the net ashore, with its 153 large fish. (The number has prompted all sorts of guesses about what, if anything, it symbolizes; maybe it simply makes the large catch vivid.) The breakfast of fish and bread recalls the time when Jesus fed a whole crowd with a boy's lunch consisting of five loaves and two fish (6:8-11), but this time there is no miracle and no "sign." When Jesus invites the disciples, "Come and have breakfast," they respond but eat in silence: "None of the disciples dared to ask him, 'Who are you?' because they knew it was the Lord." Nor did they confess that they knew who he was or greet him with joy. But their behavior, understandable as it is, doesn't stop Jesus, who "came and took the bread and gave it to them, and did the same with the fish." At this awkward moment, Jesus showed himself as the Lord who was not deterred by what they did not do or say. He took the initiative and fed them. That too is how he shows himself to be the Lord.

Episode 3: The Painful Moment (John 21:15-19). The meal is finished, and Jesus breaks the silence by questioning "Simon son of John" (not Peter the Rock). In the presence of the other six, Jesus asks, "Do you love me more than these?" With this "more than these," Simon Peter is again "naked";

for if he answers yes, he exposes not only his sense of superiority but also the glaring contradiction—namely, the others had not denied Jesus but Simon had—three times—and now he claims to love Jesus *more* than they do? Simon's reply is both forthright and defensive: He ignores the "more than these" part of the question and implies that Jesus need not even ask the question, "Yes, Lord; you know that I love you." (Why do you ask, especially in front of the others?) Remarkably, Jesus comes back with a task: "Feed my lambs." The story has no interest in Simon's response to such an assignment but instead presses on relentlessly to report Jesus' second question, "Do you love me?" And to Simon's reply, Jesus responds with "Tend my sheep." (*Tend* renders a Greek word meaning "be a shepherd" and appears to use the language of 2 Samuel 5:2, "The LORD said to you [David]: 'It is you who shall be shepherd of my people Israel' "; see also Psalm 78:70-72.) Jesus is not finished, asking yet a third time, "Do you love me?" Now Simon Peter "felt hurt" and exasperated because Jesus does not seem to believe him. So he says, "Lord, you know everything; you know that I love you." (Why do you keep asking? What more can I say?) Jesus comes back, "Feed my sheep."

Here Jesus discloses himself as the shepherd who does not abandon his flock but provides for it by appointing Simon as its shepherd to care for the sheep. He is to be the pastor, not the rock on which Jesus will build his church (Matthew 16:18). With this triple exchange the Lord cancels Peter's triple denial, showing himself forgiving—in keeping with his giving the disciples the ministry of forgiveness on Easter night (John 20:23). Jesus also confirmed Simon Peter's word, "Lord, you know everything"; for the Lord went on to predict Simon's future when he would be led "where you do not wish to go." The narrator explains that Jesus was talking about "the kind of death by which he would glorify God"—namely, Simon's martyrdom would glorify God as Jesus' own execution had. No wonder Jesus adds simply, "Follow me." That says it all. We recall that at the supper Jesus told Simon Peter, "Where I am going, you cannot follow me now; but you will follow me afterward." Simon, not realizing that Jesus was talking about his return to the Father but nevertheless sensing that Jesus was talking about his own impending death, protested, "Lord, why can I not

"Follow me"

follow you now? I will lay down my life for you." "Really?" Jesus in effect asked. Actually before daybreak "you will have denied me three times" (13:36-38). The words *not now* were indeed fulfilled. Now at this daybreak exchange the risen one foresees that the shepherd Simon too will lay down his life for the flock (10:11), and so he says ominously, "Follow me." John's readers know that he did.

Episode 4: The Lord's Will (John 21:20-23). Only now do we learn that some of the exchange between the departing shepherd and the next shepherd occurred as they walked along the shore, for Simon Peter now sees the beloved disciple is following them. Repeatedly (except at the cross) this mysterious figure appears with Peter. Are they companions? Or are they rivals? (See 20:1-10.) Now Simon, still absorbing Jesus' somber words about his future, asks, "Lord, what about him?" That is, will he face the same future, or will he fare better (because Jesus loved him?)? Jesus replies curtly, in effect saying, "It's none of your business. You follow me." And so Jesus shows himself to be the Lord of both of them; their destiny is in his hands: "If it is my will that he remain until I come, what is that to you?" Simon Peter's obedience is not to be measured by comparing it with that of the beloved disciple but by the Lord's will.

Because Jesus' reply started a rumor that the beloved disciple would not die, the writer sets the record straight (21:23). We can surmise that the beloved disciple did in fact outlive Peter and that this fact reinforced the rumor that the writer corrects. Alas, controversy over what Jesus really did and said began early.

So Then

One feature that makes this story so remarkable is its extraordinary ordinariness: Seven men fish at night but catch nothing; their unusually large catch that follows from heeding Jesus' directive is marvelous but not a miracle, and certainly not a "sign" like those Jesus had done before his death. Jesus' request for some of the catch to add to what he already had on the fire is very down-to-earth, not a repetition of the multiplication of the loaves and fish. So too Simon Peter's "hurt," like his question about the beloved disciple, is realistic, not symbolic. From now on, the disciples must look to the future, until he "comes." Compared with those apocryphal gospels that claim to report the teaching of the post-Easter Jesus—teachings withheld from the general public but reserved for the elite—here we are in the real, ordinary world. And precisely here, where there is failure, foolishness, embarrassment, and rivalry, Jesus hosts a simple breakfast and speaks simply, directly—distressingly so, in fact. Here the risen, glorified Jesus shows himself in the ordinary. That's where most people discover him.

At the same time this story points also to the future, doubly so: Jesus mentions his future coming and for the meantime makes provision for his community by commissioning Simon Peter to shepherd the sheep. The forward look of John 21 supports that of John 20, where Jesus not only gives the disciples the ministry of forgiveness but also pronounces blessed those who believe without having seen Jesus with their own eyes—that is, he blesses the readers who believe. The other Gospels too, each in its own way, end with a forward look. They all imply that when the resurrected Jesus exited the tomb, he entered the future as its Lord. Is it surprising that in John, Jesus' last word is "Follow me"?

Do You Want to Become His Disciples, Too?

To be a disciple is to follow the Jesus to whom God gave the future. Following cannot be done by proxy. Each of us must decide whether or not to follow whenever we hear his voice. That voice is insistent; it allows no negotiating (What about him or her? or what about this or that condition?) before getting an answer. Jesus' summons is simple and straightforward. He earned the right to expect an unequivocal answer.

Describe your perception, image, understanding of Jesus as you complete this study. Who is the Jesus you take with you from this study? (Before responding, review and reflect on what you wrote in Lesson 1, page 14.)

Prayer

The LORD is merciful! He is kind and patient,
    and his love never fails.
The LORD won't always be angry and point out our sins;
    he doesn't punish us as our sins deserve.

How great is God's love for all who worship him?
        Greater than the distance between heaven and earth!
How far has the LORD taken our sins from us?
        Farther than the distance from east to west!

(Psalm 103:8-12)

Worship

Having studied Jesus in the Gospels for the past thirty weeks, we gather now to worship that same Jesus. We gather to proclaim the Jesus who comes to us through and as God's Word. We gather to respond to the Jesus who calls us to follow him in his life, death, and resurrection. And we gather to bear witness to the Jesus who promises to meet us here and be with us, even to the end of the age.

Our worship moves along two paths. First, it follows the narrative of Jesus' appearance to the disciples at the Sea of Galilee in John 21: The disciples **gather** to fish; they **hear** Jesus' word of invitation to fish in another place; they **recognize** Jesus as they marvel at the surprising catch of fish; they **eat** a meal together provided and blessed by Jesus; and they (as represented by Peter) **respond** as followers of the risen Christ. Second, our worship follows a basic pattern: Gathering (in praise); Hearing (the Word); Remembering (the Lord's Supper); and Going Forth (in response of discipleship).

GATHERING

Now I would remind you, brothers and sisters, of the good news that I proclaimed to you, which you in turn received, in which also you stand, through which also you are being saved, if you hold firmly to the message that I proclaimed to you—unless you have come to believe in vain.

For I handed on to you as of first importance what I in turn had received: that Christ died for our sins in accordance with the scriptures, and that he was buried, and that he was raised on the third day in accordance with the scriptures, and that he appeared to Cephas, then to the twelve. Then he appeared to more than five hundred brothers and sisters at one time, most of whom are still alive, though some have died. Then he appeared to James, then to all the apostles. Last of all, as to one untimely born, he appeared also to me.

(1 Corinthians 15:1-8)

LIGHTING THE CHRIST CANDLE

A table, covered with a simple white cloth runner topped with a layer of sand, holds a white Christ candle. The candle is positioned in the center, on the sand, with small crosses, one for each participant, placed around its base. The leader or another participant lights the Christ candle.

GOSPEL READING
John 21:1-13

PRAYER OF BLESSING
Gracious God,
accept our presence before you
as an offering of praise
for your glorious acts in Jesus Christ our Lord.
Bless this meal we share together
as a confirmation of our study and fellowship,
in keeping with that early morning breakfast
shared by those first disciples on the Galilean shore.

Make known to us, in our breaking of bread,
the presence, the power, and the love of the Risen Christ.
And give us ears to hear his call
to follow him anew as his disciples.
Amen.

HYMN
"Be Present at Our Table, Lord" **or**
"Come, Sinners, to the Gospel Feast"

THE MEAL
After the hymn, eat a simple meal together. During the meal, it is appropriate to eat in silence as the disciples may have done during their breakfast with Jesus, or the group may talk about the Jesus they encountered during this study. After the meal, continue with the service of worship as printed.

GOSPEL READING
John 21:15-19

VIEW VIDEO SEGMENT 30

SILENCE

PRAYER OF REMEMBRANCE
Let us remember Jesus:
Who, though he was rich,
  yet for our sakes became poor and dwelt among us.
Who was content to be subject to his parents,
  the child of a poor couple's home.
Who lived for thirty years the common life,
  earning his living with his own hands and declining no
    humble tasks.
Whom the people heard gladly, for he understood their ways.
May this mind be in us which was in Christ Jesus.

Let us remember Jesus:
Who was mighty in deed, healing the sick and the disordered,
  using for others the powers he would not invoke for himself.
Who refused to force people's allegiance.
Who was Master and Lord to his disciples,
  yet was among them as their companion and as one who
    served.
Whose desire was to do the will of God who sent him.
May this mind be in us which was in Christ Jesus.

Let us remember Jesus:
Who loved people, yet retired from them to pray,
  rose a great while before day, watched through the night,
  stayed in the wilderness, went up into a mountain, sought a
    garden.
Who, when he would help a tempted disciple, prayed for him.
Who prayed for the forgiveness of those who rejected him,
  and for the perfecting of those who received him.

Who observed the traditions,
   but defied convention that did not serve the purposes of God.
Who hated the sins of pride and selfishness, of cruelty and
      impurity.
May this mind be in us which was in Christ Jesus.

Let us remember Jesus:
Who believed in people and never despaired of them.
Who through all disappointment never lost heart.
Who disregarded his own comfort and convenience,
   and thought first of others' needs,
   and, though he suffered long, was always kind.
Who, when he was reviled, uttered no harsh word in return,
   and when he suffered, did not threaten retaliation.
Who humbled himself and carried obedience to the point of
      death,
   even death on the cross,
Wherefore God has highly exalted him.
May this mind be in us which was in Christ Jesus.

Let us unite in prayer that Christ may dwell in our hearts.
O Christ, our only Savior,
   so come to dwell in us that we may go forth
      with the light of your hope in our eyes,
   and with your faith and love in our hearts. Amen.

HYMN
   "Savior, Like a Shepherd Lead Us" **or**
   "Just a Closer Walk With Thee"

LITANY OF WITNESS
The prophet Micah said, "He shall be the one of peace" (Micah 5:5).

Jesus said to his disciples, "But who do you say that I am?"

The prophet Isaiah said, "The spirit of the Lord shall rest on him" (Isaiah 11:2).

Jesus said to his disciples, "But who do you say that I am?"

An angel of the Lord said, "To you is born this day in the city of David a Savior, who is the Messiah, the Lord" (Luke 2:11).

Jesus said to his disciples, "But who do you say that I am?"

John the Baptizer said, "Here is the Lamb of God who takes away the sin of the world!" (John 1:29).

Jesus said to his disciples, "But who do you say that I am?"

The demoniac said, "What have you to do with me, Jesus, Son of the Most High God?" (Mark 5:7).

Jesus said to his disciples, "But who do you say that I am?"

Simon Peter said, "You are the Messiah, the Son of the living God" (Matthew 16:16).

Jesus said to his disciples, "But who do you say that I am?"

Martha the host said, "I believe that you are the Messiah, the Son of God, the one coming into the world" (John 11:27).

Jesus said to his disciples, "But who do you say that I am?"

The centurion at the cross said, "Truly this man was God's Son!" (Mark 15:39).

Jesus said to his disciples, "But who do you say that I am?"

Thomas who was called the Twin said, "My Lord and my God!" (John 20:28).

Jesus said to his disciples, "But who do you say that I am?"

TESTIMONY
Invite group members to respond to Jesus' question.

PRAYERS FOR THE PEOPLE
Offer brief intercessions, petitions, and thanksgivings.

HOLY COMMUNION

INVITATION
Christ our Lord invites to his table
   all who answer his question,
   "But who do you say that I am?"
   in the words and spirit of Martha or Peter or Thomas;
he invites all who heed his call to repent and believe the good
      news,
all who commit to follow his way,
all who seek to make disciples of all nations, and
all who obey his command to love God and neighbor.
Therefore, as members of such a community, let us confess our
      sin before God and one another.

CONFESSION AND PARDON
   Merciful God,
      we confess that we have not loved you with our whole
         heart.
   We have failed to be an obedient church.
   We have not done your will,
      we have broken your law,
      we have rebelled against your love,
      we have not loved our neighbors,
      and we have not heard the cry of the needy.
   Forgive us, we pray.
   Free us for joyful obedience,
      through Jesus Christ our Lord. Amen.

SILENCE

Hear the good news:
   Christ died for us while we were yet sinners;
   that proves God's love toward us.
In the name of Jesus Christ, you are forgiven!

In the name of Jesus Christ, you are forgiven!

Glory to God. Amen.

THE PEACE
Offer one another the peace of Christ.

HYMN
"Jesus Calls Us"
(Words by John Bell & Graham Maule
Tune: HOLY MANNA)

Jesus calls us here to meet him
As, through word and song and prayer,
We affirm God's promised presence
Where his people live and care.
Praise the God who keeps his promise;
Praise the Son who calls us friends;
Praise the Spirit who, among us,
To our hopes and fears attends.

Jesus calls us to confess him
Word of Life and Lord of All,
Sharer of our flesh and frailness
Saving all who fail or fall.
Tell his holy human story;
Tell his tales that all may hear;
Tell the world that Christ in glory
Came to earth to meet us here.

Jesus calls us to each other:
Found in him are no divides.
Race and class and sex and language—
Such are barriers he derides.
Join the hand of friend and stranger;
Join the hands of age and youth;
Join the faithful and the doubter
In their common search for truth.

Jesus calls us to his table
Rooted firm in time and space,
Where the church in earth and heaven
Finds a common meeting place.
Share the bread and wine, his body;
Share the love of which we sing;
Share the feast for saints and sinners
Hosted by our Lord and King.

THE GREAT THANKSGIVING
The Lord be with you.
And also with you.
Lift up your hearts.
We lift them up to the Lord.
Let us give thanks to the Lord our God.
It is right to give our thanks and praise.

It is right, and a good and joyful thing,
    always and everywhere to give thanks to you,
    Almighty God, creator of heaven and earth.
    You formed us in your image
        and breathed into us the breath of life.
    When we turned away, and our love failed,
        your love remained steadfast.

You delivered us from captivity,
    made covenant to be our sovereign God,
    and spoke to us through the prophets.

And so,
    with your people on earth
    and all the company of heaven
    we praise your name and join their unending hymn:

Holy, holy, holy Lord, God of power and might,
heaven and earth are full of your glory.
    Hosanna in the highest.
Blessed is he who comes in the name of the Lord.
    Hosanna in the highest.

Holy are you, and blessed is your Son Jesus Christ.
Your Spirit anointed him
    to preach good news to the poor,
    to proclaim release to the captives
        and recovering of sight to the blind,
    to set at liberty those who are oppressed,
    and to announce that the time had come
        when you would save your people.
He healed the sick, fed the hungry, and ate with sinners.
By the baptism of his suffering, death, and resurrection
    you gave birth to your Church,
    delivered us from slavery to sin and death,
    and made with us a new covenant
        by water and the Spirit.
When the Lord Jesus ascended,
    he promised to be with us always,
        in the power of your Word and Holy Spirit.

On the night in which he gave himself up for us,
    he took bread, gave thanks to you, broke the bread,
    gave it to his disciples, and said:
"Take, eat; this is my body which is given for you.
Do this in remembrance of me."

When the supper was over, he took the cup,
    gave thanks to you, gave it to his disciples, and said:
"Drink from this, all of you;
    this is my blood of the new covenant,
    poured out for you and for many
    for the forgiveness of sins.
Do this, as often as you drink it,
    in remembrance of me."

And so,
in remembrance of these your mighty acts in Jesus Christ,
we offer ourselves in praise and thanksgiving
    as a holy and living sacrifice,
    in union with Christ's offering for us,
as we proclaim the mystery of faith.

Christ has died; Christ is risen; Christ will come again.

Pour out your Holy Spirit on us gathered here,
  and on these gifts of bread and wine.
Make them be for us the body and blood of Christ,
that we may be for the world the body of Christ,
  redeemed by his blood.

By your Spirit make us one with Christ,
  one with each other,
  and one in ministry to all the world,
until Christ comes in final victory,
  and we feast at his heavenly banquet.

Through your Son Jesus Christ,
with the Holy Spirit in your holy Church,
all honor and glory is yours, almighty Father,
  now and for ever. **Amen.**

THE LORD'S PRAYER
And now, with the confidence of children of God, let us pray:

Our Father in heaven,
  hallowed be your name,
  your kingdom come,
  your will be done,
    on earth as in heaven.
  Give us today our daily bread.
  Forgive us our sins
    as we forgive those who sin against us.
  Save us from the time of trial,
    and deliver us from evil.
  For the kingdom, the power, and the glory are yours
    now and for ever. Amen.

GIVING THE BREAD AND CUP

With these or other words being exchanged:

The body of Christ, given for you. **Amen.**
The blood of Christ, given for you. **Amen.**

PRAYER AFTER COMMUNION
O give thanks to the LORD, for he is good;
  His steadfast love endures forever! . . .
  The stone that the builders rejected
  has become the chief cornerstone.
  This is the LORD's doing;
  it is marvelous in our eyes.
  This is the day that the LORD has made;
  let us rejoice and be glad in it.

(Psalm 118:1, 22-24)

TAKING UP THE CROSS
Participants come forward one by one during the singing of the hymn to take a cross, emblem of discipleship, from the table.

HYMN
  "Tú Has Venido a la Orilla" ("Lord, You Have Come
    to the Lakeshore") **or**
  "When I Survey the Wondrous Cross"

GOING FORTH
  Now may the God of peace, who brought back from the dead our Lord Jesus, the great shepherd of the sheep, by the blood of the eternal covenant, make you complete in everything good so that you may do his will, working among us that which is pleasing in his sight, through Jesus Christ, to whom be the glory forever and ever. **Amen.**

(Hebrews 13: 20-21)

Glossary

Acts of John

One of the oldest of several apocryphal Acts, The Acts of John was written between 150 and 180 A.D. It chronicles the apostle John's missionary journeys to Ephesus and through Asia Minor, concluding with an account of his death. The chapters featuring John's preaching are notable in their accounts of Christ's appearing in various bodily shapes to the apostles and leaving behind no footprints. The text also includes a hymn of Christ set to music in the nineteenth century by Gustav Holst.

Allegorical Interpretation

Allegorical interpretation came before the creation of allegory itself—a type of communication, written or visual, in which the literal meaning conceals the real meaning. Several centuries before the Christian era, Greek thinkers developed allegorical interpretation in order to find the true philosophical or moral meanings in the stories of the gods whose escapades were considered offensive when taken at face value. Allegorical interpretation holds that while the story says A, it really means X. At the beginning of the Christian era, Philo* used allegorical interpretation to explain what the Pentateuch (in the Septuagint*) really meant to educated Greek-speaking Jews who were puzzled by its unusual Greek and strange laws. By explaining each detail allegorically, Philo claimed that what Moses wrote actually anticipated what sophisticated modern first-century persons understood to be true. For example, according to Genesis 2:10-14, from Eden flowed a great river that became four rivers. Philo explained that the big river is goodness, from which come the four cardinal virtues that have been widely emphasized ever since Plato—prudence, self-control, courage, and justice.

Philo's way of interpreting Scripture was picked up by Christian theologians, especially in Alexandria. Famous is Augustine's allegorical interpretation of the parable of the good Samaritan: the man (Adam) went down from Jerusalem (the heavenly city) toward Jericho (the moon, symbol of mortality because it grows and dies); the thieves (the devil and his angels) stripped him (of his immortality); the priest and Levite (the Old Testament priesthood) did nothing for him, but the Samaritan (the Lord Jesus) put him on his beast (the Incarnation) and took him to the inn (the church) whose innkeeper is Paul. Thus the point of Jesus' parable—who is the neighbor?—is turned into a story that teaches Christian doctrine in code.

While Philo and Augustine used allegorical interpretation to explain texts that were not allegories to begin with, others used the same principle (real meaning is hidden beneath the literal meaning) to create allegories to convey Christian teaching. For example, the second-century work known as *The Shepherd of Hermas* reports a vision of a great tower (the church) being built on water (baptism) by six young men (the angels) who use square stones (the apostles, bishops, and teachers), as well as stones from the sea (those who suffered persecution), but rejected stones with cracks (those who have malice in their hearts) and stones that are too short (those who have insufficient righteousness); they also set aside round stones until they could be squared (those whose wealth must be cut away first). The most famous allegory of the Christian life is John Bunyan's *Pilgrim's Progress.*

Some of Jesus' parables are not allegories (for example, the secretly growing seed, Mark 4:26-29); some parables, such as the parable of the soils in Mark 4:3-8, invite allegorical interpretation (given in Mark 4:14-20); but the parable of the wicked tenants (Mark 12:1-11) is an allegory of Israel's treatment of God's messengers.

Apocrypha

This word identifies those writings (and parts of writings such as the Additions to the book of Daniel) that are not part of the Hebrew Bible or Protestant Old Testament but are considered "deuterocanonical" (secondary canon) in the Roman Catholic Old Testament. Most of these writings are found at various places in the Septuagint,* but Martin Luther brought them together and placed them at the end of the Old Testament and called them "Apocrypha" (hidden writings), saying that they could be read with profit even though not part of the Old Testament proper. In response, in 1546 the Council of Trent included most of these books in the Old Testament (leaving out 1 and 2 Esdras [4 Ezra] and the Prayer of Manasseh). Although many Protestant Bibles later omitted the Apocrypha, today many of them include it, following Luther's practice. However, *The New Interpreter's Bible* includes these books where they are found in the Roman Catholic Bible. These writings are indispensable for understanding the Jewish thought-world in which early Christianity emerged. The Apocrypha is not to be confused with another group of Jewish writings, mostly from the same era, that were never part of any canon,* the so-called Pseudepigrapha (false writings).

Canon

The word (from Greek *kanon*, reed, and then measuring stick) refers to those writings that Jews and Christians, separately, decided would be included in their "Bible." Exactly when and how these decisions were made is not clear, partly because we have no records of proceedings from the beginning of the process, partly because the writings' authority in worship, moral instruction, and doctrine had been recognized long before they were canonized formally. The order of the three parts of the Hebrew Bible—Law; Prophets (including Joshua through Second Kings except for Ruth); Writings (including everything else)—probably reflects the sequence in which each part came to be regarded as authoritative, a process that apparently was concluded only after the fall of Jerusalem in A.D. 70. The oldest known list of authoritative (canonical) Christian writings that agrees with the contents of our New Testament today is found in an Egyptian bishop's Easter letter written in A.D. 367. Even so, in other areas, some books, such as Hebrews and Revelation, would not be accepted as part of the canon until much later. Two things should not be overlooked: (1) No writer of the New Testament books was commissioned to produce a piece for the canon, the way a composer is commissioned to produce music for an orchestra. Canonization always came later, after the book had proved its value by being used widely and repeatedly. (2) Because a great variety of early Christian literature was available to the faithful, canonization was necessary in order to specify which texts the church would heed above all others. In principle, all canons are closed; otherwise, the list would contain only preferences, not unlike a list of "best sellers" of the day. Nothing prevented Christians from continuing to read those writings that did not become canonical.

Diaspora

Diaspora is the Greek word meaning scattered and is sometimes translated as Dispersion. It refers to the Jews who lived outside Palestine after the Babylonian Exile (586 B.C.). In New Testament times, Diaspora Jews were found in most parts of the Roman Empire, especially in Syria, Mesopotamia, Egypt, and Asia Minor. The letter of James is addressed to "the twelve tribes in the Dispersion [Diaspora]," but this may be a way of referring to Christian Jews.

Didache

The full title of this writing is "The Teaching [*didache*] of the Lord to the Gentiles by the Twelve Apostles." This book was discovered in 1873. Perhaps written at the beginning of the second century, this work contains various moral teachings as well as instructions for Christian practices such as baptism, fasting, and the treatment of traveling teachers. Though neither the author nor the place of writing is known, the book throws important light on Christianity as it was developing at the end of the New Testament period.

Epistle of Barnabas

Despite the title, this early second-century work was not written by the Barnabas known in the New Testament (Acts 4:36-37; 9:26-27; 13:1-3), but by an unknown author. In one important biblical manuscript (Codex Sinaiticus), it appears right after the book of Revelation, as if it were part of the New Testament (it never was, of course). The author insists that the Old Testament must be interpreted in such a way that Christians will "not be shipwrecked by conversion to their [Jews'] law" (Barnabas 3:6).

2 Esdras

The book called 2 Esdras in the Apocrypha of Protestant Bibles is known as 4 Esdras in an appendix to Roman Catholic Bibles. The book is an apocalypse that attempts to explain why God allowed the Temple in Jerusalem to be destroyed in A.D. 70. The central section (Chapters 3–14) reports seven visions of Ezra the scribe concerning ethical issues and the problem of good and evil and the interpretations of those visions by the angel Uriel. This section is thought to have been written in Hebrew or Aramaic late in the first century A.D. by an anonymous Palestinian Jew. The two other sections (Chapters 1–2 and 15–16), written in Greek, are considered second-century and third-century Christian additions.

Evangelists

Because our English word *gospel* translates the Greek *euangelion* and the Latin equivalent, *evangelium*, the authors of the Gospels are called Evangelists (normally capitalized) to avoid confusing them with "evangelists"—those who preach the gospel message in order to elicit conversion.

Gospel According to the Hebrews

This Jewish Christian work is lost, but brief quotations from it are found in several Christian writings from the third and fourth centuries. It may have been written in Egypt, probably in the first half of the second century.

Gospel of the Nazaraeans

The long lost *Gospel of the Nazaraeans* (or *Nazoreans*, also spelled *Nazarenes*) was probably written in Aramaic before A.D. 150 for use by Jewish Christians in Syria. What we know of it depends on references to it and brief quotations from it in fourth and fifth century writers who noted where it differs from the canonical Gospels. For example, Jerome's* commentary on Matthew 12:9-14 reports that this gospel says that the man with the withered hand was a mason who *asked* Jesus to restore his hand so he need no longer beg for bread.

Gospel of Peter

Also called *The Lost Gospel According to Peter*, this book was probably written in Syria between 100 and 130 A.D. The *Gospel of Peter* is an important source for anti-Semitic ideas common in the early church. It was used by the church of Rhossus and often quoted by Christian writers in the late second century. Relying heavily on references to Jewish messianic prophecy, it describes Jesus' trial, burial, and resurrection but contains no references to post-Resurrection appearances. Scholars long assumed this gospel depended on the four canonical Gospels, but recently some scholars have begun to think that this writing may be the earliest Passion account. The gospel eventually was branded heretical because it seems to deny the suffering of Jesus on the cross, saying that he remained silent.

Gospel of Thomas

Two quite different writings, both probably produced in the second century, have this same title. One is in Greek, the other in Coptic (a language developed in Egypt, drawing on both Egyptian and Greek). The Greek *Infancy Gospel of Thomas* contains short stories about the precocious, miracle-working boy Jesus, and ends when the twelve-year-old appears in the Temple

(Luke 2:41-51). The Coptic *Gospel of Thomas*, probably translated from a now lost Greek original, contains no stories at all but claims to be "the secret sayings which the living Jesus spoke and which Didymus [twin] Thomas wrote down." Some of these sayings are similar to those in the New Testament Gospels, while others are totally different (for example, "Jesus said, 'If the flesh came into being because of spirit, it is a wonder. But if spirit came into being because of the body, it is a wonder of wonders. Indeed, I am amazed at how this great wealth has made its home in this poverty' "). The Coptic *Gospel of Thomas* was found in Egypt in 1945.

Hillel

Rabbi, legal scholar, and possibly the most important figure in postbiblical Judaism. Born in Babylonia, Hillel came to Jerusalem to study Torah in the first century B.C., becoming head of the Sanhedrin* during the reign of Herod the Great. Hillel is considered a central founder of rabbinic Judaism and was both a contemporary of Jesus and (indirectly, through his grandson, Gamaliel I), a teacher of Paul (Acts 22:3). Of his many accomplishments, his systematization of the rules for interpreting and applying Scripture was likely used by the Pharisees Jesus encountered.

Incarnation

Literally "enfleshment," this word, while not actually used in the New Testament, is the long-standing technical theological term for what John 1:14 says: that "The Word became flesh." The doctrine of the Incarnation assumes that an eternal being (in John, the Word) became a historical, human person, who was named Jesus.

Jerome

Jerome (A.D. 347-420), while living in Bethlehem, used his command of Latin, knowledge of Greek, and facility in Hebrew to produce (begun at the request of Pope Damasus) the Latin version of the Bible, the Vulgate, that replaced the many, divergent Latin translations that had been used. He also wrote commentaries on books of the Old and New Testaments and was the first to insist that only those books originally written in Hebrew should be in the Old Testament. Durer's famous engraving shows him sitting in his study, his pet lion beside him.

Josephus

Born into a priestly family in A.D. 37, Josephus led the Jewish forces in Galilee when the revolt against Rome began in 66. Captured a year later, he switched sides and then predicted that the general Vespasian would become emperor—which in fact happened. After the war he moved to Rome where he died around A.D. 100. There he wrote *The Jewish War*, which he blamed on Jewish fanatics. He also wrote the *Antiquities of the Jews*, a history from the beginning to his own time. Historians still find these works indispensable. He also wrote *Against Apion*, in which he defended the Jewish religion against slanders, and a brief autobiography, the *Life*.

L

Scholars use L to identify those Gospel passages found only in Luke. We have no evidence that Luke found these passages in a single written text. Some of the L passages are sayings of Jesus such as Luke 6:24-26; others are stories such as Luke 24.

LORD

Modern English translations of the Bible print this word in capital letters to indicate that it renders YHWH (*Yahweh*, the Divine Name), not the Hebrew *adonai*, which also means "lord" and is used of humans as well as of God. The distinction is clear in Psalm 110:1, "The LORD [YHWH] says to my lord [*adonai*, here the king]."

M

Scholars use M to identify those Gospel passages found only in Matthew. We have no evidence that Matthew found these passages in a written document. Some of the M passages are sayings of Jesus such as Matthew 5:17-20; others are stories such as Chapters 1 and 2.

1 Maccabees

A book of the Old Testament Apocrypha, 1 Maccabees narrates the story of the Jewish revolt led by the Maccabee family in opposition to the Seleucid ruler, Antiochus IV Epiphanes during the second century B.C. Central to this book is the account of Judas Maccabees's purification and rededication of the Temple in 164 B.C., which became the basis for the Jewish feast of Hanukkah. Most likely written originally in Hebrew, then translated into Greek, the book was produced around the time of John Hyrcanus's reign (134-104 B.C.).

Mishnah

The Mishnah is the oldest part of the Talmud*; it is a compilation of rabbinic decisions that specify how the Old Testament laws are to be obeyed. The material is organized according to topics such as tithes, sabbath, marriage, and so forth. The compilation was made about A.D. 200 and gathered up what had been handed down by word of mouth for generations.

Narrator

The narrator is the storyteller through whose voice the author conveys the message to the reader. The narrator is a persona, a figure whose image is created and projected, unavoidably, in the very process of writing. Although the narrator-persona represents the author, the two are not identical, because the narrator is the persona who comes through to the reader.

The narrator not only conveys the content but also shapes the reader's understanding of it and attitude toward it by what he includes (and leaves out), by the nature of the plot (does it move forward in time to its conclusion or move backward from the conclusion to the beginning by relying on memory?), and by the way the characters are portrayed (note how Mark 3:19 introduces Judas and how John 12:6 characterizes him). The narrator knows everything the author wants to convey. The narrator in the Gospels knows what people said even in secret (Matthew 2:7-8) and what a person in the story did not know (Mark 9:6). Yet the Gospel narrator is never a disciple (never do we read, "I heard Jesus say, '...'"), yet he always is the one who knows, sees, hears, and sometimes explains (Mark 7:3-4). Being alert to the role of the narrator helps us appreciate more the artistry of the Gospels as literature. We perceive Jesus in the Gospels by listening to the narrator.

Parallelism

Parallelism is a common rhetorical form of teaching, found regularly in Hebrew poetry, proverbs, and admonitions. Characteristically, the thought is expressed in a two-part sentence in which the second line paraphrases the first line, and thereby reinforces it:

> Even fools who keep silent are considered wise;
>> when they close their lips, they are deemed intelligent (Proverbs 17:28).
> Bless those who curse you,
> pray for those who abuse you (Luke 6:28).

The second line can also reinforce the first by stating the opposite:

> All day long the wicked covet,
>> but the righteous give and do not hold back (Proverbs 21:26).

These will go away into eternal punishment, but the righteous into eternal life (Matthew 25:46).

Passion Story

The Latin word behind *passion* means suffering. So the "Passion story" is not an account of aroused emotions, but the customary designation for that part of each Gospel that reports Jesus' arrest, trial, and execution because taken as a whole, it is the account of Jesus' suffering, as in Acts 1:3.

Philo

Philo was the leading Jewish figure in Alexandria, Egypt, during the lifetimes of Jesus and Paul (he died around A.D. 50). He was a prolific writer whose commentaries on the Pentateuch (which he read in Greek) interpreted the text by claiming that Scripture, even its strange laws in Leviticus, agreed with the best of Greek philosophy once a person knew how to interpret the biblical text. No New Testament author quotes Philo, but his thought helps us understand the theology of the Prologue of John, parts of Paul, and especially the letter to the Hebrews.

Protevangelium of James

One of several apocryphal gospels produced to supply information about Jesus and the apostles not contained in the New Testament. Written in Greek sometime between the middle of the second century A.D. and early third century A.D., the *Protoevangelium of James* relies on a variety of sources—oral and written, including the Gospels of Matthew and Luke—to recount the births of Mary and Jesus. Notably, Mary's conception and birth recall the story of Hannah and Samuel: At three years old, Mary is left in the care of the priests at the Temple in Jerusalem. In addition, during Mary's delivery of the infant Jesus, she is attended to by a midwife named Salome.

Q

Scholars use Q to identify those passages that are virtually alike in Matthew and Luke but are absent from Mark (Matthew 3:7-10 and Luke 3:7-9 are a useful example). The Q passages are almost entirely words of Jesus, which probably were put into writing around A.D. 50. Most scholars think that this text of Q was used by both Matthew and Luke but in different ways and that both relied on Mark for their overall narrative. Q no longer exists (a few scholars deny that it ever did). As a collection of Jesus' sayings, Q would have resembled the Coptic *Gospel of Thomas.** Although Jesus probably used Aramaic, his sayings had been translated into Greek before they were recorded in Q, as is true also of those sayings not in Q.

Qumran

Qumran is the name of a place now in ruins on the northwestern shore of the Dead Sea where a community of Jews lived and presumably wrote and used the Dead Sea Scrolls. The scrolls were hidden in nearby caves where they were discovered in 1947 and later.

Sanhedrin

The term comes from a Greek word meaning literally, "sitting together" or "assembly." Descriptions of the composition and function of the Sanhedrin are somewhat imprecise according to rabbinic literature, Josephus, and the New Testament. The Mishnah* identifies a single court of seventy sages plus one (the high priest) that met in the Chambers of Hewn Stone in the Temple to decide various legislative and judicial matters. Elsewhere the Mishnah uses the term *sanhedrin* to refer to three courts of twenty-three judges. Josephus mentions several councils— both Jewish and Roman—by the term *sanhedrin*, each with memberships changing according to the political climate. The New Testament uses the term *sanhedrin* to refer to judicial councils in general (Matthew 10:17) and the Jerusalem council in particular (Matthew 26:59; John 11:47). In relation to Jesus in the Gospels, the most that can be said is that in the first century A.D., there likely existed a supreme court of religious leaders—Torah scholars, chief priests, elders, members of the Jewish aristocracy, Pharisees and Sadducees—charged with the governance of the Jewish people.

Second Clement

At the end of this Christian sermon, probably from the second half of the second century, we read, "The Second Epistle of Clement to the Corinthians." Its unknown author was not the Clement who wrote First Clement (about A.D. 95) from Rome to the Corinthian church. *Second Clement* teaches that "we must think of Jesus Christ the way we think of God," and insists that "if we do the will of the Father, if we keep the flesh pure, and if we observe the commandments of the Lord, we shall obtain eternal life" (2 Clement 8:4).

Septuagint

This word designates the Greek translation of the Old Testament made in the third and second centuries B.C. in Alexandria and which became the Bible of those early Christians who did not use Hebrew. The name (from the Greek word for seventy) reflects the legend that seventy-two translators came to Egypt to make the translation. Scholarly literature therefore uses LXX (Roman numerals for seventy) to refer to this Greek Bible. In some places, LXX translates a Hebrew text whose wording differs from the Hebrew behind our English translations; at other places LXX is markedly longer or significantly shorter. When New Testament writers, including Gospel writers, quote the Old Testament, they use LXX.

Sirach

Sirach is sometimes called Ben Sira, sometimes Ecclesiasticus (not to be confused with Ecclesiastes). The original Hebrew was written in Jerusalem between 200 and 180 B.C. and translated about half a century later in Alexandria by the author's grandson. Like the book of Proverbs, Sirach compiles wise sayings, and like the Wisdom of Solomon* it celebrates wisdom as God's self-expression (Sirach 24). Incomplete Hebrew texts of Sirach were found at Qumran.*

Synoptics

This word is a convenient abbreviation for "the Synoptic Gospels" (Matthew, Mark, and Luke). Scholars use this designation because these Gospels generally have the same narrative structure, and when compared with John, a common way of telling the Jesus story.

Talmud

The Talmud includes both the Mishnah* and its later interpretations called the Gemara (complete in the fifth century A.D.) One Talmud was created in Palestine, another in Babylon (complete in the sixth century A.D.). Unless the former is specified, "the Talmud" normally refers to the one developed in Babylon because it became the dominant authority for Judaism.

Tobit

Tobit is a short tale, probably written around 200 B.C., about the troubles of Tobit and his family of Jews living under the oppressive Assyrians in the 700s B.C. The book contains moral instruction like that of the wisdom literature.* Aramaic and Hebrew versions of Tobit were found among the Dead Sea Scrolls. In the fourth century A.D.

Jerome* translated Tobit into Latin in the Vulgate Version (common Latin) of the Christian Bible. In Roman Catholic Bibles it has secondary standing (deuterocanonical), but Protestants put it with the Apocrypha.* Although New Testament writers do not quote this book, reading it helps us better understand parts of the Jewish heritage of Jesus and the earliest Christians.

Wisdom Literature

The phrase refers to those writings that emphasize insight into human affairs and which often present this understanding in the form of proverbs and maxims, many of which are found in similar form in other ancient literature, especially Egyptian. The wisdom literature includes Job, Proverbs, Ecclesiastes, as well as the Wisdom of Solomon* and Sirach* in the Apocrypha.*

Wisdom of Solomon

This Jewish writing, part of the Apocrypha,* was written in Greek (probably in Alexandria, Egypt) either in the time of Jesus and Paul or earlier; it presents wisdom (*sophia* in Greek) not only as prudence but also as the means by which God created the world and guided the history of Israel. Though not actually quoted in the New Testament, Wisdom of Solomon's understanding of wisdom anticipates what Paul, John, and Hebrews say about Christ's relation to God. In fact, Hebrews 1:3 uses the same word for Christ ("reflection," NRSV) as Wisdom of Solomon 7:26 uses for wisdom.

Notes

Notes

Notes

CPSIA information can be obtained
at www.ICGtesting.com
Printed in the USA
LVHW01s0345100817
544439LV00001B/1/P

9 780687 026920